Other Books By Rick Steves:

Europe 101: Art & History for the Traveler

Mona Winks: Self-Guided Tours of Europe's Top
Museums

Asia Through The Back Door (with John Gottberg)

Itinerary Planners
22 Days In Europe
22 Days In Norway, Sweden & Denmark
22 Days In Germany, Austria & Switzerland
22 Days In Spain & Portugal
22 Days In Great Britain

Europe Through the Back Door

Eighth Edition

---

by Rick Steves

cover by Jennifer Dewey

illustrated by Melissa Meier

maps by David D. Hoerlein

The updated and expanded do-it-yourself guide to budget travel, with practical information on all aspects of European travel.

John Muir Publications
Santa Fe, NM

Thanks to Gene Openshaw (a geyser of bright ideas), Carl, Ruth, Gene, Greg, Patty, Dave, Mike, the mini-bus tours, my parents, and my wife Anne for sharing with me the excitement of European travel.

Rick Steves' lecture and travel seminar schedules are available from Europe Through The Back Door, 120 4th North, Edmonds, WA 98020 Telephone: 206-771-8303.

Library of Congress Catalog No. 87-043161

ISBN 0-912528-84-2

Printing history:

First edition, 1980
Second edition, 1981
Third edition, 1982
Fourth edition, 1984
Fifth edition, 1985
Sixth edition, 1986
Seventh edition, 1987
Eighth edition, 1988

Distributed to the booktrade by:

W.W. Norton & Company
New York, NY

Printed in the United States of America

To
The People of Europe

Also
to those
who further the
myths that inhibit
independent travel—
in hopes that their
eyes will be
opened.

Table of Contents

Europe Through The Back Door

Most people enter Europe through the front door, Europe's stuffy grand entrance for welcoming rich American tourists. In fact, seeing Europe in this way has become commonplace.

Make your trip special. Come with me—through the back door. A warm, relaxed, personable Europe will greet us as an intimate friend. We can become temporary Europeans, part of the family—approaching Europe on its level, accepting its way of life, appreciating its unique ways. We will demand nothing—nothing except that no fuss be made over us.

Spending money has very little to do with enjoying your trip. In fact, spending less money brings you closer to Europe. A lot of money forces you through Europe's grand front entrance where you receive formal, polite (and often stuffy) treatment. But through the back door—well, that's a different story—a story I'd like to tell. The most important decision you will make is which door to enter.

The first half of this book covers the skills of Back Door European travel. In the second half are the keys to some of Europe's most exciting back doors, places where you can experience pure Europe—where you'll feel its fjords and caress its castles.

Rick Steves

The Back-Door Travel Philosophy

Travel is intensified living—maximum thrills per minute. It's one of the last great sources of legal adventure.

Affording travel is a matter of priorities. Many people who "can't afford a trip" could sell their car and travel for two years. A friend marvels at my ability to come up with the money to travel as we sit on $2000 worth of living room furniture. I read my journal on a $50 sofa and spend my free time and money exploring the world.

Experiencing the real thing requires candid informality. A "Sound and Light" show at the Acropolis with six bus-loads of tourists is OK, but you'll find the real Greece down the street playing backgammon in an Athens *taverna*. Rome has plenty of temples and monuments to the dead. After your tour of the Forum, liven things up by crossing the river for a wander through Trastevere, today's Roman village. Europe is a cultural carnival, and time after time, you'll find that its best acts are free.

Traditional travel writing gives its readers an eloquent void—a thousand column-inches wide. This book fills that hole with a foundation in travel skills that will prepare and encourage you to experience Europe—as well as the world—from Walla Walla to Bora Bora. You'll experience Europe as a temporary local person—seeing a living Europe, not just a quick appraisal from the roof garden of the Inter-Continental hotel and cultural cliches kept alive only for tourists.

I'll discuss problems and offer solutions, bolstered by cocky optimism. Too much travel writing comes from free trips. But a guest of a country's tourist industry gains experience that is helpful only to other guests of the industry. I travel the way you will. My job is to make mistakes (and I'm good at my job) so you can learn from them.

This book dispels myths. It helps you conquer the fears and apprehensions that evil forces create to scare you out of your independent travel dreams and into the arms of organized travel.

Here are a few of my beliefs.

• You can travel anywhere in Europe for $35 a day, plus transportation costs. Money has little to do with enjoying your trip. In fact, spending more money builds a wall between you and what you came to see. If you spend enough, you can surround yourself with other Americans and talk baseball. A tight budget forces you to travel "close to the ground," meeting and communicating with the people, not relying on service with a purchased smile. But cheap doesn't mean lousy. I'll never sacrifice sleep, nutrition, safety or cleanliness in the name of budget. I enjoy—and prefer—the alternatives to expensive hotels and restaurants.

• I have found that if I don't enjoy a place it's often because I don't know enough about it. Seek out the truth. You don't need to settle for entrepreneurial tourist traps.

• A culture is legitimized by its existence. Give a people the benefit of your open mind. We really have no right to ridicule a starving Hindu for his fat cow. It's natural—but incorrect—to measure the world by America's yardstick of cultural values. I try to understand and this helps me to accept without judging. This attitude makes travel more fun.

• Of course, travel, like the world, is a series of hills and valleys. Be fanatically positive. Remember, Lisbon traffic jams are so much more fun than those back home! Optimism is a mental discipline, a requirement for "dream-travel".

Travel is addictive. It can make you a happier American as well as a citizen of the world. Our Earth is home to five billion equally important people. That's wonderfully humbling. Globe-trotting destroys ethnocentricity and broadens our perspectives so we can understand and appreciate the diverse cultures that grace this planet. Travel changes people, and I like the results. Many travelers assimilate the best points of different cultures into their own character. Europe is a cultural garden and "back door travelers" are fixing the ultimate salad—come join us!

1
Planning

The more you plan and prepare, the better your trip will be. A European adventure is a huge investment of time and money. Those who invest wisely enjoy tremendous returns.

Tour vs. Independent Travel

One of the first big decisions to make is whether to travel alone or with a group tour. Consider the pros and cons of each. Do you want the security of knowing that all your rooms are reserved and that a trained guide will take you smoothly from one hotel to the next? Do you require good hotels and restaurant meals, wishing at the same time to be as economical as possible? Will you forego adventure, independence and the challenge of doing it on your own in order to take the worry and bother out of traveling? Is sitting on a bus with the same group of tourists an acceptable way to spend your vacation? If the answer to these questions is "yes", then you need a good European tour company. There's a tour for just about every need. Your travel agent can help you.

For many people, tours are the most economical way to see Europe. Without a tour, three restaurant meals a day and a big, modern hotel are very expensive. Large tour companies book thousands of rooms and meals year-round and can, with their tremendous economic clout, get prices that no individual tourist could even come close to. For instance, on a recent "Cosmos" tour (one of the largest and cheapest tour companies in Europe), for $50 a day I got fine rooms (with private bath), three hot meals a day, bus transportation and the services of a European guide. Considering that each hotel room alone would have cost the tourist off the street at least $50, that all-inclusive tour price per day was great. Such

Europe is crawling with tour groups. Some are lots of fun.

comfort without a tour is very expensive. (To get the most out of your tour, read the chapter on "Bus Tour Self-Defense.")

A tour, however, is not the most inexpensive way to see Europe. The cheapest and, for me, the best way to see Europe is to travel independently. If you've read this far, you have what it takes mentally to handle Europe on your own. To the independent traveler, Europe can be a rewarding challenge and adventure as well as an enjoyable vacation. While the tour groups that unload on Europe's quaintest towns are treated as an entity, a mob to be fed, shown around, profited from, and moved out, the individual traveler enjoys Europe's warmer underbelly.

From here on, this book will focus mainly on the skills of do-it-yourself European travel. If you're destined for a tour, read on anyway. Even on a bus with 50 other people, you can and should be in control, thinking as an independent tourist—not a meek sheep in vagabondage.

Alone or With a Friend?

The independent traveler must weigh the advantages and disadvantages of traveling alone or with a friend. Here are the pros and cons.

Traveling alone gives you complete freedom and independence. You never have to wait for your partner to pack up; you never need to consider what the partner wants to see, where he wants to go, how fast he wants to travel, when he's tired, how much he wants to spend; you go where you want to, when you want to.

You meet more people when you travel alone for two reasons: you are more accessible in the eyes of a European, and loneliness will drive you to reach out and make friends. When you travel with someone, it's just too easy to focus on your partner and forget about meeting Europeans.

Solo travel is intensely personal. Without the comfortable crutch of a friend, you're more likely to know the joys of self-discovery and the pleasures found in the kindness of strangers. You will be exploring yourself as well as a new city or country.

Traveling alone can be very lonely. Hotel rooms become lifeless cells and meals are served in a puddle of silence. Big cities can be cold and ugly when the only person you have to talk to is yourself. Being sick alone in a country where no one even knows you exist is, even in retrospect, a miserable experience.

Europe is full of lonely travelers, and there are a few natural meeting places. You're likely to find a vaga-buddy in youth hostels, museums, on one-day bus tours and on trains. Eurailers meet plenty of other Eurailers on the trains.

Traveling with a partner overcomes many of these problems. Shared experiences are more fun, and for the rest of your life, there will be a special bond between you. The confident, uninhibited extrovert is better at making things happen and is more likely to run into exciting and memorable events. And when I travel with a partner it's easier for me to be that kind of "wild and crazy guy."

Traveling with a partner is cheaper. Rarely does a double room cost as much as two singles. If a single room costs $20, a double room will generally be around $30, a savings of $5 per night per person. Picnicking is cheaper and easier when you share costs, as are travel guides, banking, maps, magazines, taxis, storage lockers and much more. Besides expenses, partners can share the burden of time-consuming hassles, like standing in ticket, bank, or post office lines.

Remember, traveling together greatly accelerates a relationship—especially a romantic one. You see each other constantly, making endless decisions. The niceties go out the window. Everything becomes very real, and you are in an adventure—and a struggle—together. You can jam the

On your own, you'll have locals dancing with you—not for you.

experiences of years into one summer.

I'd be scared to death to marry someone I hadn't traveled with. A mutual travel experience is unreasonably stressful on a relationship—revealing its ultimate course. In every conceivable sense, it's the greatest way to get to know somebody.

Your choice of a travel partner is crucial. It can make or break a trip. Traveling with the wrong partner can be like a two-month computer date. I'd rather travel alone. Analyze your travel styles and goals for compatibility. Consider a trial weekend together before merging your dream trips.

Choose a partner carefully. One summer I went to Europe to dive into as many cultures and adventures as possible. The trip was a challenge, and I planned to rest when I got home. My partner wanted to get away from it all, relax and escape the pressures of the business world. Our ideas of acceptable hotels and good meals were quite different. The trip was a near-disaster.

Many people already have their partner—for better or for worse. In the case of married couples, remember to minimize the stress of traveling together by recognizing each other's needs for independence. There's absolutely nothing selfish, dangerous, insulting or wrong with taking time alone to exercise your independence, but it's a freedom too few travel partners allow themselves. After you do your own thing for a few hours or days, your togetherness will be fun again.

Traveling in a threesome or foursome is usually troublesome. With all the exciting choices Europe has to offer it's often hard even for a two-some to reach a consensus. The "split and be independent" strategy is particularly valuable here, especially if each person is strong-willed.

Another way to minimize travel partnership stress is to go communal with your money. Separate checks, double bank changes, and long lists of petty IOU's in six different currencies are a pain. Pool your resources, noting how much each person contributes, and just assume everything equals out in the long run. Keep track of major individual expenses, but don't worry who got an extra postcard or *gelati*. Enjoy treating each other to taxis and dinner out of your "kitty", and after the trip, divvy up the remains. If one person consumed $25 or $30 more, that's a small price to pay for the convenience of communal money.

Many single travelers pick up a partner in Europe.

Our Travel Industry

It's a huge business—travel. Most of what the industry promotes is decadence: lie on the beach and be catered to; hedonize those precious two weeks to make up for the other fifty; see if you can eat five meals a day and still snorkel when you get into port. That's where the money is and that's where most of the interest is. The industry caters to the rich tourist while you (anyone who's read this far in this book) are just a fringe that fits the industry like a snowshoe in Mazatlan.

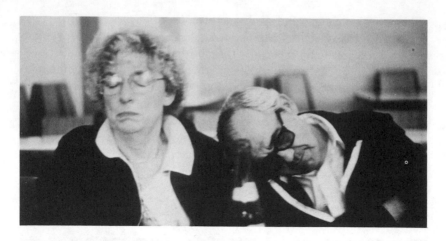

Their travel agent recommended this tour.

As a newspaper travel columnist, I've learned a lot about the politics of tourism. Advertising makes your newspaper's travel section go. Practical consumer information does not sell cruises. The advertisers (travel agencies) that support the travel section of one of the newspapers I wrote for, organized a kind of boycott and approached the editor saying that they would not advertise as long as my column was called "The Budget Traveler." I met with the editor and we decided to change the name to "The Practical Traveler"—same subversive information but with a more palatable title—and we managed to keep the ads coming in. The key to marketable travel writing is not to teach or write well—but to write stories that enthuse prospective travelers while furthering the myths that inhibit independent travel. Tales of Ugly Americanism, high costs, language barriers, theft and sickness, help fill the cruise ships and tour buses with would-be independent adventurers.

Most travel agents could not and would not travel "Through the Back Door." The most typical attitude I get when I hobnob with big-wigs from the industry in Hilton Hotel ballrooms is "If you can't go first class, it's better to stay home." I'll never forget the bewilderment I caused when I turned down a free room in Bangkok's most elegant Western-style hotel in favor of a ten dollar Thai-style hotel. That did not compute.

Of course, these comments are generalizations and there are many great travelers in the industry that do more than sell ads. These people will understand my frustration because they've also had to deal with it. Travel in a hungry world can be rich people flaunting their affluence—

taking pictures of poor kids jumping off ships for small change. Or it can promote understanding—turning our American perspective into a human perspective and making our world more comfortable in its smallness. What the industry promotes is up to each individual agent, and—consumers.

Your Travel Agent—
And How to Choose One

Travel agents: How do you find one? When do you use one? And which of their services is necessary? I start every trip by visiting my agent. So should you.

What do I need from an agent? Travel agents are, or should be, experts on the logistics of travel—getting there, getting around over there, and tour options. For independent budget international travel, I use an agent for my plane ticket, trainpass or car rental and nothing else.

While many agents can give you handy tips on Irish B&Bs and sporadic advice on the best biking in Holland, basically, use your travel agent to get you there and after that rely on a good guidebook.

It takes a full time and aggressive travel professional to keep up with the crazy and deregulated airline industry these days. You won't save money by going directly to the airlines. Most airline representatives barely know what they're charging, much less their competitors' rates and schedules. And only your agent would remind you that leaving two days earlier would get you in on the end of shoulder season—and save you $50. Agents charge you nothing. They make their money from commissions paid by the airlines—not by marking up your tickets. Take advantage of their expertise.

A good agent understands that there's no free lunch in the airline industry. Normally, for every dollar you save, you're losing a dollar's worth of comfort, flexibility or reliability. Rather than grab the cheapest ticket to Europe, I go with my agent's recommendation for the best combination of reliability, economy and flexibility for my travel needs.

Car rentals are cheaper when arranged before departure through your agent. Eurailpasses and many other rail passes must be purchased before you leave home. To get good service on small tedious items like these, do all your trip business through the agent who made a good commission on your air ticket.

When do I buy? Meet with your agent as soon as you know where you're going. Buy your plane tickets as soon as you're ready to firmly commit yourself to flight dates and ports. As you delay, dates will sell out and prices will most likely rise. Once you buy your ticket you fix the price but remember, cheap tickets are very expensive to change.

Who do I buy from? If people spent as much energy finding the right agent and cultivating a loyal relationship with him or her as they do shopping around for the cheapest ticket, they'd be much better off. A good agent can get you almost any ticket and dumping your agent for a $30 savings from a discount agent down the street is a bad move.

These days people are milking every good agent for all they're worth and then buying their tickets from their sister's friend's agency around the corner. Because of this trend, it's tough to get good advice over the phone and "browsers" usually get no respect. I thoroughly enjoy the luxury of sitting down with my agent, explaining travel plans, getting a thorough briefing on my options and choosing the best flight. I don't have time to sort through all the frustrating seemingly too-good-to-be-true ads that fill many Sunday mornings with shouts of "Come on!"

If you have a travel specialty, find an agency with the same focus. In the fast-paced and deregulated airline industry, your agency should be computerized and up-to-date. Big or specializing agencies do have more clout with the airlines and often can exercise a little more flexibility with airline rules and prices. Big city agencies have a closer working relationship with airlines and therefore, a slight advantage. But a hardworking smaller agency may give you more personal attention and be less distracted. The travel agency chains are best suited to help the business traveler. Often, but not always, the discounting agencies make too little per ticket to properly service their masses. I'd choose a no-frills flight— not a no-frills agency. Recommendations from other travelers provide excellent leads.

But the right agency doesn't guarantee the right agent. You need a particular person—someone whose definition of "good travel" matches yours. Consider his or her attitude and experience. Are you a Love Boat, eat-five-meals-a-day and see-if-you-can-still-snorkle-type traveler? Or do you travel to leave rather than flaunt your Americanness? Quiz your agent (see below). You'll learn a lot.

Know Thy Travel Agent—a Quiz

One way to be sure your travel agent is properly suited to helping you with your trip is to ask him or her a few questions. Here's a little quiz—complete with answers . . .

1. **What is "open jaws?"**
   a) Yet another shark movie sequel.
   b) A tourist in awe of the Mannekin Pis.
   c) A special interest tour of Czechoslovakia's dental clinics.
   d) An airline ticket that allows you to fly into one city and out of another.

2. **Which international boat rides are covered by the Eurailpass?**
   a) Poland to Switzerland.
   b) All of them.
   c) Ireland to France, Sweden to Finland, Italy to Greece, and Germany and Sweden to Denmark.

3. **What's the Youth Hostel membership age limit?**
   a) Five.
   b) As high as 30 if you like the Rolling Stones.
   c) There is none.

4. **What is the best way to get from London's Heathrow Airport into London?**
   a) Walk.
   b) In a Youth Hostel.
   c) Don't. Spend your whole vacation at Heathrow.
   d) By subway.

5. **What is an ISIC card?**
   a) A universal way to tell foreigners you're not feeling well.
   b) It beats three-of-a-kind.
   c) International Student Identity Card, good for many discounts at sights and museums.

6. **Is there a problem getting a "bed and breakfast" in England's small towns without a reservation?**
   a) Not if you live there.
   b) Yes. Carry No-Doze in England.
   c) No.

7. **How much does a Yugoslavian visa cost?**
   a) "How much you have, comrade?"
   b) You can just charge it on your "Visa" card.
   c) More than a Grecian urn.
   d) It's free and can be obtained easily at the border.

Answers 1-d, 2-c, 3-c, 4-d, 5-c, 6-c, 7-d.

Once you find the right agent, nurture your alliance. Be loyal, keep your traveling eggs together in the correct basket and travel with this expert on your side.

Travel Insurance—
To Insure or Not to Insure

Travel insurance is a way to buy off the financial risks of traveling. These financial risks include accidents, health, missed flights, cancelled or interrupted tours, lost baggage, emergency evacuation, and so on. Each traveler's risk and potential loss varies, depending upon how much of their trip is pre-paid, the kind of air ticket purchased, their health, the health of their loved ones, value of their luggage, where they're traveling, what health coverage they already have, the financial health of their tour company or airline and so on. For some, insurance is a good deal—for others it's not.

Travel agents will recommend travel insurance because they make a commission off of it, they can be held liable for your losses if they don't explain insurance options to you, and maybe because it's right for you. But the final decision is yours.

What are the chances of needing it, how able are you to take the risks and what's the peace of mind worth to you?

There are **package insurance** deals, like that offered by the Travel Guard Company, providing you everything but the kitchen sink for 7% of your prepaid trip cost (airfare, car rental, Eurail ticket, tour cost, etc.). This can be a better deal for those with less prepaid (those without tours) since coverage is the same regardless of your premium. This covers any deductible expense your existing medical insurance plan doesn't cover. And it also gives you a supplemental collision damage waiver on rental cars. The included insurance on a rental car normally has a $1000 deductible clause. A collision damage waiver (CDW) supplement from the car rental company cuts your deductible to zero but costs from $5 to $10 per day—great for peace of mind but tough on the pocketbook. The CDW savings alone can more than cover your 7% insurance cost on a policy like Travel Guard's. Find out if your car insurance already covers you. However you get it, the CDW insurance supplement is something I hate to do without. It's so much more fun to drive relaxed, knowing you can turn in your car an unrecognizable shambles with an apologetic shrug saying, "S-s-s-sorry"—and lose no money. Driving with this kind of confidence is safer. Note: Lately car rental agencies have been making the "deductible" amount the total value of the car which is way over the maximum coverage (usually $2500) given by travel insurance companies. This racket almost forces you to go with their CDW deal.

The problem with a Travel Guard-type package is that you must take the whole works—dental care, hotel overbooking, CDW supplement and all—whether you need it or not. It's comprehensive, but not necessarily cheapest.

If you want more control, you can order your **travel insurance a la carte** through a policy like Mutual of Omaha's. This insurance menu includes four sections: medical, baggage, trip cancellation and flight insurance. Tailor it to your needs, then compare it with the package deal explained above.

Medical insurance may be unnecessary. Most health insurance policies (Blue Cross, Group Health and Blue Shield for instance) cover emergency medical expenses wherever you break your toe. Before your trip, check your coverage and know what information to collect to be properly reimbursed when you get back home.

Baggage insurance costs about $2 or $3 per day per $1000 coverage. If you're traveling with all your valuables in your moneybelt or left at home, this coverage is unnecessary.

Trip cancellation or interruption insurance covers your losses if you must cancel or interrupt your trip. This policy covers all your losses if your travel partner or a family member cannot travel due to sickness or a list of other acceptable reasons; if your tour company or airline goes out of business or can't perform as promised; or, if for a good reason you miss a flight or need an emergency one. This costs about five and a half per cent of the amount you want covered (e.g., $1500 tour and $500 airfare is fully insurable for $110). This is a good deal if you figure there's a better than one in twenty chance you'll need it. The rugged, healthy, unattached and gung-ho traveler will probably skip this coverage. Someone with questionable health taking an organized tour (which is very expensive to cancel) should consider getting this coverage.

Flight insurance (crash coverage) is great for your heirs. But statistically it's a rip-off. Over 30,000 airplanes take off and land safely every day. The chances of being in an airplane crash are minuscule.

Your travel agent has insurance brochures. Ask her which she recommends for your travels and why. Study the brochures. Consider how insurance fits your travel and personal needs, compare the likelihood of your using it and your potential loss to its cost—and then decide. In 17 European vacations I have never insured myself and I've suffered no expenses that would have been covered by insurance. But if I play this game long enough, sooner or later I'll lose. Every traveler can and should make an informed decision on whether or not to travel insured.

Information Sources

Books

Too many people spend their vacations stranded on a Paris street corner. They thought they could manage without a guidebook—or maybe they didn't think at all. You need a good directory-type guidebook. You can't fake it in Europe. Those who get the best trip for the least expense and with minimal headaches not only have a good guidebook—they *use* it. I can step off the plane for my first time in Bangkok and travel like an old pro by taking full advantage of a good guidebook.

Before buying a book, study it. How old is the information? The cheapest books are often the oldest—no bargain. Who wrote it? What's his experience? Is it readable? Many guidebooks are practical only as a powerful sedative. It should be fun but not wordy.

Don't believe everything you read. The power of the printed word is scary. Most books are peppered with information that is simply wrong. Incredibly enough, even this book may have an error (but I could be wrong). Many "writers" succumb to the temptation to write guidebooks based on hearsay, travel brochures and other books.

There are many handy books. Find a bookstore that specializes in travel books. Ask the salesperson's opinions. Browse—books are a traveler's most valuable tool.

Here are a few books that I've found very helpful.

Let's Go: Europe   Aptly subtitled "The Bible of the Budget Traveler," I wouldn't travel without it. *Let's Go* covers the big cities, towns and countryside of all European countries as well as North Africa and the USSR. You'll find listings of budget accommodations and restaurants, info on public transportation, capsule social, political and historical run-downs and a refreshingly opinionated look at sights and tourist activities. It doesn't teach "Ugly Americanism" like many prominent Europe guidebooks.

Although written by Harvard students for young travelers, it's the best book available for anyone wanting to travel as a temporary European in search of cultural intimacy on a budget. It is updated each year and hard to find in Europe (always use the current edition—I've bought the last twelve).

Let's Go also publishes books covering these countries individually: Britain and Ireland, Spain, Portugal and Morocco, France, Greece, Italy, Israel and Egypt. If you'll be spending two weeks in any of these areas and like Let's Go's style, these editions are for you. Offering ten times the coverage of *Let's Go: Europe* and giving you some elite info (very few people use these compared to *Europe*), these are easily the best guides available for these countries. The new Morocco, Israel and Egypt books fill a void.

Europe on $30 a Day, Arthur Frommer   This classic guide is the best around for the big cities but totally ignores everything else (and there's so much more!). It is full of reliable and handy listings of budget hotels, restaurants, and sightseeing ideas compiled by the father of budget independent travel himself. I take along only the chapters on the cities I plan to visit as supplemental information. This book is in tune to the needs of older travelers.

Frommer books on specific countries offer a much more thorough coverage of each country—regions, towns and villages as well as cities. Some of these are "wordy" at the expense of practical help and most overemphasize hotel and restaurant listings, neglecting sights and culture. I hate to see 80% of a book's pages spent listing places to eat and sleep when any B & B will do. This conditions readers to think that 80% of their concern will be on finding room and board. Frommer's $X a Day books have a budget focus, while his *Dollarwise* guides are for pricier travel.

Discovery Trips in Europe   This Sunset guide is great pre-trip reading offering "Discovery Trips" (their "back doors") to every corner of Europe. It has a snatch here and snippet there approach rather than attempting comprehensive coverage. It can give you some unique ideas for your itinerary. Well written and worth studying and taking applicable photocopies or notes with you.

The Whole World Handbook   By the Council on International Educational Exchange, this is, without any doubt, the greatest sourcebook for those interested in working or studying in Europe. CIEE is the biggest and most energetic student travel service in the USA—well worth taking advantage of.

Michelin Green Guides   These famous tall green books, available in dryly translated English all over Europe, ignore hotels and eating but are a gold mine of solid practical info on what to see, covering many regions in Europe. English editions I've used are: Paris, London, southwest England, Italy, Spain, Portugal, Greece, Germany, Austria, Switzerland, The Loire Valley, Normandy, Brittany, French Riviera and Provence. Each book includes comprehensive general chapters on history, lifestyles, art, culture, customs, economy and so on. My favorite feature is the large map with places listed according to their touristic importance rather than their population. An exciting village appears bolder on the map than a big, dull city.

Rough Guides   This series by Englishman Mark Ellingham includes books on Spain, Portugal, Morocco, Greece, Yugoslavia, and Holland. They are great sources of hard-core go-local-on-a-tight-budget info. Ellingham has accumulated an incredible amount of practical info but is unable to update annually. Check the print dates.

Blue Guides   This series of books (which has nothing to do with European brothels) takes a very dry and scholarly approach to the countries of Europe. Blue Guides are ideal if you want to learn as much as you possibly can about each country (architecture or art history, for instance). With the Blue Guide to Greece I had all the information I would ever need about any sight in Greece. There was no need ever to hire or buy a guide.

Rick Steves' Books   *22 Days in Europe*, 3rd Edition, 1987, 144 pages. Europe's best three weeks—in recipe form. This book lays out the most efficient and exciting mix of "must see" sights, intimate "back door" nooks and off-beat crannies. It's a step-by-step handbook complete with city maps, day plans, train schedules and everything you need to know to be your own tour guide. Also available: *22 Days in Great Britain, 22 Days in Spain & Portugal, 22 Days in Germany, Austria & Switzerland,* and *22 Days in Norway, Sweden & Denmark.*

Europe 101: History and Art for the Traveler, 2nd edition, 1987, 370 pages, is the first and only fun traveler's guide to Europe's history and art. Full of boiled-down, practical information to make your sightseeing more meaningful and enjoyable. The perfect companion to all the "survival guides," *Europe 101* is your "passport to culture" in a practical and easy-to-read manual.

Mona Winks: Self-guided Tours of Europe's Top Museums by Rick Steves and Gene Openshaw. Don't assume you can buy good English guidebooks on the spot for Europe's sights and museums. Those that are available are so dry that if you read them out loud your lips would chap. *Mona Winks* is a breezy, step-by-step, painting-by-sculpture walk through the best hour or two of the Louvre, the Uffizi, the Prado, the Roman Forum, etc. Essential for those who know a lot about everything but art. (See the back of this book to order other Rick Steves books.)

While adequate travel information is what keeps you afloat, too much info can sink the ship. You can always find good travel books in English in Europe. I rip my books up, bringing with me only the chapters that will be needed on my trip. There's no point in carrying around 120 pages of information on the British Isles if you're not going there. When I finish seeing a country, I give my stapled-together chapter on that area to another traveler or leave it at my last hotel.

Your public library has a lifetime of valuable reading on European culture. Look under Dewey Decimal #914 for plenty of books on your destination. Versailles came to life after I read a Newsweek book on the court of Louis XIV. If travel partners divide up their studying they can take turns being "guide" and do a better job.

Talk With Other Travelers

Both in Europe and here at home, travelers love to share their mental souvenirs and the lessons they've learned. Grab every opportunity you can to learn from other tourists. Firsthand, fresh information is the best kind anywhere, and it just waits to be harvested. Keep in mind, however, that all assessments of a place's touristic merit (including my own) are a product of that person's time there and his personality. It could have rained, he could have met the meanest people or he may have been sick in "that lousy, overrated city." Or, he may have fallen in love in that "wonderful" village. All opinions are just that—opinions.

As you travel remember that many of the best guidebooks are not sold in the USA. Take advantage of every opportunity (train or bus rides, etc.)

to swap information with travelers you meet from other parts of the English-speaking world. This is particularly important when traveling beyond Europe.

Classes

The more you understand something, the longer it stays interesting. For instance, everyone enjoys their first Gothic cathedral. But those with no background in medieval architecture are the first to get "cathedraled out." Whether you like it or not, you'll be spending lots of time browsing through historic buildings and museums. Trust me, you'll have more fun sightseeing in Europe if you prepare by doing some reading or taking some classes beforehand.

There are plenty of worthwhile classes on many aspects of Europe. While you can get by with English, a foreign language—even a few phrases—can only add to your enjoyment of Europe. History makes Europe come alive. A basic modern European history course turns a dull museum into a trip highlight.

Eastern Europe is a demographic nightmare. An Eastern European studies class will bring a little order to that chaos. Art history is probably the most valuable course for the prospective tourist. Please don't go to Europe—especially Italy or Greece—without at least having read something on art and architecture.

National Tourist Offices

Tourism is an important part of Europe's economy. Each country has a National Tourist Office with a healthy promotional budget. They are happy to send you a free package of information on their country. Just send them a postcard. Ask for info about your specific interests (e.g., hiking in Austria, castles in Germany, maps, calendar of festivals) to get exactly what you need along with the general packet.

Europe

Austrian National Tourist Office, 500 5th Ave., Suite 2009-2022, New York NY 10110, (212) 944-6880

British Tourist Authority, 40 W. 57th St. 3rd floor, New York NY 10019, (212) 581-4700

Belgian National Tourist Office, 745 5th Ave., New York NY 10151, (212) 758-8130

Bulgaria: Balkan Holidays, 161 E 86th St., New York NY 10028. (212) 722-1110

Czechoslovakia Travel Bureau, 10 East 40th St. #1902, New York NY 10016, (212) 689-9720

Denmark (see Scandinavia)

Finland (see Scandinavia)

French Tourist Office, 610 Fifth Ave., New York NY 10020-2452, (212) 757-1125

German National Tourist Office, 747 Third Ave., New York NY 10017, (212) 308-3300

Greek National Tourist Organization, 645 Fifth Ave., New York NY 10022, (212) 421-5777

Hungarian Travel Bureau IBUSZ, 630 5th Ave., #2455, New York NY 10111, (212) 582-7412

Irish Tourist Board, 757 3rd Ave., New York NY 10017, (212) 418-0800

Italian Government Travel Office, 630 Fifth Ave., #1565, New York NY 10020, (212) 245-4822

Luxembourg National Tourist Office, 801 Second Ave., New York NY 10017, (212) 370-9850

Netherlands National Tourist Office, 355 Lexington Ave., 21st floor, New York NY 10017, (212) 370-7367

Norway (see Scandinavia)

Polish Travel Bureau, 130 E 7th, New York NY 10009, (212) 674-3652

Portuguese National Tourist Office, 548 Fifth Ave., New York NY 10036, (212) 354-4403

Rumanian National Tourist Office, 573 Third Ave., New York NY 10016, (212) 697-6971

Scandinavian National Office, 655 3rd Ave., 18th Floor, New York, NY 10017, (212) 949-2333

Spanish National Tourist Office, 665 Fifth Ave., New York NY 10022, (212) 759-8822

Sweden (see Scandinavia)

Swiss National Tourist Office, 608 Fifth Ave., New York NY 10020, (212) 757-5944

Turkish Tourism Office, 821 United Nations Plaza, New York NY 10111, (212) 687-2194

USSR: Intourist, 630 Fifth Ave., #868, New York NY 10111, (212) 757-3884

Yugoslavia National Tourist Office, 630 Fifth Ave., #280, New York NY 10111, (212) 757-2801

Middle East and North Africa

Egyptian Tourist Office, 630 Fifth Ave., New York NY 10111, (212) 246-6960

Israel Government Tourist Office, 350 Fifth Ave., New York NY 10118, (212) 560-0650

Jordan Information Bureau, 2319 Wyoming Ave., NW, Washington DC 20008, (202) 265-1606

Moroccan National Tourist Office, 20 East 46th St., #1201, New York NY 10017, (212) 557-2520

Pack Light Pack Light Pack Light

The importance of packing light cannot be overemphasized—but for your own good, I'll try. You'll never meet a traveler who after several trips brags, "Every year I pack heavier." The measure of a good traveler is how light he travels. You can't travel heavy, happy and cheap. (Pick two.)

Limit yourself to twenty pounds in a "carry-on" sized bag (9" × 22" × 14" fits under the airplane seat). You're probably muttering, "Impossible," but believe me it can be done and after you enjoy that sweet mobility and freedom you'll never go any other way. I've taken several hundred people of all ages and styles to Europe in mini-groups. Only one carry-on bag was allowed and now these former non-believers are the fanatic nucleus of my pack-light cult.

You'll walk with your luggage more than you think. Before leaving home, give yourself a test. Pack up completely, go into your hometown and be a tourist for an hour. Fully loaded, you should enjoy window shopping—if you can't, go home and thin out.

When you carry your own luggage, it's less likely to get lost, broken or stolen. It sits on your lap or under your seat on the bus, taxi and airplane. You don't have to worry about it, and when you arrive, you leave—immediately. It's a good feeling. When I land in London, I am

Pack light and travel mobile. These travelers are using a convertible suitcase/rucksack.

virtually downtown before anyone else on the plane even knows if their bags made it through.

Too much luggage slams the "back door" shut. Serendipity suffers and changing locations becomes a major operation. Porters are only a problem to those who need them. One bag hanging on your back is nearly forgotten. Take this advice seriously. Don't be one of the thousands of tourists who return home cursing their luggage and vowing never again to travel with so much stuff.

Backpackademia—What to Bring?

How do you fit a whole trip's worth of luggage into a small suitcase or rucksack? The answer is simple—bring very little.

Spread out everything you think you'll need on the living room floor. Pick up each item and scrutinize it—look at it critically. Ask yourself, "Will I really use this snorkel and fins enough to justify carrying it around all summer?" Not "will I use it" but "will I use it *enough?*" I'd buy them in Greece before I'd carry that extra weight through the Alps.

Think in terms of what you can do without—not what will be handy on your trip. The key rule of thumb is, "When in doubt, leave it out." I've seen people pack a whole summer's supply of deodorant, nylons or razors, thinking you can't get it there. Europeans are civil. The world's getting awfully small—I bought Herbal Essence shampoo in Sicily a few years ago. You can get anything in Europe. Tourist shops in major international hotels are a sure bet whenever you have difficulty finding some personal item. Whether I'm traveling for 3 weeks or 3 months, I pack exactly the same. Rather than take a whole trip's supply of toiletries, I take enough to get started and look forward to running out of toothpaste in Bulgaria. Then I have the perfect excuse to go into a Bulgarian department store, shop around and pick up something I think might be toothpaste.

Rucksack or Suitcase?

Whether you take a small suitcase with a shoulder strap (wheels are silly for independent international travel), or rucksack is up to you. Packing light applies equally to suitcase or rucksack travelers. Most young travelers go the rucksack route. If you are a "suitcase" person who would like the ease of a rucksack without foregoing the "respectability" of a suitcase, look into the new and very popular convertible, suitcase/rucksacks with zip-away shoulder straps. These carry-on sized bags give you the best of both worlds. I live out of one of these for three months at a time. (See The Back Door Catalog at the back of this book.)

I used to carry a frame pack because I had a sleeping bag. Unless you plan to camp or sleep out a lot, a sleeping bag is a bulky security blanket. Even on a low budget, bedding will be provided. I'd rather risk being cold one or two nights out of the summer than carry my sleeping bag for ten weeks—just in case I might need it. Don't pack to camp unless you're going to camp.

Without a sleeping bag, a medium sized rucksack is plenty big. Start your trip with it only two-thirds full to leave room for picnic food and things travelers always tend to pick up. Also, of course, bags don't pack so compact and orderly once you actually start living out of them. Sturdy stitching, front and side pouches, padded shoulder straps and a low-profile color are rucksack virtues. A simple, rugged bag for your trip needn't cost more than $60 or $70.

Clothing

The bulk of your luggage is clothing. Minimize by bringing less and washing more often. There is no need for more than three pairs of socks (unless you enjoy carrying a bag full of dirty laundry). Every night you'll spend two minutes doing a little washing. This doesn't mean more washing, it just means doing a little washing as you go along.

Bring dark clothes that wash and dry quickly and easily. You should have no trouble drying clothing overnight in your hotel room. I know this sounds barbaric, but my body dries out a damp pair of socks or shirt in a jiffy.

It's always fun to buy clothes as you travel. This is just another reason to pack only a minimal amount of clothing. Last summer I put away my Yankee-style jeans and enjoyed the European-style comfort of a light baggy pair of cotton pants I bought in Amsterdam.

For winter travel, I pack just as light. The only difference is a down coat, long johns, mittens and an extra pair of socks and underwear since things dry slower. Pack with the help of a climate chart. (See Appendix.)

Europe is casual. I have never felt out of place at symphonies, operas, plays, wearing a new pair of jeans and a good-looking sweater. Cultural events seem to be more formal outside of the tourist season. Of course, there are situations where more formal attire would be in order, but the casual tourist rarely encounters these. Older travelers may have different taste in clothing (keep in mind I'm a 33-year-old who's never appeared on a best-dressed list).

Many travelers are concerned about appropriate dress. European women wear dresses more than pants. American women will generally feel fine in pants but in certain rural and very traditional areas they'll fit in better and more comfortably in their dress. Tennis shoes and jeans mark you as an American. Frankly, so what? Europeans will know you're a Yankee anyway. I fit in and am culturally sensitive by watching my manners—not the cut of my pants.

There is a handful of sacred places mostly in Southern Europe which have modest dress requirements. This is basically no short pants or bare shoulders. While these dress codes deserve respect, it's usually easy to improvise some modesty (even a hairy-legged man can wear a nearby tablecloth as a kilt in order to be allowed in.)

Go casual, simple and very light. Remember, in your travels, you'll meet two kinds of tourists—those who pack light . . . and those who wish they did.

Recommended Clothing (for summer travel)

One pair long pants, light weight, light colored cotton

Walking shorts with plenty of pockets—doubles as a swimsuit

Two T-shirts or short-sleeved shirts, cotton/polyester blend

Long-sleeved shirt, same blend

Dark, warm sweater—for warmth and for dressing up; it never looks wrinkled and is always dark—no matter how dirty it is.

Light, waterproofed windbreaker jacket—folds up into pocket, "Gortex" is good.

Underwear and socks—three sets, quick dry

One pair of shoes—sturdy vibram-type sole, good traction, well-broken in, light, cool. I like "Rockports." Sturdy low-profile colored tennis shoes with a good tread are fine too.

Especially for Women—summer dress or skirt, swimsuit, sandals, robe, or nightshirt.

Extras You May Want to Pack

Hostel sheet. Youth hostels require you to use a sheet. You can bring your own or rent one there for about $2 per night. If you plan to do a lot of hosteling, bring your own regular bed sheet or buy a regulation hostel sheet (basically, a normal bed sheet sewn together like a sleeping bag) at the first hostel you visit. This sheet can double as a beach or picnic blanket, is handy on overnight train rides and will save you money in other dorm-type accommodations which normally charge extra for linen.

Poncho or Parka. A plastic poncho, large enough to protect you and your pack in a rainstorm, that can open flat to serve as a ground cloth for sleeping on or for a beach or picnic blanket is ideal for the hard core vagabonds. Otherwise, a good weatherproof parka is your best bet.

Rucksack. Small size for day trips. These nylon sacks are great for carrying your sweater, camera, literature, food, and so on, while you leave most of your luggage in your larger rucksack or suitcase at the hotel or in the train station. The little rucksack folds into a pocket-size pouch when not in use.

A good paperback. There is plenty of empty time on a trip to either be bored or to enjoy some good reading. Ideally, the novel will relate to your travels, for example *Iberia* for Spain and Portugal, *The Agony and the Ecstasy* for Italy, or *Trinity* for Ireland.

European map. An overall map best suited to your trip's needs. Get maps for specific local areas as you go.

Money belt. Essential for the peace of mind it brings; you could lose everything except your money belt, and the trip could still go on. Lightweight, beige and water-resistant is best. Use it before your trip to be sure it works. (See The Back Door Catalog at the back of this book.)

Cash. Bring American dollars (Europeans get a kick out of seeing George Washington fold up into a mushroom) for situations when you only want to change a few bucks and not a whole travelers check. I bring twenty ones and a few ten and twenty dollar bills. And bring foreign cash. I buy one bill worth about thirty dollars for each country I plan to visit so I can function easily until I can get to a bank.

Picnic supplies. A small tablecloth to give your meal some extra class (and to wipe the knife on), a mini-can opener, a corkscrew, salt and pepper, a damp face cloth in a baggie for cleaning up. A Swiss army-type knife is handy for many things.

Water bottle. Small. The plastic reusable mineral water bottles sold throughout Europe work great.

Ear plugs. If night noises bother you, you'll grow to love a good set of plugs. Europe has more than its share of night noises.

Zip-lock baggies. 1,001 uses; great for leftover picnic food, containing wetness and bagging potential leaks before they happen. Bring a variety of sizes.

First-aid kit. (See Chapter 7, Health)

Medicine. In original containers with legible prescriptions.

Wristwatch. A built in alarm is handy. Otherwise consider packing a small travel alarm clock as well.

Extra glasses, contacts and prescriptions.

Toiletries. In a small container. Minimal. Remember to put all squeeze bottles in zip-lock baggies since pressure changes in flight cause even good bottles to leak. Consider a vacation from cosmetics.

Nothing electrical. While there are good adapters available, every year some American plugs his Universal adapter into my hotel and the whole place goes universally black.

Clothesline. For hanging up clothes to dry in your hotel room.

Small towel. Not all hotels provide a towel. Hand towel size is adequate.

Soap. Not all hotels provide soap. A plastic squeeze-bottle of concentrated, multi-purpose liquid soap is handy for laundry and much more.

Sewing kit. Clothes age rapidly while traveling.

Travel information (minimal). Rip out appropriate chapters, staple them together, store in a zip-lock baggie. When you are done, give them away.

Postcards from your hometown and family pictures. A zip-lock baggie of show and tell things is always a great conversation piece with Europeans you may meet.

Address list. For sending postcards home and collecting new addresses. Taking a whole address book is not packing light. Consider typing your mail list onto a sheet of gummed address labels before you leave—you'll know exactly who you've written to and the labels will be perfectly legible.

Journal. If you fill an "empty book" with the experiences of your trip, it will prove to be your most treasured souvenir—I guarantee it. I use a hard bound type designed to last a lifetime rather than a spiral notebook.

Sony Walkman-type recorder. Partners bring one, with jacks for two stereo mini-earphones. Many travelers enjoy a micro-cassette recorder to tape tours, journal entries, etc. And some recorders have radios which add a whole new dimension to your experience.

Mini note pad and pen. Carry in back pocket—great organizer, reminder, and communication aid.

2
Planning an Itinerary

If you have any goals at all for your trip, make an itinerary. I never start a trip without having every day planned out. Your reaction to an itinerary may be, "That shackles me to a rigid plan at the expense of spontaneity and freedom!" While I have always begun a trip with a well thought out plan, I maintain my flexibility and make plenty of changes. An itinerary forces you to see the consequences of any spontaneous change you make while in Europe. For instance, if you spend two extra days in the sunny Alps, you'll see that you won't make it to, say, the Greek Isles. With the help of an itinerary, you can lay out your goals, maximize their potential and avoid regrettable changes.

By planning an itinerary, you can deal thoughtfully with issues like weather, crowds, culture shock, health maintenance, fatigue, festivals and inefficient transportation. The result is a smooth and more enjoyable trip.

Design an Efficient Plan

1. Establish a logical flight plan. You can avoid needless travel time and expense by flying "open-jaws". With "open-jaws" you fly into one port and out of another at no extra expense. You just pay half the round-trip fare for each port. A good example would be to fly into Oslo, travel south through whatever interests you in Europe, and fly home from Lisbon, eliminating the costly and time-consuming return to Oslo. Your travel agent will know which fares allow "open-jaws".

2. Make the most of the weather conditions you'll encounter. Match the coolest month of your trip with the warmest area, and vice

versa. For example, if you visit Europe in the spring and early summer, you'll have moderate temperatures throughout by starting in the southern countries and working your way north. If possible, avoid the mid-summer Mediterranean heat. Spend those weeks in Scandinavia or the Alps. (See Appendix for climate charts.)

3. Avoid tourist crowds. Europe is most crowded from about June 20 to August 20. Do what you can to avoid this peak season crush. If you're flexible, scoot your trip into the more relaxed shoulder months (May, early June and September). Or structure your trip to minimize crowds. Consider, for instance, a six week European trip starting on June

Venice is sinking under its peak season crowds.

1st, half with a Eurailpass to see the famous sights and half visiting relatives in Scotland. It would be wise to do the Eurail section first, enjoying those precious last three weeks of relatively uncrowded shoulder season and then spend time with the family during the last half of your vacation when Florence and Salzburg are teeming with tourists. Salzburg on June 10th and Salzburg on July 10th are two very different cities.

4. Punctuate a long trip with rest periods. Constant sightseeing is grueling. I try to schedule a peaceful period every two weeks. If your trip is six weeks or longer, schedule a vacation from your vacation in the middle of it. Most people need several days in a place where they couldn't see a museum or take a tour even if they wanted to. A stop in the mountains or on an island, in a friendly rural town, or a visit with a relative is a great way to revitalize your tourist spirit. Alternate intense big cities with villages and countryside.

5. Leave some slack in your itinerary. Don't schedule yourself too tightly (a common tendency). Everyday chores, small business matters, transportation problems and planning mistakes deserve about one day of slack per week in your itinerary.

6. Don't overestimate your powers of absorption. Especially on your first trip, European travel can be very intense, bombarding your senses from all sides day after day. Each day is packed with experiences and memories. It may be thrilling, but your body can only take so much. You have a saturation point. Rare is the tourist who doesn't become somewhat jaded after six or eight weeks of travel. At the start of my trip, I will seek out every great painting and cathedral I can. After two months, I find myself "seeing" cathedrals with a sweep of my head from the doorway, and I probably wouldn't even cross the street for a Rembrandt. Don't burn out on mediocre castles, palaces and museums. Save your energy for the biggies.

7. See countries in order of cultural hairiness. For instance, if you plan to see Britain, the Alps, Greece and Egypt, do it in that order so you'll grow steadily into the more intense and crazy travel. If you make that trip in reverse order, even if you do survive the culture shock of Egypt, England's culture will seem like a wet noodle compared to Egypt's.

8. Save your good health. If you plan to visit countries that may be "hazardous to your health" (North Africa or the Middle East), do so at the end of your trip so you won't needlessly jeopardize your healthy enjoyment of the safer countries. If you are going to get sick, it's best to do it at the end of your trip so you can recover at home missing more work, not vacation.

9. Assume you will return. This Douglas MacArthur approach is a key to touristic happiness. You'll never satisfy your thirst for Europe with one trip. Don't try to. Enjoy what you're seeing. Forget what you won't get to on this trip. If you worry about things that are just out of reach, you won't appreciate what's in your hand. I'm planning my 18th three-month European vacation, and I still need more time. I'm happy about what I can't get to. It is a blessing that we can never see all of Europe. The day when there is no more to see will be a sad one.

The nine factors listed above must be weighed and thoughtfully juggled until you arrive at a plan that gives you the optimal mix. There are several trade-offs (for instance, you may have to choose between optimal weather and minimal crowds), and you can't have the best of each point. Design the trip that best fits your needs.

Your Best Itinerary—In Eight Steps

1. Read up on Europe, talk to travelers, study. What you want to see is determined by what you know (or don't know)—identify your personal interests. WWII buffs will study up on battle sites, and McGregors will locate their clan in Scotland.

2. List all the places you want to see. Minimize clutter and redundancy. (A so-so sight, breaking a convenient night train into two half-day journeys is clutter. On a quick trip, focus on only one part of the Alps. Oxford and Cambridge are redundant—choose one.) Have a reason for every stop. Don't go to places just because they're famous. Carefully consider travel time required. When you must cut something, cut to save the most mileage. For instance, if Amsterdam and Berlin are equally important to you and you don't have time for both, cut the more distant destination, Berlin.

3. Establish general structure or framework: how long you'll stay, and where you'll fly in to and out of. Research flights for cheapest and most convenient dates and ports.

4. Determine mode of transportation, not solely on economical terms but by analyzing what is best for the trip you envision.

5. List the sights you want to see in a logical order, considering: efficient transportation (minimizing miles), an "open-jaws" flight plan, your mode of transportation, getting maximum overnight train rides (if you want them), weather and crowds. Pin down any places that you have to be on a certain date.

6. Write in the number of days you'd like to stay in each place, considering transportation time. Eurailers often use night trains (N/T) to save time and money whenever possible.

7. Add up the number of days. Adjust by cutting, streamlining or adding to fit or fill your time limitations. Consider economizing on car rental or Eurailpass. For instance, try to manage a 23-day trip on a 15-day train pass by doing London, Paris and Amsterdam outside of its validity.

8. Fine tune. Study guidebooks. Be sure crucial sights are open the day you'll be in town. Maximize festival and market days. Ask your travel agent which flight departure days are cheapest. Write out a day by day itinerary.

9. Resist the temptation to clutter your itinerary with additional sights. Be satisfied with your efficient plan and focus any more study and preparation on those places only.

Sample Itinerary Worksheet

Step 1. Study notes.

Step 2. Places I want to see:

London	Alps	Bavaria	Florence	Paris
Amsterdam	Rhine	Rome	Venice	Greece

Step 3. I can escape for 23 days. Cheapest places to fly to: London, Frankfurt, Amsterdam.

Step 4. Since I'm traveling alone, going so many miles and will spend the majority of my time in big cities, I'd rather not mess with a car. I'll use a Eurail Pass.

Steps 5 and 6. Logical order, and desired time in each place:

DAYS	
3	London
1	English Channel crossing
5	Paris
3	Alps
2	Florence
3	Rome
7	Greece
2	Venice
3	Munich/Bavaria
3	Romantic Road/Rhine Cruise
4	Amsterdam

36   Note: if I eliminate Greece, I'll still need to cut 6 days.

Note: "Open-jaws" into London and out of Amsterdam is economical.

Step 7. Itinerary adjusted to time limitations:

DAYS	
4	London (Night Train)
3	Paris (N/T)
3	Alps (N/T)
1	Florence
2	Rome (N/T)
2	Venice (N/T)
3	Munich/Bavaria
2	Romantic Road/Rhine Cruise
3	Amsterdam

23   days with a 15-day Eurailpass from last day in Paris until first day in Amsterdam

Step 8. Day-by-Day Fine-Tuned Plan

According to my guidebook, I must keep these points in mind as I plan my trip. London: theaters closed on Sundays, Speaker's Corner is Sunday only. Paris: most museums are closed on Tuesdays, Versailles and the Orsay Museum closed on Mondays. Florence: museums closed Mondays. Rome: Forum closed Tuesdays, Pantheon closed Mondays. Dachau: closed Mondays. Amsterdam: museums closed on Mondays and most shops closed on Monday mornings.

S	1	Leave home. (You'll always arrive the next day in Europe).
S	2	Arrive in **London.** Buy train ticket to Paris and a Tuesday eve theater ticket at Victoria Station. See Speaker's Corner. Take orientation bus tour.
M	3	Sightsee all day London.
T	4	Sightsee all day London. Leave bags at station. See play. N/T.
W	5	Arrive early in **Paris.** Find hotel. Explore Latin Quarter, Champs Elysees, take bus orientation tour.
T	6	Sightsee all day Paris, Louvre, Orsay museum, Notre Dame; Eve: Montmartre.
F	7	Early side trip to Versailles. Afternoon in Paris. N/T.
S	8	Arrive early in Interlaken. All day **Alps** hike (Back Door).
S	9	Free in Alps, Lauterbrunnen, Gimmelwald, Schilthorn.
M	10	Cruise Swiss lakes, afternoon and evening in city. N/T.
T	11	**Florence.** Check museum hours carefully. David closes at 1:00, Uffizi open all day.
W	12	Early train to **Rome.** Set up near station. Explore classical Rome.

T	13	Visit Vatican, St. Peter's, famous night spots. N/T.
F	14	Arrive early in **Venice.** Slow boat (#1) down Grand Canal to St. Marks. All day free.
S	15	All day free in Venice. N/T.
S	16	Arrive early in **Munich.** Reserve Romantic Road bus tour at station. Sightsee all day. Evening beerhall.
M	17	All-day side trip to Neuschwanstein (Castle Day Back Door).
T	18	Most of day in Salzburg (90-minute train from Munich).
W	19	Romantic Road bus tour from Munich to Wiesbaden stopping at Rothenburg and Dinkelsbuhl. Short train to Bingen. Check boat schedule.
T	20	Cruise the Rhine, Bingen to Koblenz (10:30-1:20) for the best castles.
F	21	Early train to **Amsterdam.** Call to reconfirm flight home. Orientation canal tour, nightlife.
S	22	All day free in Amsterdam for museums, shopping, or, bike ride into countryside.
S	23	Catch plane, Amsterdam-USA.
M	24	Relax at home, put on a fresh set of clothes, enjoy your own bed, fridge, shower, stereo and try not to think about work tomorrow. (Note: my *22 Days in Europe* book develops this itinerary in reverse order.)

Itinerary Miscellany

Hit as many festivals, national holidays and arts seasons as you can. This takes some study. Ask the national tourist office of each country you'll visit for a calendar of events. (See the festival listing, Appendix II.) An effort to hit the right places at the right time will reward you with some real highlights.

Carefully consider travel time. Driving, except on superfreeways, is generally slower than in the USA. Borrow a Thomas Cook Continental Timetable from your travel agent and get an idea of how long various train journeys will take (see Appendix III). Learn which trains are fast and avoid minor lines in countries with less-than-good railroad systems (e.g., Spain and Portugal).

Remember that most cities close many of their major tourist attractions for one day during the week. It would be a shame to be in Milan only on a Monday, for instance, when Leonardo da Vinci's "Last Supper" is out to lunch. Mondays are closed days for tourist sights in many cities, including Amsterdam, Brussels, Munich, Vienna, Lisbon, Florence, Milan, Rome and Naples. Paris closes the Louvre and most other sights on Tuesdays.

Minimize "mail stops." Arrange mail pickups before you leave. Some American Express offices offer a free clients' mail service for those who have an AmExCo card or travelers' checks. Friends or relatives (unless they live in Eastern Europe) are fine for mail stops. Every city has a general delivery service. Pick a small town where there is only one post office and no crowds. Have letters sent to you in care of "General Delivery" (or "Poste Restante" in French speaking cities). Tell your friends to print your surname in capitals and omit your middle name. If possible, avoid the Italian mail.

Don't design your trip around stale mail. Every year my mail stops are farther apart. Once a month is comfortable. If you get homesick, mail just teases you, stirring those emotions and aggravating the problem. The best remedy for homesickness is to think of Europe as your home. Until you return to the United States, your home is right where you are.

High-Speed Town-Hopping

When I tell people that I saw four or five towns in one day, many either say or think: "That guy must be crazy! Nobody can really see four or five towns in a day!" Of course, it's folly to go too fast, but many stop-worthy towns take only an hour or two to cover. Don't let guilt feelings tell you to slow down and stay longer if you really are finished with a town. There's so much more to see in the rest of Europe! Going too slow is as bad as going too fast.

If you are efficient and use the high-speed town-hopping method, you will amaze yourself at what you can see in a day. Let me explain with an example:

You wake up early in Town A. Checking out of your hotel, you have two sights to cover before your 10:00 train. (You checked the train schedule the night before.) Before getting to the station you visit the open-air market and buy the ingredients for your brunch, and pick up a brochure on town B at town A's tourist office.

From 10:00 to 11:00 you travel by train to Town B. During that hour you'll have a restful brunch, enjoy the passing scenery and prepare for Town B by reading your literature and deciding what you want to see. Just before your arrival you put the items you need (camera, jacket, tourist information) into your small daypack and, upon arrival, check the rest of your luggage in a locker. Every station has storage lockers.

Before leaving Town B's station, write down on a scrap of paper the departure times of the next few trains to Town C. Now you can sightsee as much or as little as you want and still know when to comfortably catch your train. You're ready to go. You know what you want to see. You aren't burdened by your luggage. And, you know when the trains are leaving.

Town B is great. After a snack in the park you catch the 2:30 train. By 3:00 you're in Town C where you repeat the same procedure as you did in Town B. Town C just isn't what it was cracked up to be, so after a walk along the waterfront and a look at the church you catch the first train out.

By 5:30 you arrive in D, the last town on the day's agenda. The man in the station directs you to a good budget *pension* just two blocks down the street. You're checked in and unpacked in no time, and after a few horizontal minutes, it's time to find a good restaurant and eat dinner. After a meal and an evening stroll you're ready to call it a day. Thinking back, it really was quite a day—you spent it high-speed town-hopping.

The Home-Base Strategy

The home-base strategy is a clever way to make your trip itinerary smoother, simpler and more efficient: set yourself up in a central location and use that place as a base for day trips to nearby attractions.

Here are four advantages of using this approach to European travel:

1. The home-base approach minimizes setting up time (usually over an hour). Searching for a good hotel can be exhausting, frustrating, and time-consuming.

2. You are freed from your luggage. Being able to leave your luggage in the hotel enhances your mobility. You will enjoy yourself more without your luggage and with the peace of mind that you are set up for the night.

3. You will feel comfortable and "at home" in your home-base town. This feeling takes more than a day to get, and when you are changing locations every day or two, you may never enjoy this important rootedness.

4. The home-base approach allows you to spend the evening in a city, where there is some exciting nightlife. Most small countryside towns die after 9:00 p.m. If you are not dead by 9:00, you will enjoy more action in a larger city.

Europe's generally frequent and punctual train and bus systems make this home-base strategy very practical. With a train pass, the round-trips are free; otherwise, the transportation is reasonable, often with reductions offered for round-trip tickets. Take advantage of the time you spend on the train. Use it productively.

Here are some of my favorite home-base cities and some of their best day trips:

Madrid   Toledo, Segovia, Avila, El Escorial

Amsterdam   Alkmaar, The Hague, Haarlem, The Arnhem Folk Museum, Scheveningen, Delft, most of the Netherlands

Copenhagen	Lund, Malmo, Roskilde, Helsingor, Odense
Paris	Reims, Versailles, Chartres, Fontainebleau, Chantilly
Bregenz, Austria	Lake Constance (Bodensee) area, Lindau, Meersburg, Vorarlberg, Bregenzerwald, Feldkirch
London	Oxford, Stratford, Cambridge, Salisbury (Stonehenge), Bath, and fifty others as explained in a handy guidebook called *Day Trips from London* (Hastings House).
Avignon	Nimes, Arles, The Rhone Valley
Florence	Pisa, Siena, San Gimignano, Arezzo, many small towns
Munich	Salzburg: Berchtesgaden, Augsburg, Neuschwanstein, Linderhof and Herrenchiemsee (three of King Ludwig's castles), many small Bavarian towns including Oberammergau, Wies Church.

Minimizing Peak Season Crowds

If you must travel in July and August here are a few crowd-minimizing tips that I've learned over many peak seasons in Europe.

Get off the beaten path. So many people so energetically jockey themselves into the most crowded square of the most crowded city in the most crowded month (St. Mark's Square, Venice, in July) and complain about the crowds. You could be in Venice in July and walk six blocks behind St. Mark's Basilica, step into a cafe and be greeted by the open arms of a Venice that acts like it's never seen another tourist.

Be an early bird. Walk around Rothenburg's ancient wall before breakfast. Joggers and crack-of-dawn walkers enjoy a special look at wonderfully medieval cities as they yawn and stretch and prepare for the daily onslaught of the 20th century.

Arrive at the most popular sights early or late. Mid-days are normally congested by tour groups.

On Rothenburg's medieval wall, the old days are alive and well, before breakfast.

Residential neighborhoods rarely see a tourist, much less a crowd of them. Dance with the locals while your pizza cooks.

Spend the night. Popular places near big cities and resorts like Toledo (near Madrid), San Marino (near huge Italian beach resorts) and Rothenburg (near Frankfurt) take on a more peaceful and enjoyable atmosphere at night when the legions of day trippers return to their home bases. Small towns normally lack tour-worthy hotels and are often inaccessible to large buses. So they will experience mid-day crowds at worst.

Study. Keep in mind that accessibility and promotional budgets determine a place's fame and popularity just as much as its worthiness as a tourist attraction. For example, the beaches of Greece's Peloponnesian Peninsula offer the same weather and water as the highly promoted isles of Mykonos and Ios, but are out of the way, not promoted—and have none of the crowds.

Develop a minimize-the-crowd mentality. Avoid museums on their weekly free days when they're most crowded. And, since nearly all Parisian museums are closed on Tuesday, nearby Versailles, which is open, is predictably very, very crowded. And it follows that Parisian museums are especially crowded on Mondays and Wednesdays. While crowds at the Louvre can't be avoided altogether, some thought before you start your trip can help. If you're traveling by car or bike, take advantage of your mobility by leaving the well-worn tourist routes. The Europe away from the train tracks seems more peaceful, relaxed and one step behind the modern parade.

Off-Season Europe? The Pros and Cons

Each summer Europe greets a stampede of sightseers and shoppers with its cash registers open. Before jumping into the peak season pigpile, consider an *off*-season trip.

In travel industry jargon, the year is divided into peak, shoulder, and off-season. Each time has its pros and cons. While shoulder season is the best mix of decent weather and minimal crowds, off-season (November through February) is still worth considering.

The advantages of winter travel are many. Off-season airfares are much cheaper. With fewer crowds in Europe you'll sleep cheaper. Off-season adventurers wander all alone through Leonardo's home, sit quietly in Rome's Forum, stroll desolate beaches, and enjoy log fires and a cup of coffee with the guards in French chateaux. Lines in tourist offices and at bank exchange desks will be gone. While Europe won't be geared up for you and many popular tourist-oriented parks, shows and tours will be closed, the real arts seasons, like the Vienna Opera, will be rolling and the people you deal with will be more relaxed.

Winter travel has several problems. Since much of Europe is in Canadian latitudes, the days are very short. It's dark by 5:00. The weather can be miserable—cold, windy and drizzly. But, just as summer can be wet and gray, winter can be crisp and blue—and even into mid-November, hillsides blaze with colorful leaves. Off-season hours are limited. Some sights close down entirely, most operate on shorter hours (such as 10:00-5:00 rather than 9:00-7:00) with darkness often determining the closing time. Winter sightseeing is fine in big cities, which bustle year round, while it's more frustrating in small tourist towns (beach resorts, Rhine villages, etc.) which often shut down entirely. Europe's wonderful outdoor evening ambience, a fair weather phenomenon, hibernates each winter. English language tours, common in the summer, are quite rare off-season when most visitors are natives. Tourist information offices normally stay open year round, but with shorter hours in the winter. A final disadvantage with winter travel is loneliness. The solo traveler won't have the built-in comradery of other travelers that he'd find in peak season.

To thrive in the winter, you'll need to get the most out of your limited daylight hours. Start early, eat a quick lunch, and telephone the tourist offices before they close (usually 5:00 pm) to double-check hours and confirm your plans. Pack for the cold and wet—layers, rainproof parka, gloves, wool hat, long johns, waterproof shoes and an umbrella. Remember, cold weather is colder when you're outdoors trying to enjoy yourself all day long. Use undershirts to limit the washing of slow-drying heavy shirts.

Accommodations will be easy to find—but not always heated. I conducted an 18-day November tour of Germany, Italy and France with 22 people and no room reservations. We'd amble into town around 5:00 pm and always found 22 beds with breakfast for our $10 per bed budget.

Most hotels charge less in the winter. To save some money arrive late, notice how many empty rooms they have, let them know you're a hosteler (student, senior, honeymooner, or whatever) with a particular price limit and bargain from there. Big city business centers, on the other hand, are busiest and most expensive outside of summer holiday time.

Italy, so crowded in peak season, is back to normal—its hill towns are brisk and glorious. The Alps are crowded with skiers. It's easy to rent gear but the snow often comes late. Off-season hiking is disappointing. Travel north of the Alps suffers more in the winter. It can be bitterly cold with many sights closed down. Big cities bubble on but small tourist towns become drab and dull. I could get excited about a winter anywhere along the Mediterranean.

3
Transportation

Flying to Europe

Flying to Europe is a great travel bargain—for the well-informed. The rules and regulations are confusing and always changing but, when you make the right choice—the price is right.

The key to budget flying is a good travel agent. You'll never beat the prices he can get. You'll save money and headaches if you put your energy into finding the right agent, not the cheapest flight. I can't (and don't want to) keep up with the ever-changing world of airline tickets. I rely on the experience of my agent who specializes in budget European travel to come up with the best combination of economy, reliability and convenience.

There is no great secret to getting to Europe for next to nothing. Basically, you get what you pay for—or less. Remember this equation:

A dollar saved = More restrictions, less flexibility or more risk.

There's no such thing as a free lunch (or a good lunch, for that matter) in the airline industry.

Your flight options include regular fare, Advanced Purchase Excursion Fare (APEX), standby and charter flights. Regular fare is very expensive. You get the ultimate in flexibility—but I've never met anyone spending his own money who flew that way.

The popular **APEX** is the most flexible of the budget fares. You can pick your dates and ports, but must pre-purchase your ticket and meet minimum and maximum stay requirements. (In England, it's a liberal 7 to 180 days.) APEX allows "open-jaws" plans (flying into one city and home from another) for no financial penalty. The major drawback of APEX is that you can't change your ticket once you buy it. The only way

52

to change your date is to refund your ticket (usually at a $50 loss) and buy a new one (if seats are still available) at the current fare, which is usually higher.

Standby fares are the cheapest way to go. Your savings over the APEX fare is a function of the risk you'll incur. During the busy season there is a big risk that you won't get a seat, but the savings are substantial. During the off season, the risk is low and so are the savings. If you have a very tight budget and don't mind the insecurity and possible delays, go standby. Ask your agent about the current situation. Many times when I fly I meet someone spending fifty to a hundred dollars less than I on the plane. We're flying just as fast and eating the same food. The difference was that I went to bed the night before knowing I'd be on that flight. My friend went to the airport—and stood by. Obviously, in the case of an air controllers' strike or something similar, those "cheapskates who scrounged up unsold seats at rockbottom prices" (standby passengers) are rockbottom in the airline's list of concerns.

The **charter** scene has its ups and downs. Some years offer exciting charter savings. Do some research. Remember, a charter flight can be cancelled if it doesn't fill. Anyone selling charters promotes an air of confidence, but at the last minute any flight can be "rescheduled" if it won't pay off. Those who "saved" by booking onto that charter are left all packed with nowhere to go. Get an explicit answer to what happens if the flight is cancelled. "It won't be cancelled," is not good enough.

Scheduled airlines are very reliable. If for some reason they can't fly you home, they find you a seat on another airline. You won't be stranded in Europe.

Flights Within Europe

Europe is a small continent with big plane fares. There are a few economical flights available (London to Paris, and to and from Athens), but unless you have a lot more money than time, you are generally better off on the ground. Special budget fares for inter-European flights can be purchased only in Europe—not in the USA. Remember, extending your flight from the USA deeper into the Continent (without stopovers) can be very cheap. Look into "open-jaws" possibilities before purchasing your ticket.

London and Athens have many "bucket shops"—agencies that clear out plane tickets at super-discounted prices. If your travel plans fit the tickets available, *and* you're flexible enough to absorb delays, these can be a great deal. Any flight from London usually must be bought in London to enjoy this savings. Your local library should have a London newspaper. Look in the classifieds under "Travel" to see what's available. Tickets from London to the Mediterranean can be incredibly—and reliably—cheap. Athens also has some great buys on tickets to London, Western Europe and the Middle East.

Trains and Eurailpass Skills

The European train system makes life easy for the American visitor. The great trains of Europe shrink that already small continent making the budget whirlwind or far-reaching tour an exciting possibility for anyone.

Generally, European trains are fast, frequent and inexpensive (faster and more frequent in the north, less expensive but not as fast in the south). By using the train you could easily have dinner in Paris, sleep on the train and have breakfast in Rome, Madrid, Munich or London.

The Eurailpass

For the average independent first-timer planning to see lots of Europe (from Norway to Portugal to Italy for instance) the Eurail is probably the best way to go.

The Eurailpass is available in these forms (1988 prices—see Back Door Catalog):

Eurailpass First-Class: 15 days $298; 21 days $370; 1 month $470; 2 months $650; 3 months $798; Children under 12—half price, under 4— free.

Eurail Youthpass, Second-Class (for those under 26); 1 month $320, 2 months $420

Eurail Saver Passes—15 days. First class travel for 3 people traveling together for $210 each rather than $280 (off-season, Oct. 1-March 31, two traveling together qualify). The only difference with this pass is that partners *must* travel together.

Flexipass—a new type of Eurailpass gives you unlimited first class travel in any nine days out of twenty-one for $310.

If you're traveling just barely enough to justify getting the pass, get one. There's more to it than economy. With the unlimited pass you'll travel more, not worrying about the cost of spontaneous side-trips. And the con-

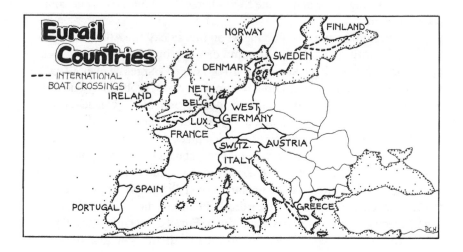

Eurail covers all countries on this map (except Britain)—over 100,000 miles of track!

venience of a train pass is worth a lot. You'll never have to worry about getting the best train ticket deal, no changing extra money to buy tickets and you'll avoid the dreadful ticket lines that exasperate so many travelers. Train stations can be a mess. It's maddening to stand in line beating off all the Spaniards for half an hour and then learn you waited in the wrong line. Many trains are missed because of ticket line frustrations.

The Eurailpass gives you unlimited first-class travel on all public railways in all the countries named on this map. It's open-dated. You validate it at any train station ticket window just before you catch your first train.

The Eurailpass gives you Europe (except Britain) by the tail—you travel virtually anywhere, anytime without reservations. Just step on the proper train, sit in an unreserved seat, and when the uniformed conductor comes, flash your pass.

A few special trains require reservations as do all long runs in Spain and Norway. Otherwise, worrying about reservations on Europe's trains makes as much sense as calling ahead for a Big Mac.

Know your extras. You get much more than just train travel with your Eurailpass. Your Eurail manual (included with purchase) lists all the free and discounted extras that come with a Eurailpass: international boats from Ireland to France, Italy to Greece, Sweden to Finland, cruises on the

Rhine, Mosel, Danube and all the Swiss lakes, local buses in some countries and more.

The Eurailpass must be purchased on this side of the Atlantic. If you are already in Europe a friend at home can buy one for you (your legal name and money is all it takes) and mail or Federal Express it over. (That's risky, like mailing cash, but I do it routinely without problems.) The pass is irreplaceable and, after it's validated, non-refundable. If you never start it you can get a refund less 15 percent within one year.

While Eurail says the passes are irreplaceable, you can probably, after much delay and hassle, get a replacement pass if you lose yours. The passes have a small receipt tab that is ripped off and given to you when you validate it in Europe. Save that tab. If you do lose your pass, take the tab and a good story to the nearest Eurail aid office where, after telegraphing your travel agent to verify your claim to Eurail ownership, they'll generally give you a second lease on Eurail life. If this gets out of hand, Eurail has every right to say "Sorry, Charlie." (My travel partner and I carry each other's "proof tabs" in our own plastic Eurail case.)

Eurail passes must be validated within six months. They increase in price on January 1st. If you're traveling early in the year, buy in December and save money. They cost the same everywhere. Buy your pass from an agent who can help you on your budget-independent Europe plans. Agents who do a lot of Eurail business can issue passes on the spot or within two days. Others take about one week to process an order.

Validate your pass thoughtfully. A 21-day pass can often cover a 30-day trip if you plan carefully. For example, many people start their pass at the French coast between London and Paris to cover the fourteen dollar ride to Paris. Then they spend four days in Paris, not using their pass. At the end of their trip they wish they had four more days of train pass coverage. To get the most use out of your pass, start it when you're really ready to move (in this case, when you leave Paris). A train pass is not worthwhile in the Low Countries—distances are too short to justify a pass. So if your pass expires when you arrive in Amsterdam, that's no problem.

A **Youthrail** pass is a second-class Eurailpass available only to those who will be under 26 on the day they validate their pass. Those 26 or over have no choice but a first-class pass—forced luxury. First-class passes are good on second-class, and "second-class people" can pay extra to travel with stuffier first-class passengers. If you're under 26 and money matters, go second-class. (The Inter-rail pass for European youths is explained in Appendix IV).

Virtually all trains have both **first and second-class** cars and both go the same speed. First-class cars are filled with wealthy "first-class" Europeans, who paid 50% more than the second-class ticket cost to get away from the crowds, and other Eurailers. Second-class cars are where the soldiers, students and nuns are partying. Second-class is where your picnic will most likely sprout into a Bruegelian potluck.

Physically, first and second class compartments are fairly similar. The major advantage of first-class is it's less crowded than second. This is most important for peak season night travel. Many people complain about over-crowded trains. I've felt like a sardine many times, and spent more than my share of hours sitting on someone's suitcase in a crowded aisle. But more often than not there's a nearly empty car on the same train, unnoticed by the complainers. Complainers are usually too busy being miserable to find answers to their problems. Look around. People get off and new cars are often added to ease the crowding.

When I was under 26 I always traveled second class. Now that I have no choice but to Eurail with a first class pass, I have to admit the roomy and less crowded first class cars are great. I can pass pleasant hours reading, writing, eating, enjoying the view and quietly daydreaming. Still, when I need to buy an individual ticket, I go second class.

By the way, classless travel has a certain nobility or appeal, even to a democratic capitalist like myself. I'll never forget the irate American I met in the Bangkok airport the day before Christmas. He booked first-class to L.A. It wasn't available. He refused to get a four hundred dollar refund to sit "economy" with regular people for 8 hours. Instead, he chose to be very angry, go back downtown and wait two days—missing Christmas at home—so he could fly first-class. What is that Thai lady behind the desk, whose countrymen labor in the fields to support a family on $300 a year, supposed to think about Americans? Incidents like that are commonplace as Americans mingle with the "natives."

The Eurailpass isn't best for every tourist. In fact, I'd estimate that 20% of the people who buy a pass don't travel anywhere near enough to justify the purchase. That's an expensive mistake. Determine what it would cost if you simply buy second-class tickets for each of your expected journeys. Your travel agent can calculate this for you or use the chart in Appendix III.

Second-class tickets from Amsterdam to Rome to Madrid and Amsterdam will cost about as much as a two-month Eurail Youthpass ($420). First-class tickets would cost the same as a two-month first-class Eurailpass. Remember, only those under 26 can buy the second-class Eurailpass but anyone can buy individual second-class rail tickets.

Travel Without Eurail

Consider the alternatives to Eurail. If you know where you want to go, you can tailor your own "personalized train pass" at any European station. Just buy a second-class ticket connecting the cities you plan to visit. You'll get one ticket listing your route and up to a year to complete the journey, with unlimited stopovers. This can be very economical (see sample prices listed in Appendix III), for instance, if you plan to travel Amsterdam-Brussels-Paris-San Sebastian-Madrid-Lisbon, you can buy the second-class ticket, with unlimited stopovers for $180—about half the cost of a 21-day Eurailpass.

You can buy tickets in train stations or at European travel agencies (same price, usually faster and easier). Buying tickets through your agent at home is unnecessary and probably more expensive. Always ask about special (night, family, senior, round-trip, weekend, etc.) prices.

Most countries have their own mini-version of a Eurailpass. The *Beyond Eurail* in Appendix IV explains the Britrail, Finrail, Francerail, Swissrail, Scandiarail and Germrail. (I'm still waiting for the Israil.) The new Scandiarail (Nordturist) pass, given the high cost of train travel up there and the popularity of Scandinavian trips among Americans, is worth a good look.

Only the **Britrail pass** among these single country train passes, is a big seller. England attracts more Americans than any other country and Eurail doesn't cover the British Isles. Worthwhile if you're traveling from London to Edinburgh and back, the Britrail pass has just about the same rules and regulations as the Eurailpass.

The Britrail pass can be purchased in the States or on the Continent— not in Britain—and is available for from eight to thirty days. This pass differs from the Eurail in that seniors get a discount and people of any age can take advantage of a second-class economy pass. Britrail has some complexities, but everything is adequately explained in its brochure. The Sealink coupon, a discount ticket for the ride from London to the Continent across the Channel confuses many. It's a bargain only for people over 26 who plan to cross the English Channel during the day (youth and night tickets bought at the Sealink office in Victoria Station are cheaper).

To travel from London to the Continent, simply buy a train ticket (at the Sealink office in London's Victoria Station, not in the USA) from London to the European city of your choice. Many people agonize over which English Channel port to use and then worry about missing the boat if their train is late. Relax, don't worry, the boat is figured into the train ride.

You'll get the most efficient boat and it won't leave until the scheduled train butts up against it and all the people file on board. When you dock at the French or Belgian port, find the train with your destination label and you're home free. Eurail travelers generally buy tickets just to the coast of Europe, validate their pass at that station and Eurail away.

Off the Track—Train Miscellany

Multi-Station Cities. Most large European cities and some small ones have more than one train station. For instance, there is "Brussels Nord," "Brussels Midi," and" Brussels Central." Be sure you know which station your train leaves from, even if that means asking what may seem like a stupid question. A city's stations are easily connected by train, subway or bus.

Train-splitting. Never assume the whole train is going where you are. Each car is labeled separately, because cars are usually added and dropped here and there all along the journey. Sometimes you'll be left sitting in your car on the track for ten minutes, watching your train fade into the distance, until another train comes along and picks up your car. To survive all of this juggling easily, just check to be sure that the city on your car's nameplate is your destination. The nameplate lists the final stop and some (but not all) of the stops in between.

Baggage. Baggage has never been a problem for me on the trains. Every car has plenty of room for luggage, so the average tourist never checks baggage through. I've seen Turkish families moving from Germany back to Turkey without checking a thing. They just packed all their worldly belongings into the compartment they reserved, and they were on their way. People complain about the porters in the European train stations. I think they're great—I've never used one. Frankly, I don't feel sorry for anyone who travels with more luggage than he or she can carry.

Use Train Time Wisely. Train travelers, especially Eurailers, spend a lot of time on the train. This time can be dull and unproductive, or you can make a point to use travel time productively. This will free up more leisure time away from the train. Besides, the time spent busy on the train passes faster and more enjoyably. It makes no sense to sit on the train bored and then arrive in Rome only to sit in the station for an hour reading your information and deciding where to go for hotels and what to do next.

Spend train time studying, reading, writing postcards or journal entries, eating, organizing, cleaning, doing anything you can so you don't have to do it after you arrive. Talk to local people or other travelers. There is so much to be learned. Europeans are often less open and forward than Americans. You could sit across from a silent but fascinating and friendly European for an entire train ride, or you could "break the ice" by offering him a cigarette or some candy, showing him your Hometown, USA postcards or by asking him a question. This may start the conversation flowing and the friendship growing.

Station Facilities. Europe's train stations can be one of the independent traveler's best and most helpful friends. Take advantage of the assistance they can offer. All stations have a luggage checking service where, for about a dollar, you can leave your luggage. People traveling light can usually fit two rucksacks into one storage locker, cutting their storage costs in half.

Most stations have comfortable waiting rooms. The bigger stations are equipped with day hotels for those who want to shower, shave, rest, etc. If you ever, for one reason or another, need a free, warm and safe place to spend the night, a train station (or an airport) is my choice.

Every station has a train information office eager to help you with your scheduling. I usually consult the timetables myself first and write down my plan, then confirm this with the information desk. Written communication is easiest and safest.

Tourist information and room-booking service is usually either in the station (in the case of major tourist centers) or nearby. This is my first stop in a new city. I pick up a map with sightseeing information and, if I need it, advice on where to find budget accommodations. Oftentimes, the station's money-changing office is open long after others have closed for the night. Train stations are major bus stops, so connections from train to bus are generally no more difficult than crossing the street. Buses go from the stations to the nearby towns that lack train service. If you have a bus to catch, be quick, since many are scheduled to connect with the train and leave promptly.

Thomas Cook Continental Timetable is a handy tool that has become my itinerary planning bible. Published several times a year, it has every European train schedule in it, complete with maps. Borrow your travel agent's. Or see if he'll give you an old one. (To order the up-to-date *Cook Timetable*, $19.95 postpaid, and/or to get their fine travel guide catalog, call the Forsyth Travel Library 1-800-FORSYTH.) I find the schedules vary more with the season than the year. I don't rely on it for the actual train I'll take, but I use it at home before I leave to familiarize myself with how to read train schedules and to learn the frequency and duration of train trips I expect to take. Every station and most trains will be equipped with the same schedule, updated. While I don't carry the bulky "Cook Book" with me, those who do find it very handy and enjoy tremendous popularity on the train.

Managing on the trains is largely a matter of asking questions, letting people help you, assuming things are logical, and *thinking*. I always ask someone on the platform if the train is going where I think it is. (Point to the train and ask, "Munich?") Uniformed train personnel can answer any question—if you can communicate. Speak slowly, clearly and with caveman simplicity. Be observant. If the loudspeaker comes on, gauge by the reaction of those around you if the announcement concerns you, and if it's good or bad news. If, after the babble, everyone dashes across the station to track 15, you should assume your train is no longer arriving on track 2.

Luggage is never completely safe. There is a thief on every train (union rules) planning to grab a bag (see chapter on theft). Don't be careless. Before leaving my luggage in a compartment, I establish a relationship with everyone there. If they didn't know each other before the ride, I'm safe leaving it among mutual guards rather than a pack of vultures.

A typical European train station scene. This is track 10. It's 3:39. At 3:45 this train leaves for Aachen.

Safety. Physically I feel completely safe on trains. Women should use discretion, however, in choosing a compartment for an overnight ride. Sleeping in an empty compartment in southern Europe is an open invitation to your own private Casanova. Choose a room with a European grannie or nun in it. That way you'll get a little peace—and he won't even try.

Train Schedules—Breaking the Code

Train schedules are a great help to the traveler—if you can read them. Many Eurail travelers never take the time to figure them out. Here are a few pointers and a sample map and schedule to practice on. Understand it—you'll be glad you did.

You'll find these confusing looking charts and maps in the *Cook Timetable* and in display cases in every station. Find the trip you want to take on the appropriate train map. Your route will be numbered, referring you to the proper time-table. That table is the schedule of the trains traveling along that line, in both directions (arr. = arrivals, dep. = departures).

As an example, let's go from Venice to Rome (the local spellings are always used, in this case, Venezia and Roma). This is #389 on the map. So refer to table 389. Locate your starting point, Venezia. Reading from left to right, you will see that trains leave Venice for Rome at 6:10, 9:40, 10:25, 11:28 and so on. Those trains arrive in Rome at 13:45, 17:08, 18:20 and 17:20 respectively. (European schedules use the 24-hour clock.) As you can see, all departures don't go all the way to Rome. For example, the 8:25 train only goes to Bologna, arriving at 10:38. From there the 11:51 train will get you to Rome by 17:08.

This schedule shows overnight trains in both directions. You could leave Venice at 22:52 (10:52 p.m.) and arrive in Rome by 7:05, just in time for breakfast. Traveling from Rome to Venice, your trip would start at 0:35 and end at 8:15.

Train schedules are helpful in planning your stopovers. For instance, this table shows a train leaving Venice at 8:05, arriving in Florence (Firenze) by 10:57. You could spend the middle of the day exploring that city and catch the 16:37 train to Rome (arr. 20:05).

Remember each table shows just some of the trains that travel along that track. Other tables feed onto the same line and the only person who knows everything is the one at the train station information window. Let her help you. She'll fix mistakes and save you many hours. (The book entitled *The Eurail Guide* is often misleading in this respect.) Each table

TABLE 389

Table 389 — (WIEN) - VENEZIA - BOLOGNA - ROMA — State Rlys. (75, 85)

has three parts: a schedule for each direction and a section explaining the many exceptions to the rules (not shown here). You never know when one of those confusing exceptions might affect your train. Schedule symbols also indicate problem-causing exceptions, such as which trains are first-class only, sleepers only, charge supplements, require reservations, or leave only on certain days. Use the tables but always confirm your plans with the person at the information window. Just show her your plan on a scrap of paper (i.e., Venezia-Firenze, 8:05-10:57; Firenze-Roma, 16:37-20:05) and ask, "Okay?" If your plan is good, the information person will nod, direct you to your track, and you're on your way. If there's a problem, she'll solve it. Uniformed train employees on the platforms or on board the trains can also confirm your plans.

Another kind of schedule you'll need to understand is the listings of all trains that come to and go from a particular station each day. These are clearly posted in two separate listings: departures (the one we're concerned with, usually in yellow) and arrivals (which you'll rarely use, normally in white.)

You'll also find airport-type departure schedules that flip up and list the next eight or ten departures. These often befuddle travelers who don't realize that all over the world there are four easy to identify columns listed and these are always: destination, type of train, track number and departure time. I don't care what language they're in, you can accurately guess which column is what.

This is a French train station. Arrivals and departures are clearly listed. Can you read the French?

How to Sleep on the Train

The economy of night travel is tremendous. You slaughter two birds with one stone. Sleeping while rolling down the tracks saves time and money, both of which, for most travelers, are limited resources. The first concern about night travel is, "Aren't you missing a lot of beautiful scenery? You just slept through half of Sweden!" Well, there are very few train rides that will have you looking out the windows most of the time. (Chur to Martigny in Switzerland and Oslo to Bergen in Norway are very scenic.) In other words, nearly every eight-hour train ride will be a bore unless you spend it sleeping. Obviously, you will miss a few beautiful sights, but that will be more than made up for by the whole extra day you gain in your itinerary.

For $12 you can rent a "couchette" (bunkbed, pronounced "Ku SHETT") on your overnight train.

If you anticipate a very crowded train and must get some sleep, you can usually reserve a sleeping berth known as a *couchette* (pron. "Ku SHETT") a day in advance at the ticket counter or, if there are any available, from the conductor on the train. For about the cost of a cheap hotel bed ($12) you'll get sheets, pillow, blankets, a fold-out bunkbed and, hopefully, a good night's sleep. It's best (and easy) to book your couchette at the station the day you arrive in a city.

The Economy of Night Travel

The typical traveler:

Friday   Finish sightseeing in Copenhagen.

Friday night   Sleep in Copenhagen. Room costs $30.

Saturday   Spend entire day on train traveling to Stockholm.

Saturday night   Arrive when most rooms are booked. Find acceptable but expensive room for $30.

Sunday   Free for sightseeing in Stockholm.

The clever traveler:

Friday   Finish sightseeing in Copenhagen

Friday night   22:00–0:800 sleep on the train traveling to Stockholm.

Saturday   Arrive early when plenty of budget beds are available. Get set up in a hotel. Saturday is free for sightseeing in Stockholm!

The efficient traveler saved $60 and gained a whole day of sightseeing by sleeping on the train.

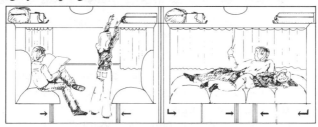

Some train seats make into a bed.

A major concern is, "How do you sleep?" Sleeping on an overnight train ride can be a waking nightmare. One night of endless bouncing of the head, with swollen toes and a screaming tailbone, sitting up straight in a dark eternity of steel wheels crashing along rails, trying doggedly— yet hopelessly—to get comfortable, will teach you the importance of finding a spot to stretch out for the night. This is an art that night travelers cultivate. Those with the greatest skill at this game, sleep. Those not so talented will spend the night gnashing their teeth and squirming for relief.

A traditional train car has about ten compartments, each with six or eight seats (three or four facing three or four). Many of these rooms have seats that pull out and arm rests that lift allowing you to turn your compartment into a bed on wheels. This is only possible if you have more seats than people in your compartment. A compartment that seats six can sleep three. It can be an overcrowded prison or your own private bedroom—depending on how good you are at encouraging people to sit elsewhere. There are many ways to play this game (which has few rules and encourages creativity). Here are my two favorite techniques.

The Big Sleep. Arrive thirty minutes before your train leaves. Walk most of the length of the train, but not to the last car. Choose a car that is going where you want to go and find an empty compartment. Pull two seats out to make a bed, close the curtains, turn out the lights and pretend you are sound asleep. It's amazing. At 9:00 p.m., everyone on that train is snoring away! The first thirty people to get on that car have room to sleep. Number thirty-one will go into any car with the lights on and people sitting up. The most convincing "sleepers" will be the last to be "woken up."

The Hare Krishna Approach. A more interesting way that works equally well and is more fun is to sit cross-legged on the floor and chant religious-sounding, exotically discordant harmonies, with a far-away look on your face. People will open the door, stare in for a few seconds— and leave, determined to sit in the aisle rather than share a compartment with the likes of you. You'll probably sleep alone—or with 5 other religious fanatics who want to chant the night away.

These tricks work not to take advantage of others but to equal out the train load. When all compartments are lightly loaded and people continue to load in, the game is over. To minimize the misery on a full train sit opposite your partner, pull out the seats and share a single bed.

Another trick is to use the reservation cards to your advantage. Each compartment will have a reservation board outside the door. Never sit in a seat that is reserved, because you'll be "bumped out" just before the train leaves. Few people realize that you can determine how far the people on a train will travel by reading their reservation tags. Each tag explains which segment of the journey that seat is reserved for. Find a compartment with three or four people traveling for just an hour or two, and then for the rest of the night you will probably have that compartment all to yourself.

Remember that trains add and lose cars throughout the night. A train could be packed with tourists heading for Milan, and at 1:00 a.m. an empty Milan-bound car could be added. The difference between being packed like sardines and stretching out in your own fishbowl could be as little as one car away.

For safety, sleep with your valuables either in a money belt or, at least, securely attached to your body. For good measure, I clip and fasten my rucksack to the luggage rack. If one tug doesn't take the bag, a thief will usually leave it rather than ask you how your luggage is attached. You'll hear stories of entire train cars being gassed and robbed in Italy. It happens—but I wouldn't lose sleep over it.

For a more thorough and complete rundown on Eurail travel skills see Appendix IV.

Losers in the "sleep-stakes."

Driving in Europe

Horror stories about European traffic abound. They're fun to tell, but really, driving in Europe is only a problem to those who make it one. Any good American driver can cope with European traffic.

Europe is a continent of frustrated race car drivers. You'll find highly skilled maniac drivers in any country, but the most dangerous creature on the road is the timid American. Be aggressive, observe, fit in, minimize big city driving, wear your seat belt and pay extra for zero-deductible insurance.

Behind the wheel you are totally free. You go where you want to, when you want to—you're not limited by tracks and schedules. You can carry more luggage (if you didn't like the "Pack Light" chapter, you can even tow a trailer) and it's very economical for small groups.

Solo car travel is expensive, but three or four people sharing a **car rental** travel cheaper than three or four using train passes. The super-mobility of a car saves you time and money in locating budget accommodations—a savings I use to help rationalize the "splurge" of a car rental. You can also play it riskier, arriving in a town late with no reservation. If it's full you simply drive to the next town.

Gas in Europe is expensive—as much as four dollars a gallon—but their little puddle-jumpers get great mileage. Europe's superhighways are *wunderbar* but the smaller roads are slow and often congested. You'll make slower time in Europe than in the USA but distances are short and you'll be impressed by how few miles you need to travel to enjoy the diversity of Europe.

Car travel is best for a group focusing on one area (seven or eight people do wonderfully in a VW or Ford mini-bus; dirt cheap per person). The British Isles are good for driving—inexpensive rentals, no language barrier, exciting rural areas, fine roads, not covered on Eurail, and, after one near head-on collision scares the bloody heck out of you, you'll have no trouble remembering which side of the road to drive on.

To avoid driving in big cities like London, pick up and drop off your car at the airport even if you're not flying in or out. It's best to take the subway or bus out of town and get used to driving in the easier-going countryside. Scandinavia (beware of long waits at ferry crossings), Belgium, Holland and Luxembourg (yield for bikes—you're outnumbered), Germany, Switzerland and Austria (driving down sunny Alpine valleys with yodelling on the tape deck is auto-ecstasy) and Spain and Portugal (with their exasperating public transportation system, I spell relief—

C.A.R.) are all regions that are especially suited to car travel. The whirlwind, see-Europe-from-top-to-bottom-type trip is best by train.

The big American companies offer reasonable rentals in Europe but "Auto Europe" and "Europe by Car" are a bit cheaper. Your travel agent has plenty of information worth studying. Read the brochures completely. Prices will vary up to 40% from country to country depending on tax and insurance costs. A weekly rate with unlimited mileage is most economical. Rental rates are usually much cheaper when arranged in the USA except in Greece, where I found on-the-spot rates cheaper. Personally, I like the luxury of walking into the Marseilles Avis office and finding my name on that envelope with the car prepaid and ready to go.

Spontaneous car rental (with a major credit card) is easy, virtually at any date, anywhere in Europe. Even if you're doing Europe with a train pass, there are places—like the hill town region of Tuscany and Umbria— where train travel is frustrating and two days in a car is fifty dollars very well spent.

Ask about drop-off privileges and take advantage of a large company's willingness to let you drop the car at their nearest office when your time's up. Avis has about a hundred offices in France alone—a tremendous convenience. If you drop the car where you pick it up, ask for the economy plan. So often discounts are there, but "no takey, no getty."

While Americans rarely consider this budget option, Aussies and New Zealanders routinely **buy used cars** for their trip and sell them when they're done. The most popular places to buy one are London, Amsterdam and from U.S. military bases. Before your trip, or once in Europe, you can check the classified ads in the armed forces' Stars and Stripes newspaper.

When buying or renting a vehicle, consider the advantage of a van or station wagon which gives you the flexibility to drive late and just pull over and camp for free.

Driving Miscellany

Adapt, be observant and try to drive European. After a few minutes on the Autobahn you'll learn that you don't cruise in the passing lane. In Rome my cabbie went through three red lights. Curious, I asked "Scuzi, do you see red lights?" He said, "In Rome, red lights are discretionary. When I come to light, I look. If no cars come, red light stupido, I go through. If policeman sees no cars—no problem—red light is stupido."

In Rome I exercise as much "discretion" as possible. England's round-abouts work wonderfully if you take advantage of the yield system and don't stop. Stopping before a round-about is as bothersome as stopping on our freeway on-ramps.

International driver's licenses are generally unnecessary. Available, quick, cheap and easy from the AAA, they are a handy piece of legitimate but disposable photo-identity. They're basically just a translation of your American driver's license—which makes it much easier for a European cop to write you a ticket. I've never used or needed an International license.

When interested in getting there fast, always use the **toll roads.** While tolls can be very high in Italy and France, I normally figure that the gas and time saved on European super freeways justify the expense. Others prefer the more scenic and free national highway systems ("route national" in France). Small roads can be a breeze or they can be dreadfully jammed up.

Get the best maps possible. European maps are cheaper and better than those you get in the States and they use the local spellings. The popular yellow 1:200,000 scale Michelin maps are cheap and very good. I buy maps in local bookstores and always ask the person who helps me to suggest the best local drive a visitor could take. That friend will be tickled to plan your itinerary—and no travel writer could do it better. "back doors" are best found from local sources—not in guidebooks.

There is no language barrier on the roads of Europe. All of Europe uses a very easy to understand standard set of **road symbols.** Just use your common sense, a good map and assume it's logical. Autobahn rest stops have great local driving almanacs explaining such signs, roadside facilities and exits.

I drive in and out of strange towns fairly smoothly by following a few basic signs. Most European towns will have signs directing you to the "old town" or the center (*centrum, centro, centre ville,* etc.). The tourist office, which is normally right downtown, will usually be clearly signposted ("i," "tourismo," "VVV," or various abbreviations which you'll learn in each country). To leave a city I look for autobahn signs (usually green) or "all directions" ("toutes directions") signs. Try to avoid heavy traffic times. Big cities are great fun and nearly traffic-free for Sunday drives.

Don't use your car for city sightseeing. **Park it** and use public transportation. City parking is a problem. Basically, find a spot as close to the center as possible (aim for the church spire, usually near the tourist office), grab it and keep it. For short stops, I park just about anywhere my car will fit without blocking traffic (I've been towed once—a great $30 experience). For overnight stops it's crucial to choose a safe, well-traveled and well-lit spot. Nothing is certain except death, taxes and vandalism to a tourist's car parked overnight in a bad urban neighborhood. In big cities it's often worth parking in a garage. Ask your hotel receptionist for advice.

Pumping **gas** in Europe is not exotic. In fact it's easy as finding a gas station ("self-service" is universal), sticking the nozzle in and pulling the big trigger. Gas prices are listed by the liter (about a quart). "Petrol" or "benzine" is gas and "gasoil" is diesel. "Super" is super and "normal" is normal. Unleaded gas is catching on fast. It's easy to find in northern Europe and, with local info maps, no problem in most of southern Europe. Freeway stations are more expensive than those in towns but during siesta only freeway stations are open.

Remember, on the continent you'll be dealing with kilometers—to get miles, cut in half and add ten percent (90 km equals 45 plus 9 miles: 54).

Biking in Europe

While biking through Europe is about the cheapest way to go, most bikers choose to pedal for the sheer joy of it. Imagine low-gearing up a beautiful mountain road on a bike—scent of fresh-mown hay—then picture an air-conditioned Mercedes with the windows closed and the stereo on—scent of upholstery. Someone in the car might pass by and say, "Masochistic nut!" but he also might notice the biker's smiling face—that traveler who can see clear from mountain to village, smell the woods, hear birds singing, the trees breezing, see the flow of brook water while anticipating a well-earned and glorious downhill run on the other side. If this is for you, bike. Edwin McCain, who for years has gotten his travel thrills crisscrossing Europe by bike, helped me assemble these tips on biking in Europe.

Use good maps and biking guidebooks. Planning your trip is half the fun. *The Michelin Europe map* (#920) is fine for strategic planning. Once in Europe, pick up local maps that show the back roads and even some bike paths. Don't be obsessed with following a pre-planned route. Delightful and spontaneous side trips are part of the spirit and joy of biking. And when you ride off a map, don't lug it; give it to someone going the other way or mail it home.

Some recommended guidebooks are: *Europe by Bike* by Karen and Terry Whitehill, Mountaineers; *Cycle Touring Europe* by Nicholas Crane, Pan Books; *Bicycle Touring in Europe* by Karen and Gary Hawkins, Pantheon Books; *CTC Cycle Touring Book of Great Britain and Ireland, Cyclist's Britain,* Pan/Ordnance Survey.

Before setting out, get in shape. Don't rely on just an occasional ride to work or the store plus a two or three hour ride on Sunday. Try some 60-mile a day rides (5 hours at 12 mph) around home and, if possible, for several days at a time with loaded panniers. 100 km or 60 miles is a good daily target for a European tour.

You may want to join one of many good organized bike tours. These usually average an easy thirty to forty miles a day. For more info, check: The American Youth Hostels Assoc. Box 37613, Washington, DC 20013-7613; Bikecentennial Inc., Box 8308, Missoula, MT 59807; and bicycling magazines available at bike shops or newsstands. Or, you can go it alone, with occasional pickup pals on the way. As a loner you'll go where, when and as far and fast as you want. But going with one or a few good companions is more fun.

When to go depends somewhat on where you go. Ideal biking temperatures are between 50 and 68 degrees Fahrenheit, so May is a good time to bike in the Mediterranean countries. Edwin started in May in Greece before it got too hot and pedaled up through the Balkans to England where, on his arrival, 36 days later, it wasn't too cold. He had good temperatures all the way but he also had headwinds—the prevailing westerlies. The next year he set out from Lyon, France, for Helsinki and had not only just-right temperatures but also tail winds allowing him to cover as much as 130 miles in a day.

Expect rain, and bring good biker's raingear. For necessary protection from the sun, take long pants as well as shorts, long sleeves, a hat or helmet (you see very few bikers in Europe wearing helmets), gloves (not the ones with holes in their backs) and a good sunblock.

Taking your bike on an airplane is easy. Most lines don't charge for this service, considering your bike as one of two checked pieces of luggage. Some require the bike be boxed, and some provide these boxes—if not, you can get one at a bike store. Check with the individual airlines concerning their requirements. Many lines will take an unboxed bike if you sign a "fragile" waiver. Baggage handlers seem less liable to pile a lot of luggage on top of an unboxed bike. Prepare your bike by turning the lowered handlebars 90 degrees, lowering the seat, taking off the odometer and pedals and unhooking the cantilever brakes. Leave on the panniers—good added protection. This way you can bike right into and out of the airports.

The bikes you see in Europe are quite different from those you see in the U.S. In Western Europe, you'll see touring bikers and racers as well as ladies biking in the rain with open umbrellas. Bike repair shops are hard to find in the eastern countries where most bikes are simple and heavy one-speeds. A European touring bike has fenders, lights and bells. Lights and a horn or bell are generally required on all but racers. Even if you never ride at night, having lights both fore and aft is very comforting for those unavoidable, long, and dark tunnels. And bells are used to say a multilingual "Hi!" to other bikers as well as, "Look out, here I come!"

The small Penta valves are standard in Europe, so if you take a bike over with the automotive-type Shraeder valves, it's wise to take along an extra tube. Since you're going to Europe to savor its differences, consider buying a bike there. France, England and Italy have good selections at reasonable prices. Oddly, Holland does not. You can rent ten speeds, but not fifteen or eighteen speeds whose low gears are really appreciated on those long steep grades and when bucking headwinds.

Smart bikers travel very light. While many go with full panniers, front and rear (and in Sweden Edwin met a couple on a tandem and towing a well-laden trailer), you'll enjoy your biking trip much more toting much less. Don't bring cooking and camping gear unless you'll be nearly always camping. Youth hosteling and biking are a wonderful budget mix.

Bike thieves abound in Europe, especially at a youth hostel after midnight. Precautions: use a good bike lock; never leave your pump, water bottle or computer on your bike when you can't see it and take your bike inside whenever possible; at hostels always ask if there is a locked bike room and, if not, ask or even plead for a place inside to put your bike overnight; and remember that hotels don't really have rules against taking a bike up to your room. Just do it unobtrusively. You can even use the elevator. You can also usually walk your bike right into banks, post offices and telephone exchanges. Stores, rarely; restaurants, hardly ever.

Traffic rules in Europe apply to bikers. The closer one gets to Holland the more bike signs one sees; a one-speed in a blue circle for a bike route, in a red circle where bikers are not allowed. Be alert, and the blue bike signed paths, which are mandatory, will get you through even some of the most complicated highway interchanges. Beware of the silent biker who might be right behind you, and use hand signals before stopping or turning. Stay off the freeways. "Little roads" are nicer for biking anyway. Not enjoyable but often unavoidable are the cobblestones and stone paving blocks found in older cities across Europe.

If you decide to see less of Europe but want to be able to stop on the way and pick berries and cherries, go by bike. And may the wind always be at your back!

Hitchhiking—Rules of Thumb

Hitching, sometimes called "auto-stop" or "tramp," is a popular and acceptable means of getting around in Europe. Without a doubt, hitching is the cheapest means of transportation in Europe. It's also a great way to meet people. Most people who pick you up are genuinely interested in getting to know an American.

After picking up a Rhine river boat captain and running him back to his home port, I realized that hitchhiking doesn't wear the same "hippie hat" in Europe that it does in the USA. The farther you get from the militant self-sufficiency pushed by our culture, the more volunteerism you'll encounter. Bumming a ride is a perfect example. In the Third World— rural Europe in the extreme—anything rolling with room will let you in. You don't hitch, you just flag the vehicle down.

Hitching has two drawbacks. First, it can be terribly time-consuming. Some places will have twenty or thirty people in a chorus line of thumbs, just waiting their turns. Once, I said what I thought was a goodbye forever to an Irishman after breakfast. He was heading north. We had dinner together that night, and I learned a lot about wasting a day on the side of a road. Second, of course, there is the ever-present danger involved in hitchhiking. I would say that if you're comfortable hitchhiking in the USA, then you should have no problem in Europe.

Personally, I don't hitchhike at home and I wouldn't rely solely on my thumb to get me through Europe. But I never sit frustrated in a station for two hours because there's no bus or train to take me 12 or 15 miles down the road. I thumb my way out of train and bus schedule problems, getting to my destination in a flash. You'll find that Germany, Ireland and Great Britain are generally good, and southern countries much slower for hitching.

Discretion makes hitching much safer. Feel good about the situation before you commit yourself to it. Keep your luggage on your lap, or at least out of the trunk, so if things turn sour you can excuse yourself

Hitchhiking at the Bulgaria-Greece border or whenever the train and bus schedules leave you stranded.

quickly and easily. Women should not sit in the back seat of a two-door car. A fake wedding ring and modest dress are indications that you're interested only in transportation.

Your success as a hitchhiker will be determined by how well you follow several rules. The hitchhiking gesture is not always the outstretched thumb. In some countries you ring an imaginary bell. In others you make a downward wave with your hand. Observe and learn. Consider what the driver will want to let into his car. Arrange your luggage so it looks as small and desirable as possible. Those hitching with very little or no luggage enjoy a tremendous advantage.

Look like the Cracker Jack boy or his sister—happy, wholesome and a joy to have aboard. To get the long ride, take a local bus out of town to the open country on the road to your destination and make a cardboard sign with your destination printed big and bold in the local language. Long rides are often advertised on hostel bulletin boards or with ride-finding agencies in many cities. Ask about these at student travel and tourist information offices.

Speed and safety are a trade-off when it comes to hitching. A single woman maximizes speed and risk. Two women travel safer and nearly as fast. A man and a woman together are the best combination. A single man with patience will do fine. Two guys go slow and three or more should split up and rendezvous later. Single men and women are better off traveling together and these alliances are easily made at hostels.

When I'm doing some serious hitchhiking I work to create pity. I walk away from town and find a very lonely stretch of road. In a lot of cases I feel that the more sparse the traffic, the quicker I get a ride. On a busy road, people will assume that I'll manage without their ride. If only one car passes in five minutes, the driver senses that I might starve to death or die of exposure if he doesn't stop. Look clean, safe and respectable. Establish eye contact. Charm the driver. Stand up. Pick a good spot on the road, giving the driver both plenty of time to see you and a safe spot to pull over.

When you're in a hurry, there are two sure-fire ways of getting a ride fast. Find a spot where cars stop and you can encounter the driver face to thumb. A toll-booth, border, gas station or best of all, a ferry ride, each give you that chance to smile and convince him that he needs you in his car or truck. A car's license plate is often a destination label as well. While it's easy to zoom past a hitchhiker at 60 mph and not feel guilty, it's much more difficult to turn down an in-person request for a ride. A man and a woman traveling together have it easy. If the woman hitches and the guy steps out of view around the corner or into a shop, you should both have a ride in a matter of minutes. (Dirty trick, but it works.)

With this "hitch when you can't get a bus or train" approach, you'll find yourself walking down lovely mountain or rural roads out of a village. You get rides from small-town folk—fanatically friendly and super safe. I can recall some "it's great to be alive and healthy" days riding my thumb from tiny town to waterfall to desolate Celtic graveyard to coastal village and remembering each ride as much as the destinations.

Sometimes hitching almost becomes an end in itself. In the British Isles, especially Ireland, I've found so much fun in the front seat that I'd drive right by my planned destination to carry on with the conversation. In rural Ireland, I'd stand on the most desolate road in Connemara and hitch whichever way the car was coming. As I hopped in, the driver would ask, "Where you goin'?" I'd say "Ireland."

Walking (and Dodging)

You'll walk a lot in Europe. It's a great way to see cities, towns and the countryside. Walking tours are the most intimate look at a city or town. A walker complements the place she walks through by her interest and will be received warmly. Many areas, from the mountains to the beaches, are best seen on foot. Be very careful. Pedestrians are run down every day. Over 300 pedestrians are run down annually on the streets of Paris. The drivers are crazy, and politeness has no place on the roads of Europe and pedestrians enter only at their own risk. If you wait for a break in the traffic, you may never get a chance to cross the street. Look for a pedestrian underpass or, when all else fails, find a heavy-set local person and just follow him or her like a shadow—one busy lane at a time—across that seemingly impassable street.

Hiking

Hiking in Europe is a joy. Travelers explore entire regions on foot. The Jungfrau is an exciting sight to those who enjoy it from their hotel's terrace cafe. But those who hike the region enjoy nature's very own strip-tease as the mountain reveals herself in an endless string of powerful poses.

The Alps are especially suited to the walking tourist. The trails are well kept and carefully marked. Very precise maps (scale 1:25,000) are readily available. You're never more than a day's hike from a mountain village where you can replenish your food supply or enjoy a hotel and restaurant meals. By July most trails are free of snow and lifts take the less rugged visitors to the top in a sweat-free flash.

The Alpine countries have hundreds of mountain huts to provide food and shelter to the hiker. I know a family that hiked from France to Yugoslavia spending every night along the way in Alpine huts. The huts are generally spaced four to six hours apart. Most serve hot meals and provide bunk-style lodging. If you plan to use the huts, it's a good idea to join an Alpine club. Membership in one of these European or American clubs entitles you to discounts on the cost of lodging and priority over non-members. The club can provide information about the trails and huts and where reservations are likely to be necessary.

Do some research before you leave. Buy the most appropriate guidebook for your hiking plans. Ask for maps and information from the National Tourist Offices.

Tenderfeet high in the Alps. The highest ridge is a $10 gondola ride away.

4
The Budget—Eating and Sleeping on $35/Day

In the twelve years I've been teaching travel, my notes on budgeting for a European vacation have had to be continuously revised. It looked for a while like "Europe on the Cheap" was on the road to extinction. We saw Mr. Frommer's book grow from *Europe on $5 a Day* to *Europe on $35 a Day* and many were predicting that *Europe on $35 a Rest Stop* was just around the corner.

Then, from 1980 to 1985, the dollar grew stronger and stronger. Life in Europe was very easy for the budget traveler. But since 1985 the value of our dollar dropped drastically against most European currencies and once again surviving on a budget requires some artistry.

While the dollar has "plummeted" in value lately, it is still well above the value I grew up thinking was "standard." I'd say it's not high or low, it's fair. Overall, most of Europe is about as expensive as the USA now and the sloppy traveler can blow a small fortune in a hurry. Still, smart travelers can thrive on $30 a day in the South and $40 daily in the North. The information in this chapter will give you a solid foundation in the skills necessary to have a blast—within your budget.

My idea of "cheap" is basic, but not sleazy. My budget morality is to never sacrifice safety, reasonable cleanliness, sleep or nutrition to save money. I go to safe, central, friendly, local-style hotels, shunning decadence, TV's, swimming pools, people in uniforms, and transplanted American niceties, in favor of an opportunity to travel as a temporary European.

With these standards, $35 a day for room and board in 1988 is not farfetched. Civil people have a blast in Europe spending much less than that. This budget is realistic, and the feedback I get from back door travelers bolsters my confidence. It can be done—by you.

In 1988 you can travel comfortably for eight weeks for around

$3,000: $1,300 for round-trip plane ticket and a two-month Eurailpass, and $1,700 for room and board. Add $400 or $500 for souvenirs, personal incidentals, admissions and sightseeing costs.

There are two halves to any budget—transportation, and room and board. Transportation expenses are rather fixed. Flying to Europe is a bargain. Get a good agent, understand all your options and make the best choice. This cost cannot be cut. Transportation in Europe is reasonable if you take advantage of a Eurailpass or split a car rental between three or four people. This is also a fixed cost. Your budget should not dictate how freely you travel in Europe. If I want to go somewhere, I will, taking advantage of whatever money-saving options I can. I came to travel.

The area that will make or break your budget—where you have the most control—is in your eating and sleeping expenses. People who spend $5,000 for their vacation spend about the same on transportation as those whose trips cost half as much. Room and board is the beaver in your bankbook. If you have extra money it's more fun to spend it in Europe, but if your trip will last as long as your money does and you develop and deploy a good strong SDI (spending defense initiative)—figure about $35 per day plus transportation.

I traveled for 3 months a year for years on a part-time piano teacher's income. I ate and slept great by learning and using the skills that follow. For the last few years I've been running around Europe with mini-groups (8 to 25 people). By following these same guidelines in 1987 we played it by ear, thriving on this budget. I bought over 3,000 hotel beds last summer—averaging less than $15 per night per person including breakfast. It can be done!

Sleeping Cheap

Finding a Hotel Without Reservations— At a Price You Won't Lose Sleep Over

Hotels are the most expensive way to sleep and, of course, the most comfortable. With a reasonable budget, I spend most of my nights in hotels. Hotels, however, can rip through a tight budget like a grenade in a doll house.

I always hear people complaining about that "$160 double in Frankfurt" or the "$200 a night room in London." They come back from their vacations with swollen, bruised and pilfered pocket books telling

In the Back Door-style hotel, you get more by spending less.

stories that scare their friends out of international travel and back to Florida or Hawaii one more time. True, you can spend $150 for a double —but I never have. That's five days accommodations budget for me.

As far as I'm concerned, spending more for your hotel just builds a bigger wall between you and what you came to see. If you spend enough, you won't know where you are. Think about it. "In-ter-con-ti-nen-tal"— that implies uniform sterility, a lobby full of stay-press Americans with wheels on their suitcases, English menus, boiled water, lamps bolted to the tables—and all the warmth of a submarine.

Europe is full of European hotels—dingy, old-fashioned, a bit run-down, central, friendly, safe, and government regulated, offering good-enough-for-the-European-good-enough-for-me beds for $10 to $20 a night ($20-$40 doubles). No matter what your favorite newspaper travel writer or travel agent says, these are hard-core Europe: fun, cheap and easy to find.

What's a Cheap Room?

A typical cheap room in Europe (one star, $25 double in Paris, $30 simple guesthouse-type hotel double in Germany, $20 double for a pension in Madrid, or $40 room in a mission-owned hotel in Oslo) is very basic. It has a simple bed, usually firm enough to meet the needs of modern travelers (but always check), a rickety old or plastic new chair and table, a free-standing closet, small window, old wallpaper, good sink, mysterious bidet, peeling plaster, and a tile or wood floor. The light fixtures will be very simple, often with a weak and sometimes even bare and dangling ceiling light bulb. Some travelers BYOB when they travel. A higher wattage kills a lot of dinginess. Naked neon is common in the south. You won't have a TV or telephone and, while more and more European hotels are squeezing boat-type prefab showers and toilets into their rooms, the cheapest rooms give you only a shared WC and shower or tub down the hall.

The bottom of the line European hotel usually has clean-enough but depressing shower rooms with hot water normally free and constant (but occasionally available only through a coin-op meter or at certain hours). The WC or toilet is reliably clean and provides good toilet paper but is often missing its lid or has a cracked or broken plastic lid. In some hotels you pay about two dollars for a towel and a key to the shower room.

The cheapest hotels are run by and filled with people from what we call the "Third World." While the rooms themselves lack *en suite* facilities, in the lobby there is nearly always a living room with a good TV, a couple of phone booths, and a man at the desk who is at your service

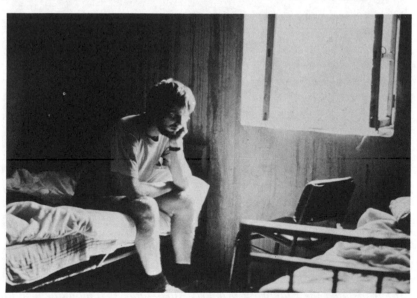

Cheap hotels aren't this bad—unless you're in Eastern Turkey.

and a good information source. You'll climb lots of stairs as elevators are rare and often broken in cheap hotels. You'll be given a front door key since the desk is not open all night.

I want to stress there are many places that I find unacceptable. I don't mind dingy wallpaper, climbing stairs and "going down the hall," but the place must be clean, central, friendly, safe, quiet enough to sleep well and provide good beds. The hotel described above is appalling to many Americans; colorful, charming or funky to others. It's good enough for Europeans, luxurious compared to the rest of the world and fine for me. An extra $10 or $15 per night will buy you into a cheerier class of hotel.

Make No Reservations

Reservations are a needless and expensive security blanket. They'll smother your spontaneity. Know how to manage without and make reservations only if you require a specific hotel or location or if you're hitting a crowded festival or event.

The problems with reservations are three. First, you can't see what you're getting before accepting. Second, booking ahead destroys your

If I translated the Bulgarian properly, this statue is a monument to the tourist "freeing himself from the chains of needless hotel reservations".

flexibility. Nobody knows how long they'll enjoy Paris or what the weather will be like in the Alps. Being shackled into a rigid calendar of hotel reservations all summer would be a crushing blow to the spontaneity and independence that makes travel such good living. And finally, reservations are much more expensive than playing it by ear. Through my agent, it was impossible to book a room in Madrid for less than $60. I'm sure it would have been a fine room, but I don't have $60 for a fine room. I went on my own and had no trouble finding a double for $20. Your agent is telling you the truth when she says there's nothing available, or, "This is the cheapest room possible." But she's been taught to think all of Madrid is listed in her little book. Not so! Pedro's Pensions never made it in any American travel agency's book of accommodations. You must have the courage and spirit to go there bedless and find it yourself.

I make a reservation only when I know where I want to stay and I do not need flexibility. I do it personally with a phone call.

Basic Bed-Finding

In over 1500 unreserved nights in Europe, I've been shut out twice. That's a 99.8% bedding average earned in peak season and very often in crowded, touristy or festive places. What's so traumatic about a night without a bed anyway? My survey shows those who have the opportunity to be a refugee for a night have their perspectives broadened and actually enjoyed the experience—in retrospect.

The cost of a wonderfully reservation-free trip is the remote chance you'll end up spending the night on a bench in the train station waiting room. As in capitalism, the threat of losing gives an on-the-ball person the necessary incentive to win. Knowing the basic skills of bed-finding is much more valuable than having the best hotel list.

Use the ideas below and you'll have no trouble finding a room when you arrive.

1. Hotel lists. Have a good guidebook's basic listing of hotels and budget alternatives. These lists, whose recommendations are often crowded with people using the same book, are reliable and work well. Never expect the prices to be the same. Very few guidebooks have the guts to list the very least expensive options. Tourist information services usually have a better list of local hotels and accommodations.

2. Room-Finding Services. Popular tourist cities usually have a room-finding service at the train station or tourist information office. For a dollar or two they'll get you a room in the price range and neighborhood of your choice. They have the complete listing of that town's available accommodations and their service is usually well worth the price when you consider the time and money saved by avoiding the search on foot. Room-finding services are not above pushing you into their "favored" hotels, and kickbacks are powerful motivators. Room-finding services only give dormitory, hostel and "sleep-in" (circus tents, gyms with mattresses on the floor and other $3 a night alternatives to the park or station) information if you insist. Remember, many popular towns open up hostels for the summer that are not listed in your books. (If the line at the room-finding service is too long, ask someone who just got a room where he or she is going.)

3. Use the Telephone. If you're looking on your own, telephone the places in your list that sound best. Not only will it save the time and money involved in chasing down these places with the risk of finding them full, but you're beating all the other tourists—with the same guidebook—who may be hoofing it as you dial. It's rewarding to arrive at a hotel when people are being turned away and see your name on the reservation list—because you called first. If the room or price isn't what you were led to believe, you have every right to say, "No, thank you." (See later chapter on Telephoning.)

Remember, a hotel prefers a cash deposit with reservations. But if you call and assure them you'll arrive before 6 p.m., they'll usually hold your room with no money deposited. If you'll be a little late, call again to assure them you're coming. Also, cancel if you won't make it. If someone cancels after 6 p.m. and the room-finding service is closed, the room will probably go unfilled that night. When that happens too often, hotel managers start to get really surly and insist on cash deposits.

4. Hotel Runners. Sometimes you'll be met by hotel runners as you step off the bus or train. My gut reaction is to steer clear, but these people are usually just hard-working entrepreneurs who lack the location or write-up in a popular guidebook that can make life easy for a small hotel owner. If you like the guy and what he promises, follow him to his hotel. You are obliged only to inspect the hotel. If it's good, take it. If it's not, leave—you're probably near other budget hotels anyway.

5. The Early Bird Gets the Room. If you anticipate crowds, go to great lengths to arrive in the morning—when the most (and best) rooms are available. If the rooms aren't ready until noon, take one anyway; leave your luggage behind the desk; they'll move you in later and you're set up—free to relax and enjoy the city. I would leave Florence at 6:30 a.m. to arrive in Venice (a crowded city) early enough to get a decent choice of rooms. One of the beauties of overnight train rides is that you arrive bright and early. Your approach to room-finding will be determined by the market situation—if it's a "buyer's market" or a "seller's market". Sometimes you'll grab anything with a pillow and a blanket. Other times you can arrive late, be selective and even talk down the price.

6. Leave the Trouble Zone. If the room situation is impossible, don't struggle—just leave. Thirty minutes by car, train or bus from the most miserable hotel situation anywhere in Europe is a town—Dullsdorf or Nothingston—that has the Dullsdorf Inn or the Nothingston Gasthaus just across the street from the station or right on the main square. It's not full—never has been, never will be. There's a guy sleeping behind the reception desk. Drop in at 11:00 p.m., ask for 14 beds and he'll say, "Take the second and third floors, the keys are in the doors." It always works. Oktoberfest, Cannes Film Festival, Pampalona bull-run, Easter at Lourdes—your bed awaits you in nearby Dullsdorf.

7. Taxi-tips. A great way to find a place in a tough situation is to let a cabbie take you to his favorite hotel. They are experts. Cabs are also handy when you're driving lost in a big city. Many times I've hired a cab, showed him that elusive address, and followed him in my car to my hotel.

8. Let Hotel Managers Help. Nobody knows the hotel scene better than local hotel managers. If one hotel is full, ask for help there. Often they have a list of neighborhood accommodations or will even telephone a friend who rarely fills up just around the corner. If the hotel is too expensive, there's nothing wrong with asking where you could find a "not so good place". I've always found hotel receptionists understanding and helpful.

The most expensive hotels have the best city maps and an English-speaking staff that can give advice to the polite traveler in search of a cheap room. You may get nowhere but it doesn't hurt to try.

Remember, my experience is based on budget European-style situations. People who specialize in accommodating soft, rich Americans are more interested in your money than your happiness. The staffs of Europe's small hotels, guesthouses and "bed and breakfast" places may have no room service and offer only a shower down the hall, but they are more interested in seeing pictures of your children than thinning out your wallet.

To Save Money, Remember . . .

Large hotels, international chains, big city hotels and those in the North are more expensive. Prices usually rise with demand during festivals and in July and August. Off-season, many hotel people will take an offer. If the place is too expensive, tell her your limit; she may meet it. In Scandinavia, on the other hand, fancy "business hotels" are desperate in the summer and on weekends when their business customers stay away. They offer some amazing deals through the local tourist offices.

Many national governments regulate hotel prices according to class or rating. To overcome this price ceiling (especially in peak season when demand exceeds supply) hotels often require that you buy dinner and/or lunch there. Breakfast almost always comes with the room. One more meal (demi- or half-pension) or all three meals (full-pension) is usually uneconomical (although not always) since the hotel is skirting the governmental hotel price ceilings to maximize profit. I prefer the freedom to explore, experiment and sample the atmosphere of restaurants in other neighborhoods.

When going door-to-door, rarely is the first place you check the best. It's worth ten minutes of shopping around to find the going rate before you accept a room. You'll be surprised how prices vary as you walk farther from the station or down a street strewn with "B & B's." Never judge a hotel by its exterior or lobby.

Ask to see the room before accepting. Then the receptionist knows the room must pass your inspection. He'll have to earn your business. Notice the little boy is given two keys. You only asked for one room. He's instructed to show the hard-to-sell room first. If you insist on seeing both rooms, you'll get the best. Check out the rooms, snarl at anything that deserves displeasure. The price will come down or they'll show you a better room. Think about heat and noise. I prefer climbing a few stairs to cheaper rooms higher off the noisy road. Some towns never quiet down. A room in back may lack a view but it will also lack night noise. I accepted a bedroom without seeing it first and complained to the receptionist. He looked at me and said, "tough sheet."

Room prices are determined not by room quality but by hotel features, like: if the reception desk stays open all night, if there's an elevator, how classy the lobby is, shower-to-room ratio and age of facilities. If you can climb stairs, use the night key, manage without a TV in the room and find a small old hotel without a modern shower in each room, you'll sleep well and save enough money to buy a memorable dinner.

A person staying only one night is bad news to a hotel. If, before telling you whether there's a vacancy, they ask you how long you're staying, be ambiguous. Some hotels offer a special price for a long stay.

Avoid doing outside business through your hotel. It's much better style to go to the bull ring and get the ticket yourself. You'll learn more, save money, and you won't sit with other tourists who drown your Spanish fire with Yankee-pankee. So often, tourists are herded together by a conspiracy of hotel managers and tour organizers and driven through touristy evenings—500 tourists in a gymnasium drinking cheap sangria and watching flamenco dancing on stage to the rhythm of their automatic rewinds—and leave disappointed. You can't relive your precious Madrid nights; do them right—on your own.

Always, when checking in, pick up the hotel's business card or address. In the most confusing cities they come with a little map. Even the best pathfinders get lost in a big city and it's scary not knowing where your hotel is. With the card, you can hop into a cab and be home in minutes.

Always establish the complete and final price of a room before accepting. Know what's included and what taxes and services will be added on. More than once I've been given a bill that was double what I expected. Dinners were required and I was billed whether I ate them or not; so I was told—in very clear Italian.

Showers

Showers are a Yankee fetish. A night without a shower is traumatic to many of us—it can ruin a day. Here are some tips on survival in a world that doesn't start and end with squeaky hair.

First of all, get used to the idea that you won't have a shower every night. The real winners are those who manage with three showers a week and a few sponge baths tossed in when needed.

Many times you'll have a shower—but no pressure or hot water. When you check in, ask when the best time to take a hot shower is. If a shower is important to you, take it while you can. Many have water pressure or hot water only during certain times. Heating water twenty-four hours a day is a luxury many of us take for granted.

Americans are notorious energy gluttons—wasting hot water and leaving lights on as if electricity is cheap. What country besides us sings in the shower, or would even dream of using a special nozzle to take a hot water massage? European electric rates are shocking and some hotels have had to put meters in their showers to survive. You'll pay about 50 cents for five minutes of hot water. It's a good idea to have an extra token handy to avoid that lathered look. A "navy shower," using the water only to soap up and rinse off, is a wonderfully conservative method, and those who follow will more likely enjoy some *warm wasser*.

I think about half of all the cold showers Americans take in Europe were cold only because they didn't know how to turn the hot on. Study the always-different system and before you shiver, ask the receptionist for help. There are some very peculiar tricks. You'll find showers and baths of all kinds. They are part of traveling—an adventure.

Nearly every hotel room in Europe comes with a sink and a bidet. Sponge baths are fast, easy and European. A bidet is that mysterious porcelain thing that looks like an oversized bed pan. Tourists use them as anything from a laundromat to a watermelon rind receptacle to a urinal. They are used by locals to clean the parts of the body that rub together when they walk—in lieu of a shower. Give it a whirl.

Europe's budget hotels rarely provide a shower or toilet in your room. Each floor shares a toilet and a shower "down the hall." To such a bathoholic people, this sounds terrible. Imagine the congestion in the morning when the whole floor tries to pile into that bathtub! You must remember, there are only two peoples on earth who believe a bath a day keeps the fleas away—the Japanese and the Americans. Shower-crazy tour groups don't stay in these "local" hotels; therefore, you've got a private bath—down the hall. I spend four months a year in Europe—shower a time or two—and I never have to wait.

Many budget hotels and most dorm-style accommodations don't provide towels or soap. BYOS. In some Mediterranean countries private baths are rare. People routinely use public baths. (There's one in Venice between the AmExCo office and St. Mark's.) These are a great experience and often come with full service scrubbers and a massage.

If you're vagabonding or sleeping several nights in transit you can buy a shower in train station "day hotels", in public baths or swimming pools, or even, if you don't mind asking, from hostels or small hotels. Most Mediterranean beaches have free, fresh water showers all the time.

Europe's 2000 Hostels

Europe's cheapest beds are in hostels. Two thousand youth hostels provide beds throughout Europe for three to ten dollars a night.

Hostels are not hotels—not by a long shot. Many people hate hostels. Others love hostels and will be hostelers all their lives—regardless of their financial status. Hosteling is a philosophy. A hosteler trades service and privacy for a chance to live simply and communally with people from around the world.

A youth hostel is not limited to young people. You may be ready to jump to the next chapter because, by every other standard, you're older than young. Well, a few years ago the Youth Hostel Association came out with a new card giving "youths" over the age of 59 a discount. People of any age can youth hostel if they have a membership card, available through Europe Through the Back Door, your local student travel office or youth hostel office. (Bavaria is the only exception with a strictly enforced 26 year old age limit.)

A hostel provides "no frills" accommodations in clean dormitories. The sexes are segregated, with four to twenty people packed in a room.

One of Europe's 2000 hostels—$3 a night, your own kitchen, a million dollar view of the Jungfrau, and lots of friends. Note the worldwide triangular hostel symbol.

Many hostels have doubles for couples and family rooms. The buildings are usually in a good, easily accessible location, and come in all shapes and sizes. There are castles (Bacharach, Germany), cutter ships (Stockholm), Alpine chalets (Gimmelwald, Switzerland), huge modern buildings (Frankfurt), old tunnel-diggers' barracks (Chamonix), bomb shelters (Friburg, Switzerland) and former royal residences (Holland Park, London).

The facilities vary, but most provide more than you would expect. Hearty super-cheap meals are served, often in family style settings. A typical dinner is meat and potatoes seasoned by conversation with people from Norway, New Zealand, Canada and Spain. The self-service kitchen complete with utensils, pots and pans, is a great budget aid that comes with most hostels. Larger hostels even have a small grocery store. Many international friendships rise with the bread in hostel kitchens. Very good hot showers (often with meters) are the norm, but simpler hostels have cold showers or even none at all. The hostel's recreation and living rooms are my favorite. This is where conversational omelettes are made with eggs from all over the world. People gather, play games, tell stories, share information, read, write and team up for future travels. Solo travelers find a family wherever they go in hostels. Hostels are ideal meeting places for those in search of a travel partner.

The latest *International Youth Hostel Handbook Vol. I* is essential. That small directory, available where you get your card or at any European hostel, lists everything you could ever want to know about each of Europe's 2000 hostels. In it you'll find which day the hostel is closed, what bus goes there, distance from the station, how many beds, its altitude, phone number with area code, and a great map locating all the hostels. And each country has an even more informative directory or handbook.

There seem to be nearly as many unofficial or independent hostels as official (International Youth Hostel Federation) ones. Many wardens and student groups prefer to run their own show and avoid the occasionally heavy-handed bureaucracy of the IYHF. These hostels are generally looser and more casual but not as clean or organized. Ireland has a great network of these maverick independent hostels. Many large cities have wild and cheap student-run hostels which are popular with wild and cheap student travelers. In the Alps, look for the word *lager* which means they have a loft full of $5 a night mattresses. As in IYHF hostels, you'll usually save money if you provide your own sheets.

And now the drawbacks: hostels have strict rules. They lock up during the day (usually from 10:00-5:00) and they have a curfew at night (10:00, 11:00 or 12:00) when the doors are locked and those outside stay there. These curfews are for the greater good—not to make you miserable. In the mountains, the curfew is early because most people are early-rising hikers. In London the curfew is 11:45, giving you ample time to return from the theatre. Amsterdam, where the sun shines at night, has a 1:45 a.m. curfew. Pillows and blankets are provided, but no sheets. You can bring a regular single bed sheet (sewn into a sack if you like), rent one each night ($2 each) or buy a regulation hostel sheet-sack at the first hostel you hit (light, ideal design at a bargain price).

Many school groups (especially German) turn hostels into a teeming kindergarten. Try to be understanding (many groups are disadvantaged kids); we were all noisy kids (I hope) at one time. Get to know the teacher and make the best of it.

Hostel rooms can be large and packed. The first half hour after "lights out" reminds me of Boy Scout camp—giggles, burps, jokes and strange noises in many languages. Snoring is permitted and practiced openly.

Theft is a problem in hostels, but the answer is simple—don't leave valuables lying around (no one's going to steal your tennis shoes or journal). Use the storage lockers that are available in most hostels.

In a youth hostel you'll have bunkbeds and roommates.

Hostels were originally for hikers and bikers, but that isn't the case these days. Still, you might give your car a low profile and arriving by taxi is just plain bad taste. Traditionally, every hosteler does a chore before his card is returned to him. These duties are becoming very rare and most remaining duties are token duties, never taking more than a few minutes.

The hostel is run by a "warden" or "house parent". They do their best to strictly enforce no-drinking rules, quiet hours and other regulations. Some are rather loose and laid back, others are like marine sergeants, but all are hostel wardens for the noble purpose of enabling travelers to better appreciate and enjoy that town or region. While they are often overworked and harried, most wardens are great people who enjoy a quiet cup of coffee with an American and are happy to give you some local travel tips or recommend a special nearby hostel. Be sensitive to the many demands on their time and never treat them like a hotel servant.

Big city hostels are the most crowded and institutional. Rural hostels, far from train lines and famous sights, are usually quiet and frequented by a more mature crowd. If you have a car, use that mobility to enjoy some of Europe's overlooked hostels.

Hostel selectively; there are some hostels that are ends in themselves. Survey other hostelers and hostel wardens for suggestions. I hostel much more in the North where hostels are generally more comfortable and the savings over hotels are more exciting. I rarely hostel in the South, where hostels are less common and two or three people can sleep just as cheaply in a budget hotel.

Getting a hostel bed in peak season can be tricky. The most popular hostels fill up every day. Written reservations are possible but I've never bothered. Telephone reservations work wonderfully where the warden will take them—about 50% of the time. I always call ahead to try to reserve and at least check on the availability of beds. Without a reservation you can count on landing a bed if you arrive in the morning before the hostel closes. If you miss that, line up with the scruffy gang for the 5:00 opening of the office when any remaining beds are doled out. Hostel bed availability is very unpredictable. Some obscure hostels are booked out on certain days two months in advance. But I stumbled onto Oberammergau one night during the "jam-packed" Passion Play festival and found beds for a group of eight.

Pensions, Zimmers, Bed and Breakfast and the Like

Between hotels and youth hostels or campgrounds in price and style are a special class of accommodations. These are small, warm, family run and offer a personal touch at a budget price. They are the next best thing to staying with a local family, and even if hotels weren't more expensive, I'd choose this budget alternative.

Each country has these friendly accommodations in varying degrees of abundance. They have different names and offer slightly different facilities from country to country, but all have one thing in common; they satisfy the need for a place to stay that gives you the privacy of a hotel and the comforts of home at a price you can afford. While information on some of the more established places is available in many budget travel guidebooks, I've always found that the best information is found locally, through tourist information offices, room-finding services or even from the local man waiting for his bus or selling apples. In fact, many times the information is brought to you. I will never forget struggling off the bus upon my arrival in Dubrovnik, Yugoslavia. Fifteen women were begging me to spend the night. Thrilled, I made a snap decision and followed the most attractive offer to a very nice, budget, *Zimmer*-type accommodation.

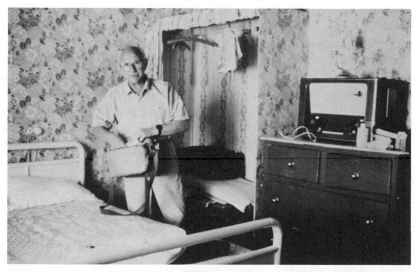

All over Europe people rent spare bedrooms to budget travelers. Bed and breakfasts give you double the cultural experience for half the price of a hotel.

These places are called *Gastehaus, Zimmer,* or *Fremdenzimmer* in Germany, Switzerland and Austria; *Gites or Chambres d' Hotes* in France; *camas* in Spain; *sobe* in Yugoslavia; *pensao* or *casa particular* in Portugal; *pension, locanda* or *camera* in Italy; *pension* or *domatio* in Greece, *husrom* in Scandinavia; and bed and breakfast in the British Isles.

Britain's bed and breakfast places are the best of all. Very common throughout the British Isles, they are a boon to anyone touring England, Scotland, Wales or Ireland. As the name indicates, a breakfast comes with the bed, and this is no ordinary breakfast. Most women "doing B and B" take pride in their breakfasts. Their guests sit down to an elegant and very British tablesetting and feast on cereal, juice, bacon, sausages, eggs, broiled tomatoes, toast, marmalade and coffee or tea, always an impressive meal. While you are finishing your coffee, the landlady (who by this time is probably on very friendly terms with you) will often present you with her guest book, pointing out the other guests from your state that have stayed in her house and inviting you to make an entry.

Your hostess will usually cook you up a simple dinner for a pittance and, if you have time to chat, you'll undoubtedly get tea and biscuits.

When you bid her farewell and thank her for the good sleep and full stomach, it is, more often than not, difficult to get away. Determined to fill you with as much information as food, she wants you to have the best day of sightseeing possible.

A list of recommended B&B's is unnecessary and very likely out of date. The scene is constantly changing, with B&Bs coming and going as easily as they can put out or take in their signs. Except in big cities the quality varies only in degrees of wonderful and you really don't need a travel writer's particular recommendation. If you arrive by mid-afternoon you won't need reservations (except in London and a few very touristy instances). I normally let the local tourist office find me a room or I find it on my own near the train station or town center and shop around. I have a personal rule never to take a B&B until I've checked out three. Styles and atmosphere vary from house to house—and I enjoy looking through European homes.

Camping European-Style

Few Americans consider taking advantage of Europe's 10,000-plus campgrounds. Camping is the cheapest way to see Europe and every camper I've talked to gives it rave reviews.

Every town has a campground with enough ground for the average middle class European to pitch his tent or park his "caravan" (trailer), good showers and washing facilities, a grocery store and restaurant, and a handy bus connection into town, all for just a few dollars per person per night.

"Camping" is the universal word for campground. Unlike the American campground, European camping forbids open fires and you won't find a picturesque riverfront lot with a stove, table and privacy. A "Camping" is more functional—near or in the town—a place to sleep, eat, wash and catch a bus downtown. They rarely fill up and if they do, the "Full" sign usually refers to trailers (most Europeans are trailer campers). A small tent can almost always be squeezed in somewhere.

"Campings" are well sign-posted and local tourist information offices have guides and maps listing nearby campgrounds. Every country has good and bad campgrounds. Campgrounds mirror their surroundings. If the region is overcrowded, dusty, dirty, unkempt and generally chaotic, you're unlikely to find an oasis behind the campground's gates. A sleepy Austrian valley will most likely offer a sleepy Austrian campground.

Many campgrounds offer "bungalows" with four to six beds. These are very comfortable and much cheaper than hotels. Scandinavian bungalows are especially popular.

Camping with kids has many advantages. A family sleeps in a tent a lot cheaper than in a hotel. There's plenty to occupy children, and many campings have playgrounds that come fully equipped with European kids. As your kids make European friends, your campground social circle will naturally widen.

European campgrounds come well equipped. Showers and washing facilities, while often over-crowded, are usually very good. Hot water, as in many hostels and hotels, is metered and you'll learn to carry coins and "douche" European style, lathering up and scrubbing with the water off, then rinsing quickly.

European tenters appreciate the in-camp grocery store, cafe and restaurant. The store, while high priced, stays open longer than most, offering late-comers a budget alternative to the restaurant. The restaurant or cafe is a likely camp "hangout" and Americans enjoy mixing in this easygoing European social scene. I've scuttled many nights on the town so I wouldn't miss the fun right in the camp. Camping, like hosteling, is a great way to meet Europeans. If the campground doesn't have a place to eat, you'll find one nearby.

Silence reigns in European campgrounds after the ten or eleven o'clock curfew. Noisemakers are dealt with strictly. Many places close the gates to cars after 10:00. If you do arrive after the office closes, set up quietly and register in the morning.

Campgrounds, unlike Youth Hostels, are remarkably theft-free. "Campings" are full of basically honest middle-class European families and someone's at the gate all day. Most people just leave their gear zipped inside their tent.

Prices vary from country to country, and within countries according to facilities and style. Expect to spend two to five dollars per night per person. You'll often pay by the tent, so four people in one tent sleep cheaper than four individual campers. (Beware, Italian campgrounds can be shockingly expensive.)

Camp registration is easy. As with most hotels, you show your passport, fill out a short form and learn the rules. Check-out time is usually noon. English is the second language of "campings" throughout Europe and most managers will understand the monoglot American.

The "International Camping Carnet," a kind of international campground membership card, is required at some sites, handy at others. It is available for $20 through the National Campers and Hikers Association, Inc. or at many European campgrounds. The "Carnet" will get you an occasional discount or preferential treatment in a very crowded situation. Sometimes you are required to leave either your passport or your camping Carnet at the office.

European sites called "week-end campings" are rented out on a yearly basis to local urbanites. Too often "week-end" sites are full or don't allow what they call "stop and go" campers (you). Your camping guidebook will indicate which places are the "week-end" type.

Even if you don't have a car or trailer, but are a camper at heart, a camping may still be the way to go. Europe's campgrounds mix well with just about any mode of transportation.

Tent and train is a winning combination for many. Nearly every train station has a tourist office nearby. Stop by and pick up a map with campgrounds marked, local camping leaflets and bus directions. While some are frustrating, buses normally shuttle campers from station to a campground with ease. Every station has lockers where those with limited energy can leave unneeded bulk. (Very light modern campgear makes this approach to camping better than ever.) *How to Camp Europe by Train* by Bakken is a popular guide on this subject. The *Let's Go Guide* gives good instructions on getting to and from the campgrounds.

Hitch-hikers find camping just right for their tender budget. Many campgrounds are located near the major road out of town where long rides are best snared. Any hitching camper with average social skills can find a friend driving his way with an empty seat. A note on the camp bulletin board can be very effective.

Tents and bikes also mix well. Bikers enjoy the same we-can-squeeze-one-more-in status as hikers and will rarely be turned away.

Camping by car is my favorite combination. A car carries all your camp gear and gets you to any campground fast and easy. Road maps always pinpoint "campings" and when you're within a few blocks, the road signs take over. In big cities the money you save on parking will almost pay for your camping. I usually take the bus downtown, leaving the car next to my tent.

Commit yourself to a camping trip or to a no-camping trip and pack accordingly. Don't carry a sleeping bag and a tent "just in case".

Your camping trip deserves first class equipment. Spend some time and money outfitting yourself before your trip. There are plenty of stores with exciting new gear and expert salespeople to get you up-to-date in a hurry. European campers prefer a very lightweight "three season" sleeping bag (consult a climate chart for your probable bedroom temperature) and an ensolite closed-cell pad to insulate and soften your bed. A campstove is right for American-style camping, but probably not your cup of tea in Europe. Start without a stove. If you figure you need one, buy one there. In Europe it's much easier to find fuel for a European camp stove than for its Yankee counterpart. (If you take one from home it should be the "gaz" variety.) I kept it simple, picnicking and enjoying food and fun in the campground restaurant. (For a good catalog full of camping gear call REI at 1-800-426-4840.)

Informal camping, or "camping wild", is legal in most of Europe. Low profile, pitch-the-tent-after-dark-and-move-on-first-thing-in-the-morning informal camping is usually allowed even in countries where it is technically illegal. Use good judgment and don't pitch your tent informally in carefully controlled areas like cities, resorts or Eastern European states.

It's always a good idea to ask permission when possible. In the countryside, a landowner will rarely refuse a polite request to borrow a patch of land for the night.

Many cities, especially in France, allow camping in local stadiums. Formal camping is safer than camping wild. Never leave your gear and tent unattended without the gates of a formal campground to discourage thieves.

There are several good camping guidebooks out. The comprehensive *Europa Camping and Caravanning* catalog is available in many bookstores. *Gypsying After 40* by Robert W. Harris is a new book from John Muir Publications, my publisher, full of practical and ingenius ideas, and guidance on self discovery and adventure. Each country's national tourist office in the U.S.A. will send you plenty of helpful information on camping in its country.

Camping allows you to explore Europe cheaply. You'll have no trouble finding a spot and you'll meet plenty of Europeans. Camping in Europe has its discomforts just like it does here. If you can put up with those, a camping adventure in Europe is just a plane ticket away.

Sleeping Free

There are still people traveling in Europe on $5 a day—and less. The one thing they have in common is that they sleep free (another thing is B.O.). If even cheap *pensions* and youth hostels are too expensive for your budget, you too can sleep free. I once went twenty-nine out of thirty nights without paying for a bed. It's neither difficult nor dangerous, but it's not always comfortable and convenient. This is not a vagabonding guide, but any traveler may have an occasional free night. Faking it until the sun returns can become, at least in the long run, a good memory.

Europe has plenty of places to throw out your sleeping bag. This sort of vagabonding is a bad idea, however, in police states like those in Eastern Europe. Some large cities like Amsterdam and Athens are flooded with tourists during peak season, and many of them spend their nights in a city park. Some cities enforce their "no sleeping in the parks" laws only selectively. Away from the cities, in forests or on beaches, you can pretty well sleep where you like. I have found that summer nights in the Mediterranean part of Europe are mild enough that I am comfortable with just my jeans, sweater and hostel sheet. I no longer lug a sleeping bag around Europe, but if you'll be vagabonding a lot, bring a light bag.

Trains and stations are great for sleeping free. On the trains, success hinges on getting enough room to stretch out, and that can be quite a trick. See "How to Sleep on the Train" in the train transportation chapter.

When you have no place to go for the night in a city, you can always retreat to the station for a warm and safe place to spend the night for free (assuming the station stays open all night). Most popular tourist cities in Europe have stations that are painted nightly with a long rainbow of sleeping bags. This is allowed, but everyone is cleared out at dawn before the normal rush of travelers converges on the station. In some cases you'll be asked to show a ticket. Any ticket or your Eurailpass entitles you to a free night in a station's first class waiting room—you are simply waiting for your early train. Whenever possible, avoid the second class lounges; first class hobos are more comfortable in first class lounges.

It's tempting, but quite risky to sleep in a train car that's just sitting there going nowhere. No awakening is more rude than having your bedroom jolt into motion and roll towards God-knows-where—although many would argue it's more pleasant to sleep on a train to God-knows-where than to be stuck in the station all night.

An airport is a large, posh version of a train station, offering a great opportunity to sleep free. After a late landing, I crash on a comfortable sofa, rather than wasting sleeping time looking for a place that will sell me a bed for the remainder of the night. I usually spend the night before a very early flight in the airport as well. Many cut-rate inter-European flights leave or arrive at ungodly hours. The Frankfurt airport is served very conveniently by the train and is great for sleeping free—even if you aren't flying anywhere.

Imaginative vagabonds see Europe as one big free hotel (barns, churches, buildings under construction, ruins, college dorms, etc.). Just carry your passport with you, attach your belongings to you so they don't get stolen and use good judgment in your choice of a free bed.

Friends and Relatives

There is no better way to really enjoy a strange country than as the guest of a local family. And, of course, a night with a friend or relative is very easy on the budget. I've had nothing but good experiences (and good sleep) at my "addresses" in Europe. There are two kinds of addresses: European addresses from home and those you pick up in Europe.

Before you leave, do some research. Find out where your relatives are in Europe. No matter how distant they are, unless you are a real slob, they're tickled to have an American visitor. I always send mine a card announcing my visit to their town and telling them when I will arrive. They answer, writing either "please come visit us" or "have a good trip." It is obvious from their letter (or lack of letter) if I am invited to stop by. Follow the same procedure with indirect contacts. I have dear "parents away from home" in Austria and London. My Austrian "parents" are really the parents of my sister's ski teacher. In London, they are the parents of a

The Europeans you visit don't need to be next of kin. This Tyrolian is the father of my sister's ski teacher. That's close enough.

friend of my uncle. Neither relationship was terribly close—until I visited. Now we are friends for life.

The other kind of address is one you pick up during your travels. Exchanging addresses is almost as common as a handshake in Europe. When people meet, they invite each other to visit sometime. I warn my friend that I may very well show up someday at his house, whether it's in Osaka, New Zealand, New Mexico or Dublin. When I have, it's been a good experience.

This is not cultural free-loading. Both parties benefit from such a visit. Never forget that a Greek family is just as curious and interested in you as you are in them. Equipped with home town postcards and pictures of my family, I make a point to give as much from my culture as I am taking from the culture of my host. In this sort of cultural intercourse there are only winners. I insist on no special treatment, telling my host that I am most comfortable when no fuss is made over me. I try to help with the chores, I don't wear out my welcome, and I follow up each visit with postcards to share the rest of my trip with my friends.

House Swapping

Many families enjoy a great budget option year after year. They trade houses (sometimes cars and pets too—but you've got to draw the line somewhere) with someone in the destination of their choice. Ask your travel agent for information or read Arthur Frommer's *Swap and Go* guide to house swapping.

Eating Cheap

Many vacations revolve around great restaurant meals, and for good reason: Europe serves some of the world's top cuisine at some of the world's top prices.

I'm no gourmet, so most of my experience lies in eating well cheaply. Galloping gluttons thrive on eight dollars a day—by picnicking. Those with a more refined palate and a little more money can mix picnics with satisfying, atmospheric and enjoyable restaurant meals and eat just fine for fifteen dollars a day.

This $15 a day budget includes a $2-$3 continental breakfast (usually figured into your hotel bill), a $3-$5 picnic mid-day feast, and an $8-$10 restaurant dinner.

European restaurant meals are about as expensive as those in America. The cost of eating is determined not by the local standard—but by your personal standard. Many Americans can't find an edible meal for less than $15 in their hometown. Their neighbors enjoy eating out for half that. If you can enjoy an eight-dollar meal in Boston, Detroit or Seattle, you'll eat well in London, Rome, or Helsinki for the same price.

Forget the scare stories. People who spend $40 for a dinner in Dublin and complain either enjoy complaining or are fools.

Let me fill you in on filling up in Europe.

Restaurants

Restaurants are the most expensive way to eat. They can rape, pillage and plunder a tight budget—but it would be criminal to pass through Europe without sampling the local specialties served in good restaurants. You should relish a country's high cuisine—it's just as important culturally as its museums.

When I splurge on a restaurant meal (about one a day—less in the expensive north and more in the cheaper Mediterranean countries), I require good value.

Average tourists are attracted, like flies to cowpies, to the biggest neon sign that boasts "we speak English and accept Visa cards." Wrong! The key to finding a good meal is to find a restaurant filled with loyal, local customers enjoying themselves. After a few days in Europe, you'll have no trouble telling a local hangout from a tourist trap. Take advantage of local favorites.

Restaurants listed in your guidebook are usually fine, but too often when a place becomes famous this way it goes downhill. You don't need those listings to find your own good restaurant. Leave the tourist center, stroll around until you find a happy crowd of locals eating. Ask your hotel receptionist, or even someone on the street, for a good place.

European restaurants post their menus outside. Check the price and selection before entering. If the menu's not posted, feel free to go inside and ask to see one.

Finding the right restaurant is half the battle. Then you need to order a good meal. Ordering in a foreign language can be fun or it can be an ordeal. Any restaurant may have an English menu lying around. Ask for one—if nothing else, you may get the waiter who speaks the goodest English. Most waiters can give at least a very basic translation—pork,

A fun neighborhood restaurant; no VISA cards, no English menus, but good food, good prices and a friendly chef.

chicken, *zuppa,* green salat, etc. A pocket phrase book or menu reader is very helpful for those who want to avoid ordering sheep stomach when all they want is lamb chops.

If you don't know what to order go with the waiter's recommendation, or look for your dream meal on another table and order by pointing. You can't go wrong. People are usually helpful and understanding to the poor monoglot tourist. If they aren't, you probably picked a place that sees too many of them. Europeans with the most patience with tourists are the ones who rarely deal with them.

People who agonize over each word on the menu, season the whole experience with stress. Get a basic idea of what's cooking, have some fun with the waiter, be loose and adventurous and just order something.

To max out culturally, I never order the same meal as my partner. We share, sampling twice as many dishes. My groups cut every dish into bits and our table becomes a lazy susan. If anything, the waiters are impressed by our interest in their food and very often they'll run over with a special treat for all of us to sample—like squid eggs.

I like to order a high risk and a low risk meal with my partner. At worst we learn what we don't like and split the veal and fries.

The *menu turistico* (tourist menu) or *prix fixe* menu is very popular and normally a good value. For a set price you get the "special of the day" multi-course meal complete with bread, wine and service. When I'm lazy and the price is right, I go for it, and it usually turns out OK.

The best values in European entrees are fish, veal and chicken. Drinks and desserts are the worst value. Skipping those, I can enjoy some very classy meals for nine or ten dollars.

Before the bill comes, make a mental tally of roughly how much your meal should cost. When the bill comes (get it by catching the waiter's eye and, with raised hands, scribble with an imaginary pencil on your palm), it should vaguely resemble the figure you expected. It should have the same number of digits. If the total is a surprise, ask to have it itemized and explained. All too often waiters make the same "innocent" mistakes repeatedly, knowing most tourists are so befuddled by the money and menu that they'll pay whatever number lies at the bottom of the bill.

Fast food places are everywhere. You'll find Big Macs in every language—not exciting (and double the American price), but at least at McDonald's you know exactly what you're getting—and it's fast. A hamburger, fries and shake are fun half way through your trip. Each country has its equivalent of the hamburger or hot dog stand. Whatever their origin, they're a hit with the young locals and a handy place for a quick cheap bite. A sure value for your dollar, franc or shilling, is a department store cafeteria. These places are designed for the shopping housewife who has a sharp eye for a good value and that's what you'll get—good values and housewives with sharp eyes.

While fast food has gained a foothold in Europe, a real Continental meal is a leisurely experience, the focus of the evening. In a good restaurant, service will be slower and you won't get your bill until you ask for it. A European will spend at least two hours enjoying a good dinner and, for the full experience, so should you.

Tipping

I'm not known for flashy tipping (in fact I think it's a pretty archaic way of paying people) and tipping is a minuscule concern of mine during a European trip. Traveling through the back door, the only tipping I do is in restaurants when service isn't included, rounding the taxi bill up and when someone assists me in seeing some sight and is paid no other way (like the man who shows people an Etruscan tomb that just happens to be in his backyard).

In restaurants a service charge of about 15% is usually either included in the menu price or added on automatically to your bill. If that's the case, a tip is not expected. (It should say so on the menu or bill, *service compris* for included, or *service non compris*.) Rounding up the bill is a nice touch for good service. Over-tipping is an ugly-American act that does a disservice to the local people. Waiters who are over-tipped begin to expect the same treatment from other tourists and locals who follow. Americans in the days of the big buck shaped an image that Yankees in the days of the smaller dollar are having a hard time living down. If bucks talk for you at home, muzzle them in Europe. As a matter of principle, if not economy, the local price should prevail. Don't over tip.

Morsels—One Country at a Time

Greece   The menus are all Greek to me. Go into the kitchen and physically point to the dish you want. This is a good way to make some friends, sample from each kettle, get things straight and have a very memorable meal. (The same is true in Turkey.) This is a common and accepted practice among tourists. Be brave; try the local food. My favorite Greek snack is a tasty shish kebab in a muffin called a *souvlaki*. Souvlaki stands are all over Athens. On the islands, eat fresh seafood. If possible, go to a wine festival. The Dafni Wine Festival (nightly July-September) just outside of Athens is best. Eat when the locals do—late, and for American-style coffee order "Nescafe."

Italy   Italy is no longer so cheap. In fact, it's caught up with and passed much of Europe price-wise. Florence, Venice and Rome are most expensive, elsewhere it's easy to find a decent meal for five dollars.

Italians eat huge meals consisting of a first course of pasta, a second plate of meat plus a salad, fruit and wine. The pasta course alone is enough to fill the average tourist. While some restaurants won't serve just pasta, I usually find one that will, and enjoy reasonably priced lasagna and a salad. Any time you sit down you'll be charged a cover *(coperto)* charge of a dollar or two. That, plus service makes a cheap restaurant meal rare. The most inexpensive Italian eateries are called *tavola calda, rosticceria, trattoria, pizzeria,* or, recently, "self-service." A big pizza and a cold beer are my idea of a good, fast, cheap Italian meal. Look for a "Pizza Rustica" (which serves pizza by the slice sold by weight) for a stand-up super bargain meal. Just point to the best looking pizza, tell them how much you want; they heat it up and it's yours.

Gelati! Delizioso! Say "lick a little Italy" three times.

One of the most important words in your Italian vocabulary is *gelati,* probably the.best ice cream you'll ever taste. A big cone with a variety of flavors costs about a dollar. Cappuccino, rich coffee and milk with a marshmallow-like head, is everywhere, and it should be. Tiny coffee shops are tucked away in just about every street. All have a price list and most have a system where you pay the cashier first and take the receipt to the man with the drinks. Experiment, try coffee or tea *freddo* (cold) or a "frappe". Discover a new specialty each day. Bar hopping is fun. A bottle of wine serves six or eight people for four dollars and most bars have delicious *chequitas* (munchies).

Spain   The greatest pleasure in Spanish eating is the price tag. Take advantage of the house wine. It is very important to fit the local schedule— lunch late (noon-3:00) and dinner later (8:30-11:30). Restaurants are generally closed except at meal times. At other times, bars and coffee spots serve snacks of *bocadillos* (sandwiches) and *tortillas* (omelets) along with *tapas* (hors d'oeuvres). On my last trip I found myself eating at least one easy (what you see is what you get), quick and very cheap tapa meal a day.

Portugal   Portugal has some of the best and cheapest food I've found in Europe. Find a local sailors' hangout and fill up on fresh seafood. It's delicious, especially clams and cockles. While Portuguese restaurants are not expensive, food stands in the fairs and amusement parks are even cheaper. *Vinho verde* (green wine) is an addictive local specialty.

Switzerland   A fondue is a must. I order one steak-and-potatoes dish and a cheese fondue for two people. Swiss chocolates are deservedly famous. The Migros and Co-op grocery stores sell groceries for about the same price as you'd find in American stores—cheap by European standards. Youth hostels usually serve large family-style dinners at a low, low price. Expensive Swiss restaurant prices make these budget food alternatives especially attractive. The remote mountain huts you'll run across as you hike offer more than shelter. Eat there. Many have provisions helicoptered in, are reasonably priced, and bubble with Alpine atmosphere. Swiss wine *(Fendant)* is expensive and worth every franc. Local beer is cheap and good.

The Netherlands   My favorite Dutch food is Indonesian. Indonesia, a former colony of the Netherlands, fled the nest, leaving behind plenty of great Indonesian restaurants. The cheapest meals, as well as some of the best splurges, are found in Holland's many Indonesian restaurants. The famous *rijstafel* (rice table) is the ultimate Indonesian meal, with as many as thirty-six delightfully exotic courses, all eaten with rice. One meal will stuff two large men, so order carefully. The Bali Restaurant in Scheveningen is, according to many Hollanders, the best Indonesian restaurant in Holland. I've eaten there on four different trips and have no reason to disagree.

In a budget restaurant rijstafel can be a great bargain—12 exotic courses with rice for less than six dollars. Indonesian restaurants are found all over Holland. In Amsterdam, the best budget ones are on Bantammerstraat, just beyond the sailors' quarters (Red Light District.)

Scandinavia   Most Scandinavians avoid their highly taxed and very expensive restaurants. Some of the most expensive restaurants in Europe are found in Scandinavia. The key to budget eating in Nordic Europe is to take advantage of the smorgasbord. For about seven dollars (cheap in Scandinavia), the breakfast smorgasbords of Denmark, Norway and Sweden will fill you with plenty of hearty food. Smorgasbords do not provide "doggie bags," but I have noticed many empty rucksacks (or zip-lock baggies) being brought in and not many empty ones carried out. Since my stomach is the same size all day long and both meals are, by definition, all-you-can-eat, I opt for the budget breakfast meal over the fancier and more expensive ($15) *mid-dag* (mid-day) smorgasbord.

Many train stations and boats serve smorgasbords. The boat from Stockholm to Helsinki, Bergen's Hotel Norge and, best of all, the lovely Centralens restaurant right in the Stockholm train station all serve up especially good smorgasms. No seasoned traveler leaves the Stockholm station after his overnight train ride from Oslo or Copenhagen without enjoying a smorgasbord breakfast. If you don't smorgasbord, Stockholm could very well break your budget.

"Kro" restaurants in Denmark and "Bundeheimen" (literally, "farmer's house"), found all over Norway serve, like their name suggests, good hearty "meat-and-potatoes" meals that a peasant would like and could afford. Alcohol-free restaurants enjoy a special tax status and can serve cheaper meals. And you can normally have all the vegetables, normally potatoes, you want when you order a restaurant's entrée. Just ask for seconds. The cheapest cafeterias often close at 5:00 or 6:00 pm. Fresh produce, colorful markets and efficient supermarkets abound in Europe's most expensive corner. Picnic.

Germany   Germany is ideal for the "meat-and-potatoes" person. With straightforward, no nonsense food at budget prices, I eat very well in Deutschland. Small town restaurants serve up wonderful plates of hearty local specialties for $6 to $8. The wurst is the best anywhere and kraut is entirely different from the stuff you hate at home. Eat ugly things whenever possible. So many tasty European specialties come in gross packages.

Drink beer in Bavaria and wine on the Rhine, choosing the most atmospheric *brauhaus* or *weinstubes* possible.

Browse through supermarkets and see what Germany eats when there's no more beer and pretzels. Try Gummi Bears, a bear-shaped jelly bean with a cult following, and *Nutella,* a choco-nut spread that will turn anything into a first class dessert. Fast food stands are labeled *Schnellimbiss*.

France   France is famous for its cuisine—and rightly so. Surprisingly, dining in France is easy on a budget, especially in the countryside. Small restaurants throughout the country love their local specialties, and take great pride in what they serve up. Wine is the cheapest drink (more expensive labels run upward of five dollars) and every region has its own wine and cheese.

Degustation gratuite is not a laxative, but an invitation to sample the wine. You'll find "D.G." signs throughout France's wine-growing regions. When buying cheese, be sure to ask for samples of the local specialties. Croissants are served warm with breakfast and *baguettes* (long, skinny loaves of French bread) are great for budget munching.

Picnicking is, appropriately, a French word and, as you spread out your tablecloth, every passerby will wish you a cheery "bon appetit!"

French food deserves the coverage normally reserved for Europe's inedible attractions so I've included a back door later in the book on French Cuisine.

More Morsels

Mensas   When you're in a European university town, with a wallet as empty as your stomach, find a "mensa". Mensa is the universal word for a government-subsidized institutional (university, fire station, union of gondoliers, etc.) cafeteria. If the place welcomes tourists, you can fill yourself with a plate of dull but nourishing food in the company of local students or workers for an unbeatable price.

University cafeterias are often closed during summer holidays. A meal here is a sure-fire way to meet educated English-speaking young locals with open and stimulating minds. They're often anxious to practice their politics and economics as well as their English on a foreign friend. This is especially handy as you travel beyond Europe.

The Continental Breakfast   On the Continent (except for Holland and Scandinavia) breakfast is a roll with marmalade or jam, occasionally a slice of ham or cheese, and coffee and tea. Even the finest hotels serve the same thing—on better plates. It's the European way to start the day. I supplement my CB's with a piece of fruit and a separately wrapped chunk of cheese from my rucksack stash. If you're a coffee drinker, remember this is the only cheap time to caffeinate yourself. Most hotels will serve you a bottomless cup of a rich brew only with breakfast. After that, it'll cost you a fortune to support your habit—one costly little cup at a time.

I'm a big breakfast person at home. When I feel the urge for a typical American breakfast in Europe, I beat it to death with a hard roll. You can find bacon, eggs and orange juice in the morning, but it's nearly always overpriced and a disappointment.

Breakfast, normally "included" in your hotel bill, can sometimes be skipped and deducted from the price of your room. Ask what it includes and costs. You can usually save money and gain atmosphere by buying a coffee and roll or croissant at the cafe down the street, or by brunching picnic-style in the park.

Drinks   As I'll discuss in the health chapter, European water has a different bacterial content than what our systems are accustomed to. Many (but not all) people will have some problem adjusting—not because their water is dirty, but because our systems are weak.

The trouble involved in avoiding European water outweighs the benefits. As long as my sources are obviously for drinking, I drink the water—even in Italy, Sicily, Greece, Spain and Portugal. Generally, avoid water in North Africa and east of Bulgaria.

Restaurants play on the tourists' fears of getting sick. Even in places as safe as Switzerland, they caution the tourist about the water. This is done to scare you into a $2 Coke or beer at their restaurant. Don't believe them. Order water "natural". If you are not careful, you may get mineral water. Insist on tap water if you want a free drink.

Tap water in five languages
Italian—*l'agua di rubinetto*
French—*l'eau du robinet*
German—*leitungswasser*
Spanish—*agua del grifo*
Portuguese—*agua a torneira*

In all other languages just do the international charade: hold imaginary glass in left hand; turn on tap with right, make sound of faucet. Stop it with a click and drink it with a smile.

Many who see Europeans buying bottled water conclude that the tap water is unsafe. Europeans drink bottled water mainly because it tastes better. You get colder sparkling clear water and happier waiters when you order and pay for Europe's fine bottled waters. In the south where ordering cold bottled water makes the most sense, a liter bottle is normally quite cheap. The big questions is *con gas* or *senza gas*. Bubbles are an acquired taste and, much like kissing a man with a moustache, once you've tried it, it's just not right any other way.

If your budget is tight and you want to save $3 to $4 a day, never buy a restaurant drink. Scoff if you have the money, but remember—the drink is, along with the dessert, the worst value on any menu. Water is jokingly called "the American champagne" by the waiters of Europe.

Drink like a European. Cold milk, orange juice and ice cubes are American habits, either over-priced or non-existent in European restaurants. Insisting on cold milk or ice cubes will get you nothing but strange looks and a reputation as the ugly—if not downright crazy—American (see section on "The Ugly American"). Order local drinks, not just to save money, but to experience that part of the culture and to get the best quality and service. If you must have them, the "American waters" (Coke, Fanta and Seven-Up) are sold everywhere these days.

Buying local alcohol is much cheaper than insisting on your favorite import. A shot of the local hard drink in Portugal should cost fifty cents while an American drink would cost several dollars. Drink the local stuff with the local people in the local bars; a better experience altogether than a gin and tonic in your hotel with a guy from L.A. Drink wine in wine countries and beer in beer countries. Sample the local specialties. Let a local person order you her favorite. You may hate it, but you'll never forget it.

Youth hostelers picnicking on a Swiss mountaintop.

Picnic—Spend Like a Pauper, Eat Like a Prince

There is only one way left to feast for three or four dollars anywhere in the world—picnic. I am a picnic connoisseur. (After four months in Europe, the first thing I do when I get home is put some cheese on a hard roll.) I think I eat better while spending $8 to $10 a day less than those who eat exclusively in restaurants.

While I am the first to admit that restaurant meals are an important aspect of any culture, I picnic almost daily. This is not solely for budgetary reasons. I love to dive into a marketplace and actually get a chance to do business. I can't get enough of Europe's varied cheeses, meats, fresh fruits, vegetables and still-warm-out-of-the-bakery-oven bread. Many of my favorite foods had their debut in a European picnic. I pride myself in my ability to create unbeatable atmosphere for a meal by choosing just the right picnic spot.

I don't like to spend a lot of time looking for a decent restaurant, then waiting around to get served. And, nothing frustrates me more than to tangle with a budget-threatening menu, finally ordering a meal, then walking away feeling unsatisfied, like my money could have done much more for my stomach if I had invested it in a marketplace. So, let me talk a bit about picnicking.

Every town, large or small, has at least one outdoor marketplace. This is the most colorful and natural place to go to assemble a picnic. The unit of measure throughout the Continent is a kilo, which is 2.2 pounds. A kilo has 1000 grams. One hundred grams of cheese or meat tucked into a chunk of French bread gives you about a quarter pounder. Make an effort to communicate with the merchants in the markets. Know what you are buying and what you are spending.

You may want only one or two pieces of fruit. Sometimes merchants refuse to deal in such small quantities. The way to get what you want and no more is to estimate about what it would cost if he were to weigh it, and then just hold out a coin worth about that much in one hand and the apple, or whatever, in the other. Rarely will he refuse the deal. Timidity will get you nowhere.

If no prices are posted, be wary. I've seen terrible cases of tourists getting ripped-off by market merchants in tourist centers. I find places that print the prices. I suspect that any market with no printed prices has a double price standard—one for locals and a more expensive one for tourists. If all else fails, I watch carefully while a local woman buys her groceries. Even if I don't totally understand what went on, the merchant thinks I do and he's less likely to take advantage of me. If I don't like the price, I just say, "No thanks."

I'll never forget a friend of mine who bought two bananas for our London picnic. He grabbed the fruit, held out a handful of change and said "How much?" The merchant took two 50 pence coins. My friend turned to me and said, "Wow, London really is expensive." People like this go home and spread these wild misleading rumors: "Bananas sell for a buck a piece in London!" Any time you hold out a handful of money to a banana salesman you've had it.

Picnic Drinks   There are plenty of cheap ways to wash down a picnic. Milk is always cheap, available in quarter, half or whole liters. Be sure it's normal drinking milk. More than once I've been stuck with buttermilk

Picnic on the train—cheap, hearty, scenic.

or something I didn't want. Look for local words for whole or light, such as *voll* or *lett*. Nutritionally, milk can't be beat. Half a liter provides about twenty-five percent of your daily protein needs. Cold milk is rare in most countries. You will often find a "long-life" kind of milk that needs no refrigeration. This milk will never go bad—or taste good.

Liter bottles of Coke are cheap, as is wine in most countries. The local wine gives your picnic a very nice touch. Fruit juice (look for 100% no sugar to avoid stuff that's closer to Fanta without the fizz) comes in handy boxes costing about a dollar per quart. Any place that serves coffee has free boiling water. Those who have more nerve than pride get their plastic water bottle (a sturdy plastic bottle will not melt) filled with free boiling water at a cafe, then add their own instant coffee or tea bag later.

Picnic Atmosphere   There is nothing second class about a picnic. A few special touches will even make your budget meal a first class affair.

Proper site selection can make the difference between just another meal and *le picnic extraordinaire*. Since you've decided to skip the restaurant, it's up to you to create the atmosphere. I try to incorporate a picnic brunch, lunch or dinner into the day's sightseeing plans. For example, I'll start the day by scouring the thriving market with my senses and my camera. Then I'll fill up my shopping bag and have brunch on a river bank. I combine lunch and a siesta in a cool park to fill my stomach, rest my body and escape the early afternoon heat. It's fun to eat dinner on a castle wall enjoying a commanding view and the setting sun.

It's very efficient to plan a picnic meal to coincide with a train or boat ride. This is a pleasant way to pass time normally wasted in transit. When you arrive, you are nourished, fat, happy, rested and ready to go, rather than weak and in search of food. Mountain hikes are punctuated nicely by picnics. Food tastes even better on top of a mountain. Europeans are great picnickers, and I've had many a picnic become a potluck. By the time the meal is over, I have a new friend as well as a full stomach.

Nutritionally, a picnic is unbeatable. Consider this example: 100 grams of cheese, 100 grams of thin-sliced salami, fresh bread, peaches, carrots, a cucumber, a half liter of milk and fruit yogurt for dessert. When sandwiches get old, there are plenty of variations such as cooked fish or chicken and quiche. A pizza to go is fun. Cold cereal is not outside the realm of possibility. Cornflakes can be found in any small grocery store. European yogurt is delicious and can be drunk right out of its container.

"Table Scraps" and Miscellaneous Tips   Bring zip-lock baggies (large and small), a little can opener and a good knife; a dish towel serves as a small tablecloth and comes in very handy. Bread has always been cheap in Europe. (Leaders have learned from history that when stomachs rumble so do the mobs in the streets.) Cheese is a specialty nearly everywhere and is, along with milk, one of the cheapest sources of protein.

In many countries outside of Europe, eating can be hazardous to your health. In these cases, eat only peelable fruit and vegetables. A travelers' guidebook to health or your doctor can tell you where you'll have to be careful. Don't worry in Europe. Tourists who have been in a country for a while usually know how to stay healthy and are excellent information sources.

Know which foods in each country are reasonably priced and which are expensive by doing quick market surveys. For instance, tomatoes, cucumbers and watermelons are good deals in Italy. Citrus fruits are terribly expensive (and not very good) in Eastern Europe, while the Eastern countries have some of the best and cheapest ice cream anywhere. Ice cream is costly in Scandinavia (what isn't?) and wine is a best buy in France. Anything American is usually expensive and rarely satisfying. Europeans have not yet mastered the fine art of the American hamburger, although each has its own variation on McDonald's: I saw a "MacCheap" in Switzerland.

A quick dashboard picnic halfway through a busy day of sightseeing.

My big meal of the day is a picnic lunch. Only a glutton can spend more than four dollars for this mid-day feast. In a park in Paris, on an Norwegian ferry, high in the Alps, or on your dashboard at an autobahn reststop, picnicking is the budget traveler's key to cheap eating.

Vegetarians

Vegetarians find life a little frustrating in Europe. Very often Europeans think "vegetarian" means "no red meat" or "not much meat." If you are a strict vegetarian, you'll have to make things very clear. Write the appropriate phrase below on the back of a business card and show it to each waiter before ordering:

German: *Wir sind vegetarian. Wir essen kein fleisch, fisch oder geflugel. Eir und kase ok.*

French: *Nous sommes vegetarian. Nous ne mangons pas des viandes, des poissons or des poullets. Oeuf et fromage ok.*

Italian: *Noi siamo vegetariani. Non mangiamo carne, pesci o polli. Uovo e formaggio ok.*

Dutch: We are vegetarian. We do not eat meat, fish or chicken. Eggs and cheese ok. (Most Dutch speak English.)

Vegetarians have no problem with continental breakfasts which are meatless anyway. Meat-free picnic lunches are delicious—bread, cheese and yogurt are wonderful throughout Europe. It's in restaurants that your patience may be minced. Big city tourist offices list restaurants by category. Just look under "V." While Italy seems to sprinkle a little meat in just about everything, German cooking normally keeps the meat separate from the vegetables. Hearty salads, with beets, cheese and eggs, are a vegetarian's delight. Vegetarians enjoy Third World cuisine and ethnic restaurants throughout Europe.

Eating and Sleeping on a Budget—
The Five Commandments

You could get eight good hours of sleep and three square meals in Europe for $20 a day if your budget required it. If you have any budget limitations at all, keep these rules of thumb in mind:

1. Minimize the Use of Hotels and Restaurants. Enjoying the sights and culture of Europe has nothing to do with how much you're spending to eat and sleep. Learn about and take advantage of the many alternatives to hotels and restaurants.

If your budget dictated, you could feel the fjords and caress the castles without hotels and restaurants—and probably learn, experience and enjoy more than the tourist who spends in a day what you spend in a week.

2. Budget for Price Variances. Prices as much as triple from south to north. Budget more for the north and get by on less than your daily allowance in Spain, Portugal and Greece. Exercise those budget alternatives where they'll save you the most money. A hostel saves three dollars in Crete and twenty in Finland. I walk, sleep on trains and picnic in Sweden and live like a king in the south where my splurge dollars go the farthest. And, if your trip will last only as long as your money does, travel fast in the north and hang out in the south.

3. Adapt to European Tastes. Most unhappy people I meet in my travels could find the source of their problems if they examined their own stubborn desire to find the USA in Europe. If you accept and at least try doing things the European way, besides saving money, you'll be happier and learn more on your trip. You cannot expect the local people to be warm and accepting of you if you don't accept them. Things are different in Europe—that's why you go. European travel is a package deal, and you have no choice but to accept the good with the "bad." If you require the comforts of home . . . you'd better stay there.

4. Avoid the Tourist Centers. The best values are not in the places that boast, in neon signs, "We Speak English." Find local restaurants and hotels. You'll get more for your money.

5. Swallow Pride and Save Money. This is a personal matter, depending largely upon how important pride is to you and how much money you have. Many people cringe every time I use word "cheap"—others appreciate the directness. I'm not talking about begging and groveling around Europe. I'm talking about being able to ask a hotel for its least expensive room; order water even if the waiter wants you to order wine; ask how much something costs before ordering it, and say "no thanks" if the price isn't right. Expect equal and fair treatment as a tourist, when appropriate fight the price, set a limit and search on. Remember, even if the same thing would cost much more at home, the local rate should prevail.

5
Finances and Money

Travelers Checks

Smart travelers use travelers checks. These checks function almost like cash but are replaceable if lost or stolen. Before you buy your checks, choose the best company, currency and mix of denominations.

What Company? Choose a big well-known company—American Express, Cooks, Barclays or First National City. Travelers checks only cost 1-2% of their face value and it's not worth getting obscure checks to save. Ask around; there are plenty of ways to avoid that extra charge. Any legitimate check is good at banks, but it's nice to have a well-known check that private parties and small shops will recognize and honor. (In some countries travelers checks get a 2-3% better exchange rate than cash so they even save you money.)

Check into refund policies and services provided. I like AmExCo for its centrally located "landmark" offices, travel service, clients' mail service, refund policy—and they're free through AAA. The American Express company has two services very helpful to people planning long term trips or carrying lots of money. You can keep your money belt thin by using their $500 checks which can be broken at no charge into smaller checks (in dollars) at their foreign offices. And those with AmExCo cards can travel anywhere buying, as they go, up to $1000 a month of travelers checks with checks from their personal bank account from AmExCo offices abroad.

You'll hear many stories about slow or fast refunds. None of them matters. Extenuating circumstances—not the company—dictate the refund speed. If you wear a money belt and aren't too scatter-brained you won't lose your checks anyway. Choose the cheapest well-known company.

If you're only traveling in England go with Barclays—a British bank with a branch in every town. They waive the service charge if you have their checks, saving you two dollars per transaction.

What Kind of Currency? Travelers checks come in US dollars, Swiss francs, British pounds, Deutsche marks and even Japanese yen. When the dollar is shaky and unpredictable many travelers consider bailing out early and buying travelers checks in another, more stable, currency. The problem with that, since banks always buy low and sell high, is you lose 5% with this transaction and then you'll lose 5% more when you change your strong currency into the local currency you need. The dollar's drop is not drastic or predictable enough to merit this move. I get my travelers checks in US dollars for this reason and because merchants around the world generally know what their currency is worth in dollars, and it's simpler—I think in dollars.

If, on the other hand, my trip is mostly in one country, and the dollar is on a downward trend, I buy my checks in the currency of that country.

Which Denominations? Large bills and small bills each have advantages and disadvantages. Large checks ($100, $500) save on signing and bulk. Small checks ($10, $20, $50) are more exact and, in some cases, easier to cash. If you're only passing through a country, you may want just ten dollars. If you have only $100 checks, you'll have to change back $90. (You'll be changing a total of $190) at that uniform 4 or 5 % loss for the privilege of spending ten expensive dollars. If you're out of cash and the banks are closed it's easy to find a merchant or even another traveler who will change a $10 or $20 travelers check. Changing a large check in such a situation would be tough.

For $1000 in checks, I would choose three $100, ten $50 and ten $20 checks.

Remember, travelers checks are replaceable if lost or stolen—but you must keep track of the serial numbers. Leave a copy of all your check numbers (along with your passport number, flight number, and any other vital statistics) with someone at home, and carry a copy in your luggage and in your wallet. Update your list once a week so, if you lose them, you'll know exactly which checks to claim.

Changing Money in Europe

Remember, it's expensive and time-consuming to change money. You lose money and time every time you change so estimate carefully what you'll need and get it all at once at a bank when you enter a new country.

Rather than risk having to endure another round of bank hassles and expenses on my last day in a country, I usually change a little more than what I think I'll need. If I leave the country with some extra local money I can always change over later.

The cost of changing can be measured by the percent split between a bank's buying and selling rates. You'll normally lose about 4%. If both

SORTEN		ANKAUF DM	VERKAUF DM
BELGIEN	100 BFR	4,80	5,05
DÄNEMARK	100 DKR	27,25	2 9,25
ENGLAND	1 £	4,23	4,38
FRANKREICH	100 FF	34,50	36,50
ITALIEN	1000 LIT	1,74	1,84
JUGOSLAWIEN	100 DIN	3,60	4,60
NIEDERLANDE	100 HFL	90,00	92,00
ÖSTERREICH	100 ÖS	14,13	14,36
SCHWEIZ	100 SFR	116,25	119,25
SPANIEN	100 PTS	2,13	2,28
USA	1 $	2,43	2,53

REISESCHECKS AN U. VERKAUF ZU TAGESKURSEN

GOLDMÜNZEN

Banks that change money normally display their buy and sell rates in the window. You always lose. Notice U.S. dollars—4% loss.

rates aren't shown, be wary. Many banks, especially in touristy places, levy an extra service charge for each transaction. This added charge is usually higher for checks than cash, but many banks give a slightly better exchange rate for checks than cash (cash is a bigger headache to process). Remember, an added cost is the time you'll spend looking for a bank and waiting in the exchange line—up to an hour in peak-season madhouses like Venice.

You normally need your passport to change a check. Whenever possible, avoid the lousy exchange rates at hotels, shops and nightclubs.

Many Americans exclaim with glee, "Gee, they accept bank cards and dollars! There's no need ever to change money." Without knowing it, they're changing money every time they buy something—at a loss. Use the local money and get it at banks.

Paper money of any western country is good anywhere. The dollar is just one of many currencies all floating in the international exchange market. If you leave Italy with paper money, that 10,000 lire note is just as good as dollars in any European bank or exchange office. Many people change excess local money back to dollars before they leave a country. Then they change those dollars into the next country's money. This double-changing makes no sense and is expensive.

Coins, on the other hand, are generally worthless outside their country. Since many countries have coins worth over $2 each, exporting a pocket full of change can be an expensive mistake. Spend them or change them into paper before you cross the border. Otherwise you've just bought a bunch of souvenirs.

Most border towns use both currencies interchangeably. For instance, waiters in Salzburg keep German money in one side of their coin bags, Austrian in the other and give a fair rate for both.

Credit cards are widely accepted throughout Europe. This is exciting news to the people who have put an extra middleman into all our financial lives. Plastic fans gloat that you get a better exchange rate by using your card. While this may be true, credit card users are buying from companies that have enough slack in their prices to absorb the bank's hefty charge for the service. They are getting a better rate on a lousy price. (As more and more consumers naively believe they are getting "free use of the bank's money," we're all absorbing the 4% the banks are making in higher purchase prices.) Credit cards work in Europe—but not in the market or at Pedro's Pension. They slam the "back door" in your face.

Be careful when you use your plastic money. Many people have been terribly ripped off. Take one (Visa, Mastercard and AmExCo are all widely accepted—I use Visa) for cash advances, major purchases (car rentals, plane tickets, etc.) and for car rental security. But it's best to rely basically on cash.

While paper money from any western country is good at banks in every other country, the money of Eastern Europe is "soft"—falsely valued at several times its true worth. You can't avoid buying this money when you're in Bulgaria, Romania, Hungary, Czechoslovakia, East Germany or Poland. It's a government-sponsored rip-off designed to get "hard" western currency—desperately needed to purchase western goods on the international market. This money is worthless in western Europe so exchange it, spend it—or give it away if you have to—but don't take it out of its country.

Carry Cash

Carry plenty of cash. In some places it's getting expensive or difficult to change a travelers check—but hard cash is cash. You don't need a bank—people always know roughly what a dollar, mark or pound is worth and, for a price, you can sell it. Several hundred dollars cash in your money belt (completely safe) comes in handy for emergencies, such as when banks go on strike. I've been in Greece and Ireland when every bank went on strike—shutting down without warning.

Bring one day's budget in each country's currency with you from home. Your bank can sell you one bill worth about $30 from each country for the same price you'll pay in Europe. For no extra cost, risk or bulk (six bills—for six countries—hidden safely in the money belt) you'll have enough money to get settled in each new country without worrying about banking. This is a wonderful convenience—especially if you arrive at night or when the banks are closed. Most stations have a bank open when others are closed, but lines there after normal hours can be horrendous.

"Tip Packs," sold by many banks, are an ingenious way to lose 20 to 40% on your dollar. They are unnecessary. I'd be embarrassed to spend $10 for the privilege of carrying around $7 worth of coins and paper so I could practice in advance and tip upon arrival. Get a good sampling of coins after you arrive and in two minutes you'll be comfortable with the "nickels, dimes and quarters" of each new currency.

Many Americans refuse to understand the "funny money" of Europe. You won't find George Washington or Abe Lincoln but it's all logical. Each system is decimalized just like ours. There are a hundred "little ones" (cents, pence, centimes, pfennig, etc.) in every "big one" (dollar, pound, franc, mark, etc.). Only the names have been changed—to confuse the tourist. I do not find a currency converting calculator worth the trouble. Upon arrival, make a point to figure out the money. Very roughly figure out what the unit of currency (franc, mark, krona, or whatever) is worth in American cents. (For example, if there's one and a half Deutsche marks in a dollar, each DM is a 70-cent piece.) If a hot dog costs 5 marks, then it costs five 70-cent pieces or $3.50. Fifty little ones (pfennig) is half a mark (35 cents). If mustard costs 10 pfennig (a tenth of a 70 cent piece), it costs the equivalent of 7 cents. Ten marks is $7, 250 DM = $175 (250 × .7 or 250 less 1/3). Quiz yourself. Soon it will be second nature. You can't survive on a budget until you are comfortable with the local currency.

The Black Market—
Soft Currency and Hard Facts

Sooner or later in your travels—in Eastern Europe and the Third World—you'll be approached by a local person wanting to buy or sell money or goods from you. This is the "Black Market."

While most of the world's currencies have their true value determined by the international exchange market, some countries artificially overvalue their money. At a bank you'll be charged the "official" rate of exchange—more than that money is really worth. When this happens, the currency becomes "soft"—difficult or impossible to change outside of that country. "Hard," realistically valued currency, like dollars and all Western European currencies, are in high demand in that country for purchasing imported goods. A second economy or "black market" is created, and people everywhere seem to be in search of "real money" and the special items only it can buy. Tourists are known to have plenty of hard money and will commonly be approached by people who are trying to gather enough hard cash to buy a car or stereo or camera that cannot be purchased with that country's soft money.

Most Eastern European countries tie their currencies to the Russian ruble. The ruble is soft as a month-old banana, and as a result, these countries have a thriving black market. Even though factory workers make just a few hundred dollars a month, many have a difficult time spending their money. What they want can only be purchased with hard foreign currency, so they will pay up to triple the official rate to acquire hard dollars. That means a Polish or Bulgarian worker will trade one month's pay for $100 US to save for his imported dream. Governments continue to artificially control the value and flow of money and goods. And they allow their black markets to thrive knowing this is bringing a substantial amount of much needed currency into their economy.

Dealing in the black market is illegal and obviously risky. Nevertheless, in many countries, the underground economy is the one that keep things going. You will be tempted by the black market. When traveling in the USSR, Eastern Europe or elsewhere, the black market is the forbidden fruit—don't mess with it thoughtlessly. You should, however, know something about it.

Many people finance their travels by playing the black market. They know what to buy, what to sell—and where. I'm not talking about drugs and Ouzi machine guns. I'm talking pettiness: a bottle of gin, a Beatles record, a pair of Levis, $20 bills. Here are some examples of black market activity. Names won't be used, to protect the guilty.

In a Warsaw nightclub, a man wearing a large money pouch—complete with "change maker"—sits down with a couple of Americans and loudly announces that he will pay them triple the official exchange rate for their dollars. Poland is Eastern Europe's bargain basement—even at the government's inflated exchange rate.

In Moscow, a traveler sells a Playboy magazine for $50 (that's $50 worth of Russian currency at the official rate), a Beatles "White Album" for $70, and a Bible (in Russian) for $100. The total paid was well over one month's local wages.

In East Berlin's most popular disco, a young American pays the five mark ($3) cover charge in West German marks rather than East German soft marks. For his hard currency he is given hard drinks—free, all night long.

On a Bulgarian train, the conductor checks the tickets. Then, with the excitement of a little boy, he asks eagerly, "Black market? Change dollars?" The tourist follows him to the train's WC where the conductor gives him triple the going rate. He is undoubtedly a middle-man who makes more money buying and selling hard currency than he does punching tickets. He'll have no trouble selling those dollars at a profit to Bulgarians in need of hard cash.

The governments of these countries often require tourists to spend a minimum amount of hard currency per day. In Romania, as you enter by train you are issued a seven-day visa only after changing seven times their minimum daily expenditure requirement. To extend your visa you must show a bank slip proving that you changed enough money—legally. In the USSR and several other countries there are special shops, gas stations, tours and hotels that are especially for foreign visitors and accept only hard currency. In some cases, these are the only hotels, tours or gas stations the guests are allowed to use.

Countries with soft currencies generally require proof that you changed your money through official channels before you're allowed to make a major purchase. This includes hotel bills, plane tickets and car rentals. Because of this tight control, many tourists who "make a killing" on the black market have a very difficult time spending all their local wealth. That money can't be exchanged again for hard currency, and it becomes "funny money" once it crosses the border. It's a strange feeling, not knowing how to blow your money. You can only eat so many ice cream cones (fancy restaurant meals and long taxi rides are about the only substantial ways to consume any black marked windfalls).

Certain items that are very popular but can't be purchased with local currency make wonderful gifts for East European locals—if you can get them across the border. If the customs official sees your gifts and determines that they aren't for your personal use, he will probably confiscate them—and take them home. I once brought a Romanian friend well-chosen gifts costing $60 in America; a blank Sony recording tape, a pair of jeans, a rock and roll album (the "harder" the better), and a pocket calculator. That Romanian glowed with pride as he wore his "real American jeans." Within two days his record was taped a dozen times—all over the village. He figured the value of those gifts at two month's wages.

Black market dealings are illegal, and a tourist is expected to understand and obey the laws of the country he is visiting. I just thought you might be interested.

Keys to Successful Bargaining

In much of the world the price tag is only an excuse to argue. Bargaining is the accepted and expected method of finding a compromise between the wishful thinking of the merchant and the tourist.

Prices are "soft" in much of the Mediterranean world. In Europe bargaining is common only in the south. You should fight the price in "flea markets" and with people selling handicrafts and tourist items on the streets in all but the most developed countries.

While bargaining (if you're traveling beyond Europe) is important from a budgetary standpoint, it can also become an enjoyable game. Many travelers are addicted hagglers who would gladly skip a tour of a Portuguese palace to get the price down on the black-clad lady's handmade sweater.

Here are the ten commandments of the successful haggler:

1. Determine whether or not bargaining is appropriate. It's bad shopping etiquette to "make an offer" for a tweed hat in a London department store. It's foolish not to at a Greek outdoor market. To learn if the price is fixed, fall in love with that item right in front of the merchant. Look longingly into the eyes of that porcelain Buddha, then decide that "it's just too much money." You've put him in a position to make the first offer. If he comes down even two percent there's nothing sacred about the price tag. Now you're free to haggle away.

2. Determine the merchant's cost. Many merchants will settle for a nickel profit rather than lose the sale entirely. Promise yourself that, no matter how exciting the price becomes, you won't buy. Then work the cost down to rock bottom. When it seems to have fallen to a record low, walk away. That last price he hollers out as you turn the corner is usually about a nickel above cost. Armed with this knowledge you can confidently demand a fair price for the same item at the next souvenir stand— and probably get it.

3. Find out what the locals pay. If the price is not posted, you should assume that there is a double price standard—one for locals and one for tourists. If only tourists buy the item you're pricing, see what an Arab, Spanish or Italian tourist would be charged. I remember thinking I did very well in Istanbul's Grand Bazaar until I learned my Spanish friend bought the same shirt for thirty percent less. Many merchants just assume American tourists have more money to spend.

4. Pre-price each item. Remember that the price tags are totally meaningless and can serve only to distort your idea of an item's true worth. The merchant is playing a psychological game. People often feel that if they can cut the price fifty percent, they are doing great. Well, the merchant responds by quadrupling his prices. Then the tourist haggles the price in half and happily pays twice what that souvenir should sell for.

The best way to deal with crazy price tags is to ignore them. Before you even see the price tag, pre-price the item that you are interested in: determine what it's worth to you, considering the hassles involved in packing it or shipping it home. This value, not the price tag, should be your guide in determining a souvenir's worth.

5. Don't hurry. Get to know the shopkeeper. Accept his offer for tea, talk with him. Leave him to shop around and get a feel for the market. Then return. He'll know you are serious.

6. Be indifferent—never look impressed. As soon as the merchant perceives the "I gotta have that!" in you, you'll never get the best price. He knows you have plenty of money to buy something you really want. He knows about USA prices. Never be openly crazy about an item. (Commandments 1 and 6 are contradictory, but then, as Emerson said, "Consistency is the hobgoblin of little minds." Which one you obey depends on the situation.)

7. Impress him with your knowledge—real or otherwise. This way he respects you, and you are more likely to get good quality. Istanbul has very good leather coats for a fraction of the USA cost. I wanted one. Before my trip, I talked to some leather coat salesmen and was much better prepared to confidently pick out a good coat in Istanbul for $50.

8. Employ a third person. Use your friend who is worried about the ever-dwindling budget, or who doesn't like the price or who is bored and wants to return to the hotel. This trick may work to bring the price down faster.

9. Show the merchant your money. Physically hold out your money and offer him "all you have" to pay for whatever you are bickering over. The temptation will be greater for him just to grab your money and say, "Oh, all right."

10. If the price is too much—leave. Never worry about having taken too much of the merchant's time and tea. They are experts at making the tourist feel guilty for not buying. It's all part of the game. Most merchants, by local standards, are financially well off.

If the merchant does accept your offer, it is very bad style and insulting to him if you refuse to buy. Bid seriously.

A final point for the no-nonsense budget shopper: you can generally find the same souvenirs in large department stores at fair and firm, often government-regulated prices. Department store shopping is quicker, easier, often cheaper—but not nearly as much fun.

Theft and the Tourist

Thieves plague tourists throughout the world. As the economy gets tighter, pick-pockets and purse-snatchers get hungrier, and the tourist becomes a very tempting target.

Many countries depend on the USA economically. When we're in a recession they feel it, too. In much of the world, your camera is worth one year of hard labor to the man on the street. Gross inequities like this enable many thieves to rationalize their crimes.

If you're not constantly on guard, you'll have something stolen. One summer, four out of five friends I traveled with lost cameras in one way or another. (Don't look at me.) I've heard countless stories of tourists getting ripped-off: pickpocketed in a bad neighborhood in London; shoulder bag snatched by a motorcycle bandit in Rome; suitcase taken from the train during a long, dark French tunnel; camera slipped right off the neck of a fellow napping in Barcelona. And so on.

You can't be too careful. A tourist is an easy target. Loaded down with all his valuables in a strange new environment, he is a favorite victim of thieves—many of whom specialize solely in "the tourist trade." I read of people whose trips are ruined by thieves who snatch their purse or wallet. There is no excuse for this kind of vulnerability. Nearly all crimes suffered by tourists are non-violent and are avoidable simply by thinking. If you exercise the proper caution and are not overly trusting, you should have no problem.

Here are some hints on how not to be ripped-off during your trip:

First of all, don't bring things that will ruin your trip if they are lost, broken or stolen. Everything that is crucial should fit into your money belt. Purses and wallets are fine for odds and ends and one day's spending money but not for irreplaceables. Luxurious luggage lures thieves like a well-polished flasher lures fish. Why brag to the thief that your luggage is the most expensive? The thief chooses the most impressive suitcase in the pile.

Your moneybelt, containing just your essential documents, is worn comfortably around your waist, under your skirt or pants.

My key to peace of mind is my money belt. (Buckle up for safety.) I'll never again travel without one. The money belt is a small, nylon, zipper bag that ties around the waist under your pants or skirt. It costs only a few dollars (see Back Door catalog). In it, I keep my passport, cash, travelers checks, train pass, airline ticket and any very important documents, vouchers or identity cards. Bring only one credit card and keep it in your money belt. I keep bulky or replaceable documents in a second money belt or small zipper bag (a three-ring notebook pencil bag) that I tie or sew to the inside of my rucksack or suitcase. It's important to keep the money belt slim so it's comfortable and hidden. I wear it all summer, even sleeping with it when necessary, and it is never uncomfortable.

With a money belt, all your essential documents are on you as securely and thoughtlessly as your underpants. Have you ever noticed that every morning you put on your underpants and they stay there all day long. You don't even think about them. And every night when you take off your pants, sure enough, there they are, exactly where you put them. It's a luxury to travel with your valuables just as securely out of sight and out of mind. My camera is, to a potential thief, the most tempting item in my luggage. I never leave it lying around where hotel workers and others can see it and be tempted. It's either around my neck or safely out of sight.

If I ever sleep in public (on a train or at an airport or wherever), I clip or fasten my pack (or suitcase) to the chair or the luggage rack or to me. Even the slight inconvenience of undoing a clip foils most thieves.

Be on guard for the imaginative modern-day "artful dodgers". Thief teams often create a fight or commotion to distract their curious victims. Groups of Gypsy girls with big eyes and colorful dresses play a game where they politely mob the unsuspecting tourist, beggar-style. As their pleading eyes grab yours and they hold up their sad message scrawled on cardboard, your purse or rucksack is being delicately rifled. (This is particularly common in Paris and Rome.) Keep things zipped, buttoned and secure. Be alert and aware! Somewhere, sometime, when you least expect it most—you'll meet the thieves.

Cars are a favorite target of thieves. Be very careful never to leave anything even hinting of value in view in your parked car. Put anything worth stealing in the trunk. Leave your glove compartment open so the thief can look in without breaking in. Choose your parking place carefully. Cars get ripped off *anywhere* at night. Over half of the work that European automobile glass shops get is repairing wings broken by thieves. Before I leave my car, I notice how many crumbled wing windows litter the parking lot's asphalt. In Paris I was warned to take absolutely everything inside my hotel. I did. They stole my mirror! In Rome my favorite *pension* is next to a large police station—a safe place to park, if you're legal.

Invest in an extra key. Most rental cars come with only one, and that is needlessly risky. Besides, it's more convenient for two people to have access to the locked car.

Photocopy your valuable documents and tickets. It's a lot easier to replace a lost or stolen plane ticket, passport, Eurailpass or rental voucher if you have a picture proving that you really owned what you are claiming is lost. This is especially helpful if you lose your Eurail pass.

Now that you've taken these precautions, there's one more thing— relax and have fun. There's no sense in letting fear limit your vacation. Most people in every country are on your side. If you exercise adequate discretion, aren't overly trusting, and don't put your self into risky situations your travels will be about as dangerous as home-town grocery shopping. Please don't travel afraid—travel carefully.

6
Hurdling the Language Barrier

Communicating in a Language You Don't Speak

That notorious language barrier is about two feet tall. While it keeps many people out of Europe, with a few tricks, you can step right over it. I speak only English. My linguistic limitations have never hindered my travels. Of course, if I spoke more languages, I could enjoy a much deeper understanding of the people and cultures I visit, but logistically speaking—getting transportation, rooms, eating and seeing the sights—I can manage fine.

We English-speakers are the one linguistic group that can afford to be lazy. English is the world's linguistic common-denominator. When a Greek meets a Norwegian, neither speaks the other's language. They'll communicate in English.

While Americans are terrible monoglots, Europeans are very good with languages. Most young North Europeans speak several languages. Scandinavian students of our language actually decide between English and "American." My Norwegian cousin speaks with a touch of Texas, and knows more slang than I do! Most Swiss grow up tri-lingual like their country. People speaking minor languages (Dutch, Belgians, Scandinavians) have more reason to learn German, French or English since very few people outside their small states speak their tongue.

Imagine if each of our states spoke its own language. That's the European situation. They've done a great job of minimizing the communication problems you'd expect to find in a small continent with such a babel of tongues. Not only are most educated people multi-lingual, but most signs that the traveler must understand (road signs, menus, telephone instructions, museum info, etc.) are printed either in several languages or in universal symbols. Europe's uniform road sign system enables drivers to roll right over the language barrier.

English may be Europe's "lingua franca," and we don't need to be afraid of the language barrier, but communicating does require some skill. How well you communicate with the Europeans you meet depends on how well you can get a basic idea across—not how many words you know in that language.

Here are some keys to communicating with people who don't speak your language.

Speak slowly, clearly and with carefully chosen words. The "Voice of America" is in business to communicate and they use what they call "simple English". You're dealing with someone who learned English out of a book, reading British words, not hearing American ones. Choose easy words and pronounce each letter (Cris-py po-ta-to chips.) Borrow a singer's enunciation exercises and exaggerate each letter. Realize your lips are being read. When they aren't understood, most Americans speak louder. If they still can't communicate, they toss in a few extra words. Listen to other tourists and you'll hear your own shortcomings.

Use no contractions. Cut out all slang. Our American dialect has become a super-deluxe slang pizza not found on any European menu. The sentence "Cut out all slang," for example, would baffle the average European. "Speak no idioms" would be better understood. If you learned English in school for two years how would you respond to the American who exclaims, "What a day!" Listen to yourself. If you want to be understood, talk like a Dick and Jane primer. For several months out of every year, I speak with simple words, pronouncing every letter. When I get home my friends say (very deliberately), "Rick, you can relax now, we speak English."

Keep your messages and sentences very simple. Make single nouns work as entire sentences. When asking for something, a one word question ("Photo?") is much more effective than an attempt at something more grammatically correct. ("May I take your picture, sir?") Be a caveman. Keep it grunt simple. Your first priority when communicating in Europe is to strip your message naked and transmit only the basic ideas.

Don't be afraid to look like a fool. Even with no common language, rudimentary communication is easy. Butcher the language if you must— but communicate. I'll never forget the lady in the French post office who flapped her arms and asked, "Tweet, tweet, tweet?" I understood immediately, answered with a nod, and she gave me the air mail stamps I needed. If you're hungry, clutch your stomach and growl. If you want milk, "moo" and pull two imaginary udders. If the liquor was too strong, simulate an atomic explosion starting from your stomach and mushrooming to your head. If you're attracted to someone, pant.

Pick up gestures. Every culture has peculiar—and fun—hand and face gestures. In Turkey you signal "no" by jerking your eyebrows and head upward. In Bulgaria, "yes" is indicated by happily bouncing your head back and forth as if you were one of those oriental dolls with a spring neck and someone slapped you. "Expensive" is often shaking your hand and sucking in like you just burned yourself.

Figure things out. Most major European languages are related, coming from Latin. With that awareness and an effort to make some sense of the puzzle, lots of words become meaningful. *Lundi* (lunar), means Monday (moonday). *Sonn* is sun so *Sonntag* is Sunday. If *bongiorno* means good day, *suppa del giorno* must mean soup of the day. If *tiergarten* is zoo (literally "animal garden") in German, then *stinktier* is "skunk". Think of *kindergarten* (children's garden), *vater, mutter, trink, gross, gut, nacht, rapide, grand, economico, delicioso,* and you can *muy comprendo.*

Many letters travel predictable courses as one language melts into the next over the centuries. For instance, "p" often becomes "v" or "b" in the next language. Italian menus always have a charge for *coperto*—a "cover" charge.

Practice your understanding. Read time schedules, concert posters, multi-lingual signs in bathrooms and newspaper headlines. It's a puzzle and the more you play it, the better you get.

Be melodramatic, exaggerate the accent of the language you're working with. In France, if you sound like Maurice Chevalier you're much more likely to be understood. The locals won't be insulted—they'll be impressed. Even English, spoken with a sexy French accent, will make more sense to the French ear. In Italy be melodic, exuberant, and wave those hands. Go ahead, try it: *Mama Mia!* You've got to be uninhibited. Self-consciousness kills communication.

A small note-pad works wonders in a tough spot. The written word or number is understood much easier than when it's spoken—and mispronounced. (My backpocket notepad is one of my handiest travel buddies.) If you need to repeatedly communicate something difficult and important (like medical instructions, "I'm vegetarian", "boiled water", "well-done meat", "your finest ice cream", etc.), have it written in the local language on your notepad.

Confessions of a Monoglot   Many Europeans are self-conscious about their English and would prefer not to speak rather than speak broken English. If you are determined to communicate, and butcher their language doggedly enough, sooner or later they'll break down and surprise you with some English. After what you've done to their language, they will be more comfortable working in less-than-perfect English.

Your communicating job is made much easier if you choose a multi-lingual person to start with. Business people, urbanites, young well-dressed people, and anyone in the tourist trade is most likely to speak English.

If you draw a complete blank with someone but you want to communicate, just start hurling bits and pieces at each other. Consider this profound conversation I had with a cobbler in Sicily:

"Spaghetti" I said with a very saucy Italian accent.

"Ronald Reagan," was the old man's reply.

"Mama mia!" I said tossing my hands and head into the air.

"Yes, no, one, two, tree," he returned slowly and proudly.

Then I whispered secretly, "Molto buono, ravioli."

He spit, "Be sexy, drink Pepsi!"

Step over that language barrier. This says "Sentralsyke house" and that's just what it is.

And I waved goodby saying, "Arrivederci."

"Ciao," he smiled.

You are surrounded by expert, native-speaking tutors in every country. Let them teach you. Spend bus and train rides learning. Start learning the language when you arrive. Psychologically, it's hard to start later because you'll be leaving so soon. I like to learn five new words a day. You'd be surprised how handy a working vocabulary of 20-50 words is. The practical phrase lists following this chapter are a good place to start.

The Berlitz *14 European Languages Phrasebook* is ideal for the average traveler. Their separate books for each individual language provide more information than most people will ever need. While phrase books can be helpful in your efforts to communicate, I find them more fun than practical. I can't imagine anyone ever hauling out their phrase book to say, "I've broken my leg. Can you please show me to the nearest hospital?" In that case, a point and a scream works in any language. A phrase book is more helpful in a situation like when you are sitting, bored, in a restaurant waiting for your meal. Call the waitress over and, with a pained look, ask for a shampoo.

Assume you understand. My master key to communication is to see most communication problems as multiple choice questions, make an educated guess at the meaning of a message—verbal or written—and proceed confidently as if I understood it correctly. This applies to rudimentary things like instructions on custom forms, museum hours, menus, questions the hotel maid asks you, and so on. With this approach, I find that 80% of the time I'm correct. Twenty percent I misunderstand the message. Half of the time that I am wrong I never know it, so it doesn't really matter. So 10% of the time I really blow it. That makes my trip easier—or more interesting.

Let's take a border crossing as an example. I do not speak any Bulgarian. At the border, a uniformed guard struts up to my car and asks a question. Not understanding a word he said, but guessing what the average border guard would ask the average tourist, I look at him and answer with a solid "Nyet." He steps back, swings his arm open like and gate and says, "OK." I'm on my way, quick and easy. I could have got out of the car, struggled with the phrase book and made a big deal out of it, but I'd rather fake it, assuming he was asking if I'm smuggling anything in, and keep things simple. It works.

International Words

As our world shrinks, more and more words leap their linguistic boundaries and become international. Sensitive travelers develop a knack for choosing words most likely to be universally understood ("auto" instead of "car", "kaput" rather than "broken", "photo" not "picture"). They also internationalize their pronunciation. "University", if you play around with its sound (Oo nee vehr see tay) will be understood anywhere. The average American is a real flunky in this area. Be creative. Analogy communication is very effective. In every language on earth, "Attila" means "the crude bully". When a big Italian crowds in front of you say, "Scuzi, Ah-tee-la" and retake your place. If you like your haircut and want to compliment your Venetian barber, put your hand sensually on your hair and say "Casanova". Nickname the hairstylist "Michelangelo", or "Rambo" if appropriate.

Here are a few internationally understood words. Remember, cut out the Yankee accent and give each word a Pan-European sound.

Stop	Kaput	Vino
Restaurant	Ciao	Bank
Hotel	Bye-Bye	Rock 'n' Roll
Post, Par Avion	Camping	OK
Auto	Picnic	Amigo
Autobus (boos)	Nuclear	English (Engleesh)
Yankee, Americano	Tourist	Mama mia
Michelangelo (artistic)	Beer	Oo la la
Casanova (romantic)	Coffee	America's favorite
Disneyland (wonderland)	Tea, Chai	four-letter words
Hercules (strong)	Coke, Coka	Elephante (a big clod)
Attila (mean, crude)	Sexy	Europa
Self-serve	Toilet	Police
Super	Taxi	Telephone
Photo	Central	Information
Mañana	University	Passport
Chocolate	Pardon	Fascist
Rambo (tough guy)		

A Yankee-English Phrase Book

Oscar Wilde said, "The English have really everything in common with the Americans—except, of course, language." On your first trip to England you'll find plenty of linguistic surprises. I'll never forget checking into a small town Bed and Breakfast—a teenager on my first solo European adventure. The landlady cheerily asked me, "And what time would you like to be knocked up in the morning?" I looked over at her husband, who winked, "Would a fry at eight be suitable?" The next morning I got a rap on the door at 7:30 and a huge British breakfast a half hour later.

Traveling through England is an adventure in accents and idioms. Every day you'll see babies in "prams", sucking "dummies", as mothers change wet "nappies". Soon the kids can trade in their "nappies" for "smalls" and "spend a penny" on their own. "Spend a penny" is British for a visit to the "loo" (bathroom). Older British kids enjoy "candy floss" (cotton candy), "naughts and crosses" (tic-tac-toe), "big dippers" (roller coasters), "sultanas" (blanched raisins), "iced lollies" (popcicles), and are constantly in need of an "elastoplast" (band-aid).

In Germany, this is what they call their tour buses.

If you're just "muckin' about", it's fun to browse through an "iron mongers" (hardware store), "chemists shop" (pharmacy) or Woolworths and notice the many familiar items with unfamiliar names. The school supplies section includes "sticking plaster" (adhesive tape), "rubbers" (erasers) and "scribbling blocks" (scratch pads). Those with "green fingers" (a green thumb) might pick up come "courgette" (zucchini), "swede" (rutabaga) or "aubergine" (eggplant) seeds.

In England, "chips" are fries and "crisps" are potato chips. A hamburger is best on a toasted "bap" and if you ask for a napkin, you'll get a funny look but no more (that's what the British call our "sanitary napkins"). You wipe your fingers with a serviette—never a napkin!

The English have a great way with names. You'll find towns with names like Upper and Lower Piddle. Once Brewed and Itching Field. I saw a hair salon called "Curl Up and Dye". This cute coziness comes through in their language as well. Your car is built with a "bonnet" and a "boot" rather than a hood and trunk. You drive it on "motorways", and when the freeway divides, it becomes a "dual carriageway". Gas is "petrol", a truck is a "lorry", and when you hit a traffic jam, don't "get your knickers in a twist" (make a fuss), just "queue up" (line up) and study your American-English phrase book.

A two-week vacation in England is unheard of, but many locals "holiday for a fortnight" in a "homely" (pleasant) rural cottage. They'll pack a "face flannel" (wash cloth), "torch" (flashlight), "hoover" (vacuum cleaner), and "hair grips" (bobby pins) before leaving their "flat" (apartment). The cottage can be lovely. Every day I'd "post" a letter in the "pillar box" and give my "bird" (girl friend) a "trunk" (long distance) call, "reversing the charges" (collect), of course. On a cold evening it's best to pick up a "pimp" (bundle of kindling) and make a fire or take a walk wearing the warmest "mackintosh" (raincoat) you can find or an "anorak" (parka) with "press studs" (snaps).

Many times after "washing up" (doing the dishes) I'd go up to the first floor (second floor) with a "neat" (straight) Scotch and a plate of "biscuits" (sweet cookies) with "desiccated" (shredded) coconut and just enjoy the view. It's a "smashing" view, guaranteed to give you "goose pimples" (goose bumps) every time.

All across the British Isles, you'll find new words, crazy local humor and countless accents. Pubs are colloquial treasure chests. Church services, sporting events, The House of Parliament, live plays featuring local comedy, the streets of Liverpool, the docks of London and children in parks are playgrounds for the American ear. One of the beauties of tour-

ing the British Isles is the illusion of hearing a foreign language and actually understanding it—most of the time.

European Travel Glossary

ATS. Airplane type seats, advertised for buses and boats, they recline just
enough so you can't sleep solidly, like those on airplanes.

The American Waters. Coke, Pepsi, Fanta, Sprite and Seven-Up. Found
(and bottled) all over Europe. Five-year-olds in Turkey greet foreigners
with "Be sexy, drink Pepsi!"

Auto-stop. The most common European term for hitchhiking; also called
"tramp" in some countries.

Balkans. The name for the Greece, Bulgaria, Yugoslavia region.

Celtic. The Irish, Welsh and Scottish people and those who live in Brittany, France.

The Continent. Continental Europe. England is an island and not really
part of what she thinks of as "The Continent".

Etruscans. The highly civilized people who inhabited Italy from Rome to
Florence in the thousand years before Christ. Rome was originally an
Etruscan town.

Germanic Countries. Those countries that speak German—Germany,
Switzerland, and Austria.

Hard and Soft Currency. Hard currency is sold at its true value at home
and is accepted at banks in other countries. Soft currency is falsely valued
at home and is impossible or very difficult to change outside its borders.
All of Western Europe has hard currency.

Homesick. A problem suffered by people who don't mentally travel with
their home with them. Be "at home" on the road—it works wonderfully.
As Carl Franz advises in *The People's Guide to Mexico*, "Where ever you
go—there you are."

Iberia. The peninsula of Spain and Portugal.

The Industry. Organized tourism, all the facets of the business side of travel working together.

Lerks and Perks. A popular topic of conversation among tour guides and bus drivers in parking lots—kick backs and special incentives they enjoy for encouraging a group of stark raving shoppers to consume in a certain direction.

Low Countries. Belgium, Netherlands, and Luxembourg (Benelux). They're called low because they are. Half of Holland is below sea level, reclaimed from the sea.

Mensa. The European word for university cafeteria, usually government subsidized, always cheap.

Moors. The Muslim Arabs that flourished in Spain and Portugal from 711 until 1492.

Open-jaws. Flying into one European city and home from another. A very efficient itinerary strategy.

Option. The half-day or evening tours or activities that are not included in a bus tour's price. In many cases, they are barely "optional".

Peak season. The busiest tourist season. In Europe, about June 20 through August 20. It's so crowded you can only "peek" at the most popular sights.

Shoulder season. Still crowded, but not quite "peak". Shoulder season is between "peak" and "off" season. In Europe, roughly May 20 to June 20 and August 20 to September 30. You've got elbow room in shoulder season.

Sound and Light Shows. Very popular with sedentary tourists, these are evening shows in a romantic and historic setting where bus tours gather, sit on folding chairs and listen to a recorded narration with a musical and dramatic touch while colored lights play on the surrounding buildings. Generally not worth the time or money.

WC. Water closet, international symbol for toilet. Also "loo".

Practical Foreign Phrases
FRENCH

1. hello	bonjour	bohn-ZHOOR
2. goodbye	au revoir	oh reh-VWAH
3. see you later	a bientot	ah byuhn-TOH
4. goodnight	bonne nuit	bohn NWEE
5. please	s'il vous plait	seel voo PLAY
6. thank you	merci	mehr-SEE
7. yes/no	oui/non	wee/noh
8. one/two/three	un/deux/trois	uh/DOO/twah
9. cheap/expensive	bon marche/cher	bohn mar-shay/shehr
10. good/bad	bon/mauvais	bohn/mo-VAY
11. beautiful/ugly	joli/laid	zho-LEE/lay
12. big/small	grand/petit	grahn/pehTEE
13. fast/slow	rapide/lent	rah-PEED / lah
14. very	tres	tray
15. where is . . . ?	ou est . . . ?	oo ay
16. how much . . . ?	combien	kohm-bee-ah
17. I don't understand	je ne comprends pas	zhuh neh KOHM-prahn PAH
18. What do you call this?	qu'est-ce que c'est?	KESS koo SAY
19. I'm lost	je me suis perdu	zhuh meh swee pehr-DOO
20. complete price (everything included)	tout est compris	toot-ay cohm-PREE
21. Im tired	je suis fatigue	zhuh swee fah-tee-GAY
22. I'm hungry	j'ai faim	zhay fah
23. cheers!	sante!	sahn-TAY
24. food	nourriture	new-ree-TOOR
25. grocery store	epicerie	eh-PEES-REE
26. picnic	pique-nique	peek-neek
27. delicious	delicieux	de-lee-syoh
28. market	marche	mar-SHAY
29. drunk	saoul	SOO
30. money	argent	ar-ZHA
31. station	gare	gar
32. private accommodations	chambre	shambr
33. toilet	w.c.	VAY say
34. I	je	zhuh
35. you	vous	voo
36. love	amour	ah-MOOR
37. sleep	sommeil	so-MAY
38. train	train	tran
39. The bill, please	L'addition, s'il vous plait	lah-dee-see-OHN, see voo play
40. friend	ami	ah-MEE
41. water/tap water	eau/eau douce	OH/OL dooss
42. castle	chateau	shat-TOH
43. How are you?/I'm fine	ca va?/ca va	sah VAH
44. Tourist Information	syndicat d'initiative	san-dee-KAH dee nee-see-ah-TEEV

GERMAN

1. hello	guten tag	goo-ten tock
2. goodbye	auf wiedersehn	awf VEE-der-sayn
3. see you later	bis bald	beess bald
4. goodnight	gute nacht	gooteh nahkt
5. please	bitte	BIT-teh
6. thank you	danke schon	DONG-kuh shurn
7. yes/no	ja/nein	yah/nine
8. one/two/three	eins/zwei/drei	aintz/tzvy/dry
9. cheap/expensive	billig/teuer	BIL-ikh/TOY-err
10. good/bad	gut/schlecht	goot/shlehkht
11. beautiful/ugly	schon/hasslich	shurn/HESS-leek
12. big/small	gross/klein	groass/kline
13. fast/slow	schnell/langsam	shnel/LONG-zahm
14. very	sehr	zair
15. where is . . . ?	wo ist . . . ?	voh ist
16. how much . . . ?	wieviel	vee-FEEL
17. I don't understand	ich verstehe nicht	ikh vehr-SHTAY-eh nicht
18. what do you call this?	wie heisst das?	vee HEIST dahss
19. I'm lost	ich habe mich verirrt	ikh hah-beh mikh fehr-IRT
20. complete price (everything included)	alles ist inbegriffen	alles ist IN-ber-grif-ern
21. I'm tired	ich bin mude	ikh bin MEW-duh
22. I'm hungry	ich habe hunger	ikh hah-beh HOONG-guh
23. cheers!	prosit!	proast
24. food	speise	SHPY-zuh
25. grocery store	supermarket	supermarket
26. picnic	picknick	pik-nik
27. delicious	lecker	LECK-uh
28. market	markt	markt
29. drunk	betrunken	bay TROON kin
30. money	geld	geld
31. station	bahnhof	BAHN-hof
32. private accommodations	zimmer	TSIMM-er
33. toilet	klo	kloh
34. I	ich	eekh
35. you	du	doo
36. love	liebe	LEE-beh
37. sleep	schlaf	shloff
38. train	zug	tsoog
39. The bill, please	die Rechnung, bitte	dee RECK-nung, BIT-teh
40. friend	freund	froint
41. water	wasser	VOSS-ehr
42. castle	schloss	shlohss
43. How are you/ I'm fine, thanks	wie geht es?/ Es geht mir gut, dahnke	vee GATES/ ess GATE mehr GOOT, DONG-kuh
44. Tourist Information	Reiseburo	RIE-suh-BYOO-ro

GREEK

1.	hello	YAHSS-ahss
2.	goodbye	YAHSS-ahss
3.	see you later	EESS to ehpahneeDHEEN
4.	goodnight	kahleeNEEKtah
5.	please	pahrahkahLO
6.	thank you	ehvkhahreeSTO
7.	yes/no	neh/O-khee
8.	one/two/three	EHnah/DHEEo/TREEah
9.	cheap/expensive	ftee-NOHSS/ah-kree-VOHSS
10.	good/bad	kah-LOHSS/kah-KOHSS
11.	beautiful/ugly	or-AY-ohss/AHSS-kee-mahss
12.	big/small	meh-GAH-lohss/mee-KROHSS
13.	fast/slow	GREE-gor-ohss/ahr-GOHSS
14.	very	poLEE
15.	where is . . . ?	poo IN-neh
16.	how much . . . ?	POH-so
17.	I don't understand	DEN kah-tah-lah-VENN-o
18.	What do you call this?	poss LEHyehteh ahvto
19.	I'm lost	KAHtheekah
20.	complete price (everything included)	Olah pehreelahmVAH-nondheh
21.	I'm tired	EEmeh koorahSMEHnoss
22.	I'm hungry	peeNO
23.	cheers!	YAH-sahss
24.	food	tro-FEE
25.	grocery store	mah-gah-ZEE
26.	delicious	thaumasios
27.	market	aGORa
28.	money	lep-TAH
29.	station	stathmos
30.	private accommodations	doeMAHteeo
31.	toilet	meros
32.	I	AY-go
33.	you	eh-SAYSS
34.	love	ah-GAH-pay
35.	sleep	kim-MOM-may
36.	train	TREN-no
37.	The bill, please	Toh log-a-ree-ahz MO, pah-rah-kah-LOH
38.	friend	FEE-lohss
39.	water	neh-RO
40.	Tourist Information	toor-is-MOHSS

ITALIAN

1. hello	buongiorno	bohn-JOOR-no
2. goodbye	ciao	chow
3. see you later	ci vediamo	chee vey-dee-OMM-o
4. goodnight	buona notte	BWONN-ah NOT-tay
5. please	per favore	pair fah-VOR-ay
6. thank you	grazie	GRAH-tsee-ay
7. yes/no	si/no	see/no
8. one/two/three	uno/due/tre	oo-noh/doo-ay/tray
9. cheap/expensive	e tropo caro/caro	ay tropo CARR-0/CARR-o
10. good/bad	buone/cattivo	BWON-o/kaht-TEE-vo
11. beautiful/ugly	bello/brutto	BEHL-lo/BROOT-to
12. big/small	grande/piccolo	GRAHN-day/PEEKkoh-lo
13. fast/slow	rapido/lento	RAHH-pee-do/LÉHN-to
14. very	molto	MOHL-to
15. where is . . . ?	dov'e . . . ?	do-VAY
16. how much . . . ?	quanto?	KWAHN-to
17. I don't understand	Non capisco	nohn kay-PEESS-ko
18. what do you call this?	che cosi questo?	kay KO-zay KWAY-sto
19. I'm lost	mi sono perso	mee SOH-no PEHR-so
20. I'm tired	sono stanco	SOH-no STAHNG-ko
21. I'm hungry	ho fame	oh FAH-may
22. food	cibo	CHEE-bo
23. grocery store	alimentari	al-ee-men-TAR-ee
24. picnic	picnic	picnic
25. delicious	delizioso	day-leet-see-OH-so
26. market	mercato	mayr-COT-to
27. drunk	ubriacarsi	oo-bree-ah-KAR-see
28. money	denaro	day-NAHR-ro
29. station	stazione	STAHT-see-OH-nay
30. private accommodations	camera affittata	CAH-may-rah ah-fee-tah-tah
31. toilet	toilet	toy-LET
32. I	io	ee-OH
33. you	lei	lay
34. love	amore	ah-MOH-ray
35. sleep	dormire	dor-MEER-ay
36. train	treno	TRAY-no
37. The bill, please	Il conto, prego	ell KON-to, pray-go
38. friend	amico	ah-mee-ko
39. water/mineral water	acqua/acqua naturale	AH-kwa nah-toor-ALL—ay
40. castle	castello	kah-STELL-o
41. church	chiesa	kee-AY-za
42. How are you?	come va?	KO-may VAH
43. Tourist Information	ufficio informazioni	oo-FEE-cho EEN-for-MATZ-ee-OH-nee
44. You're welcome	prego	PRAY-go
45. Doing sweet nothing	dolce far niente	DOL-chay far nee-YEN-tay

PORTUGUESE

1. hello	bom dia	bohm DEE-ah
2. goodbye	adeus	eh-DAY-oosh
3. see you later	ate logo	eh-TAY LO-go
4. goodnight	boa noite	BOH-eh NOY-teh
5. please	por favor	poor feh-VOR
6. thank you	obrigado	obree GAHdhoo
7. yes/no	sim/nao	see/NAH-oh
8. one/two/three	um/dois/tres	uh/doysh/traysh
9. cheap/expensive	barato/caro	beh-RAW-to/CARR-o
10. good/bad	bom/mau	BOHM/MAH-oh
11. beautiful/ugly	belo/feio	BEHloo/FAYoo
12. big/small	grande/pequeno	GRAHN-day/peh-KAYN-yo
13. fast/slow	rapido/lento	RAHpeedo/LENN-to
14. very	muito	MOO-to
15. where is . . . ?	donde esta . . . ?	OHN-deh eesh-TAH
16. how much . . . ?	quanto?	KWAHN-to
17. I don't understand	nao compreendo	NAH-oh kohm-pree-AYN-do
18. what do you call this?	como se chama isto?	KO-moo sehr SHAR-ma EESH-to
19. I'm lost	estou perdido	esh-TOH-ah perr-DEE-do
20. complete price (everything included)	tudo incluido	TOO-do ANN-kloo-EE-do
21. I'm tired	estou cansado	esh-TOH-ah cahn-SAH-do
22. I'm hungry	tenho fome	TEN-no FO-meh
23. cheers!	saude!	sah-OO-duh
24. food	alimento	ah-lee-MEN-tu
25. grocery store	mercearia	mehr-say-ah-REE-ah
26. picnic	piquenique	PEEK-ah-NEEK
27. delicious	delicioso	deh-LEE-see-OH-zuh
28. market	mercado	mehr-KA-du
29. drunk	bebado	be-BA-du
30. money	dinheiro	dee-NEER-u
31. station	estacao	eh-stah-SAH-oh
32. private accommodations	case particular	casa parr-teek-u-LARR
33. toilet	retrete	ray-TRAY-tay
34. I	eu	yo
35. you	tu	tu
36. love	amor	a-MOHR
37. sleep	dormir	dor-MEE
38. train	trem	trehm
39. The bill, please	A conta, por favor	ah KOHN-tah, poor feh-VOR
40. friend	amigo	eh-MEE-go
41. water	agua	AH-guah
42. castle	castelo	coss-TELL-o
43. Tourist Information	informacao turistico	ann-for-mah-SAH-o too-REE-stee-ko
44. How are you?	Como vi?	CO-MO VIE

SERBO-CROATIAN

1. hello	dobar	DO-bar DUN
2. goodbye	dan	DUN
3. see you later	dovidjenja	do-vee-TEN-ya
4. goodnight	laku noc	LAH-koo NOACH
5. please	molim	MO-leem
6. thank you	hvala	HVAH-lah
7. yes/no	da/ne	dah/neh
8. one/two/three	jedan/dva/tri	YEH-dahn/dvah/tree
9. cheap/expensive	jeftino/skupo	YEHF-tee-no/SKÒO/po
10. good/bad	dobro/lose	DObro/LOsheh
11. beautiful/ugly	lepo/ruzno	LEHpo/ROOzhno
12. big/small	veliko/malo	VEHleeko/MAHlo
13. fast/slow	brzo/sporo	BERzo/SPOro
14. very	vrlo	VERlo
15. where is . . . ?	gde je . . . ?	g'DAY-yeh
16. how much . . . ?	koliko?	koLEEko
17. I don't understand	ne rezumem	neh rah-ZOO-mem
18. What is that?	Sto je to?	SHTAH yeh-toh
19. I'm lost	zalutao sam	zah-LOOT-ow sahm
20. complete price (everything included)	sve je uracunato	sveh yeh OOrachoonahto
21. I'm tired	umoran sam	OOmorahn sahm
22. I'm hungry	gladan sam	GLAHdahn sahm
23. cheers!	ziveli	ZHEEvehlee
24. food	hrana	HRA-na
25. grocery store	bakalnica	bah-KAHL-nee-kah
26. picnic	izlet	EEZH-let
27. delicious	ukusan	OO-koo-shawn
28. market	trg	turg
29. drunk	pijan	PEE-yahn
30. money	novac	NOH-vak
31. station	stanica	STAHN-eetz-ah
32. private accommodations	podesavanje	poh-deh-sah-VAHN-yeh
33. toilet	toaleta	toh-LET-tah
34. I	ja	yah
35. you	vi	vee
36. love	ljubav	LYOO-bahv
37. sleep	spavati	SPAH-va-tee
38. train	voz	voze
39. The bill, please	Racun, molim	RAW-choon, MO-leem
40. friend	prijatelj	PREE-yah-tell
41. water	vode	VO-day
42. Tourist Information	turisticki ured	TOO-rist-eech-kee-OO-red
43. How are you?	kako ste?	KOCK-O stay

SPANISH

1. hello	hola	OH-lah
2. goodbye	adios	AH-dee-OHSS
3. see you later	hasta luego	AHSS-tah LWAY-go
4. goodnight	buenas noches	BWAY-nahss NOH-chayss
5. please	por favor	por fav-VOHR
6. thank you	gracias	GRAH-see-ahss
7. yes/no	si/no	see/no
8. one/two/three	uno/dos/tres	OO-no/dohs/trayss
9. cheap/expensive	barato/caro	bah-RAH-to/KAH-ro
10. good/bad	bueno/malo	BWAY-no/MAH-lo
11. beautiful/ugly	bonito/feo	bo-NEE-to/FAY-o
12. big/small	grande/pequeno	GRAHN-day/pay-KAYN-yo
13. fast/slow	rapido/lento	RAH-pee-do/LAYN-to
14. very	muy	mwee
15. where is . . . ?	donde esta . . . ?	DOHN-day ayss-TAH
16. how much . . . ?	cuanto?	KWAHN-to
17. I don't understand	no comprendo	no kom-PRAYN-do
18. what do you call this?	como se llama esto?	KO-mo say YAH-ma AYSS-to
19. I'm lost	me he perdido	may ay pehr-DEE-do
20. complete price	todo esta incluido	TOH-doh ayssTAH eenklooEEdo
(everything included)		
22. I'm hungry	tengo hambre	TAYNG-go AHM-bray
23. cheers!	a su salud!	ah soo sah-LOOD
24. food	alimento	ah-lee-MAYN-to
25. grocery store	abaceria	ah-bah-say-REE-ah
26. picnic	comida a escote	ko-ME-da AH eskoy-tay
27. delicious	delicioso	day-lee-see-OH-so
28. market	mercado	mayr-KAH-do
29. drunk	borracho	boh-RAH-choh
30. money	dinero	dee-NAY-ro
31. station	estacion	ay-STAH-see-OHN
32. private accommodations	casa particular	KAH-ssah pahr-tee-koo-LAHR
33. toilet	retrete	ray-TRAY-tay
34. I	yo	yo
35. you	usted	usted
36. love	amor	ah-MOHR
37. sleep	sueno	SWAYN-yo
38. train	tren	train
39. The bill, please	La cuenta, por favor	lah KWAYN-tah, por fah-VOHR
40. friend	amigo	ah-MEE-go
41. water	agua	AH-gwah
42. castle	castillo	coss-TEE-yoh
43. How are you?/I'm fine, thanks	Como esta?/Estoy bien, gracias	co-mo STAH/stoy bee-AYN, gracias
44. Tourist Information	Informacion turistica	EEN-for-MAH-see-OHN too-REES-tee-kah

SWEDISH

1. hello	god dag	goo dagh
2. goodbye	adjo	ah JUR
3. see you later	vi ses	vee SAYSS
4. goodnight	god natt	goo NACHT
5. please	varsagod	VAHR-sah-gude
6. thank you	tack	tock
7. yes/no	ja/nej	yah/nay
8. one/two/three	ett/tva/tre	eht/tvoh/tray
9. cheap/expensive	billig/dyr	BIL-lig/deer
10. good/bad	god/dalig	goat/DAW-lig
11. beautiful/ugly	vacker/ful	VAHkeer/fewl
12. big/small	stor/liten	stoor/LEE-tern
13. fast/slow	snabb/langsam	snob/LONG-sahm
14. very	mycket	MEWkert
15. where is . . . ?	var ar . . . ?	VARR ahr
16. how much . . . ?	hur mycket?	hewr MEWkert
17. I don't understand	jag forstar inte	yawg furr-SHTOAR IN-ter
18. what do you call this?	vad heter det har?	vod HET-ter det HARE
19. I'm lost	jag har gatt vilse	yawg harr got VIL-ser
20. complete price (everything included)	allt ingar	ahlt in-GOAR
21. I'm tired	jar ar trott	yog ayr TRUTT
22. I'm hungry	jag ar hungrig	jog ayr HEWN-rig
23. cheers!	skal!	skoal
24. food	naring	NAYR-ing
25. grocery store	specerihandel	SPEES-er-ee-HAN-del
26. picnic	utflykt	OOT-flekt
27. delicious	harlig	HAR-lig
28. market	torg	torg
29. drunk	drucken	DROO-ken
30. money	pengar	PENG-yar
31. station	station	stah-SHONE
32. private accommodations	husrom	HOOSS-rum
33. toilet	toalett	to-ah-LET
34. I	jag	yog
35. you	du	doo
36. love	karlek	SHAR-lik
37. sleep	sova	SO-vah
38. train	tag	towg
39. The bill, please	var vanlig ge mig notan	var VAYN-lig yay mee NO-tahn
40. friend	van	venn
41. water	vatten	vott-en
42. castle	borg	borg
43. How are you?	Hur star det till?	hoor STOAR det till
44. Are you rich and single?	Ar du rik och ogift?	
45. I am rich and single.	Jag ar rik och ogift.	

DUTCH / FLEMISH
(For The Netherlands and North Belgium)

	English	Dutch/Flemish	Pronunciation
1.	hello	Goedendag	goo den dahch
2.	goodbye	Tot ziens	tot zeenz
3.	see you later	Tot straks	tot straks
4.	sleep well	slaaftwel	slaapt wel
5.	please	Alsdubleift (A.U.B)	als doo bleeft
6.	thank you	Dank U	dank oo
7.	yes, no	ja, neen	yah, nayn
8.	one, two, three	een, twee, drie	ayn, tvay, dree
9.	cheap	goedkoop	goot kope
10.	expensive	duur	duer
11.	good, bad	goed, slecht	goot, slekt
12.	beautiful	mooi	mow ee
13.	ugly	lelijk	lay lick
14.	big, small	groot, klein	groat, kline
15.	fast, slow	snel, langzaam	snell, langzaam
16.	very	zeer	zehr
17.	where is. . .?	waar is	wehr is
18.	how much	hoe veel	who veel
19.	I don't understand	ik versta u niet	ik verSTA oo neet
20.	what do you call this?	Hoe noemt u dat	who noomt oo dat
21.	I'm lost	Ik ben verloren gelopen	Ik ben vehrloren geloopen
22.	complete price	De totale prijs	Deh totaleh prize
23.	I'm tired	Ik ben moe	ik ben moo
24.	I'm hungry	Ik hep hoonger	ik hep hoonger
25.	cheers!	Gezondheid	geh zond heit
26.	food	Eten	ay ten
27.	grocery store	Voedingswinkel	Vod ings venkle
28.	delicious	heerlijk	hair lick
29.	market	markt	markt
30.	drunk	zat	zat
31.	money	geld	geld
32.	station	station	stah sheon
33.	private accommodations	kamer	kam er
34.	toilet	WC	vay say
35.	I/you	ik/jij	ik-yay
36.	love	liefde	leef da
37.	sleep	slapen	sla pen
38.	train	trein	train
39.	the bill, please	De Rekening	dah Ray kaning
40.	friend	vriend	vreend
41.	tap water	Kraatjewater	krantges water
42.	castle	Kasteel	ka steel
43.	tourist info	toeristische informatie	toor is tische in for mat see
44.	how are you?	Hoe gaat het	who gaat het
45.	church	kerk	ker ek
46.	the sweetness of doing nothing.	Het is fijn niets tedoen.	het is fayn neetz tch doon.

TRAIN PHRASES

English	French	German
1. National Railway	SNCF	DB/OBB
2. station	gare	Bahnof
3. information	resignements	Auskunft
4. Tourist Office	Syndicat D'Initiative	Auskunft
5. currency exchange	change	Wechsel
6. lockers	consigne-automatique	Spinde
7. check room	consignee	Garderobe
8. toilets	toilettes	Toiletten
9. men	messieurs	Herren
10. women	dames	Damen
11. waiting room	salle d'attente	Wartesaal
12. entrance	entre	Eingang
13. exit	sortie	Ausgang
14. timetable	horaire	Fahrplan
15. arrival	arrivee	Ankunft
16. departure	depart	Abfahrt
17. train	train	Zug
18. tickets	billet	Fahrkarten
19. reservation	reservation	Platzkarte
20. one way/round trip	aller/retour	Einfache/Zuruck
21. 1st/2nd	premiere/deuxieme	erster/zweiter
22. change	change	Umsteigen
23. ferry	bateau	Schiff
24. track	quai	Gleis
25. car	wagon	wagen
26. seat	place	platz
27. smoking	fumeurs	Raucher
28. couchette	couchette	Liegewagen
29. sleeping	wagon-lit	Schlaufwagen
30. restaurant	wagon-restaurant	Speisewagen

Italian	Spanish	Danish
1. FS	RENFE	DSB
2. stazione ferroviario	estacion	bandgarden
3. informazioni	informacion	oplysning
4. (EPT)	informacion turistica	turistbureau
5. cambio	cambio	veksling/valuth
6. armadietto	casilleros	autobousene
7. deposito	la consigna	oppbevaring-boks
8. gabinetto	servicios	toilet
9. uomini	caballeros	herrer
10. donne	senoras	damer
11. sala d'espetto	sala de espera	ventesalen
12. entrata	entrada	indgang
13. uscita	salida	udgang
14. orario	horarios	timeplan
15. arrivi	llegada	ankomst
16. partenze	partida	afgang
17. treno	tren	tog
18. biglietto	billetes	billet
19. prenotazione	reserva	pladsbestillingen
20. andata/andata e ritorno	ida/ida y vuelta	enkelt/retur
21. prima/seconda	primera/segunda	forste/anden
22. cambio	cambio	skifte
23. traghetto	balsadero	faerge
24. binario	andennes	perron/spor
25. carrozza	vagon	vogn
26. posto	place/asiento	sete
27. fumatori	coche-fumador	roker
28. cuccetta	coche-litera	liggevogn
29. vagone letto	coche-cama	sovevogn
30. ristorante	coche-restaurante	spisvogn

The insults that follow are taken from **The Insult Dictionary — How to Snarl Back in Five Languages,** *which can be ordered through James H. Heineman, Inc., 475 Park Ave., New York, NY 10022 (To be used in jest.)*

English	German	French	Italian	Spanish
Hairy creep	Oller Leisetreter (Oller lysetrayter)	Troglodyte (Troglodeet)	Stupido scimmione (Stoo-peedoh scheemee-ohneh)	Espantapajaros (Spantahpahharos)
Moron	Nackter Wilder (Naackter veelder)	Cretin (Craytan)	Deficiente (Deh-fee-chenteh)	Carcamal (Carcamahll)
Ass	Narr (Naarr)	Ane bate (Ann battay)	Somaro (Soh-mah-roh)	Asno (Assnoh)
Donkey	Esel (Ayzel)	Bourricot (Booreeko)	Asino (Ah-zeenoh)	Burro (Boorroh)
Crazy in the head	Schwach Kopf (Shvaach kopf)	Dingue (Dang)	Pazzoide (Pah-tzo-ee-deh)	Majareta (Mahharetah)
Ugly	Hasslich (Haesslich)	Laideron (Laidron)	Brutto (Broot-toh)	Asqueroso (Askehrosoh)
Useless vampire	Blutsaugendes Gespenst (Blootsaogendes geshpenst)	Vampire a la gomme (Vampeer a la gom)	Vampiro innutile (Vam-peeroh in-ootee-leh)	Vampiro caduco (Bahm-peeroh cadookoh)
Blood-sucking leech	Schmarotzer (Shmaarotser)	Sangsue (Sansi)	Sanguisuga (Sangoo-ee-sooga)	Tacano (Tahkanyoh)
Repulsive, evil-smelling dog	Widerlicher Lump (Veederlicher loomp)	Repugnant voyou (Raipinian vvahyoo)	Repulsivo vagabondo puzzolente (Ree-pul-see-vo vagabond-oh poot-zolehnteh)	Ronoso (Ronyosso)
Dribbling, senile fool	Bloder Sabberer (Bloeder zaabberer)	Vieux baveux (Vyer bavehr)	Stupido vecchio rincitrullito (Stoopeedoh veh-keeoh reen-chee-trool-leeto)	Viejo baboso (Beeyehho babbosoh)

7
Health

Before Your Trip

See your doctor

Just as you'd give your car a good check-up before a long journey, it's a good idea to meet with your doctor before your trip.

Get a general check-up. Tell the doctor everywhere you plan to go and anywhere you may go. Then you can have the flexibility to take that impulsive swing through Turkey or Morocco knowing that you're prepared medically and have the required shots. At the time of this printing, no shots are required for basic European travel (although some shots are recommended), but it's always best to check. Get advice on maintaining your health and about drinking the water. Obtain recommended immunizations and discuss proper care of any medical conditions. Take a letter from your doctor describing your special problem. If you plan to travel beyond Europe, ask your doctor about gamma globulin, the anti-diarrheal medicines and special precautions necessary.

Investigate the weather conditions you expect to encounter and pack proper clothing. Will you need an umbrella or a sunscreen ointment?

Remember, your GP is not a specialist in travel medicine and probably doesn't keep entirely up-to-date on conditions around the world. While travel in Europe is as safe as the USA, those traveling to more exotic destinations should consult a specialist.

Have a dental check-up. Emergency dental care during your trip is time and money consuming, and it can be hazardous and painful.

Assemble a Traveler's First Aid Kit

My kit contains soap, supplemental vitamins, aspirin, bandages and medications—antibiotic, anti-diarrheal and motion sickness.

Soap prevents and controls infections. Young travelers concerned about acne (which can be especially troublesome when traveling) should wash with soap five times a day, six if you're touring the Swiss chocolate factories.

Supplemental vitamins (with iron, for women) are most effective when taken with the day's largest meal. Aspirin is a great general pain reliever for headaches, sore feet, sprains, bruises, hangovers and many other minor problems.

If you have a fever, you should seek medical help. (To convert from Celsius to Fahrenheit, use the formula $F = [(C \times 9/5) + 32]$. Ninety-eight degrees Fahrenheit equals 37 degrees Celcius. To be effective, medication for motion sickness ("Dramamine") should be taken several hours before the upsetting motion is expected to begin. This medication can also serve as a mild sleeping pill. Ask your doctor to recommend an anti-diarrheal medication.

If you have any cooking instructions or serious dietary restrictions (like no wheat products), have a multilingual friend write it in the local language on the back of a business card and use it to order in restaurants.

Bandages help keep wounds clean, but are not a substitute for thorough cleaning. A piece of clean cloth can be sterilized by boiling for ten minutes or by scorching with a match. Bandages, tape or two pairs of socks can prevent or retard problems with the feet. Cover any irritated area before it blisters.

Those with corrected vision should bring extra glasses in a solid protective case, as well as the lens prescription. Contact lenses are used all over Europe and the required solutions for their care are easy to find. Soft lenses can be boiled like eggs. (Be sure to remind your helpful landlady to leave them in their case.) Do not assume that you can wear your contacts as comfortably in Europe as you can at home. I find that the hot, dusty cities and my style of travel make contacts impossible, and every summer I end up wearing my glasses and carrying my contacts.

Jet Lag and the First Day of Your Trip

Flying halfway around the world is stressful. If you leave frazzled after a hectic last night and a wild *bon voyage* party there's a good chance you won't be healthy for the first part of your trip. Just a hint of a cold coupled with the stress of a long flight will mean a sniffly first week. Once you're on the road it's pretty hard to slow down enough to fight that cold properly.

Leave home well rested. An early trip cold used to be a regular part of my vacation until I learned a very important trick. Plan from the start as if you're leaving two days before you really are. Keep that last 48-hour period sacred even if it means being hectic before your false departure date. Then you have two orderly peaceful days after you've packed and are physically ready to fly. Mentally, you'll be comfortable about leaving home and starting this adventure. You'll fly away well-rested and 100% capable of enjoying the bombardment of your senses that will follow.

Anyone who flies through time zones has to grapple with the bio-rythmic confusion known as jet lag. When you switch your wristwatch eight hours forward your body says, "Hey, what's going on?" Body clocks don't reset so easily. All your life you've done things in a twenty-four hour cycle. Now, after crossing the Atlantic your body wants to eat when you tell it to sleep and sleep when you tell it to enjoy a museum. You can't avoid jet lag, but with a few tips you can minimize the symptoms.

You dehydrate during a long flight so drink plenty of liquids. I ask for "two orange juices with no ice" every chance I get. Eat light, no coffee, minimal sugar until the flight's almost over. Alcohol is stressful to your body and will aggravate jet lag. The in-flight movie is good for one thing—nap time. With three hours of sleep during the trans-oceanic flight you will be functional the day you land. (I take one sleeping pill a year— on my flight to Europe.) Upon arrival make yourself stay awake until an early local bedtime. Your body may beg for sleep but refuse. You must force your body's transition to the local time. Then, after a solid ten hours of sleep you should wake up feeling like "super-tourist".

Too many people assume their first day will be made worthless by jet lag. Don't prematurely condemn yourself to zombie-dom. Most people, of all ages, that I've traveled with have enjoyed very productive—even hyper—first days. Most people wake very early on their first morning. Trying to sleep later is normally futile. Jet lag is a joke to some and a major problem to others. It's hard to predict just how serious your jet lag will be. Those who keep strict twenty-four hour schedules will probably feel more jet-lag than those who work swing shift or keep crazy hours.

You'll read about many jet lag "cures". Most are "worse than the disease". Just leave un-frazzled, minimize jet lag's symptoms and give yourself a chance to enjoy your trip from the moment you step off the plane. Remember, this is the first day of the rest of your trip.

Health in Europe

Europe is generally safe. All the talk of gamma globulin, doxycycline and treating water with purification tablets is applicable only south and east of Europe.

Many people might disagree with me, but I'd say that, with discretion and common sense, you can eat and drink whatever you like in Europe. If any area deserves a little extra caution it is rural areas in the southern countries of Spain, Portugal, Italy and Greece. As our world becomes more chemical, reasons for concern and caution will increase on both sides of the Atlantic.

I was able to stay healthy while traveling from Europe to India. By following these basic guidelines, I never once suffered from "Tehran Tummy" or "Delhi Belly".

Outside of Europe, use good judgment when eating. Avoid unhealthy-looking restaurants. Wash and peel all fruit. When in serious doubt, eat only thick-skinned fruit (uh, peeled). Even in the worst places, anything cooked and still hot is safe. Meat should be avoided or at least well-cooked. Have "well-done" written on a piece of paper in the local language and use it when ordering. Avoid possibly-spoiled foods, and remember, pre-prepared foods gather germs. The train station restaurants are India's safest because they have the fastest turnover. Germs just don't have time to congregate.

Honor your diet. An adequate diet is very important for a traveler. The longer your trip, the more you will be affected by an inadequate diet. Budget travelers often eat more carbohydrates and less protein to stretch their travel dollar. This is the root of many nutritional problems encountered by travelers. Protein is necessary for resistance to infection and to rebuild muscles. Protein should be consumed with the day's largest meal because that is when the "essential" amino acids are most likely to be present to allow complete protein utilization. I bring supplemental vitamins and take them religiously.

Drink the Water

I drink the water in Europe. Read signs carefully, however, because some taps, like those on the trains, are not for drinking. A decal showing a glass with a red "X" over it or a skull and crossbones should be taken as a subtle hint that it is not *trinkwasser*. Water served in a restaurant is obviously drinking water. A new game is being played all over Europe. Many waiters are telling tourists that the water is no good. "It's only for brushing your teeth." This is a lie to scare you into ordering a two-dollar drink.

East of Bulgaria and south of the Mediterranean, do not drink the water without treating it. Water can be treated by boiling it for six minutes. Outside of Europe I use the two percent tincture of iodine treatment. I carry it in an eye-dropper bottle. Eight drops per quart or liter or one drop per glass (left to stand for 15 minutes) will purify the questionable water. This is very handy in a restaurant, because my glass of water is purified in time to drink it still cold with my meal. Iodine is fast, easy, kills just about everything (except giardia) and doubles as a good disinfectant.

Beer, wine, boiled coffee and tea, and bottled soft drinks are safe. Coca-Cola products (if the top is on and the carbonation is still there) are safe to drink anywhere in the world.

You Will Get Sick—Loosen Up

Get used to the fact that travel is a package deal. You will get sick in Europe. You'll have diarrhea for a day. (Practice that thought in front of the mirror tonight.) When you get the runs, take it in stride, and if you stay healthy, you'll feel lucky.

The water may, sooner or later, make you sick. It is not necessarily dirty. The bacteria in European water is different from that in American water. Our systems are the most pampered on earth. We were raised, proudly, on bread that rips in a straight line. We are capable of handling American bacteria with no problem at all, but some people can go to London and get sick. Some French people visit Boston and get sick. Some Americans travel around the world, eating and drinking everything in sight, and don't get sick—others spend weeks on the toilet. It all depends on the person.

"Traveling makes a man wiser, but less happy." Thomas Jefferson

If (or when) you do get diarrhea, it will run its course. Revise your diet, don't panic, and keep "plugging" along. When I get diarrhea, I make my diet as bland and boring as possible for a day or so (bread, rice, baked potatoes, clear soup, weak tea). Keep telling yourself that tomorrow you'll feel much better. You will. Most conditions are self-limiting. I have found that the bland diet is the best remedy. If your loose stools persist, be sure to replenish all lost liquids and minerals. (Bananas are very effective in replacing potassium which is lost during a bout with diarrhea.) If you have a prolonged case of diarrhea (especially dangerous for an infant), a temperature greater than 101 degrees (38.8 degrees C), or if you notice blood in your stools, contact a doctor for help. Europeans use a pill called Enterovioform to get you solid. American doctors warn that it can harm your eyesight. Don't use it.

I visited the Red Cross in Athens after a miserable three-week tour of the toilets of Syria and Jordan, and the remedy that finally stopped all of my troubles was simply boiled rice and plain tea. After five days on that dull diet, I was as good as new—and constipated.

Constipation, the other side of the intestinal pendulum, seems to be nearly as prevalent as diarrhea. Know what roughage is and everything will come out all right in the end.

A basic hygiene hint is to wash your hands often, keep your nails clean and never touch your fingers to your mouth.

If You Do Get Sick

Throughout Europe, people with a health problem go first to the local pharmacy, not to their doctor. European pharmacists will diagnose and prescribe a remedy for most simple problems. They are usually friendly and often speak English.

If you need serious medical treatment in Europe it's generally of high quality. To facilitate smooth communication, it's best to find an English-speaking doctor. Information leading you to these doctors can be obtained through agencies that deal with Americans, such as embassies, consulates, American Express Companies and large hotels.

American embassies and consulates have lists of American or British trained doctors. This is most important outside of Europe.

A physical injury is often accompanied by swelling which is painful and retards healing. For 48 hours after a sprain or bruise occurs, you should apply ice to and elevate the injured area. An "ace" bandage is useful to immobilize, stop swelling and later provides support. It is not helpful to "work out" a sprain.

Venereal disease has reached pandemic proportions. Obviously, the best way to prevent V.D. is to avoid exposure. A condom is fairly effective in preventing transmission for those who are unable to avoid exposure. Cleaning with soap and water before and after exposure is also helpful if not downright pleasurable. AIDS has been reported in Europe's heterosexual population.

Keeping fit. Physically, travel is great living—healthy food, lots of activity, fresh air and all those stairs! Still, you may want to work out during your trip. Jogging, while not as popular in Europe, is nothing weird. Lots of travelers enjoy Europe from a special perspective—running at dawn. Europe has plenty of good inexpensive public swimming pools. Whatever your racket, if you want to badly enough, you'll find ways to keep in practice as you travel. Most big city private tennis and swim clubs welcome foreign guests for a small fee. This is a good way to make friends as well as exercise.

Traveler's Toilet Trauma

Any traveler has one or two good toilet stories. Foreign toilets can be traumatic. And they can be hard to find. But, in the long run, they are one of those little things that make travel so much more interesting than staying home. Before you dive into that world of memorable porcelain experiences, let me prepare you for toilet-shock, and pass on a few tips on finding a WC quickly when you need one.

First, about toilet-trauma. While most European toilets are reasonably similar to our own, be prepared for some toilets that are dirtier and different than what you're used to. Only Americans need disposable bibs to sit on and a paper strip draped over their toilet, assuring them that no one has sat there yet. In fact, those of us who need a throne to sit on are in the minority. Most humans sit on their haunches and nothing more. When many Asian refugees are oriented (or de-oriented) in the USA, they have to be taught not to stand on our rims.

So, if you plan to venture away from the international-style hotels in your Mediterranean travels and become a temporary local person, "going local" will take on a very real meaning. Experienced travelers enjoy recalling the shock they got the first time they opened the door and found only porcelain foot-prints and a squat-and-aim hole in the ground—complete with flies in a holding pattern. When confronted by the "non-toilet" remind yourself that if a Western-style toilet was there it would be so filthy you wouldn't want to get near it.

Toilet paper (like spoons and forks) is another Western "essential" that most people on our planet do not use. What they use varies. I won't get too graphic here, but remember that a billion people in South Asia never eat with their left hand.

A week's supply of toilet paper—don't leave home without it. When you run out, tour a first-class hotel or restaurant and borrow ten or twelve more yards of good soft stuff. Local grade TP used to be closer to wax or crepe paper—good for a laugh but not much more. The TP scene has improved markedly in the last few years, but you'll still find some strange stuff worth taking home to show your friends.

Finding a decent public toilet can be frustrating. I dropped a group off in a town for a potty stop, and when I picked them up 20 minutes later, none had found relief. Most countries have few public restrooms. You'll need to develop a knack for finding a private WC.

I can sniff out a biffy in a jiffy. Any place that serves food or drinks has a restroom. No restaurateur would label his WC so those on the street can see, but you can walk into nearly any cafe or restaurant, politely and confidently, and find a bathroom somewhere in the back. It's easiest in places that have outdoor seating, because waiters will think you're a customer just making a quick trip inside. Some call it rude, I call it survival. If you feel like it, ask permission. Just smile, "Toilet?" I'm rarely turned down. Timid people buy a drink they don't want in order to leave one. That's unnecessary. American-type fast food places are very common these days and always have a decent and fairly "public" restroom. When nature beckons and there's no restaurant or bar handy, look in parks, train stations, on trains, in museums, hotel lobbies, government buildings and on upper floors of department stores.

Large, classy, old hotels are as impressive as many palaces you'll pay to see. You can always find a royal retreat here and plenty of very soft TP. These are an oasis in Third World countries where a pleasant western sit-down toilet experience is rare.

After you've found and used a toilet, you're down to your last challenge—flushing it. Rarely will you find the basic handle you probably grew up with. Find some protuberance and push, pull, twist, squeeze, step on or pray to it until the waterfall starts. Electric-eye sinks and urinals are increasingly popular.

In many countries you'll need to be selective to avoid the gag-a-maggot variety of toilets. Public toilets like those in parks are often repulsive. I never leave a museum without taking advantage of its restrooms—free, clean and full of artistic graffiti. Use the toilets on the train rather than in the station to save time and money. Toilets on first-class cars are a cut above second-class toilets. I go first-class even with a 2nd class ticket. Train toilets are located on the ends of cars, where it's most jiggly. A trip to the train's john always reminds me of the rodeo. Never use a train WC while stopped in a station.

Tipping or paying to use a public WC is a European custom that irks many Americans. Some, practicing ugly Americanism, will tip with coins from a previously visited country since they no longer need them. Such coins, to the WC attendant, are useless. Many times the toilet is free but the woman in the corner sells sheets of toilet paper. Most common is the tip dish by the entry. The equivalent of about 25 cents is plenty. Remind yourself that the fee keeps the place clean and, trust me, it's a small price to pay for a more pleasant WC experience. The keepers of the WC are sometimes known to be crabby. You would be too if you lived under the street in a room full of public toilets. Humor them, understand them and leave them a coin.

The women who seem to inhabit Europe's WCs are a popular topic of conversation among Yankee travelers. Sooner or later a man is minding his own business at his urinal and the lady brings him his change, or sweeps under his feet. Yes, it is distracting, but you'll just have to get used to it—the WC attendants have.

And finally, there are countries where the people don't use restrooms at all. I've been on buses that have just stopped, and fifty people scatter. Three minutes later they reload, relieved. It takes a little adjusting, but that's travel. When in Rome, do as the Romans do—and before you know it . . . Euro-peein'.

8
The Woman
Traveling Alone

Every year more and more single women are traveling alone around Europe. Women outnumber the men in the travel classes I teach. And many are asking: "Is it safe for me to travel alone in Europe?" This is a topic that is best understood and discussed by a woman. Pam Kasardi, who has traveled more than any woman I know, has agreed to share her thoughts on the subject in this chapter.

A woman traveling alone faces two special problems. First off, the usual danger associated with solo travel, crime may be greater because a woman is seen as more vulnerable than a man. And secondly, a woman traveler may have to endure more sexual harassment while on the road than she would find acceptable at home. Aside from these problems, however, the lone woman traveler enjoys some great advantages.

If you have the desire to travel alone in Europe, do it. While I don't recommend traveling alone in North Africa or the Middle East, I have never regretted traveling alone in Europe. My feeling (as well as the general consensus of the solo woman travelers I've met) is that you will be safe as long as you are careful and exercise the same common sense you would in any big American city. Be very wary of the people you meet. Withhold your trust much longer than you would at home. To put it bluntly, Europe has more than its share of horny men roaming about with no other purpose in mind than to hustle women tourists.

As far as crime and your safety are concerned, I would say Europe is on par with the US. If you don't feel safe traveling alone in America, think twice before embarking on a solo European adventure. You are most likely to run into problems in the Mediterranean world. The Moslem countries, while not necessarily a criminal threat, are generally considered the leaders of the pack in hassling women travelers. In these coun-

tries you are safest in the more touristed areas, where the Western traveler is a relatively common sight.

Fit in. Women's Liberation has yet to reach Southern Europe. When you enter a new country, observe. See how the women are treated and how they are expected to act. Don't forget that you are in a different culture with different morals and mores. Just as you must learn to fit in as a guest, you must learn to adapt to the local expectations of proper relations between the sexes. Learn to see your actions as the local people see them. Don't flaunt your relative liberation. If you wear skimpy cut-offs and a tight tee-shirt amidst women shrouded from head to toe in black, you will be certainly be calling attention to yourself, offending people and asking for trouble. In a situation such as this, a skirt or long pants would be more appropriate—even if less comfortable.

Don't be a temptation. The flashy female tourist is often equated with the dreamy women the Southern European man sees in American movies. You may be considered "loose" just because you are American. Work hard to fit in so you don't encourage that sort of appraisal of your character. Be especially careful with your clothing and physical movements (eye contact, smiles, winks and so on). I'll never forget the day I left my Naples hotel wearing a cool tank top. Within a few minutes I realized that, heat or no heat, I would have to wear something much less interesting.

Many foreign men will look at you for anything they can interpret as a sexual invitation. I have found that the most harmless gesture, like a warm smile or eye contact, can be misinterpreted. Sadly, you will sometimes have to act colder than you really are to remain unharassed.

No matter how you dress or act, you will probably be the object of much admiration, some advances and plenty of less-than-discreet stares. Try not to let gestures of appreciation (whistles and so forth) bother you. I have found them to be generally harmless (if annoying) compliments as well as invitations. The best policy is to ignore them and keep on walking. If things get out of hand, a harsh scolding, in any language, especially in the presence of onlookers, will usually work wonders. Basta! means "enough" in Italian.

Stares are a fact of traveling. The farther off the beaten path you get, the more you'll be stared at. In the countryside of Spain, foreigners of any sex are stared at constantly. Admittedly, stares, wolf whistles, pinches and macho come-ons are not to your or my liking, but they are as much a part of Italian and Spanish culture as spaghetti and bullfights. Even if you don't like it, accept it as inevitable.

Southern European women have a habit of strolling arm in arm to let men they pass know that they are in no need of "companionship". When traveling in the South with another woman, I do the same thing. It works very well in reducing harassment.

If you find yourself in a conversation that is leading in the wrong direction, you may want to tell the man or men involved about your husband or children—even if they are imaginary. One summer I wore a fake wedding band whenever I wanted to be considered unavailable and uninterested. When I want to sit unpestered in a cafe, I write in my journal. If you are doing something, you don't look like you're just waiting to be picked up.

In Europe it's macho to try. Train conductors may lie down next to you on the train, hotel managers may try to escort you farther than your room, shoe shine boys may polish your thighs. These are not rape attempts. These are frustrated men asking for a date with a very impressive woman from a skyscraper land that speaks and thinks a strange language. Don't overreact—just firmly refuse.

Be very careful who you trust. Believe me, European men, especially the ones who get a lot of practice, can be incredibly smooth and impressive. I've heard several stories about women travelers who joined up with some "classy" European only to wake up abandoned and left without any of their belongings. This unfortunate condition can be avoided by withholding your trust.

Women traveling in pairs are less likely to find themselves in difficult situations than those traveling alone. Many people start their trips alone, intending to pick up partners as they go along. This is easy since there are many solo travelers of both sexes all over Europe traveling with the same intention—befriending and teaming up with a compatible travel partner. I find this particularly easy in youth hostels. European hotels don't care if the couples they rent to are married or not.

You will enjoy rewarding experiences and wonderful hospitality because you are a woman—dinner invitations, escorted tours, rides, cups of tea and so on. American women are often looked upon with awe by foreign men. While there may be hassles, I think these hassles are more than compensated by the generous offers of hospitality. You will have many advantages over your male counterpart. Most men would have to travel months to receive the same amount of tangible hospitality that a woman receives in a few days. Needless to say, this sort of friendliness can make a visit to any country special. As you travel beyond Europe you will notice even greater hospitality and attention. I'll never forget the Egyptian man who let me ride his donkey. As I rode sleepily up the bank of the Nile he begged me to stay with him in Egypt. He promised to build me "a castle on the hilltop".

The problem of course is that all too often those things come with strings attached. (My Egyptian friend fondled my leg while he promised me the world.) I find that these amount to little more than minor irritations. Before you curse the attention you are getting, remember that you may actually miss it a little after you get home.

A woman who finds herself in any sort of serious trouble should know that a few well-placed tears will often do wonders to clear things up. While a man could conceivably starve on the street corner, a "damsel in distress" is never far from help.

I think the most common negative result from this kind of harassment is that the woman escapes to more comfortable terrain, like England or Germany, and takes with her a disdain for "those rude men in the south"

Now that you've read this chapter, keep in mind that, if anything, I have made the situation sound worse than it really is. Proceed with a cautious but positive attitude and you'll have a great trip.

Pam Kasardi

9
Travel Photography

My most prized souvenirs are the pictures I've taken. Every year I ask myself whether it's worth the worry and expense of mixing photography with my travels. After my film is developed and I re-live my trip through those pictures, the answer is always, "Yes!" Here are some tips and lessons that I've learned from the photographic school of hard knocks.

The Camera

Good shots are made by the photographer—not the camera. For most people, a very expensive camera is a bad idea. Your camera is more likely to be lost, stolen or broken than anything else you'll travel with. A very expensive model may not be worth the risks and headaches that accompany it.

A good basic 35mm single lens reflex camera provides everything I need. (like my Pentax ME.) When buying a camera, think about size, weight and durability.

Those who want an extremely simple lightweight camera that takes good pictures enjoy the popular mini-automatics. These are far better than instamatic snapshot cameras, have handy built-in flash attachments, fit comfortably in your coat pocket, and cost around $150. But the point-and-shoot automatics limit your creative control since the focus, exposure, depth of field and shutter speed is given to you—automatically. With one of these very simple cameras most of what follows is not required knowledge. But even a point-and-shoot photographer should understand the basics.

Research before you buy. Camera owners love to talk photography. Learn from them. Visit some camera shops and ask questions. Most people are limited not by the shortcomings of their camera but by their lack of knowledge. You may put a lot of expense and energy into your travel photography. If you don't understand ASA numbers, "f-stops" or "depth of field" find a photography class or book and learn. Camera stores offer many good books on photography and even on travel photography. I shutter to think how many people are underexposed or at least lacking depth in this field.

Lenses

Most cameras come with a "normal" 50-55 mm lens that does "down" to about" f-2." To start with, this is all you need. The "f-stop" numbers indicate how wide you can open the aperture. A better and more expensive lens can be opened wider (set at a lower "f-stop"), enabling you to take a picture when less light is available. Your lens should go at least as low as "f-2."

The length of the lens (e.g., 55 mm) determines the size of the image it takes. A wide-angle lens is shorter (28 or 35 mm), letting you fit more into your picture. This is especially useful when photographing interiors where it's impossible to back up enough to get much in. A lense with a very wide angle distorts the picture. A 28 mm lens is considered as wide as you can go before the distortion becomes very noticeable.

A longer telephoto lens (e.g., 150 mm) allows you to get a closer shot of your subject. A telephoto lens is especially handy for taking portraits inconspicuously. The longer or more powerful the lens, the more it magnifies any vibrations, thus requiring a faster shutter speed for a good, crisp shot.

A zoom lens has an adjustable length. A common size zoom lens has a range from 70 to 205 mm. You could fit your subject's entire body in the picture (at 70 mm), then "zoom" right in to get just the face (at 205 mm). This is a lot of fun, but, like the telephoto, it's substantially bulkier and heavier than either the regular or the wide-angle lenses.

I would say that for travel photography, unless you are particularly interested in candid portraiture, the wide-angle is a more valuable second lens than the telephoto or zoom.

There is a mid-range zoom lens that gives the photographer a range from about 35 to 70 mm. Many travelers are very happy with this three-lens-in-one concept. Remember, the capacity to "zoom" adds weight and limits your "f-stop" range. There is also a device called a "doubler" which is attached between the body of the camera and the lens. This doubles the power of that lens' magnification, but also doubles the loss of light.

Filters

There is a wide variety of filters available for the photographer to play with. Every lens should have a clear, ultraviolet or a haze filter to protect the lens. The only other filter I use is a polarizer to intensify colors. A polarizer will sharpen the contrast between the white and blue of a cloudy sky, giving you more intense colors and a more powerful landscape.

Film

Travel photographers around the world debate the merits of different kinds of film. There's no real right or wrong choice—just trade-offs and a personal preference.

Each brand is a little different. For instance, Kodak yields pictures that are bluer, while Agfa is a little stronger in its treatment of reds. Rather than trying to evaluate all films, I'll simply explain what I buy and why.

A good eye is more important than an extra lens.

Prints are much more expensive so I take slides, and get prints made only of the shots I really like. I buy rolls of 36 rather than 20 exposures. It's cheaper, less bulky and you don't have to change film as often.

Films come with different ASA numbers or "speeds". The average traveler carries film with ASA numbers ranging from 25 to 400. The ASA number indicates how sensitive to light the film is. Greater light sensitivity (higher number ASA) allows you to take pictures with less light. There is a trade-off, however, since greater light sensitivity produces pictures with a "grainy" quality. In choosing your film, you must decide how "fast" you need it and how important it is for you to minimize graininess. I have never found graininess to be a problem. In a small print or on a slide projected on a screen, I see no difference in graininess between ASA 400 and ASA 64. Graininess does become a factor in large prints. Colors seem to vary a little from one ASA numbered film to another. It's a confusing field. You will make the best choice if you understand the trade-offs between speed, color and graininess. Kodachrome 64 is the best selling slide film and is the best general purpose film on the market. I get Kodak film in ASA 64 or 400.

Film prices vary, and if you find a good price you can stock up. Film is much more expensive in Europe. (Keep what film you don't use fresh by freezing it.) Before buying film or any photographic equipment it's wise to pick up a photography magazine and read the advertisements. Wholesale warehouses all over the country sell cameras, accessories and film at prices no retail outlet can match.

Galaxy of Gadgets

Like many hobbies, photography is one that allows you to spend endless amounts of money on a galaxy of gadgets. I have some favorites that are particularly useful to the traveling photographer.

First of all you need a gadget bag. The most functional and economical one is simply a small nylon stuff bag made for hikers. When I'm in a market or somewhere taking a lot of pictures, I like to wear a nylon belt pouch (designed to carry a canteen). This is a handy way to have your different lenses and filters accessible, allowing you to make necessary changes quickly and easily. A formal camera bag attracts thieves and is unnecessary.

A mini C-clamp/tripod is a great gadget. About 5 feet high, this tool screws into most any camera, sprouts three legs and holds the camera perfectly still for slow shutter speeds and time exposure shots. (It looks like a small "lunar landing module".) The C-clamp works where the tripod won't, such as on a fence or a hand rail. A conventional tripod is much too large to lug around Europe. A cable release is a gadget that allows you to snap a shot or hold the shutter open without moving the camera. Proper use of this and a C-clamp/tripod will let you take some exciting time exposures and night shots.

A lot of time exposure photography is guesswork. The best way to get good shots of difficult lighting situations is to "bracket" your shots by trying several different exposures of the same scene. You'll have to throw out a few slides that way, but one good shot is worth several in the garbage can. Automatic cameras usually meter properly up to eight or ten seconds, making night shots easy and bracketing unnecessary. A "no-frills" camera like the Pentax K-1000 will not have a timed shutter release.

An accessory self-timer is fun and reasonably priced. If you are traveling with a friend and want to share lenses, it's possible to buy an adapter ring that will make lenses of different mounts compatible. A dust blower, lens cleaning tissue and a small bag of cleaning solution are wise additions to any gadget bag. I take my camera without its protective case and protect my lens with a cap that dangles on its "cap-keeper" when I'm shooting. For most people, a camera case is unnecessary.

Tricks for a Good Shot

A sharp eye with a wild imagination is more valuable than a third lens. Develop an eye for what will look good and be interesting after the trip. Weed out dull shots before you take them, not after you get them home. It's cheaper. Postcard-type shots are boring. Everyone knows what the Eiffel Tower looks like. Find a unique or different approach to sights that everyone has seen. Shoot the belltower through the horse's legs or lay your camera on the floor to shoot the Gothic ceiling.

Buildings, in general, are not interesting. It doesn't matter if Karl Marx or Beethoven was born there, a house or building is as dead as they are. As travel photographers gain experience, they take more "people shots" and fewer buildings or general landscapes. Show the personal and intimate details of your trip: how you lived, who you met, what made each day an adventure (a close-up of the remains of a picnic, your leech bite, a local schoolboy playing games with his nose or a shot of how you washed your clothes).

Vary the perspective of your camera—close, far, low, high, day, night, etc. Break rules and be gamey. For instance, we are told never to shoot into the sun. Some into-the-sun shots bring surprising results. Try to use bad weather to your advantage. Experiment with strange or difficult light situations. Buy a handbook on photographing in existing light.

People are interesting subjects. It takes nerve to walk up to someone and take their picture. It can be difficult, but if you want some great shots, be "nervy". Ask for permission. The way to do this in any language is to point at your camera and ask, "Photo?" Your subject will probably be delighted. You most likely just made his day, as well as a good picture. Try to show action. A candid is better than a posed shot. Even a posed "candid" is better than a posed shot. Many photographers take a second shot immediately after the first portrait to capture a looser, warmer subject. If the portrait isn't good, you probably weren't close enough. My best shots are so close that the entire head can't fit into the frame.

I traveled through Spain and Morocco with a professional photographer. One of the lessons I learned from him was not to intimidate your subject. If you walk right up, shake his hand and act like a bloody fool, he will consider you just that and ignore you while you feast on some great material.

It's very important to be able to take a quick shot. Know your camera, practice setting it, understand depth of field and metering. In a marketplace situation, where speed is crucial, I preset my camera. I set the meter on the sunlit ground and focus at, let's say, 12 feet. Now I know that, with my depth of field, anything from about 10 to 15 feet will be in focus and, if it's in the sunshine, properly exposed. I can take a perfect picture in an instant, provided my subject meets these preset requirements. It's possible to get some good shots by presetting the camera and shooting from the waist. Ideally, I get eye contact while I shoot from the hip.

You will hear that the focal length of your lens will dictate the slowest safe hand-held shutter speed you can use. For instance, a 50 mm lens should shoot no slower than a 50th of a second. That rule is a bit conservative. I have been able to get fine shots out of my 50 mm lens at a 30th of a second, even a 15th. Don't be afraid to hand-hold a slow shot, but do what you can to make it steady. If you can lean against a wall, for instance, you become a tripod instead of a bipod. If you have a self-timer, hold the camera still and let that mechanism click the shutter rather than your finger. Using these tricks, I can get good-looking pictures inside a museum at an 8th of a second. I don't use a flash. With ASA 400 film I manage fine even indoors.

Contrary to what you may think, you won't be able to remember the name of every monastery and mountain that you take a picture of. I record the name of anything I want to be sure to remember.

When you put your slide show together, remember to limit the length of your show. Nothing is worse than to sit through an endless parade of lackluster shots. Set a limit (maximum two carousals of 140 slides each) and prune your show down even if you've had to leave out some shots that you really like. Keep it tight. Keep it moving. Leave the audience crying for more.

10
Museums

Culture Beyond the Petri Dish

Europe is a treasure chest of great art. Many of the world's greatest museums will be a part of your trip. Here are a few hints on how to get the most out of these museums.

I have found that some studying before the trip makes the art I see in Europe much more exciting. It's criminal to visit Rome or Greece with no background in those civilizations' art. I remember touring the National Museum of Archeology in Athens as an obligation, and it was really quite boring. I was convinced that those who were enjoying it were actually just faking it—trying to look sophisticated. Two years later, after a class in ancient art history, that same museum was a fascinating trip into the world of Pericles and Socrates—all because of some background knowledge.

A common misconception is that a great museum has only great art. A museum like the Louvre in Paris is so big (the building itself was, at one time, the largest in Europe), you can't possibly cover everything properly in one visit—so don't try. Be selective. Only a fraction of a museum's pieces is really "greats", and generally, it's best to enlist the services of a guide or guidebook to show you the best two hours of a museum. Brief guide pamphlets recommending the best basic visit are available in some of Europe's great museums. With this selective strategy, you'll appreciate the highlights when you're fresh. If you still have any energy left, you can explore other areas of specific interest to you. For me, museum going is the hardest work I do in Europe, and I'm rarely good for more than two or three hours. If you are determined to cover a large museum thoroughly, the best strategy is to tackle one section a day for several days.

If you are especially interested in one piece of art, spend half an hour

A victim of the Louvre.

studying it and listening to each passing tour guide tell his or her story about "David" or the "Mona Lisa" or whatever. They each do their own research and come up with different information to share. There's really nothing wrong with this sort of tour freeloading. Just don't stand in the front and ask a lot of questions.

Upon arrival, I always thumb through a museum guidebook index or look through the postcards to make sure I won't miss anything of importance to me. For instance, I love Dali. One time I thought I was finished with a museum, but in the postcards I found a painting by Dali. A museum guide was happy to show me where this Dali painting was hiding. I saved myself the agony of discovering after my trip was over that I was there but didn't see it.

If you're concerned that you may be overwhelmed by Europe's greatest museums be sure to pick up *Mona Winks—A Guide to Enjoying Europe's Greatest Museums*. This new book (by Gene Openshaw and me) is a collection of fun and clear take-you-by-the-hand two hour tours of Europe's 20 most important (and difficult) museums. It's just me and you together in the greatest art of our civilization. (See the back of this book for ordering instructions.)

Remember, most museums are closed one day during the week. Your local guidebook or tourist information has that information. Free admission days are usually the most crowded. In many cases, it's worth the entrance fee to avoid the crowds.

Open Air Folk Museums

Many travel in search of the old life and traditional culture in action. While we book a round-trip ticket into the archaic past, those we photograph with the old world balanced on their heads are struggling to dump that load and climb into our world. Many are succeeding.

More than ever, the easiest way to see the "real culture" is by exploring that country's Open Air Folk Museum. True, it's culture on a "lazy susan", about as real as Santa's Village in a one-stop climate-controlled shopping mall, but the future is becoming the past faster than ever and, in many places, it's the only "Old World" you're going to find.

An Open Air Folk Museum is a collection of traditional buildings from every corner of the country or region carefully reassembled in a park, usually near the capital or major city. These sprawling museums are the best bet for the hurried (or tired) tourist craving a magic carpet ride through that country's past. Log cabins, thatched cottages, mills, old school houses, shops and farms come complete with original furnishings and usually a local person dressed in the traditional costume who's happy to answer any of your questions about life then and there.

In the summer, folk museums buzz with colorful folk dances, live music performances and young craftsmen specializing in old crafts. Many traditional arts and crafts are dying and these artisans do what they can to keep the cuckoo clock from going the way of the dodo bird. Some of my favorite souvenirs are those I watched being dyed, woven or carved by folk museum craftsmen.

To get the most out of your visit, pick up a list of special exhibits, events and activities at the information center and take advantage of any walking tours. These sightseeing centers of the future were popularized in Scandinavia, and they're now found all over the world.

The best folk museums I've seen are in the Nordic capitals. Oslo's, with 150 historic buildings and a 12th century stave church, is just a quick boat ride across the harbor from the city hall. Skansen in Stockholm gets my first place ribbon for its guided tours, feisty folk entertainment and its Lapp camp complete with reindeer.

Switzerland's Ballenberg Open Air Museum near Interlaken is a good alternative when the Alps hide behind clouds.

The British Isles have no shortage of folk museums. For an unrivaled look at the Industrial Revolution, be sure to spend a day at the new Blists Hill Open Air Museum at the Iron Bridge Gorge, north of Stratford. You can cross the world's first iron bridge to see the factories that lit the fuse of our modern age.

The "Knotts Berry Farm" of Bulgaria is in Gabrovo and offers a refreshing splash of free enterprise-type crafts in a rather drab socialist world.

Every year new folk museums open. Travel with a current guide and use tourist information centers abroad. Before your trip send a card to each country's National Tourist Office in San Francisco or New York (addresses in Chapter 1). Request the general packet of trip-planning information and specifics like schedules of festivals and cultural events and lists of Open Air Folk Museums.

Folk museums teach traditional lifestyles better than any other kind of museum. As the world plunges towards 100 billion McDonald's hamburgers, these museums will become even more important. Of course, they're as realistic as Santa's Village—but how else will you see the elves?

Here is a list of some of Europe's best open air Folk Museums:

NORWAY

Norwegian Folk Museum, at Bygdoy near Oslo. *150 old buildings from all over Norway and a 12th-century stave church.*

Maihaugen Folk Museum, at Lillehammer. *Folk culture of the Gudbrandsdalen.*

Trondheim and Trondelag Folk Museum at Sverresborg fortress near Trondheim. *60 buildings showing old Trondheim, Lapp village and farm life.*

SWEDEN

Skansen, Stockholm. *One of the best museums, with over 100 buildings from all over Sweden, craftspeople at work, live entertainment and a Lapp camp complete with reindeer.*

Kulteren, Lund. *Features Southern Sweden and Viking exhibits.*

FINLAND

Seurasaari Island, near Helsinki. *Buildings reconstructed from all over Finland.*

Handicrafts Museum, Turku. *The life and work of 19th-century craftspeople.*

DENMARK

Funen Village (Den Fynske Landsby), just south of Odense.

Old Town, Arhus. *60 houses and shops show Danish life from 1580-1850.*

Lyngby Park, north of Copenhagen.

Hjerl Hede Iron Age Village, 10 miles south of Skive in northern Jutland. *Lifestyles in prehistoric times.*

Oldtidsbyen Iron Age Village, near Roskilde.

GERMANY

Cloppenburg Open Air Museum, southwest of Bremen. *Traditional life in Lower Saxony, 17th and 18th centuries.*

Unterhuldingen Prehistoric Village, on the Boden Sea (Lake Constance).

SWITZERLAND

Ballenberg Swiss Open Air Museum, just northeast of Lake Brienz. *A fine collection of old Swiss buildings with furnished interiors.*

BENELUX

Zaandijk, 30 miles north of Amsterdam. *Windmills, cheese, wooden shoes, etc.*

Netherlands Open Air Museum, north of Arnhem. *70 old Dutch buildings.*

De Zeven Marken Open Air Museum, in Schoonoord.

Bokrijk Open Air Museum, between Hasselt and Genk, in Belgium. *Old Flemish buildings and culture in a native reserve.*

GREAT BRITAIN

Blist's Hill Open Air Museum, near Coalport. *Shows life from the early days of the Industrial Revolution.*

Beamish Open Air Museum, northwest of Durham. *Life in Northeast England in 1900.*

Welsh Folk Museum, at St. Fagan's near Cardiff. *Old buildings and craftspeople illustrate traditional Welsh ways.*

Irish Open Air Folk Museum, at Cultra near Belfast. *Traditional Irish lifestyles. Buildings from all over Ireland.*

IRELAND

Bunratty Folk Park, near Limerick. *Buildings from the Shannon area and artisans at work.*

Glencolumbkille Folk Museum, Donegal. *Thatched cottages show life from 1700-1900. A Gaelic-speaking cooperative runs the folk village and a traditional crafts industry.*

BULGARIA

Gabrovo Folk Museum, Gabrovo. *Old buildings and skilled craftspeople.*

SPAIN

Pueblo Espanol, Barcelona. *Buildings from all over Spain depict regional architecture, costumes and folk craft.*

This is not a complete listing and new ones are opening every year. Ask for more information at European tourist offices.

11
Coping Abroad

City Survival

Many Americans are overwhelmed by European big city shock. Struggling with the LA's, Chicagos and New Yorks of Europe is easier, if you follow three rules: 1. Get and use information; 2. Orient yourself; 3. Take advantage of the public transportation systems.

Information

Without information and planning, you'll be Mr. Magoo in a large city. Spend the last hour as you approach by train or bus reading and planning. Know what you want to see and put it in an efficient order. Your sightseeing strategy should cover the city systematically, one neighborhood at a time, keeping closed days and free days in mind.

No matter how well I know a town, my first stop is the tourist office. Any place with a tourist industry has an information service for visitors located on the central square, in the city hall building, at the train station or at the freeway entrance. You don't need the address—just look for its many signs. An often hectic but normally friendly and multi-lingual staff will equip you with a map, general sightseeing and tour info, reserve a room for you, sell you concert or play tickets and answer your questions. I always prepare a list of needs and questions so I'm well-organized and get the most out of my visit.

All big cities have English bookstores. Large bookstores and university bookstores have English sections. Most kiosks sell local guides in English.

Find a good map. The best and cheapest map is often the public transit map. Try to get one that shows bus lines, subway stops and major sights. Many hotels can give you a free city map.

If you find yourself in a town with no information and the tourist office is closed, a glance through a postcard rack will quickly show you the most interesting and scenic town sights.

Big European cities bubble with entertainment, festivities and night life. But it won't come to you. Without the right information and not speaking the local language, it's easy to be completely oblivious to a once-in-a-lifetime event erupting just across the bridge. In this case, a periodical entertainment guide is the ticket. Every big city has one, either in English like London's "What's On", or "This Week" in Oslo, or in the local language, but easy to decipher, like the "Pariscope".

Ask at your hotel and at the tourist office about entertainment. Read posters. Events are posted on city walls everywhere. They are in a foreign language but that really doesn't matter when it reads: Weinfest, Musica Folklorico, Juni 9, 21:00, Piazza Major, Entre Libre, and so on. Figure out the signs—or miss the party.

Orientation

Get the feel of the city. Once you get oriented, you're more at home in a city—it warms up and sightseeing is more enjoyable. Study the map to understand the city's layout. Relate the location of landmarks—your hotel, major sights, the river, main streets and station—to each other. Use any viewpoint like a church spire, tower or hilltop to look over the city. Retrace where you've been, see where you're going. Back on the ground you won't be in such constant need of your map.

Many cities have fast orientation bus tours like London's famous "Round London" tour. If you're feeling overwhelmed, these make a city less so by showing you the major sights and giving you a feel for the urban lay of the land.

Public Transportation

When you master a city's subway or bus system, you've got it by the tail. Europe's public transit systems are so good that many Europeans don't own a car. Trains, buses and subways are their wheels.

The buses and subways all work logically and are run by people who are happy to help the lost tourist locate himself. Anyone can decipher the code to cheap and easy urban transportation. Too many timid tourists never venture into the subways or on to the buses and end up spending needless money on taxis or needless time walking.

Paris and London have the most extensive, and the most needed, subway systems. Both cities are covered with subway maps and expert subway tutors. Paris even has maps that show you which way to go. Just push a button and the proper route lights up! Subways are speedy and comfortable, never slowed by traffic jams. And they actually feel safe. Buses are more scenic. Some cities have one scenic and tourist-oriented bus route—cruising you by the major sights, sometimes even with a recorded narration, for the cost of a ticket.

Make a point to get adequate transit information. Pick up a map. Find out about any specials—like packets of tickets sold at a discount (Paris) or tourist tickets allowing unlimited travel for a day or several days (London). These "go as you please" passes may seem expensive, but if you do any amount of running around, they can be a convenient money-saver. And remember, they are more than economical. With a transit pass you'll avoid the often long ticket lines.

Have a local person explain your ticket to you. A dollar and a half may seem expensive for the bus ride until you learn that your ticket is good for round-trip, two hours, or several transfers. Bus drivers and local people sitting around you will generally be sure you know when to get off. Just make sure they know where you want to go.

Taxis are often a reasonable option. In southern countries they are cheap and, while expensive for the lone budget traveler in the north, a group of three or four people can often travel cheaper by taxi than by buying three or four bus tickets. Don't be bullied by cabbie con-men (common only in the south). Insist on the meter, agree on a rate or know the going rate. Taxi drivers intimidate too many tourists. If I'm charged a ridiculous price for a ride, I put a reasonable sum on the seat and say goodbye. Please be careful though. Many tourists are sure the cabbie is taking the long way around or adding unfair extras when he's going as directly as the town allows.

Bus Tour Self-Defense

Most American tourists on an organized bus tour don't even consider using a guidebook. They pay a guide to show them around.

A typical big bus tour has a professional multi-lingual European guide and 40 to 50 people, mostly from the USA, on board. The tour company is probably very big, booking rooms by the thousand and often even owning the hotels it uses.

Most bus tours come with a ready-made circle of friends.

Typically, the bus is a luxurious, fairly new 50-seater, with a high quiet ride, comfy seats, air-conditioning and a toilet on board. The hotels will be fit for American standards—large, not too personal, offering mass-produced comfort, good plumbing, and double rooms. Most meals are included, generally in un-memorable hotel restaurants which can serve large groups.

As long as people on board don't think too much or try to deviate from the plan, things go smoothly, reliably and you really do see a lot of Europe. Note I said "see" rather than "experience". If you like the itinerary, have decent weather, have a likeable guide and enjoy the people on your bus, it's a good, easy and inexpensive way to go.

The independent-minded traveler can do very well on a big bus tour if he knows how to get the most out of it and doesn't allow himself to be taken advantage of. Keep in mind that many savvy travelers take escorted coach tours year after year only for the hotels, meals and transportation provided. Every day they do their own sightseeing, simply applying the skills of independent travel to the efficient, economical base an organized coach tour provides. You can take a tour and still go "on your own".

Having escorted several European coach tours and organized some of my own, I've learned that you must understand the guide and his position. Leading a tour is a demanding job with lots of responsibility, paperwork and miserable hours. Most guides treasure their time alone and, socially, keep their distance from the group. Each tourist has personal demands and a bus load of 50 can often amount to one big headache for the tour guide.

To the guide, the best group is one that lets him do the thinking, is happy to be herded around and enjoys being spoonfed Europe. The guide's base salary is normally low, but an experienced guide can do very well when that is supplemented by his percentage of the optional excursions, kickbacks from merchants that he patronizes and the trip-end tips from his busload. The best guide is a happy one. It's very important to be independent without alienating him. If the guide wants to, he can give you a lot of unrequired extras that will add greatly to your tour—but only if he wants to. Your objective, which requires some artistry, is to keep the guide on your side without letting him take advantage of you.

Most tours don't include the daily sightseeing programs. Each day one or two special excursions or evening activities, called "options", are offered for $15 to $20 apiece. Each person decides which "options" to take and pay for. Since budget tours are so competitive, the profit margin on their base price is very thin. The tour company and guide sell these options aggressively. The profit is theirs when 40 people pay $20 each for an evening bus tour of Rome.

Discriminate among options. Some are great; others are not worth the time or money. In general, the half-day city sightseeing tours are a good value. A local guide will usually show you his or her city much more thoroughly than you could do on your own given your time limitations. Illuminated night tours of Rome and Paris can be marvelous. I'd skip most other "illuminated" tours and "nights on the town". On a typical big bus tour evening, several bus tours come together for the "evening of local color". Two hundred tourists having a glass of local wine watching Flamenco dancing on stage in a huge room with buses lined up outside isn't really local. I'd rather save the money and take a cab or a bus downtown to just poke around. One summer night in Regensburg, while most of the tour waited to get off the bus, the great-great-great grandson of Johannes Kepler bought me a beer and we drank it under the stars, overlooking the Danube.

Your guide may pressure you into taking the "options". Stand firm. In spite of what you may be told, you are capable of doing plenty on your own. Maintain your independence. Get maps and tourist information from your hotel desk (or another hotel desk) or a tourist information office. Tour hotels are often located outside the city where they cost the tour company less and where they figure you are more likely to book the options just to get into town. Some tours promise to take you downtown if the hotel is outside the city limits. Ask the man or woman behind the desk how to get downtown on the public transportation. Taxis are always a possibility, and with three or four people sharing, they're not expensive.

Team up with others on your tour to explore on your own. No city is dead after the shops are closed. Go downtown and stroll.

Do your own research. Know what you want to see. Don't just sit back and count on your guide to give you the Europe you're looking for. The guide will be happy to feed you Europe—but it will be from his menu. This often distorts the importance of sights in order to fit the tour. For instance, many tours seem to make a big deal out of a statue in Lucerne called "the Dying Lion". Most tourists are impressed upon com-

Many who take an organized bus tour could have managed fine on their own.

mand. The guide declares that this mediocre-at-best sight is great, and that's how it's perceived. What makes it "great" for the guide is that, one, Lucerne (which doesn't have a lot of interesting sights) was given too much time in the itinerary, and it's easy for the bus to park and wait. "The Last Supper" by Leonardo da Vinci, on the other hand, is often passed over as bus tours skirt Milan. It's an inconvenient sight.

Many people make their European holiday one long shopping spree. The guide is happy to promote this. According to the merchants I talked to in Venice and Florence, 15% is the standard commission that a store gives a tour guide who brings in a busload of tourists. Don't necessarily reject your guide's shopping tips; just keep in mind that the prices you see often include that 15% kickback. Shop around and never swallow the line, "This is a special price available only to your tour, but you must buy now." The salesmen who prey on tour buses are smooth. They zero right in on the timid and gullible group member who has no idea what a good buy is. If you buy—buy carefully.

When you're traveling with a group, it's fun, as well as economical, to create a kitty for communal "niceties." If each person contributes $10, the "kitty-keeper" can augment dry Continental breakfasts with fresh fruit, provide snacks and drinks at rest stops for a fraction of the exorbitant prices you'll find in the freeway restaurants, get stamps for postcards so each person doesn't have to find the post office himself, and so on.

Remember that the best selling tours are the ones that promise you the most in the time you have available. No tour can give you more than twenty-four hours in a day or seven days in a week. What the "blitz" tour can do is give you more hours on the bus. Choose carefully among the itineraries available and don't assume more is better. In Europe, pace yourself. Be satisfied with what you can see comfortably.

The groups I have escorted on typical European big bus tours have been almost universally happy and satisfied with their vacations. They got the most out of their tour—and their tour didn't get the most out of them—because they exercised a measure of independence.

Guided Day Tours in Europe

Throughout your trip you'll encounter hour-long, half-day and all-day sightseeing excursions or tours. There are several kinds. Orientation tours are fast, inexpensive and superficial. Rarely do you even get out of the bus. Their only redeeming factor is that they serve to orient the traveler, though I suppose if you only had three hours in London, for example, the "Round London Tour" would be the best you could do to "see" the place.

Walking tours are my favorite. They are thorough since they focus on just a small part of a city. They are usually conducted by a well-trained local person who is sharing his town for the noble purpose of giving you an appreciation of the city's history, people and culture—not to make a lot of money. The walking tour is personal, inexpensive and a valuable education. I can't recall a bad one. Many local tourist offices organize the tours or provide a do-it-yourself walking tour leaflet. For the avid walking tourist consider a guidebook called "Turn Right at the Fountain".

Fancy coach tours, the kind that leave from the big international hotels, are expensive and of variable quality. Some are great. Others are boring and so depersonalized, sometimes to the point of multi-lingual taped messages, that you may find the Chinese soundtrack more interesting than the English. These tours can, however, be of value to the budget-minded do-it-yourselfer. Pick up the brochure, and you have a well-thought-out tour itinerary. Now do it on your own, taking local buses at your leisure, touring every sight for a fraction of the cost. A popular trend in Europe these days is a bus route that connects all the major sightseeing attractions. Tourists buy the one-day pass and make the circuit at their leisure.

The best guides are often those whose tours you can pick up at the specific sight. These guides usually really know their museum or castle or whatever.

Telephoning in Europe

The more I travel, the more I use the telephone. I call hotels and hostels to make or confirm reservations, tourist information offices to check my sightseeing plans, restaurants, train stations and local friends. In every country the phone can save you lots of time and money. Each country's phone system is different—but each one works—logically.

The key to figuring out a foreign phone is to approach it without comparing it to yours back home. It works for the locals and it can work for you. Many people flee in terror when a British phone starts its famous "rapid pipps". They go home telling tales of the impossibility of using England's phones.

Each country has phone booths with multi-lingual instructions. Study these before dialing. Operators generally speak English and are helpful. International codes, instructions and international assistance numbers are usually on the wall or in the front of the phone book. If I can't manage in a strange phone booth, I let a nearby local person help me out.

Area codes are a common source of phone booth frustration. They are usually listed by city on the wall or in the book. When calling long distance in Europe, you must dial the area code first. Area codes start with

a zero which is replaced with the country code if you're calling internationally. Local numbers vary in length from three to seven digits.

Once you've made the connection, the real challenge begins—communication. With no visual aids, getting the message across in a language
you don't speak requires some artistry.

Some key rules are: speak slowly and clearly, pronouncing every con-
sonant. Keep it very simple—don't clutter your message with anything
less than essential. Don't over-communicate—many things are already
understood and don't need to be said. (Those last six words didn't need to
be written.) Use international or carefully chosen English words. When
all else fails, let a local person on your end do the talking after you explain
to him, with visual help, the message.

Let me illustrate with a hypothetical telephone conversation. I'm
talking to a hotel receptionist in Barcelona from a phone booth in the train
station. I just arrived, read my guidebook's list of budget hotels, and I
like "Pedro's Hotel". Here's what happens.

Pedro answers, "Hotel Pedro, grabdaboodogalaysk."

I ask. "Hotel Pedro?" (Question marks are created melodically.)

He affirms, already a bit impatient, "Si, Hotel Pedro."

I ask, "Speak Eng-leesh?"

He says, "No, dees ees Spain." (Actually, he probably would speak
a little English or would say, "moment" and get someone who did. But
we'll make this particularly challenging, not only does he not speak English—he doesn't want to.)

Remembering not to over-communicate, you don't need to tell him
you're a tourist looking for a bed. Who else calls a hotel speaking in a
foreign language? Also, you can assume he's got a room available. If he's
full, he's very busy and he'd say "complete" or "no hotel" and hang up. If
he's still talking to you he's interested in your business. Now you must
communicate just a few things, like how many beds you need and who
you are.

I say, "OK, hotel." (OK is international for "Roger, prepare for the
next transmission.") "Two people"—he doesn't understand. I get fancy,
"Dos people"—he still doesn't get it. Internationalize, "Dos pehr-son"—
no comprende. "Dos Hombre"—nope. Digging deep into my bag of international linguistic tricks. I say "Dos Yankees." "OK!" he understands,
you want beds for two Americans. He says, "Si" and I say, "Very good"
or "Muy bueno."

Now I need to tell him who I am. If I say, "My name is Mr. Steves
and I'll be checking in in a few minutes," I'll lose him. I say, "My name

Ricardo (Ree KAR do)." In Italy, I say, "My name Luigi." Your name really doesn't matter, you're communicating just a password so you can identify yourself when you walk through the door. Say anything to be understood.

He says, "OK."

You repeat slowly, "Hotel, dos Yankees, Ricardo, coming pronto, OK?"

He says, "OK."

You say, "Gracias, ciao!"

Twenty minutes later you walk up to the reception desk and Pedro greets you with a robust, "Eh, Ricardo!"

E. T. (European Traveler) Phone Home

Most European countries have direct connections to the USA now and you can get through for as little as 50 cents. Rather than write post-cards, I just call in my "scenery's here, wish you were beautiful" messages.

You can call home in three ways—your hotel's phone, post office phone or from a public phone booth. Telephoning through your hotel's phone system is easy but very, very expensive. I only do this for a quick "Call me in Stockholm at this number" message. Post offices are much cheaper, with metered international phone booths. The person who sells stamps will plug you in, assign you a booth and help you with your long distance prefixes. You'll sit in your private booth, make the call and pay your bill before you leave. I normally just get a few coins, find a public phone booth, dial direct and keep it short and sweet.

While less common in the south, nearly all European countries have "dial direct to anywhere" phone booths. US calls cost two to four dollars per minute. There is no minimum. First get a pile of coins. Then find a phone booth. International booths usually have instructions in English in the first few pages of the phone book or on the wall. Put in a coin and dial: 1) international code, wait for tone; 2) country code; 3) area code; and 4) the seven digit number. If you want to call me from France, put in a franc (20 cents) dial 19-1-206-771-8303 and talk fast. Every country has its quirks—try pausing between codes if you're having trouble or dial the English-speaking international operator for help. Remember, it's six to nine hours earlier in the states.

I start with a small coin worth 10 to 25 cents to be sure I get the person I need or can say "I'm calling back in five minutes so wake him up." Then

I plug in the larger coins. I keep one last sign-off coin ready. When my time is done I pop it in and say goodby. Most booths have a digital meter showing you how much money you've put in which diminishes as you talk warning you when you're about to be cut off.

It's cheaper and easier (coin-free) if you have your friend call you back, dialing direct from the states. Give your local area code (without the first zero) and number. They can get the international and country code from their American operator.

Calling collect is sometimes more complicated and always more expensive. More and more phone booths take telephone company credit cards or strip cards that you buy locally at tobacco shops and freeway rest stops. In countries with no large coins, like Italy, these are much easier than the coin-op phones.

Counting and Other Bug-a-boos

Europeans do many things differently than we do. Simple as these things are, they can cause needless confusion.

Their numbers 7 and 1 are slightly different from ours. European "ones" have an upswing, "[1]." To make the seven more distinctive, add a cross, "[7]."

Europeans reverse the day and month in numbered dates. Therefore, Christmas is 25-12-88 instead of 12-25-88 as we would write it. Commas are decimal points and decimals commas, so a dollar and a half is 1,50 and there are 5.280 feet in a mile.

Floors are numbered differently. The bottom floor is called the ground floor. What we would call the second floor is a European's first floor. So if your room is on the second floor (European), bad news— you're on the third floor (American).

When counting with your fingers, start with your thumb. Making a "peace" sign to indicate the number 2 is an obscene gesture in some countries.

Finally, the 24-hour clock is used in any official timetable. This includes bus, train and tour schedules. Learn to use it quickly and easily. Everything is the same until 12:00 noon. Then, instead of starting over again at 1:00 p.m., the Europeans keep on going, 1300, 1400, 2400. Eighteen hundred is 6:00 p.m. (subtract 12 and add p.m.). Using the 24-hour clock, midnight is 2400.

Europeans measure temperatures in degrees Celsius. Zero degrees C = 32 degrees F (C × 9/5 + 32 = F) A memory aid: 28 C = 82 F.

European countries (except Great Britain) use kilometers instead of miles. A kilometer is six-tenths of a mile. To translate kilometers to miles quickly, I cut the km figure in half and add 10% of the original figure (e.g., 420 km = 210 + 42 = 252 miles).

Italian lire, with 1200 to the dollar, drive visiting Yankees crazy. To translate, just cover the last three digits with your finger and cut what's left by a little more than 10% (e.g., 18,000 lire for dinner equals about $16. Forty-five thousand lire for a hotel is about $40. Six-hundred twenty thousand lire for a taxi ride is about . . . oh oh . . .)

House numbers often have no correlation to what's across the street. While odd is normally on one side and even is on the other, #27 may be directly across from #2.

Polite Paris

Let's explore this "mean Parisian" problem.

The French, as a culture, are pouting. They used to be the "creme de la creme", the definition of high class. Their language was the "lingua franca"—everyone seemed to speak, or want to speak, French. There was a time when the Tsar of Russia and his family actually spoke better French than they did Russian. Those were glorious days for the French.

Today they are reeling, lashed by Levis, crushed by the Big Mac of American culture and depressed by a wet noodle economy. The French enjoy subtleties and sophistication. American culture sneers at these fine points. We're proud, brash, and in love with rugged individualism. We are a smiley face culture whose bank tellers are fined if they forget to say, "Have a nice day." The French don't find slap-on-the-back niceness terribly sincere. And too often, we judge a people on their "niceness".

Understand that most of us see Paris in the height of hot busy summer when the Parisians see their home town flooded with insensitive foreigners who butcher their language and put ketchup on their meat. That's tough to take smiling.

If you expect rude coldness in Paris, you'll find it. I don't believe Paris is made up of millions of mean people. If you look for warmth and friendliness, you'll find it. At worst, the Parisians I meet are people struggling to be human in an oppressively large city that used to rule the world culturally. It's tough adjusting to a lesser position on our planet's totem pole of aggressive cultures.

12
Attitude Adjustment— For a Better Trip

The Ugly American

Europe sees two kinds of travelers: those who view Europe through air-conditioned bus windows, socializing with their noisy American friends and those who are taking a vacation from America, immersing themselves in different cultures, experiencing different people and lifestyles, broadening their perspective.

Europeans will judge you as an individual, not based on your government. A Greek fisherman once told me, "I can't stand Reagan—but I like you." I have never been treated like the Ugly American. I've been proud to wear our flag on my lapel. My American-ness in Europe, if anything, has been an asset.

"Ugly Americans" do exist. Europeans recognize them and treat them accordingly, often souring their vacation. "Ugly Americanism" is a disease cured by a change in attitude. The best over-the-counter medicine is a mirror.

Here are the symptoms and the cure. The Ugly American:

• **Does not respect** or try to understand strange customs and cultural differences. Only a Hindu can understand the value of India's sacred cows. Only a devout Spanish Catholic can appreciate the true worth of his town's patron saint. No American has the right, as a visitor, to show disrespect for these customs.

• **Demands the niceties** of American life in Europe—orange juice and eggs (sunny-side up) for breakfast, long beds, English menus, punctuality in Italy or cold beer in England. He should remember that he is visiting a land that enjoys its Continental breakfasts, that doesn't grow six-foot four-inch men, that speaks a different language (with every right to do so), that lacks the "fast-food efficiency" of the USA and drinks beer

193

at room temperature. Live as a European for a few week's; it's cheaper, you'll make more friends and have a better trip.

• **Is ethnocentric,** traveling in packs, more or less invading each country while making no effort to communicate with "the natives". He talks at Europeans in a condescending manner. He finds satisfaction in flaunting his relative affluence and measures well-being by material consumption. He sees the world as a pyramid with the USA on top and everyone else trying to get there. It's important to remember the average European does not envy the average but richer American.

You can be a "Beautiful American"   Your fate as a tourist lies in your own hands. A graduate of the Back Door School of Touristic Beauty:

• **Maintains a moderate sense of humility,** not flashing signs of affluence, such as over-tipping or joking about the local money. His money does *not* talk.

• **Not only accepts, but seeks** out European styles of living. He forgets his discomfort if he's the only one in a group who feels it. The customer is not "always right" in Europe.

• **Is genuinely interested** in the people and cultures he visits. He wants to learn by trying things.

• **Makes an effort to bridge** that flimsy language barrier. Rudimentary communication in any language is fun and simple with a few basic words. While a debate over the economics of Marx on the train to Budapest (with a common vocabulary of twenty words) can be frustrating, he surprises himself at how well he communicates—by just breaking the ice and trying. Don't worry about making mistakes—communicate! (See chapter on *Hurdling the Language Barrier*).

• **Is positive and optimistic** in the extreme. Discipline yourself to focus on the good points of each country. Don't dwell on problems. With a militantly positive attitude, things go great.

I've been accepted as an American friend throughout Europe, Russia, the Middle East and North Africa. Coming as an American visitor, I've been hugged by Bulgarian workers on a Balkan mountain top; discussed Watergate and the Olympics over dinner in the home of a Greek family; explained to a young frustrated Irishman that California girls aren't really goddesses; and hiked through the Alps with a Swiss school teacher, learning German and teaching English.

There is no excuse for being an Ugly American. Go as a guest, act like one and you'll be treated like one. In travel too, you reap what you sow.

Be Open Minded

"Experiencing the bazaar away from home" is "travel" in six words. Yet so many leave home and are repulsed by what they see. Between the palaces, quaint folk dancers and museums you'll find a living civilization—grasping for the future while we tourists grope for its past.

Today's Europe is a complex, mixed bag of tricks. It can rudely slap you in the face if you aren't prepared to accept it with open eyes and an open mind. Many will find that Europe is getting crowded, tense, seedy and far from the everything-in-its-place fairy-tale land it once was.

If you're not mentally braced for some shocks, local trends can tinge your travels. Hans Christian Andersen's statue has internationally understood four-letter words scrawled across its base. Whites are now the minority in London, Amsterdam's sex shops and McDonald's share the same street lamp, in Paris a Sudanese sells ivory bracelets and crocodile purses on every corner. Many a Mediterranean hotel keeper would consider himself a disgrace to his sex if he didn't follow a single woman to her room. Drunk punk rockers do their best to repulse you as you climb to St. Patrick's grave in Ireland, and Greek ferryboats dump mountains of trash into their Aegean Sea. An eight-year-old boy in Denmark smokes a cigarette like he was born with it in his mouth and, in a Munich beerhall, an old drunk spits *"sieg heil's"* all over you. The Barcelona shoeshine man will overcharge you, and people everywhere put strange and wondrous things in their stomachs.

They eat next-to-nothing for breakfast, mud for coffee, mussels in Brussels and dinner's at ten in Spain. Beer is warm here, flat there, coffee isn't served with dinner and ice cubes can only be dreamed of. Roman cars stay in their lanes like rocks in an avalanche and beermaids with the big pretzels pull mustard packets from their cleavages.

Contemporary Europe is alive and groping. Today's problems will fill tomorrow's museums. Feel privileged to walk the vibrant streets of Europe as a sponge—not a judge. Absorb, accept, learn and be open-minded.

Don't Be a Creative Worrier

Travelers tend to be creative worriers. Many sit at home before their trip, all alone, just thinking of things to be stressed by. Travel problems are always there; you just notice them when they're yours. (Like people only notice the continual newspaper ads for tire sales when they're shopping for tires.) Every year there are air controller strikes, train strikes, terrorist attacks, new problems and old problems turning over new leaves.

Travel is ad-libbing, incurring and conquering surprise problems. Make an art out of taking the unexpected in stride. Relax, you're on the other side of the world, playing games in a Continental back yard. Be a good sport, enjoy the uncertainty, frolic in the pits, have fun.

Many of my readers' most exciting travel experiences are the result of a seemingly terrible mishap. The lost passport in Yugoslavia, fell and had to find a doctor in Ireland, the blowout in Portugal, and the moped accident on Corfu were all, at least in retrospect, great experiences. In each case a museum or two were missed but local friends were made.

Tackling problems with relish opens some exciting doors. Even the worst times rosy up into cherished memories after your journal is shelved and your trip is stored neatly in the slide carousel of your mind.

The KISS Rule—
"Keep it Simple, Stupid!"

Don't complicate your trip—simplify! Travelers get stressed and cluttered over the silliest things. Here are some common complexities that in their nibbly way can suffocate a happy holiday.

Registering your camera with customs before leaving home, spending several hours trying to phone home on a sunny day in the Alps, worrying about the correct answers to meaningless bureaucratic forms, making a long distance hotel reservation in a strange language and then trying to settle on what's served for breakfast, having a picnic in pants that worry about grass stains, sending away for Swedish hotel vouchers.

People can complicate their trips with video cameras, leadlined film bags, special tickets for free entry to all the sights they won't see in England, immersion heaters, instant coffee, 65 handi-wipes and a special calculator that figures the value of the franc out to the third decimal. They ask for a toilet in 17 words or more, steal "Sweet 'n Low" and plastic silverware off the plane and take notes on facts that don't matter.

Travel more like Gandhi—with simple clothes, open eyes and an uncluttered mind.

Be Militantly Humble—
Attila Had a Lousy Trip

As one of the world's elite who are rich and free enough, you are leaving home to experience a different culture. If things aren't to your liking—don't change the "things", change "your liking".

Legions of tourists tramp through Europe like they're at the zoo—throwing a crust to the monkey, asking the guy in lederhosen to yodel, begging the peacock to spread his tail again, and bellowing Italian arias out Florentine hotel windows. If a culture misperforms or doesn't perform they feel gypped. Easy-going travelers leave the Attila-type tourists mired in a swamp of complaints.

All summer long I'm pushing a bargain, often for groups. It's the hottest, toughest time of year and tourists and locals clash. Many tourists leave soured.

When I catch a Spanish merchant short-changing me, I correct the bill and smile, "Adios." A French hotel owner can blow up at me for no legitimate reason. Rather than return the fire I wait, smile and sheepishly ask again. Asking for action, innocently assertive, but never demanding "justice", I usually see the irate ranter come to his senses, forget the problem and work things out.

"Turn the other cheek" applies perfectly to those riding Europe's magic carousel. If you fight the slaps the ride is over. The militantly humble can spin forever.

Extroverts have more interesting journals. Make things happen. If you see four cute men on a bench, ask them to scoot over.

Swallow Pride, Ask Questions, Be Crazy

If you're too proud to ask questions and be crazy your trip may well be dignified—but dull. Make yourself an extrovert, even if you aren't one. Be a catalyst for adventure and excitement. Make things happen, or often they won't.

I'm not naturally a "wild and crazy kind of guy". But when I'm shy and quiet, things don't happen. I try to keep myself out of that rut when I'm traveling. It's not easy, but this special awareness can really pay off. Let me describe the same evening twice—first, with the mild and lazy me, and then with the wild and crazy me:

The traffic held me up, so by the time I got to that great historical building that I've always wanted to see, it was six minutes before closing. No one was allowed to enter. Disappointed, I walked over to a restaurant and couldn't make heads or tails out of the menu. I recognized "steak-frites" and settled for the typical meat patty and french fries. On the way home I looked into a very colorful local tavern, but tourists didn't seem welcome, so I walked on. In a park, I was making some noise, and a couple came out on their balcony and told me to be quiet. I went back to the room and did some washing.

That's not a night to be proud of. A better traveler's journal entry would read like this:

I was late and got to the museum only six minutes before closing. The guard said no one could go in now, but I begged, joked and pleaded with him. I had traveled all the way to see this place and I would be leaving early in the morning. I assured him that I'd be out by six o'clock, and he gave me a glorious six minutes in that building. You can do a lot in six minutes when you're excited. Across the street at a restaurant that the same guard recommended, I couldn't make heads or tails out of the menu. Inviting myself into the kitchen, I met the cooks and got a first-hand look at "what's cookin'". Now I could order an exciting local dish and know just what I was getting. It was delicious! On the way home I passed a classic local bar, and while it was dark and sort of uninviting to a foreigner, I stepped in and was met by the only guy in the place who spoke any English. He proudly befriended me and told me, in very broken English, of his salty past and his six kids, while treating me to his favorite local drink. I'll never forget that guy or that evening. Later, I was making noise in a park, and a middle-aged couple told me to shut up. I continued the conversation, and they eventually invited me up to their apartment. We joked around—not understanding a lot of what we were saying to each other—and they invited me to their summer cottage tomorrow. What a lucky break! There's no better way to learn about this country than to spend an afternoon with a local family. And to think that I could be back in my room doing the laundry!

Many tourists are actually afraid or too timid to ask a local person a question. The meek may inherit the earth but they make lousy tourists. Local sources are a wealth of information. People are happy to help a traveler. Hurdle the language barrier. Use a paper and pencil, charades or whatever it takes to be understood. Don't be afraid to butcher the language.

Ask questions—or be lost. Create adventure—or bring home a boring journal. Perceive friendliness and you'll find it.

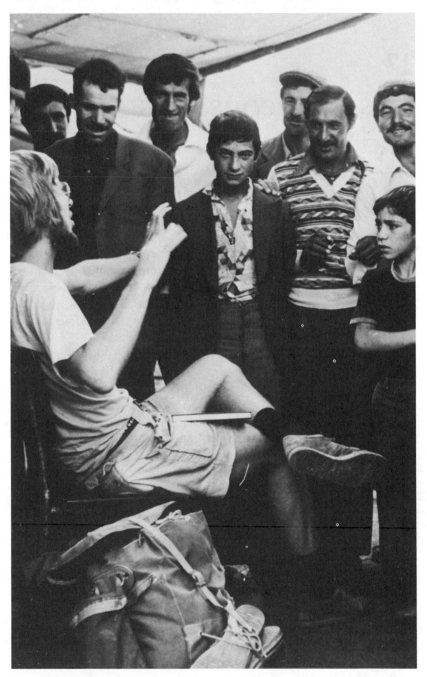

Put yourself where you become the oddity. If people stare—sing to them.

13
Miscellaneous Tips and Tricks

Political Unrest and Tourism

An awareness of current social and political problems is as vital to smart travel as a listing of top sights. Many popular tourist destinations are entertaining tourists with "sound and light" shows in the old town while quelling terrorist and separatist movements in the new. England, France, Italy and Spain are just a few countries in Europe alone that are dealing with serious or potentially serious internal threats.

Many people skip Rome because of the "Red Brigade" and avoid Spain in fear of the "militant Basques". This is unnecessary and unfortunate. Don't let these problems dictate your itinerary—they are no threat to you. Just be up on the news and exercise adequate discretion. (Don't sing Catholic songs in Ulster pubs.) I travel safely, enjoying a first-hand look at the demographic chaos that explains much of what fills the front pages of our newspapers.

Travel can broaden your perspective, enabling you to rise above the six o'clock news and see things as a citizen of our world. While monuments from the past are worthy of your sightseeing energy, travel plugs you directly into the present. There are many peoples fighting the same thrilling battles we Americans won 200 years ago, and while your globe may paint Turkey orange and Iran green, no political boundaries can divide racial, linguistic or religious groups that simply.

Look beyond the beaches and hotels in your tourist brochures for background on how your vacation target's cultural, racial and religious make-up is causing problems today or may bring grief tomorrow. With this foundation and awareness you can enjoy the nearly unavoidable opportunities to talk with involved locals about complex current situations.

If you're looking to "talk politics" you must be approachable—free from the American mob on the air-conditioned coach. Like it or not, people around the world look at "capitalist Americans" as the kingpins of a global game of Monopoly. Young, well-dressed people are most likely to speak (and want to speak) English. Universities are the perfect place to solve the world's problems in English with a liberal open-minded foreigner over a government-subsidized budget cafeteria lunch.

In Ireland "the troubles" are on everyone's mind. Hitchhiking through the Emerald Isle, I never knew if I'd get Lincoln or Douglas but I'd always get a stimulating debate. In the USSR and throughout Eastern Europe whenever I wanted some political or economic gossip I'd sit alone in a cafe. After a few minutes and some "James Bond eye-contact", I'd have company and a juicy chat with a resident dissident.

After your smashingly successful European adventure, you'll graduate to more distant cultural nooks and geographic crannies. If you mistakenly refer to a Persian or Iranian as Arabic you'll get a stern education on the distinction, and in Eastern Turkey you'll learn there is a fiercely nationalistic group of people called Kurds who won't rest until that orange and green on the globe is divided by a hunk of land called Kurdistan. In a Bangkok temple befriend a saffron-robed Buddhist monk and while you teach him some slang he'll explain to you what "guided democracy" means in Southeast Asia.

Understand a country's linguistic divisions. It's next to impossible to keep everyone in a multilingual country happy. Switzerland has four languages—German dominates. In Belgium there's tension between the Dutch and French-speaking regions. Like many French Canadians, Europe's linguistic underdogs will tell you their language receives equal treatment only on Corn Flakes boxes, and many are scheming up ways to correct the situation.

Terrorism and Tourism

It's refreshing to be so out of touch while traveling that you forget what day it is but even in areas that aren't "hot spots" it's always wise to be up on the news. American and English newspapers are available in most of the world as are English radio broadcasts. Other tourists can be valuable links with the outside world as well. Most importantly, the nearest American or British consulate can advise you on problems that merit concern. Take their advice seriously even if it means "scrubbing your mission".

Talking to people about local problems is fine. Dodging bullets isn't. I can't remember ever hearing a gun or a bomb in my travels. Many times, however, I've had the thrill of a first hand experience merely by talking with people who are personally involved.

Your tour memories can include lunch with a group of Palestinian college students, an evening walk through Moscow with a Russian dissident, listening to the "Voice of America" with curious Bulgarians in a Black Sea coast campground, and learning why the French aren't promoting the reunification of Germany. Or your travel memories can be built upon the blare of your tour guide's bullhorn in empty gothic cathedrals and polished palaces.

Terrorism in Europe has been a hot topic in recent years. Since things are quiet right now, I hesitate to even bring up the subject. But I'm concerned that people are planning their trips assuming terrorism is over. That's a dangerous approach. Terrorism has always been with us and I'm afraid it always will be a threat. It's in your best interest to plan your trip assuming there will be some terrorist activities between now and your departure date—probably in the city you're flying into. Travel understanding the risk of terrorism, and travel in a way that minimizes that tiny threat. Let me explain.

First of all, terrorism is nothing new. There have always been terrorists—Basque separatists, the Red Brigade in Italy, countless groups in France. What's new is that Americans are being targeted and our media and government reward the terrorists royally by bringing the dangers into our homes in living color and by treating it as a matter of foreign policy rather than as a common crime.

Terrorism makes headlines and sells ads. There's a great temptation for the media to sensationalize terrorism. It's tailor-made for TV—quick emotional and gruesome ninety-second spots. Consider the emotional style in which terrorism is covered.

Certainly we need to understand the terrorist threat and travel in a way that minimizes it, but it shouldn't keep us from traveling altogether. We have the option of either accepting the risks or settling for a lifetime of National Geographic specials.

Travel is accelerated living—it is risky. Terrorism is just another risk, much smaller than the ones tourists have always taken without a second thought. Let's look at it in cold unemotional statistics. In all of 1985, twenty-eight Americans, out of 25 million who traveled, were killed by terrorists. Sure, that's a risk, but Europeans wonder why we decided to stay home when, statistically, we're much more likely to be murdered on the streets of any big American city than we are in Europe—even at the height of terrorism. Plane crashes are also a greater risk. I know people die in planes, but I also know that, in the USA alone, over 30,000 planes take off and land safely every day. I take the risk. I remind myself that one plane crashes or is hijacked for every 978,000 flying hours, say a quick prayer and travel. Every year several hundred pedestrians are run down on the streets of Paris. But it's not a subject that's glamorous enough for headlines. By the way, according to our State Department, more Americans were killed by terrorists in 1974 than in 1985 but the media didn't pick up on it and we tourists didn't notice.

Okay, the risks are small. But it's smart to travel in ways which make the risks even more minuscule. Keep a low profile. While I wouldn't go wearing a Canadian flag, I wouldn't wave an American one either. Minimize your time in airports and in American business, diplomatic and military centers. Try to fly non-stop on a flight that does not originate in a "bad" area. Avoid places where American soldiers hang out.

Understand that loved ones may stand between you and your travel dreams. Family members beg and even bribe us not to go. Well-meaning loved ones often take TV news to heart and lack a broad understanding of

The graffiti you see is usually not anti-us or anti-them, it's pro-peace.

the world. If I'm in Europe and there's a train crash in Italy, my mother just assumes I was on it. I always call to let her know I survived. (It's easy, direct and cheap—two or three dollars a minute from most northern European phone booths. Fifteen seconds is all you need.) Assure those who'll worry about you that you'll call home every few days.

Anti-Americanism

Apart from the actual terrorist problem, many are concerned about anti-American sentiment in Europe. Anti-Americanism is nothing new. It rises and falls with the headlines. But people around the world understand the distance between citizens and their governments, and the vast majority of Europeans, regardless of how their banners insult Uncle Sam, will want to like you. These days, many foreigners strongly oppose what they see as callous American militarism or "imperialism". And "ugly Americans" will see an awful lot of "peace-niks" and naive wimps who lack a good healthy hatred of communism. But sensitive Americans, traveling to better understand the world, will be welcomed warmly in Europe.

Travel is a blunt teacher. It's taught me that there are values other than the Judeo-Christian, democratic and materialistic ones that America finds "God-given" and "self-evident", and that there are always local Nathan Hales willing to die for "strange notions". It's also taught me that some nationalities, like whales, are endangered species. For example, five languages become extinct every year. Why shouldn't people fight to keep their culture and their society alive?

When I think of terrorism, 1914 keeps coming to mind. History teaches us loud and clear the power of nationalism and the tragic consequences of ignorance. In 1914 a Serbian terrorist killed the Hapsburg archduke because his South Slavic people wanted a homeland. To teach the Serbs a lesson, the superpower of the day, Austria, declared war. Four years and many million deaths later, the Serbs got exactly what they wanted—the creation of "the union of the South Slavs"—Yugoslavia. In other words, there are certain problems that involve entire national groups that won't go away, can't be ignored, and one way or another, must be faced.

The world is rapidly growing smaller and every day new groups outside America try to wake us up—rightly or wrongly. They see us flooding the world with our strong values. They see Americans as only 6% of the world's population who control 40% of the world's wealth and all of its future. And they feel threatened.

That's why they lash out at the high-profile symbols of our powerful and wealthy society. The targets are predictable: airplanes, luxury cruise ships, elegant high-rise hotels, posh restaurants, military and diplomatic locations—and these have been the targets of nearly every terrorist incident to date. They don't bother the low-cost, local-style places where sensitive travelers stay. Terrorists don't bomb Pedro's pension—that's where they sleep.

The answer to the violence isn't to strike back, to kill Khadafy and sit back thinking everything will be fine. And the answer isn't to stay home in Fortress America either. The answer is to seek understanding—not to travel less, but to travel more and to travel sensitively, so we can better understand the world and the world can understand us.

Terrorism is caused by a lack of understanding. Travel teaches understanding. And since we're all trapped here on this little globe in a high-tech drama that will sooner or later force us to choose between living together or dying together, what could be better than to continue to travel and thereby help our world take a much-needed step toward global harmony?

Geriatric Globe-Trotting

More people than ever are hocking their rocking chairs and buying plane tickets. To many senior adventurers, travel is the fountain of youth. I spent six weeks last summer in Europe with a group of people who made any parent look young. They taught me many things, including the fact that it's never too late to have a happy childhood.

Special discounts in much of the world encourage many older travelers, but the trend I see lately is for energetic elders to leave their seniority at home and expect to get the same respect as budget travelers a third their age.

I spend a lot of time meeting with retired couples who were flying off to Europe with Eurailpasses, carry-on suitcases (9 by 22 by 14 inches) that convert into rucksacks, and $30 a day. Most of them are on their second or third retirement trip and each time as they walk out my door, I think, "Wow, I've got a good 40 or 45 years of travel ahead of me."

Gertrude and Vernon Johnson, both 68, are in Europe now. Nobody knows where. Before they left, I quizzed them on geriatric globe-trotting:

Was this your first major trip abroad? "Last year's trip was our first trip anywhere! We spent six weeks with a train pass and $60 a day for the both of us. Out of that $60, we spent $45 on room and board (going the Bed & Breakfast way) and $15 a day covered everything else, including miscellaneous transportation, admissions, little souvenirs and even a weekly phone call home to the kids."

Were you hesitant at first? "Yes, indeed. I remember climbing into that airplane thinking I might be making a big mistake. But when we got over there and tackled problem after problem successfully our confidence soared. Friendly people were always coming out of the woodwork to help us when we needed it."

What about theft and physical safety for a couple of retired kids like yourselves running around Europe independently? "As far as retired people go, we never felt like we were 'retired'. I never felt any different from anyone else and people accepted us as just two more travelers."

Gertrude added, "Later on, as we remembered our trip, we thought maybe people treated us 'gray-haired ruck-sackers' a little kinder because of our age. We never had a bit of a problem with theft or safety. Of course, we'd wear our moneybelts every day and choose our neighborhoods carefully. It's pretty obvious when you're getting into a bad neighborhood.

We never felt that Ugly American problem. People treated us very well—if anything, there was more help for seniors in public in Europe than we find at home."

Were the Europeans impressed by a retired couple with such an independent travel style? "I'd say they were. In fact, at one place, Rick, we were sitting down and. . . . " Then the table jolted as Gertrude grabbed Vernon's knee saying, "Nothin' doing! That's too good an anecdote." She plans, at 68, on becoming a travel writer some day—so we'll just have to wait for the rest of that story.

Do you speak any languages? "No, but we worked on a Berlitz French record for three weeks and that was helpful. We found that the best way to get along with the locals was to try to speak their language. They'd laugh a lot but they would bend over backwards to help us. They could usually speak enough English to help us out."

Did you have trouble finding rooms? "No. We traveled from May 1 to June 15 without reservations. Arthur Frommer's Guide was handy and, of course, we got help from the tourist offices and people in the towns. We had no problems. Decent budget hotels are close to the station, and that made setting up a snap.

"We always planned to arrive early. The overnight trains were ideal because they arrived first thing in the morning. We took our Frommer's

His fountain of youth is in Europe.

Guide into the tourist office, which was always in or near the station, and they'd call the hotel for us. A few times they charged extra for their service, but it was always very convenient. For older people, I would insist on arriving early in the day and having local money with you when you arrive."

Then Gertrude added, "People take mercy on you when you're in trouble."

How much did you pack? "Our luggage weighed a total of 25 pounds. Gertrude carried 11 and I packed 14. We just packed a few easy-wash and fast-dry clothes. Before our first trip you told us to bring nothing electrical. We didn't listen and we almost burnt down our hotel in Paris. (The table jolted again.) So this time we're bringing nothing electrical."

What was the most important lesson you learned on your first trip? "Pack even less. When you pack light you're younger—foot-loose and fancy free. And that's the way we like to be."

Travel Laundry

I met a woman in Italy who wore her tee-sheet frontwards, backwards, inside-out frontwards and inside-out backwards to delay the laundry day. A guy in Germany showed me his take-it-into-the-tub-with-you-and-make-waves method of washing his troublesome jeans. Some travelers just ignore their laundry needs and stink.

Anybody traveling anywhere has to wash clothes. My washer and dryer won't fit under the airplane seat so I've learned to do without. Here are some tips.

Choose a quick dry and no wrinkle travel wardrobe. Your self-service laundry kit should include a stretchable "travel clothesline". Stretch it over your bathtub or across the back of your car and you're on the road to dry clothes. Many hotel room sinks come *sans* stopper—to discourage in-room washing. Bring a universal sink stopper. That flat little rubber mat out-performs a sock in the drain. Pack a concentrated liquid detergent in a sturdy small plastic squeeze bottle wrapped in a zip-lock baggie (many squeeze bottles become ooze bottles after they leave home). A large plastic bag with a drawstring is handy for dirty laundry.

Hotel rooms around the world have multilingual "no washing clothes in the room" signs. This may be the most ignored rule on earth after "eat

your peas". Interpret this as an "I-have-lots-of-good-furniture-and-a-fine-carpet-in-this-room—and-I-don't-want-your-drippy-laundry-ruining-things" order. In other words, you can wash clothes very carefully, wring them nearly dry and hang them in an undestructive way.

Your laundry should keep a low profile. Don't hang it out the window. The maid doesn't notice my laundry. It's hanging quietly in the bathroom or shuffled among my dry clothes in the closet.

Some hotels will let your laundry join theirs on the lines out back or on the roof top. Many youth hostels have coin-op washer and dryers or heated drying rooms to ease your laundry hassles.

Wring your wet laundry as dry as possible. Rolling it in a towel can be helpful. Always separate the back and front of clothes to speed drying. Some travelers pack an inflatable hanger (especially handy in Venice or on a cruise where it doubles as a kind of laundry life-jacket). Smooth out your wet clothes, button shirts and set dollars to encourage wrinkle-free drying. If your shirt or dress dries wrinkled, hang it in a steamy bathroom. A piece of tape is a good ad lib lint brush. In very hot climates I wash my shirt several times a day, wring it and put it on wet. It's clean, refreshing and in fifteen minutes it's dry.

For a thorough washing ask your hotel to direct you to the nearest laundromat. Nearly every neighborhood has one. They can be expensive and terribly slow. Use the time to catch up on postcards and your journal or chat with the local crowd that's causing the delay. Laundromats throughout the world seem to give people the "gift of gab". Full service places are quicker—"just drop it off and come back in the afternoon"— but even more expensive. Still, every time I slip into a fresh pair of jeans I figure it was worth the hassle and expense.

Souvenir Strategy

Gift shopping is getting very expensive. I remember buying a cuckoo clock 10 years ago for $4. Now a hamburger, shake and fries at the Munich McDonald's will cost that much.

If your trip includes several countries, it's a good idea to save your souvenir shopping for the cheaper ones. You can buy an eight-foot dinghy in Portugal for the price of an eight-inch pewter Viking ship in Norway. I try to do my souvenir and gift shopping in countries like Turkey, Morocco, Spain, Portugal, Greece and Italy—in that order. By gift shopping in the cheaper countries my dollar goes two or three times as far.

In the interest of packing light, try to put off shopping until the end of the trip. Ideally, you should end your trip in a cheap country, do all of your shopping, then fly home. One summer, I had a 16-pound rucksack and nothing more until the last week of my trip when, in Spain and Morocco, I managed to accumulate two medieval chairs, two sets of bongos, a camel-hair coat, swords, a mace and a lace tablecloth.

If you do some shopping before the end of your trip, it's easy to lighten your load by sending packages home by surface mail. Postage is getting expensive. A box the size of a fruit crate costs about $25 slow boat but that's a small price to pay to substantially lighten your load. Books are much cheaper if they are sent separately. Customs regulations amount to 10 or 15 frustrating minutes filling out forms with the normally unhelpful postal clerk's semi-assistance. I've never had to pay any duty. Keep it simple (contents: clothing, carving, gifts, a poster, value $50). Post offices usually provide boxes and string or tape for about $1. Service is best from the Alps north and in France. Every box I've ever mailed has arrived— bruised and battered—but all there, within six weeks.

Large department stores often have a souvenir section with prices much less than what you would pay in the cute little tourist shops nearby. Shop around and remember that, in the southern countries, most things sold on the streets or in markets have soft prices. When appropriate, bargain like mad.

A Word of Caution to the Shopper

Shopping is an important part of the average person's trip, but be careful not to lose control. All too often, slick marketing and "cutesy", romantic window displays can succeed in shifting the entire focus of your trip toward things in the tourist shops. (It's a lucrative business. Many souvenir merchants in Italy work through the tourist season, then retire for the rest of the year.) This sort of tourist brainwashing can turn you into one of the hundreds of people who set out to see and experience Europe but find themselves wandering in a trance-like search for signs announcing "We accept Visa cards." I've seen half the members of a British Halls of Parliament guided tour skip out to survey an enticing display of plastic "bobbie" hats and Union Jack panties. Don't let your tour degenerate into a glorified shopping trip.

I think it's wise to restrict your shopping to stipulated time during the trip. Most people have an idea of what they want to buy in each country. Set aside a time to shop in each of these areas and stick to it. This way you avoid drifting through a day thinking only of souvenirs.

When you are shopping, ask yourself if your enthusiasm is merited. More often than not, you can pick up a very similar item of better quality and for a cheaper price at home. Unless you're a real romantic, the thrill of where you bought something fades long before the item's usefulness. My life has more room for a functional souvenir than for a useless symbol of a place I visited. Even thoughtful shoppers go overboard. I have several large boxes in my attic labeled "great souvenirs".

My favorite souvenirs are books (a great value all over Europe, and many impossible-to-find-in-the-US editions), local crafts (well explained in guidebooks, e.g., hand knit sweaters in Portugal or Ireland, glass in Sweden, lace in Belgium), strange stuffed animals (at flea markets), cassettes of music I experienced live, posters (one sturdy tube stores 8 or 10 posters safely), clothing and photographs I've taken.

14
The Whirlwind Tour— Europe's Best Two Month Trip

Let's assume that you have ten weeks, plenty of energy and a desire to see as much of Europe as is reasonable. It's most economical to fly to London and travel around Europe with a two-month Eurailpass. You'll spend two months on the Continent and use any remaining time in England, before or after you start your train pass. Budgeting for a $700 round trip ticket to London, a $650 two-month first-class Eurailpass and $35 a day, the entire trip will cost about $3,500. It can be done. Green, but thinking, budget travelers of all ages do it all the time—often for even less.

If I could relive my first two months in Europe this is the trip I'd take. I'll have to admit—this itinerary is exciting. Fasten your seatbelts, raise your dreams to their upright and locked position, and prepare to take off.

London is Europe's great entertainer, wonderfully historic and the best starting point for a European adventure. The English speak English but their accents will give you the sensation of understanding a foreign language. Every day will be busy and each night filled with a play and a pub. But the Continent beckons.

Paris is a quick overnight train ride away. Ascend the Eiffel Tower to survey a Paris studded with architectural gems and historical "one-of-a-kinds". You'll recognize the Notre Dame, Sacre Coeur, the Invalides and much more. A busy four days awaits you back on the ground—especially with a visit to Europe's greatest palace, Louis XIV's Versailles.

On the way to Spain, explore the dreamy chateaux of the Loire Valley. Take the train to Madrid where bullfights, shopping, the Prado museum and nearby Toledo fill your sunny days. Then sleep on the train to Lisbon, Portugal's friendly capital.

Lisbon can keep a visitor busy for days. Its highlight is the Alfama. This salty old sailor's quarter is a photographer's delight. You'll feel rich in Lisbon, where a taxi ride is cheaper than a London bus ticket.

Break the long train ride to the French Riviera with a day or two in Madrid and Barcelona. A rest on the beach is in order before diving into intense Italy.

Italy, steeped in history and art, is a bright spot in any itinerary. An entire trip could be spent climbing through the classical monuments of Rome, absorbing the art treasures of Florence and cruising the canals of colorful Venice. These cities, Pompeii, the leaning tower of Pisa, the hill towns of Tuscany and so much more just might kidnap your heart.

Your favorite place in Italy may be the Cinqueterre. Cinqueterre? Your friends will believe it only after they see your pictures. Unknown to most tourists and the ultimate Italian coastal paradise, you'll find pure Italy in these five sleepy traffic-free villages near Genoa.

Savor the old world elegance of Hapsburg Vienna for a few days and then enjoy Salzburg's unrivaled music festival. Classical music sounds so right in its birthplace.

Tour Mad King Ludwig's fairy tale castle at Neuschwanstein before visiting the Tyrolian town of Ruette and its two forgotten—yet unforgettable—hill-crowning, ruined castles. These are the Ehrenburg Ruins. (Keep them a secret.) Running along the overgrown ramparts, you'll find yourself under attack a thousand years ago.

Europe's most scenic train ride is across southern Switzerland from Chur to Martigny. Be careful, on a sunny day the Alpine beauty is intoxicating.

For the best of the Swiss Alps, establish a home base in the rugged Bernese Oberland, south of Interlaken. The traffic-free village of Gimmelwald in Lauterbrunnen Valley is everything an Alp-lover could possibly want.

Munich, the capital of Bavaria, has the world's greatest street singers. But they probably won't be good enough to keep you out of the beerhalls. Huge mugs of beer, bigger pretzels and even bigger beermaids! If you're smart, you'll skip the touristy Hofbrau House and patronize Mathauser's Beerhall for the best local crowd, a rowdy oom-pah band and thick German atmosphere.

The Romantic Road bus tour (included on the Eurailpass) is the best way to get from Munich to Frankfurt. The bus rolls through the heart of medieval Germany, stopping at Dinkelsbuhl and the always popular queen of quaint German towns, Rothenburg.

After the bus tour, take the Rhine cruise (also covered by Eurail) from Bingen to Koblenz to enjoy a parade of old castles. Sleep in Bacharach's classic castle youth hostel with a panoramic view of the Rhine for $4.

Finish your Continental experience with a visit to the capital of Scandinavia. Smorgasbords, Viking ships and healthy, smiling blondes are the memories you'll pack on the train south to Amsterdam.

After a few days in crazy Amsterdam and a bike ride through the countryside, sail for England. Any remaining time is happily spent in the English countryside.

This trip is just a sampler. There's plenty more to see but I can't imagine a better first two months in Europe. See Part Two: Back Doors for details.

The Whirlwind Tour Itinerary— Some Specifics

If I was planning my first European trip and wanted to see as much as I could comfortably in two months, (and I had the experience I now have to help me plan), this is the trip I'd take.

Days	Place	
?	London	Cheapest place in Europe to fly to, easiest place to adjust. From airport (easy RR or subway access from Gatwick or Heathrow) go to Victoria Station. Get ticket to Continent (Paris) at Sealink Office. Great tourist info office in Victoria. Round London orientation bus tour from park in front of station departs every half hour. Lay groundwork for your return to London (if ending trip there)—reserve good B&B, get tickets to the hottest play in town. Night train (N/T) and boat to Paris. 20:40-6:25.
4	Paris	Arrive in morning—easy to find budget one or two star hotel room. Don't look in famous tourist areas. Take subway to a place that sees no tourist. Use Paris subway. It's fast, easy and cheap. Walk—Latin Quarter, Notre Dame, Monument to victims of the Nazis (open 10:00), St. Chapelle, Pont Neuf, self-serve lunch in Samartaine Department store, Louvre (take intro tour), Tuileries Gardens, Champs Elysees to the Arc de Triomphe. Ask hotel to recommend small family-owned restaurant for dinner. Evening on Montmartre, soak in the spiritual waters of the Sacre Coeur, browse among the shops and artists of the Place du Tertre. Later be sure to enjoy Napoleon's Tomb, Les Invalides (Europe's best military museum), the Rodin Museum ("The Thinker" and "Kiss"), the great new Orsay Museum (Impressionism), Pompidou Modern Art Gallery, a jazz club and Latin Quarter nightlife. Pick up "Pariscope" for an entertainment guide and remember most museums are closed on Tuesdays. ST (side-trip) #1—Versailles, a must. Europe's grandest palace (take the RER train to end of line, Versailles R.G.) ST #2—Chartres, great gothic cathedral, lectures by Malcom Miller at 12:00 and 2:45.

2	**Loire Valley**	Make Tours your headquarters, Hotel de Orleans near station. Good all day bus tours of chateaux. If not really into chateaux, skip Loire. Consider ST from Paris to epitome of French chateaux, Chantilly. NT direct Paris to Madrid, 20:00-8:55.
3	**Madrid**	Upon arrival reserve train out. Reservations on long trains are required in Spain (& Norway) even with Eurail. Taxi to Puerta del Sol for central budget room. Try Plaza Santa Anna (#15, Hostel Fila, tel. 522-4056). Prado museum (Bosch, Goya, El Greco, Velesquez), Guernica and Royal Palace (Europe's most lavish interior) are musts. Bullfights on Sunday, and Thursday in summer, ask at hotel, buy tickets at arena. El Rastro (flea market), for great shopping on Sundays, ST #1— Toledo (whole city perfectly preserved, best at night, El Greco's home and masterpieces). ST #2—Segovia, Roman aqueduct. Skip Avila. NT, Lisbon, 23:30-9:45.
3	**Lisbon**	Europe's bargain basement capital, see "Back Door". ST—Sintra (ruined Moorish castle), Estoril (casino nightlife). NT—Madrid, 21:00-8:16.
1	**Madrid**	Upon arrival, reserve NT to Barcy (22:30-7:49). Spend the day here. Night travel is best in Iberia— long distances, boring, hot, crowded, slow day trains. Beds (couchettes) are cheap on these trains.
2	**Barcelona**	Picasso's house (excellent), relax, shop, Gothic Quarter, watch out for thieves. NT—19:49-7:00.
3	**Rhone Valley or French Riviera**	Avignon—(Papal Palace), Nimes and Arles (Roman ruins). Nice (where the jet set lies on rocks, great Chagall Museum), Riviera (crowded, expensive, stressful, good modern art).
2	**Cinqueterre**	Great villages, coastal Italy at its best, see "Back Door". Accommodations tight.
2	**Florence**	Europe's art capital, packed in the summer, worth the headaches.
2	**Hilltowns of Tuscany & Umbria**	See "Back Door". Most neglected and underrated side of Italy. Accommodations easy, leave Florence late, arrive Rome early.

4	**Rome**	Day #1—Classical: Colosseum, Forum, Capitol Hill (both museums), Pantheon. Evening—Piazza Navona (buy Tartufo ice cream). Day #2—Vatican, St. Peter's (catch English tour), climb the dome, Sistine (see *Mona Winks* or rent headphone guide) and Vatican Museum (great market 100 yards in front of museum entry, picnic). Buy small black and white photo essay book on Pieta in bookshops and take advantage of the Vatican's Post, much better than Italy's. Day #3—Ostia Antica, Ancient Rome's seaport (like Pompeii, but just a subway ride away from Rome). Bus from station to Tivoli, garden of fountains in front of station. Piazza Barberini, Bernini fountain, Capuchin crypt, thousands of bones in first church on Via Veneto, dinner on Campo di Fiori.) Explore Trastevere, old Rome alive today, good place for dinner. NT—Venice 0:20-7:10.
2	**Venice**	Best intro—slow boat (#1) down Canale Grande. Sit in front and soak it in. Sleep at Locanda Sturion (near Rialto, tel. 523-6243). Academy Gallery—best Venetian art. Doges Palace, St. Mark's and view from Campanile are musts, then wander, leave the tourists, get as lost as possible. Don't worry, you're on an island and you can't get off. NT 20:32-6:53.
2	**Vienna**	Paris' eastern rival. Grand capital of the mighty Hapsburg Empire. Lots of art history, and more old world charm and elegance than anywhere. Great tourist info under street in front of Opera. Sleep at Pension Columbia (tel. 426757). Consider ST to Budapest or Prague (Visas required but relatively easy in Vienna) NT—Switzerland.
6	**Switzerland**	Pray for sun. Most scenic train—Chur-Martigny (two non-Eurail segments). Best region—Bernese Oberland, south of Interlaken, see "Back Door". Best big city: Bern, lovely towns along Lake Geneva and in West (Murten and Friborg). Bodensee (Meersburg castle town, tropical isle of Mainau, Lindau—venice of North, Eurail covers boats on Swiss lakes).
2	**Tirol**	Reutte ("Back Door" castle ruins), Innsbruck, with its great Tyrolian folk museum.

2	Bavaria	Fussen, Mad Ludwig's castles, Wies Church (scaffolded 'til 1990), villages.
3	Munich	Cultural capital, great palace, museums, Mathauser's Beerhall (best, halfway between station and old town on right). Tourist info and room finding service in station (open late). Lay groundwork for departure on Romantic Road bus tour upon arrival (make reservation, if necessary, confirm place and time of departure). ST—Salzburg, only 90 minute train ride away.
1	Romantic Road	Bus tour, free with Eurailpass (see "Back Door".) Munich-Frankfurt 9:00-20:00 with stops in Dinkelsbuhl and Rothenburg. Eve on the Rhine. Consider overnight in Rothenburg.
3	Rhine/Mosel River Valleys	Cruise from Bacharach to St. Goar, best castles, free with trainpass, hike from St. Goar to Rheinfels castle, great castle youth hostel in Bacharach. Mosel Valley, including cruises, Cochem town and castle, Trier-Roman town, Berg Eltz—long walk, great castle. NT Koln or Frankfurt to Copenhagen, 22:39—9:09.
1	Copenhagen	Leave bags at station, evening at Tivoli just across the street. NT—23:21-7:46.
3	Stockholm	See "Back Door". Sleep on trains in Scandinavia—long, boring rides, capitals ten hours apart, hotels expensive. NT 23:10-7:55.
2	Oslo	See "Back Door". Consider ST to Bergen, very scenic train ride, 8 hours over, evening in Bergen, NT back, or "Norway in a Nutshell" program.
1	Copenhagen	NT—22:35-8:54 Another day in Copenhagen. NT-22:10-9:54. Train goes right on to Puttgarten ferry.
4	Amsterdam	Many great side trips. Consider headquarters in small town nearby (Delft or Haarlem) as promiscuous Amsterdam is getting awfully sleazy and seedy for many visiting Americans' tastes. Consider open-jaws flight into London, out of Amsterdam, to avoid surface return to London ($50 and 12 hours). NT—20:31-9:00.
?	London	Spend remaining time in English countryside, Bath, Cotswolds, Cambridge. Call to reconfirm flight home.

Sixty days scheduled on the Continent. Train times may be dated, use only as a rough guide. Eurailpass is good for two calendar months (e.g., the 15th through midnight on the 14th). If you validate when you leave Paris and expire (the Eurail pass, not you) upon arrival in Amsterdam you spend 52 days leaving 8 days of trainpass time to slow down or add options.

Books needed for this tour: *Let's Go: Europe, Mona Winks,* and *22 Days in Europe.*

Excursions you may want to add:

England—Oxford, Stratford, the Cotswold villages, Bath and more
Geneva, Chamonix, Aiguille du Midi, Hellbrunner, Aosta (Italy)
Berlin
Morocco and South Spain
South Italy or Greece
Finland or the Arctic
East Europe or the USSR
A day for showers and laundry
Visiting and resting
Travel days to avoid sleeping on the train
A free day here and there. Every itinerary needs some slack.

The Whirlwind Tour includes fourteen nights on the train, saving about $200 in hotel costs and fourteen days for doing more interesting things than sitting on a train.

People of all ages are letting their hair down in Europe.

Part Two:
Thirty-Eight Back Doors

Part Two: Thirty-Eight Back Doors

What Is A Back Door And How Can I Find One Of My Own? . 226

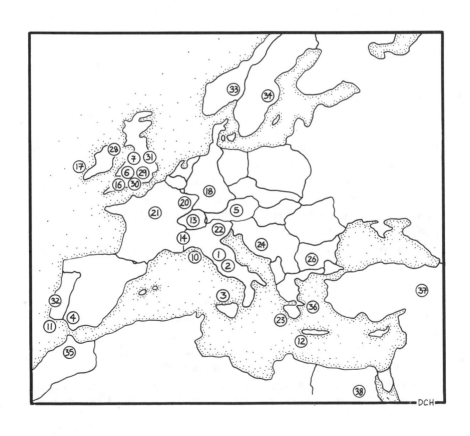

What Is A Back Door and How Can I Find One Of My Own?

The travel skills covered so far in this book enable you to open doors most travelers don't even know exist. The rest of the book is a chance for you and the travel bug to get intimate. It takes you by the hand through my favorite 38 European experiences. I hope you'll not only be able to enjoy these special places but that you'll use your travel skills to go further than museums and bus tours take you. Enjoy my back doors and, just as important, find your own.

Europe is a bubbling stew of many cultures. A back door is a steaming ladle—just one taste—of that stew. It could be an Alpine hike, an Andalusian hilltown, a French pastry, a ruined castle, a little Warsaw Pact country that everyone ignores, a new angle on a famous city, or a way to splice some beyond-Europe thrills into your trip. Each element of this delicious jumble of travel adventures is a cultural truth; taken together they create Europe.

I've organized these back doors into five groups. If you can travel with me as you read, you'll gain enough experience in each of these groupings to take the doors right off their hinges and discover your own similar, travel adventures.

The first clump is **undiscovered towns**. The big cities lead Europe's tourist parade. Discovered small towns actively promoting themselves follow right behind. But many of Europe's towns have, for various reasons, missed the modern parade. With no promotional budgets to attract us travelers, they are ignored as they quietly make their traditional way through just another century.

Then we'll explore the **natural nooks and undeveloped crannies**. These are rare opportunities to enjoy Europe's sun, beaches, mountains, and natural wonders without the glitz. Europeans are the original romantics. While they love nature, they have an impressive knack for enjoying

226

themselves in hellish crowds. There are quiet alternatives. It's possible to find forgotten stone circles, desolate castles, peaceful bike rides, and snippets of the Riviera that are not geared up to make money from visitors. While the famous fortresses and beaches grow richer and more congested, back door travelers enjoy these stars from a different angle.

Next we'll travel through a series of **misunderstood regions and countries**. Some areas lie in the shadow of a touristic superstar, like the rarely visited sights near Venice. War and other international problems have left a legacy of fascinating sights, such as the remains of Nazi Europe. Because of politics and history, Eastern Europe is busy with travelers from Angola, China, Cuba and the Socialist world while relatively few Westerners venture in. And some "countries" are forgotten entirely like the dozen or so that combined to make Yugoslavia after World War I.

There are plenty of well discovered **front door cities that need back door angles** so the visitor can get far enough away from the tourist commotion and staged culture to feel the city's real pulse. Even London has a warm underbelly where the visitor can actually hear a heart which has been beating for 2000 years.

And finally, for maximum thrills per mile, minute and dollar, it's important to look **Beyond Europe**. Europe is exciting, but a dip into Morocco, Egypt, or Turkey is easy—and rewarding beyond your wildest travel dreams.

The back doors comprise a Whitman's sampler of travel thrills. While I have listed my favorite accommodations in the chapters or, as noted, in Appendix V, these chapters are written to give you the flavor of the place. An appropriate directory-type guidebook (like our *22-Days* series or the *Let's Go* series) will give you the nitty-gritty necessary to splice your chosen highlights into a smooth trip.

Many of these places are subtle and won't hit you with their cultural razzle dazzle. The sensitive traveler will make his own fun, learning from the experiences described in each chapter. I should warn you that certain places that I really rave about will suffer from back door congestion. At least, from my experience, back door readers are pleasant people to share Europe with.

The style of travel that's developed by internalizing the countless little travel moments that I've enjoyed and compiled here lets you experience Europe with the same eternal enthusiasm that has kept me on this wonderful path for so long. And I can hardly stop dreaming about all the travel fun that awaits me in my next European adventure. I hope you'll love Europe, as I do—through the back door.

Undiscovered Towns

1: The Hilltowns of Tuscany and Umbria

Too many people connect Rome and Florence with a straight line. If you break out of the Venice-Florence-Rome syndrome, you'll find the little Italy that the splash of Venice, the finesse of Florence and the grandeur of Rome were built upon.

The hilltowns of Tuscany and Umbria hold their crumbling heads proudly above the noisy flood of the twentieth century and offer a peaceful taste of what eludes so many tourists. I find the essence of Italy in this small town package, sitting on a timeless rampart high above the traffic and trains, hearing only children in the market and the rustling of the wind aging the already aged red tile patchwork that surrounds me.

Hilltowns, like Greek islands, come in two basic varieties—touristy and untouristy. There are six or eight great touristed towns and countless ignored communities casually doing time and drinking their wine. Take time to see some of each.

Historic San Gimignano bristles with towers and bustles with tourists. Tuscany's best preserved medieval skyline is a thrilling silhouette from a distance, and it gets better as you approach. Night time's the right time to conquer the castle. Sit on its summit and imagine the battles these old cobbles and floodlit towers have endured. Even with crowds, San Gimignano is a must.

Siena, unlike its rival, Florence, is a city to be seen as a whole rather than as a collection of sights. Climb to the dizzy top of the bell tower and reign over urban harmony at its best. As you tour Siena, compare and contrast it to Florence, which was the big gun but didn't call all the shots.

Assisi, a worthy hometown of St. Francis, is battling a commercial cancer of tourist clutter. A quiet hour in the awesome Basilica of St. Fran-

228

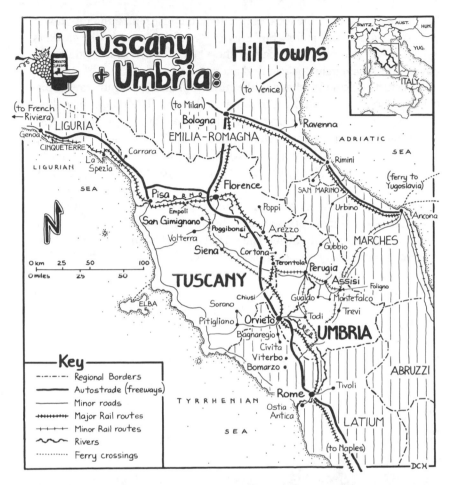

Tuscany & Umbria: Hill Towns

Key
- ---·--- Regional Borders
- ———— Autostrade (freeways)
- ———— Minor roads
- +++++++ Major Rail routes
- +++++ Minor Rail routes
- ~~~~ Rivers
- ·········· Ferry crossings

cis, some appropriate reading (there's a great bookstore next door), and a meditative stroll through the back streets can still put you in a properly Franciscan frame of mind to dissolve the tour buses and melt into the magic of Assisi.

Orvieto is the typical tourist's token hilltown. It's a nice place with a fine cathedral but, in Tuscany or Umbria, nice isn't saying much. Enjoy Orvieto wine in Rome and its impressive hill-capping profile from the train or *autostrada,* but your hilltown energy is better spent elsewhere.

Any guide book lists these and several other popular hilltowns. But if you want to dance at noon with a toothless lady while the pizza cooks, press a good luck coin into the moldy ceiling of an Etruscan wine cellar, be introduced to a less than mediocre altarpiece as proudly as if it were a

Michelangelo or have the local cop unlock the last remaining city tower and escort you to the top for a bird's-eye view of the town and the gawkers who just emptied out of the barber shop below, stow your guide book, buy the best local map you can find and explore.

Perfect back door villages, like hidden pharaohs' tombs, await discovery. Photographers delight in Italian hilltowns. Their pictorial collections are far and away the best information source (I used *Italian Hilltowns* by Norman Carver). Study these, circling the most intriguing towns on your map. Debrief those who have studied in Italy. Ask locals for their favorites. Most importantly, follow your wanderlust blindly. Find a frog and kiss it.

Gubbio, Volterra, Cortona and Arezzo are discovered but rarely visited. Civita di Bagnoregio (see next chapter), Sorano, Pitigliano, Trevi, and Poppi are virgin hill towns. The difference between "discovered" and "virgin", touristically speaking, is that "discovered" knows what tourism is and how to use it economically. "Virgin" is simply pleased that you dropped in. "Virgin" doesn't want to, or know how to, take advantage of you. It wants only to enjoy, and to be enjoyed.

Hilltowns are a vital slice of the Italian pizza—thin crust with a thick gooey culture. Leave the train lines. Take the bus, hitch, or rent a car for a few days. Don't just chase down my favorites or your guide book's

San Marino, just another magic Italian hilltown

recommendations. Be fanatic, find the treasure—the social slumber of Umbria and the human texture of Tuscany.

2: Civita di Bagnoregio

People who've been there just say "Civita," (pron: CHIV-ee-tah) with a special warmth and love. I hesitate to promote this precious chip of Italy that has somehow escaped the ravages of modernity. But it's so perfect—I have to share it. Please approach it with the same respect and sensitivity you would a dying relative, because—in a sense—that's Civita.

Eighty people live here. There's no car traffic, only a man with a donkey who works all day ferrying the town's goods across the long umbilical bridge that connects the town with a small distant parking lot and the rest of Italy. Rome is just 60 miles to the south, but may as well be on the other side of the moon.

Civita's sights are subtle and many tourists wouldn't know what to do in a town without tourism. No English menus, lists of attractions, orientation tours or museum hours. Just Italy.

Sit in the piazza. Smile and nod at each local who passes by. It's a social jigsaw puzzle and each person fits. Look up at the old woman hanging out the window. She's in charge of gossip and knows all. A tiny hunchback lady is everyone's daughter, and 2500 year-old pillars from an ancient buried Etruscan temple stick up like bar stools on the square. The bar is gone as are most of the young people, lured away by the dazzle of today to grab their place in Italy's cosmopolitan parade.

Anna introduces you to a baby donkey as if it were her child. Anna is the keeper of the keys to the church. Civita's church is the heartbeat and pride of the village. Festivals and processions start here, visitors are taken here and the town's past is honored here. Enjoy paintings by students of famous artists, relics of the hometown-boy-made-saint Bonaventura, a dried floral decoration spread across the floor, and a cool quiet sit in a pew.

Civita is a man-gripped pinnacle in a vast canyon. Erosion and the wind rule the valley and gnarled trees are time's eternal whipping boys. A lady, ignoring her eye-boggling view, took me into an ancient Etruscan cave to see her olive press. Just around the corner from the church is Domenica's cantina. Sit on a stump, enjoy a glass of her family wine. Climb into her ancient cellar. Tap the kegs to measure their fullness. Even on a blistering day, those caves are always cool and an endless supply of

The perfect hilltown, Civita di Bagnoregio

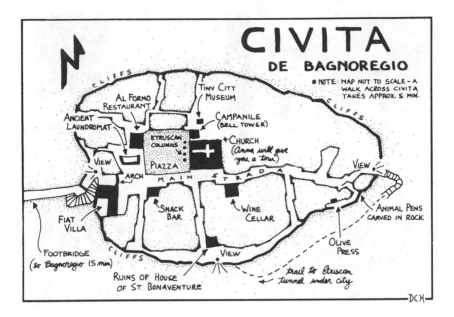

local Civita wine is kept chilled awaiting future fun.

Civita has one restaurant. You can see its green door and handmade sign from the piazza. "Al Forno" (the oven) never had a menu. You eat what's cooking. Mom and Pop slice and quarter happily through the day. I could write quite a story about the spaghetti, salad and wine I've had, cuddled by Civita on the Al Forno patio.

Civita is an artist's dream, a town in the nude. Each lane and footpath holds a surprise. Horses pose, the warm stone walls glow, each stairway is dessert to a sketch pad or camera and the grand moat does its best to keep things that way. It's changing, however, as the aggressive present eats at the last strongholds of the past. Civita will be great for years but never as great as today.

You won't find Civita on any map. Take the train to Orvieto and catch a bus to Bagnoregio. From Bagnoregio you walk to Civita.

Civita has no hotel. Stay in Bagnoregio in a local *camera,* or bed and breakfast. Bagnoregio's only hotel is a 20-minute walk out of town. Ask for Boschetto di Angelino Catarcia. Angelino is a character who runs through life like a hyper child in a wading pool. He doesn't speak English; he doesn't need to. Have an English-speaking Italian call him for you— tel. 0761/92369, address: Strada Monterado, Bagnoregio, Viterbo, Italy. His family is wonderful and if you so desire, he'll get the boys together and take you deep into the gooey, fragrant bowels of "La Cantina". Music

Travelers in search of back-street treats

and vino kill the language barrier in Angelino's wine cellar where he will teach you his theme song, "Trinka, Trinka, Trinka". Warning: descend at your own risk, there are no rules unless female participants set them. If you are lucky enough to eat dinner at Angelino's (bunny is the house specialty), ask to try the (sweet) dessert wine. Everything at Angelino's is deliciously homegrown—figs, fruit, wine, rabbit, pasta. This is the Italy you always dreamed of finding.

3: Palermo, Sicily's Urban Carnival

The European tourist boom is just a distant hum in Sicily. It took me seven trips to get down past Italy's "boot", but I finally made it. The Sicilians (along with the Irish) are the warmest and friendliest Europeans I've met.

It's well worth the overnight train ride south from Rome or Naples to escape into this rich culture living peacefully oblivious to the touristic bustle that takes such a toll on Venice, Florence and Rome.

Eating and sleeping in high style at low prices is easy. From the Palermo train station, walk straight down Via Roma for your choice of many hotels. A reservation is unnecessary. My favorite hotel is the Hotel Moderno, Via Roma 276. My double (room 23) cost $20, was large, airy and included a rooftop patio with a view. The bathroom was bigger than some entire hotel bedrooms I've stayed in. The management was friendly and eager to share lots of tourist information.

Eating in Palermo is a real treat. Colorful street markets make shopping for picnics a joy. Pizzeria Bellini on Piazza Bellini, near the central "four corners" of Palermo, was my dinnertime hangout. Over the course of several meals, I ate my way through their menu, discovering for myself why Italians like to eat. Their fanciest pizza, "Quatro Gusti con Fungi", cost three dollars and is permanently etched on my palate.

One reason Palermo lacks tourist crowds is that it has very few tourist sights as such. It does have a way of life that, in its own way, offers the tourist more than any monument or museum ever could. Don't tour Palermo—live in it.

Thriving marketplaces abound. If you've ever wondered what it would be like to be a celebrity, go on a photo-safari through the urban jungles of Palermo. The warmth and excitement will give you smile wrinkles. Scores of merchants, housewives and children compete for your attention. Cries of "Photo?" come from all corners as you venture down busy alleys. Morning markets and eternal hawkers can be found in nearly any neighborhood.

Visit a vertical neighborhood. Small apartments stack high above the side streets. If you stop to chat, six floors of balconies will fill up, each with its own waving family. I found a wobbly stack of tenements facing one another, a faded rainbow with lots of laundry and people hanging out. One wave worked wonders. The whole place became like a giant, teeming pet store full of little creatures dying to be petted. Walking around, craning my neck upward, I felt like a victorious politician among hordes of supporters. They called out for pictures and wouldn't let me go until I had filmed each window and balcony full of people: mothers holding up babies, sisters posed arm in arm, a wild pregnant woman standing on a fruit crate, holding her bulging stomach, and an old, wrinkled woman, cheery in a paint-starved window frame. I was showered with scraps of paper, each with an address on it. A contagious energy filled the air—and saying goodbye hurt.

For a strange journey through an eerie cellar of the dead, visit the Catacombs of the Capuchin Monks. This dark and dreary basement has 8000 clothed and very dead ex-monks hanging on its walls. A strange but meaningful habit.

A balcony of friends, Palermo, Sicily

For a more typical tourist attraction and a respite from the skelter and heat of Palermo, bus inland to the soothing mountain town of Monreale. Inside Monreale's Benedictine church, you'll find a collection of mosaics that rival Ravenna's. Dozens of Bible scenes, in mosaic, cover the walls of this church. Since I was wearing shorts, I was given a blanket to wear as a skirt. With my hairy, unholy legs covered, I worked my way, scene by scene, through the Bible.

Palermo has no "must-see" museum and nothing to compete with the tipsy Pisa Tower or Big Ben. Palermo lets you become a temporary Sicilian, and that's a great reason to visit.

4: South Spain's Pueblos Blancos— Andalusia's Route of the White Villages

When tourists head south from Madrid, it's generally with Granada, Cordoba, Sevilla or the Costa del Sol in mind. These places have lots to offer—as big cities. The Costa del Sol, in my mind, is a concrete nightmare, worthwhile only as a bad example. The most Spanish thing about the south coast is the sunshine—but that's everywhere. For something different and a bit more authentic, try exploring the interior of Andalusia on the "route of the white villages".

Make this an exercise in going where no tourist has gone before. If you don't know where you are—you've arrived. I spent several days driving rather aimlessly from town to village on the back roads of Southern Spain enjoying a wonderfully untouched Spanish culture. All you need is time, a car and a willingness to follow your nose, winning some and losing some. I found some great towns and learned some valuable lessons.

Estepa was my Spanish treasure chest. Below a hill crowned with a castle and a convent, spread a freshly washed and very happy town that fit my dreams of Southern Spain.

Except for the busy truck route that skirts the town, peace abounds here. Situated halfway between Cordoba and Malaga, but light years away from either, Estepa hugs a small hill. The hill is crowned by the convent of Santa Clara, worth five stars in any guidebook but found in none. Enjoy the territorial view from the summit, then step into the quiet, spiritual perfection of the church. (If it's locked find someone with a key.) Just sit in the chapel all alone and feel the beauty soak through your body.

The evening is prime time in Estepa. The promenade begins as

everyone gravitates to the central square. Estepa's spotless streets are shined nightly by the feet of ice cream-licking strollers. The whole town strolls—it's like "cruising" without cars. Buy an "ice cream bocadillo" and follow suit. There's a great barber—a real artist—located right on the square. Estepa's only drawback is its lack of decent accommodations. I found only one place, and its location on the truck route made sleeping impossible. I ended up sleeping under the stars on the porch of Santa Clara's convent. It was a beautiful night and the police agreed with my taste in impromptu campgrounds.

Don't miss Ronda. Straddling an impressive gorge and with lots of history spicing its cobbled streets, it's a joy. Nearby are the Pileta Caves. Follow the signs past groves of cork trees to the desolate parking lot. A sign says (in four languages) to "call". That means scream down into the valley, and the old man will mosey up, unlock the caves, light the lanterns and take you on a memorable, hour-long, half-mile journey through the caves. He is a master at hurdling the language barrier, and you'll get a good look at countless natural formations as well as paintings done by prehistoric "hombres" 25,000 years ago. (That's five times as old as the oldest Egyptian pyramid.) The famous caves at Altamira are closed, so as far as I know, these are the best Neolithic paintings you'll see.

From Ronda, the road to Arcos de la Frontera is a charm bracelet of whitewashed villages. You'll see Zahara (climb to its ruined castle for a

Estepa, south Spain

view that would knock Sancho Panza off his ass) and Grazalema (ideal for a picnic on its grand canyon balcony). Other memorable towns within easy striking distance are Puente-Genil and Aguilar de la Frontera with a pleasant square, outdoor dancing and people who are fascinated by tourists with hairy legs. My other favorites were Manzanares, Caratraca, hill-capping Tepa,(where people burst into hysterics when you take their picture) and the inviting village of Setenil, northwest of Ronda.

Arcos de la Frontera is a more substantial town with a labyrinthian old quarter overlooking a vast plain. (Driving here is easy if you can thread a needle when you're giggling.) This is a great overnight stop. Be sure to climb the bell towers of both churches (possibly with a picnic). You'll walk right through the keeper of the tower's living room, get the key, leave a tip, and climb to the top. Cover your ears when the giant old clappers whip into action.

Good information on small-town Andalusia is rare. There's almost nothing written on the "Pueblos Blancos". This area is unvisited, so there aren't a lot of facilities for tourists. The Michelin Guide, which is usually invaluable, skips the Andalusian countryside. Get the best map you can find, ask the people you meet for touring suggestions, and pick up the excellent "Route of the White Towns" booklet in Sevilla or at any major Spanish tourist office. The farther from the tourist trade you get, the more difficult finding a hotel becomes (See Appendix V for hotel listings).

This Andalusian adventure is best by car. The roads are fine, traffic is light. Car rental is inexpensive and public transportation is pretty bad. Gas, while expensive, is easy to get and the people are friendly. Hit the back roads and you'll find that perfect village.

5: Hallstatt, in Austria's Commune-with-Nature Lakes District

Austrians are experts at good living. They have the shortest work week in Europe (average 32 hours) and they focus their free time on the fine points of life: music, a stroll, a pastry, and a good cup of coffee. The uniquely Austrian *gemutlichkeit* (as difficult a word to translate as it is to pronounce, meaning something like a warm, cozy, friendly, focus-on-the-moment feeling) is especially evident in the Salzkammergut Lakes District, where Austrians go to relax.

Far from the urban rat race, though just 60 minutes from Salzburg, this is the perfect place for a weekend cottage, where locals commune

Hallstatt in Austria's Salzkammergut lakes district.

with nature, Austrian style. The Salzkammergut is a lushly forested playground. Trains, buses or boats lead the traveler through gentle mountains and shy lakes, winding from relaxed village to relaxed village.

The Salzkammergut's pride and joy is the town of Hallstatt. The minute it came into view I knew Hallstatt was my Alpine Oz. It's just the right size, (1200 people), and wonderfully remote—almost traffic-free. A tiny ferry takes you from the nearest train station across the fjord-like lake to Hallstatt, dropping you off on the storybook town square.

Hallstatt is tiny—bullied onto a ledge by a selfish mountain and a lovely lake. The central square is surrounded by ivy-covered guest houses and cobbled lanes. The town can be toured on foot in about ten minutes.

While there was no shortage of pleasant $10 per person zimmers, I splurged, spending $30 for a double with breakfast in the Gasthof Simony (tel 06134/231). This hotel separates the square from the lake, with balconies overlooking each. My room was rustic with a hardwood floor, rag rugs, an antique wooden bed with a free-standing closet to match, grandmother lamps and a lakeside flower-decked balcony. The view almost changed my itinerary.

Note: In August tourist crowds trample most of Hallstatt's charm.

Just three thousand years ago this town was the salt mining capital of Europe. An economic and cultural boom put this area on the map way back in Flintstone times. In fact, an entire 1000-year era is called "The Hallstatt Period".

Today you can tour the world's first salt mine, located a thrilling funicular ride above downtown Hallstatt. A humble museum next to the helpful tourist office shows off Hallstatt's ancient past.

The town outgrew its little ledge, and many of its buildings climb the mountainside, with street level on one side being three floors above street level on the other. The church cemetery in town is so old that the bones of the long dead have had to make way for those of the newly dead. The result is a fascinating chapel of decorated bones.

Passing time in and around Hallstatt is easy. The little tourist office will recommend a hike—the 9000-foot Mt. Dachstein looms overhead. Or, maybe a peaceful cruise in a rented canoe is more your style. Most people go to Hallstatt simply to relax, eat, shop, and stroll. To best cloak yourself in the cobblestones, flowers, and the rich blues and greens of Austria's "gemutlich" Salzkammergut Lakes District, visit Hallstatt.

6: The Cotswold Villages— Inventors of Quaint

Travel writers have to be careful not to overuse the word "quaint". I save my use of that word for England's Cotswold villages. These sleepy towns are the epitome of quaint. They're almost edible!

A typical Cotswold village

Cuddled by woodlands, pastures, and grazing sheep ("Cotswold" is Saxon for "the hills of the sheep's coats") and cradled by the rolling Cotswold Hills, these villages are just two hours by train west of London. The 50 by 25 mile region is officially titled an "area of outstanding natural beauty". An understatement.

This is an area of outstanding natural beauty, historic importance, touristic interest and people whose warm smiles will take the bite out of the Gloucestershire wind.

Stow-on-the-Wold is my favorite homebase town. Located in the heart of the region, any Cotswold site is within easy striking distance of Stow. Eight roads converge on Stow but none interrupt the peacefulness of its main square. The town has no real sights other than itself. There are several good pubs, plenty of B & Bs (see Appendix V), some pleasant shops and a handy little walking tour brochure called "Town Trail".

To the south, just 20 miles along what the Romans called "Foss Way" (and we call A-429) is Cirencester. Two thousand years ago, five Roman roads met here and the town, then called Corinium, was the second biggest city in Roman Britain (after Londinium). As you wander through the town's fine Roman museum and perhaps explore the nearby Chadworth Roman Villa with its impressive ancient mosaics, you'll know why they say, "if you scratch Gloucestershire, you'll find Rome."

Meanwhile, in the crafts center just down the street, craftspeople are weaving, baking and potting creative odds and old fashioned ends in the traditional ways. If possible, be in Cirencester on Friday for its bustling market.

While Cirencester may be old, it's just a baby compared with the over 70 ancient sites from the Stonehenge era—4000 years old—that litter the surrounding hills. I guess they could say "if you scratch a Roman, you'll find a Druid." *Mysterious Britain* by Janet and Colin Bord explains these fascinating glimpses of England's distant past.

To the north of Stow is Broadway, a pleasant but overcrowded town. Climb its hill for a great Cotswold panorama. Just a bit further down the road is Chipping Campden, a rich, old town that refuses to forget that, once upon a time, it was the center of this region's wool trade. In late May and early June, Chipping Campden hosts the rowdy "Dover Games" which include fun—if painful—events like "shin-kicking".

Bourton-on-the-water is very popular. I can't figure out if they call this the "Venice of the Cotswolds" because of its quaint canals, its miserable crowds or just to make more money. It's too cute—worth a drive through but no more.

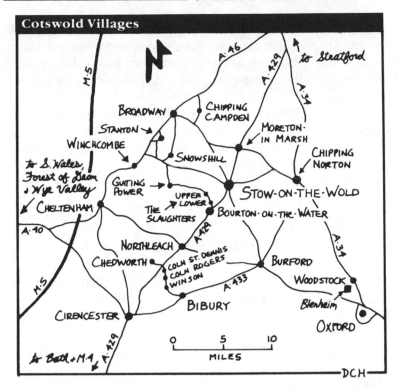

Cotswold Villages

Like many fairytale regions of Europe, the present day beauty of the Cotswolds is explained by economic ups and downs. The area grew rich on the wool trade and built lovely towns and houses. Then foreign markets stole their trade and they slumped—too poor even to be knocked down. The forgotten time-passed villages have now been discovered by us 20th century romantics, and the Cotswold villages are enjoying a new prosperity.

The charm of the Cotswolds is best savored in the tiniest towns, like Stanton, Snowshill, Upper Slaughter and its cuddly sister, Lower Slaughter near Stow. Winson, Coln St. Dennis and Coln Rogers near the entertaining town of Bibury are my finalists for the most thatch-happy and cobble-cute towns in England.

For an English dreamscape in real life, be sure to leave London for a few days in this region. There are no trains but plenty of inter-village buses. Driving is "easy as tea and crumpets" and cars rent for $140 a week with unlimited mileage. Pick up and drop your car at London's Heathrow Airport in the countryside, an easy subway ride from downtown. Don't worry about driving on the English side of the road—it's not that difficult.

Biking is a fun way to tour the villages, and the British love to walk the peaceful footpaths that shepherds walked long before polyester sheep. Hikers know that in England, just when your weary body needs it most, a village complete with a thirst-quenching and spirit-lifting pub seems to appear.

The Cotswolds have plenty of Inns, Guesthouses, Youth Hostels and "Bed and Breakfasts". You can drop into any town before dinner and make yourself at home in a B & B for $18 a night (including a huge second "B"). Local tourist information offices and gift shops have plenty of helpful booklets, maps, and tips on enjoying this most English of English regions.

7: Blackpool

England's tacky glittering city of fun, complete with bells and blinkers, is Blackpool. This middle-sized city with a six mile beach promenade is ignored by guidebooks (*Let's Go: Britain* in 500 pages of small print never even mentions Blackpool). Even the most thorough bus tour will show you castles until your brain blisters but never takes an American visitor to Blackpool.

Blackpool, located on the coast north of Liverpool, is the private playground of England's working class. When I told Brits I was Blackpool-bound, their expression soured and they asked, "Oh God, why?" Because it's the place local widows and workers go year after year

British trying to have fun in the sun at the beach, Blackpool

to escape. Tacky, yes. Lowbrow, okay. But it's as English as can be, and that's what I'm after. Give yourself a vacation from your sightseeing vacation. Spend a day just "muckin' about" in Blackpool. If you're bored here, you're tired of life.

Upon arrival, plan your stay with a visit to Blackpool's helpful tourist information office. Get the city map, pick up brochures from all the amusement centers and go over your plans. Ask for advice on rooms and about special shows and evening events. Remember, Blackpool is second only to London as a center for live theater.

Blackpool is dominated by the Blackpool Tower—much more than a tower, it's a giant fun center. Entry is $4. After that the fun is free. Working your way up from the bottom, check out the fascinating aquarium, the bad house of silly horrors, the very elegant ballroom with live music and dancing all day and the dance of discovery (funny mirrors and lots of hands-on curiosities—don't miss the "Meet Your Friends" chamber and the robot that will actually verbalize whatever you type). The finale is the tower. This symbol of Blackpool is a stubby version of its more famous Parisian cousin. Still, the view from the top is smashing. Consider a coffee break before leaving to watch the golden oldies dance to the grand pipe organ in the ballroom.

Survey Blackpool's six-mile beach promenade from a vintage trolley car. They go constantly up and down the waterfront and make much more sense than driving. The Gypsy-type spiritualists are another fixture at Blackpool. I was told I mustn't leave without having my fortune told, but at $4 per palm, I'll read them myself.

Don't miss an evening at an "Old Time Music Hall Show". There are many shows at Blackpool but its specialty is the old fashioned variety that went out with vaudeville. These are a great hit with "Twirlies" (the senior citizens who are infamous for using their senior bus passes, good only outside of rush hour, "too early"). It's definitely a corny show—neither hip nor polished—but it's fascinating to be surrounded by hundreds of partying British seniors, swooning again, waving their hankies to the predictable beat and giggling at jokes I'd never tell my grandma. Bus loads of merry widows come from all corners of England to enjoy an "Old Time Music Hall Show". Buy your ticket in the afternoon (around $5). Ask a local for the best show, probably on a pier. Try for Mike Donohoe's "Great Days of Music Hall" show.

Blackpool's "Illuminations" are the talk of England every late September and October. Blackpool stretches its season by "illuminating" its six-mile waterfront with countless lights all blinking and twinkling to the delight of those who visit this electronic festival. The American inside me kept saying "I've seen bigger and I've seen better" but I shut him up and just had some simple fun like everyone on my specially decorated tram.

For a fun forest of amusements "Pleasure Beach" is tops. These 42 acres of rides (over 80, including "the best selection of big thrill rides in Europe"), ice skating shows, cabarets and amusements attract 6 million people a year making it England's most popular single attraction.

For me, Blackpool's top sight is its people. You'll see England here like nowhere else. Grab someone's hand, a big stick of "candy floss" (cotton candy) and stroll.

Blackpool needs no reservations. It's in the business of accommodating people who can't afford to holiday in Spain. Simple B&Bs and hotels abound. The classy expensive hotels are, predictably, along the waterfront. Countless lackluster budget alternatives cluster, very handy and central, around Albert Road, near the Central Pier and the tower. These B&Bs almost all have the same design—minimal character and maximum number of beds. Double rooms (in the six or seven places I visited) are all the same small size with a small double bed, your basic English breakfast and a decent shower down the hall. Prices range from $14 (dingy) to $25 (cheery) per person.

Arriving at midday, you should have no trouble finding a place. July 15 to August 15 and summer weekends are most crowded. I stayed at the Pickwick Hotel, 93 Albert Road, Blackpool FY1 4PW, tel. (0253)24229, $16 per person. It was clean, friendly and cheery enough but nothing special.

Visit Blackpool, Britain's fun puddle where every Englishman goes—but none will admit it.

8: Europe's Best Preserved Little Towns

Every once in awhile as you travel you stumble onto a town that somehow missed the 20th-century bus. Ironically, many of these "wonderfully" preserved towns are so full of old world charm because, for various reasons, their economies failed. They became so poor that no one even bothered to tear them down to build more modern towns. Trade patterns changed (Cotswolds), their ports silted up (Brugge), the sea around them was reclaimed leaving the former fishing port high and dry (several Dutch towns), or the capital was moved to keep up with the modern world (Toledo).

Today, many of these towns enjoy a renewed prosperity as quaint "tourist dreams come true". Others slumber on, quietly keeping their own secrets. When the Old World is not performing on big city stages, it huddles in the pubs and chats in the markets of Europe's villages. Here are a few of my favorites. (Hotels are listed in Appendix V.)

Obidos, Portugal's medieval walled gem, is just a short drive north of Lisbon. Its perfectly preserved city wall circles a clutter of cobbled paths, alleys, flower-decked homes and a castle, now one of Portugal's popular *pousadas* (historic government-run hotels). While several queens used the town as a dowry, today's Obidos is a tourist's prize.

Toledo, so historic and so well preserved that Spain declared the entire city a national monument, is Spain's historic, artistic, and spiritual capital. Toledo is filled with tourists day-tripping down from Madrid, ninety minutes to the north. By all means, miss the bus and spend the night! After dark, Toledo is much more medieval—almost haunted in some corners. Explore its back streets, see the art and "home" of El Greco, and marvel at the great cathedral with its sacristy full of El Greco masterpieces. End your day with a roast-suckling pig feast somewhere in the dark tangle of nighttime Toledo.

Brugge (pron: BROOZH) is Belgium's medieval wonderland. Along with Colmar and Toledo, Brugge has more art than any other small town. Let a local guide show you Brugge's treasures. Brugge has some fun modern art, an impressive collection of Flemish paintings, a leaning tower of its own and the only finished Michelangelo statue in Northern Europe. Like many of these small town wonders, Brugge is so well pickled because its economy went sour. Formerly a rich textiles trading center riding high on the prosperity of the Northern Renaissance, its harbor silted up, the shipping was lost, and Brugge was forgotten—until the tourists of our day rediscovered it. Once again, Brugge thrives.

The Netherlands will tempt you with splashy tourist towns where the woman with the ruddiest cheeks is paid to stand on her doorstep wearing wooden shoes, a lace apron and a smile. A local boy peels eels, and there's enough cheese to make another moon. These towns (such as Volendam, Monnickendam, Edam, Marken) are designed to be fun, and they are. But make an effort to find a purely Dutch town that is true to itself—not to tourism. Rent a bike and enjoy exploring this tiny and flat country with your own wheels. In Holland, you can rent a bike at one train station and leave it at nearly any other one. My favorite Dutch village is little Hindeloopen. Silent behind its dike, it's right out of a Vermeer painting—hardcore Holland. The town of Haarlem is a pleasant small town base for side-tripping into often sleazy Amsterdam, which is just 20 minutes away by train or bus.

England loves quaintness. Every year she holds most-beautiful-town contests, and from Land's End to John O'Groats cobbles are scrubbed, flowers are planted and hedges shaved. With such spirit it's not surprising that England is freckled with more small town cuteness than any country in Europe. The cobbles, flowers, pubs and markets, combined with the townspeople, make the perfect Old English setting to enjoy tea and scones or a pint of beer.

While you're likely to find a small prize-winning town just about any-where, the Cotswold Hills and the Southeast Coast are where some of the best are tucked away. Both regions were once rich, but shifting seas and industrial low tides left them high and dry. Today their chief export is cozy cuteness with a British accent. The Southeast Coast has five former ports, the "Cinqueports", that now moor tourists for a living. One of them, Rye, is commonly called England's most photogenic village.

England's many moors are havens hiding time-passed villages that seem to have intentionally ducked out of our modern parade. Don't miss Staithes, Captain Cook's boyhood town, which is just north of Whitby near the York Moors. It's a salty tumble of ancient buildings bunny-hopping down a ravine to a cramped little harbor.

Europe has many more towns that time forgot. Passau in Germany, Rouen in France, Chechaouen in Morocco (among hundreds of others), Sighisoara in Romania, and Erice in Sicily are just a few. Remember, Europe is becoming a scavenger hunt for tourists and most of the prizes have been found. Even with tourist crowds, which are now a standard feature in the summer months, the smaller towns of Europe give the traveler the best look at Europe's old culture.

9: Bad Towns and Tourist Traps

It's generally not considered "in good style" to write negatively about tourist destinations. But since I'm the kind of guy who burps at the dinner table anyway, I'd like to give you one man's opinion on Europe's dullest places. These are the places that may be nice to live in, but I wouldn't want to visit.

Zurich and Geneva are two of Switzerland's largest and most sterile cities. Both are pleasantly situated on a lake—like Buffalo and Duluth.

And both are very famous, but name familiarity is a rotten reason to go somewhere. It's almost criminal to spend a sunny Swiss day anywhere but high in the Alps.

Bordeaux must mean boredom in some ancient language. If I were offered a free trip tomorrow to that town, I'd stay home and clean the fridge. People go there for the wine, but Bordeaux wine country and Bordeaux city are two very different things. There's a wine tourist information bureau in Bordeaux which, for a price, will bus you out of town and into the more interesting wine country nearby.

Andorra, a small country in the Pyrenees Mountains between France and Spain is as scenic as any other chunk of those mountains. People from all over Europe flock to Andorra to take advantage of its famous duty-free shopping. As far as Americans are concerned, Andorra is just a big Spanish-speaking Radio Shack. There are no great bargains here that you can't get at home.

Germany's famous **Black Forest** disappoints more people than it excites. If that's all Germany offered, it would be worth seeing. For Europeans, any large forest in a country the size of Oregon with 65 million people is a popular attraction. But I'd say the average American visitor who's seen more than three trees in one place would prefer Germany's Romantic Road and Bavaria to the east, the Rhine and Mosel country to the north, the Swiss Alps to the south and France's Alsace region to the west— all high points that cut the Black Forest down to stumps.

Stavanger, famous for nearby fjords and its new status as oil boom town, is a large Norwegian port that's about as exciting as the town in Minnesota where its emigrants finally settled. Extra time in western Norway is much better spent in and around Bergen.

Bucharest, the capital of Romania, has very little to offer. Its top selling postcard is of the Intercontinental Hotel. **Belgrade**, Yugoslavia's capital is another stop that is best not started. It's one of the few things I can think of that is more boring than the long train ride through the center of Yugoslavia. Stay on board until you're in Greece or else meander down Yugoslavia's Dalmatian coast. If you're heading from Yugoslavia to Greece, skip **Thessaloniki**, which deserves its chapter in the Bible, but doesn't belong in travel guidebooks.

Athens, while well worth visiting, is probably the most overrated city in Europe. A hundred years ago, Athens was a sleepy town of 8000 people with a pile of ruins in its backyard. Today it's a giant mix of concrete, smog, noise and tourists. See the four major attractions (the Acropolis, the Agora, the Plaka and the great National Archaeological

Museum), spend an evening at the delightful Dafni wine festival on the edge of town (open nightly mid-July through the end of August) and get out to the islands or countryside.

Probably the most common serious mistake people make in their itinerary planning is squeezing a week of Greece into their busy trip. It takes at least four, maybe five days of traveling to get from Rome to Athens and back. It's not worth rushing your whole itinerary and 4 days of hot travel for 2 days in Athens. Greece is the most touristed/least explored country in Europe. It's worthwhile but it takes time—and that time is best spent away from the noise and bustle of Athens.

Extra caution is merited in southwest England, a mine field of tourist traps. The British are masters at milking every conceivable tourist attraction for all it's worth. Here are some booby traps I've encountered.

Cornwall, England's southern-most region has more than its share of cotton candy fluff when it comes to tourism. I'll never forget driving down the road passing signs prepping me for the "Devil's Toenail." "Only five miles—The Devil's Toenail." Then, "The Devil's Toenail—next left!" Well, I figured I'd only be here once, so I better check it out. I pulled into the parking lot—paid a dollar to park. Paid another dollar to pass through the turnstile. Walked to the bottom of the ravine. And there it was, a rock the size of a watermelon, that looked just like . . . a toenail. Disappointed, and a bit embarrassed, I took a quick picture and hiked back to my car, promising myself never again to fall for such a sly snare. Predictably, **Land's End**, the far southwest tip of England, is geared up to attract, and does attract, hordes of tourists. You pay to park, walk out to the point for a photo to prove you were there, grab a postcard and take off.

Just down the coast, **Penzance** is enjoying a tourist boom of its own, capitalizing on the popularity of Gilbert and Sullivan's "Pirates of Penzance". While you won't see any salty seafarers in Penzance, you will find plenty of commercial pirates ready to pillage your pocketbook; restaurants, pubs and ye olde shoppes just bursting with smugglers' atmosphere and pirates' decor.

On the north Cornwall coast, above Land's End, are two more tourist magnets. **Tintagel** is famous for its castle—the legendary birthplace of King Arthur. The castle's exciting windswept and wave-beaten ruins are well worth exploring. Meanwhile, the town does everything in its little power to exploit this profitable Arthurian legend. There's even a pub in town called the Excali Bar.

Just up the coast is **Clovelly**. It's one of the towns I had circled in my guide book years before I ever got there. It sounded so cute—"daintily clinging to the rocky coast desperately trying not to plunge into the wicked seas". But when you arrive, reality rules. You'll park your car for a price 50 yards away and join the crowds funneling into the little town's one street. You can shop your way down one side to the waterfront and up the other side past cute knickknack shops all selling just about the same goodies—like "clotted cream that you can mail home".

England has so much to offer in so many ways. Be careful not to waste your time on worthless tourist traps. Shopping is fun but, if you're not careful, it can have a nibbly destructive impact on the cultural and educational value of your trip—especially in England. I've seen a fascinating tour of the British Halls of Parliament plundered by a table of Beefeater mugs and Union Jack underwear.

The towns and places I've mentioned here are worth skipping only because they're surrounded by so many places much more worthy of the average traveler's limited vacation time. If you have a villa in Bucharest or a cuckoo clock shop in the Black Forest, no offense is meant. Just remember to distinguish carefully between entrepreneurial ventures and legitimate sightseeing attractions.

Section 2:
Natural Nooks and Undeveloped Crannies

10: Cinqueterre, Italy's Traffic-Free Riviera

"A sleepy, romantic and inexpensive town on the Riviera without a tourist in sight." That's the mirage travelers chase in busy Nice and Cannes. Pssst! Paradise sleeps just across the border in Italy's Cinqueterre.

With larger and larger tourist crowds trampling Europe's towns and resorts every summer, it's more important than ever to trade those long lines and "no vacancy" signs in on a more real and relaxed alternative. The Cinqueterre, between Pisa and Genova, is surprisingly undeveloped.

Cinqueterre, meaning "five lands", is five pastel villages clinging to the rugged coast of the Italian Riviera. The villagers go about their business as if the surrounding vineyards were the very edges of the earth. An Italian syrup soaks every corner of this world, and it's yours to sop up.

Each town is a character. Monterosso al Mare, happy to be appreciated, boasts a great beach and plenty of fine hotels and restaurants. Its four little sisters are content to be overlooked—forgotten in their old world puddle. Little Manarola rules its ravine and drinks its wine while its sun-bleached walls slumber on. The Via dell' Amore (walkway of love) leads from Manarola to Riomaggiore. With a beauty that has seduced famed artists to live here, Riomaggiore is well worth a wander.

Corniglia sits smug on its hilltop, proudly victorious in its solitaire game of "king of the mountain". Most visitors are lured to Corniglia by the Cinqueterre's best swimming, and never tackle the winding stairs to the actual town. Those who make the Corniglian climb are rewarded by the Cinqueterre's finest wine and most staggering view—simultaneously.

Vernazza, on Italy's Riviera

Ducking into a cellar with a grape-stained local, we dipped long straws furtively into dark kegs. Wine tasting drowns the language barrier.

Vernazza is my favorite village. Its one street connects the harbor with the train station and meanders further inland, melting into the vineyards. Like veins on a maple leaf, paths and stairways connect this water-color huddle of houses with Main Street. Every day is a parade. A rainbow of laundry flags fly over barrel women wheeling fresh fish past the old men who man the bench. Little varnished boats are piled everywhere and sailors suckle salty taverns while the old world marches on to the steady beat of the crashing waves. The sun sets unnoticed—except by tourists—some who "slow down to smell the roses" so intensely that they risk choking on the petals.

The Cinqueterre is best seen on foot. A scenic trail leads you through sunny vineyards from Riomaggiore to Monterosso. The Vernazza-Monterosso trail is as rugged as the people who've worked the terraced vineyards that blanket the region. Flowers and an ever-changing view entertain every step of your hike. As you make your sweaty way high above the glistening beaches and approach each time-steeped village, you'll be glad you brought your camera.

When you run out of time or energy simply catch a train back to your home base. While most of these towns are inaccessible by car, a tunnel-train blinks open at each village and provides a quick and easy way to

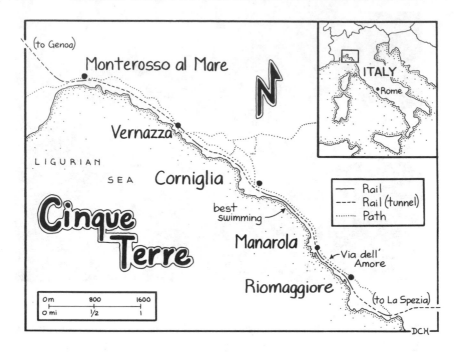

explore the region. Trains connect all five towns nearly hourly for less than a dollar.

For a great day in the Cinqueterre start by walking the Via dell' Amore from Riomaggiore to Manarola, buy a picnic in Manarola and walk to the Corniglia beach. Swim, enjoy the shady bar, picnic and take the train to Monterosso al Mare for a look at the local big town. Enjoy its sandy beach before hiking home to Vernazza. For an atmospheric and tasty finale, enjoy dinner or at least a drink at Lorenzo's Castello restaurant just below Vernazza's castle. The best bar is the umbrella-shaded balcony halfway between the castle and the surf.

While the Cinqueterre is unknown to the international mobs that ravage the Spanish and French coasts, plenty of Italians come here, so getting a room can be tough. August and weekends are bad. Avoid weekends in August altogether. (For rooms, see Appendix V.)

Five towns and the rocky surf are all that interrupt the peaceful vineyard greens and Mediterranean blues of this Riviera. The tourists are looking for it, but have yet to find Italy's Cinqueterre.

11: Salema on Portugal's Sunny South Coast

The Algarve, Portugal's south coast, has long been famous as Europe's last undiscovered tourist frontier. Any place that's famous as a "last undiscovered tourist frontier" no longer is. Portugal's south coast is a disappointment to most who come looking for fun in the sun on undeveloped beaches. Most of the Algarve is white-washed houses, sandy beaches, vacant lots, and tourists—most sunburned—all simmered in carbon monoxide and traffic noises.

But with energy, you can find places that lack fame and crowds. There are a few towns where colorful boats share the beach with a colony of sun worshippers who relax with gusto far from the tacky souvenir racks and package tour rat race.

The Algarve of your dreams survives—just barely. To catch it before it goes, find a fringe. It took me three tries. West of Lagos I tried Lux and Burgano—both offering only a corpse of a fishing village, bikini-strangled and Nivea-creamed. Then, just as darkness turned couples into lonely silhouettes, I found Salema. Any Algarve town with a beach will have tourism, but few mix tourism and realism as well as little Salema—tucked away where a dirt road hits the beach between Lagos and Cape Sagres on Portugal's southwestern tip.

Salema is a long, winding, white-washed old town—scruffy dogs, wide-eyed kids and fishermen who've seen it all. The other half was built

Salema, catch the Algarve before it's gone

for tourists. The parking lot that separates the jogging shorts from the black shawls becomes a morning market with the arrival of the trucks; a fruit and veggies mobile, a rolling meat and cheese shop, and the clothing van.

The two worlds pursue a policy of peaceful co-existence. Tractors pull in and push out the fishing boats, two-year-old sand people flop in the waves, topless women read German fashion mags and old men really do mend the nets. Tourists laze in the sun while locals grab the shade. Dogs roam like they own the place and a very dark grannie shells almonds with a railroad spike.

Salema is my kind of beach resort—four restaurants specializing in fresh fish and *vinho verde,* three hotels, lots of *quartos* (Portuguese for "Bed and Breakfast"), the beach and sun. It's quietly discovered by British and German connoisseurs of lethargy.

So often tourism chases away quaint folksiness—while the quaint folks can only survive with the help of tourist dollars. One way a fishing family speeds up the trickle down theory, with a direct shot in the pocketbook, is to rent out a spare bedroom to the ever-growing stream of tan fans from the drizzly north. I arrived at 7:00 pm with nine people and saw no "B&B" signs anywhere. I asked the gang on the street corner. "Quarto?" Eyes perked, nods okayed, and nine beds in three homes at $5 per person were arranged. I didn't feel like bargaining, but I'm sure the price was flexible downward. You'll find plenty of *quartos* along the road running left from the village center as you face the beach. For specifics see Appendix V or you can ask at the bar. We got simple rooms, showers, fine beds, glorious views of pure paradise and friendly people whose smiles assured us this was the place to be. This was the cheapest place we stayed, and after a month on the road, each member of my group called it their favorite.

In the distance a man catches short fish with a long pole. Behind him is Cape Sagres—the edge of the world 500 years ago; as far as the gang sipping Port and piling olive pits in the beachside bar is concerned—it still is.

12: Crete's Gorge of Samaria

Swarms of tourists flock to the Greek island of Crete. Many leave disappointed. Their problem was that they failed to leave the crowded cities behind and get away from the tourists. One sure-fire escape is to take the ten-mile hike through the Gorge of Samaria.

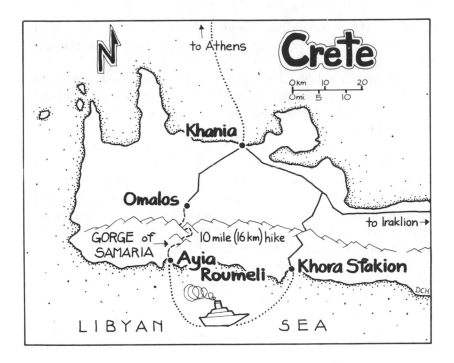

Your home-base for this circular excursion is Khania (pronounced "HAWN-yah"), a city on Crete's north coast serviced frequently by the overnight boat from Athens. Catch the earliest bus from Khania past Omalos to Xyloskala. By 7:00 a. m. after a very scenic 25-mile bus ride you'll be standing high above the wild Gorge of Samaria. Xyloskala is a small lodge, the end of the road—and the beginning of the trail. The bus will be full of hikers; no one else would come here at this early hour. The air is crisp, the fresh blue sky is cool and most of the gorge has yet to see the sun. Before you lies a downhill, ten-mile trek through some of the most spectacular scenery anywhere in Greece. This four to six hour hike down Europe's longest gorge is open from May 1 to October 31.

Pack light for this hike, but bring a hearty picnic lunch. Food can't be bought in this wonderfully wild gorge. Water is no problem, since you follow a pure mountain stream through most of the gorge. Wear light clothes, but bring a jacket for the cool morning at the top of the gorge. Come prepared to swim in one of the stream's many refreshing swimming holes. Photographers go through lots of film on this hike.

Descend to the floor of the gorge down steep switchbacks for about an hour until you come to the stream, a great place for your picnic. A leisurely meal here will do three things: bolster your energy, lighten your load, and bring you peace, as this break will let most of the other hikers get ahead of you.

Between you and the Libyan Sea on Crete's southern shore are about eight miles of gently sloping downhill trails. You'll pass an occasional deserted farmhouse, one occupied only by two lazy goats, and a small ghost town with a well. In the middle of the hike, you'll come to the narrowest (and most photographed) point in the gorge where only two or three yards separate the towering cliffs. Keep your eyes peeled for the nimble cliff-climbing agrimi, the wild Cretin mountain goats.

The cool creek trickles at your feet, reminding you that a little farther downstream you can take a cool dip in one of the stream's natural swimming holes. Find one without other hikers and jump into your own private tub complete with waterfall. It's wonderfully refreshing.

Finally, by mid-afternoon, signs of Greek civilization begin peeking through the bushes. An oleander chorus cheers you along the last leg of your hike to the coast. You'll find a tiny community with a small restaurant and a few cheap places to stay. The town, Ayia Roumeli, is accessible only by foot or by boat. Three times a day, a small boat picks up the hikers and ferries them to Kora Sfakion. Before you begin your hike, find out when the last boat leaves, so you can plan accordingly.

While you're waiting for the boat (after you buy your ticket), take a dip in the bathtub-warm, crystal-clear waters of the Libyan Sea. Africa is out there somewhere. The black sand beach is beautiful, but it absorbs the heat, so wear your shoes right to the water's edge. A free shower is available on the beach.

The hour-long boat ride to Khora Sfakion passes some of Crete's best beaches and the remote and pleasant fishing village of Loutro (several pensions). Buses meet the boat at Khora Sfakion to return you to Khania. In crossing the island of Crete, the bus goes through some lovely land and several untouched villages inhabited by high-booted, long-mustachioed, espresso-drinking Cretins, returning you to Khania by 8:30 p.m.

This day is, in every sense of the word, gorgeous.

13: The Berner Oberland, the Alps in Your Lap

In Switzerland you'll find Europe's most spectacular mountain scenery. There was a time when the only thing higher than those Alpine peaks was the prices you had to pay to see them. Switzerland has enjoyed a very low inflation rate and today it is no more expensive than its neighbors. Switzerland does suffer from tourist crowds, however, and you should keep this in mind when you choose your Swiss destination. How do you see the best of the Swiss Alps without enduring traffic jams and congested trails? The answer has two parts: Kleine Scheidegg and Gimmelwald.

Kleine Scheidegg— The Mona Lisa of Mountain Views

I had always considered Interlaken overrated. Now I understand that Interlaken is best used as a jumping-off point—the gateway to the Alps. No need to stop in Interlaken. Get an early start and catch the private train

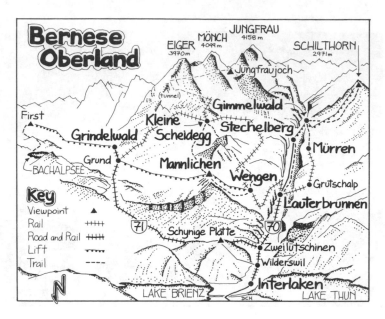

(not covered by your Eurailpass) to Grindelwald. Avoid the common mistake of making heavily-touristed Grindelwald your final destination. Take advantage of its friendly and very helpful tourist information office. Browse through the expensive tourist shops, if you like. Stop at the Co-Op grocery store and buy what you need for a first-class mountain picnic. Then ascend into a wonderland of powerful white peaks by taking the train to Kleine Scheidegg or even higher to Mannlichen where you can walk down to Kleine Scheidegg.

Now you have successfully run the gauntlet of tourist traps and reached the ultimate. Before you towers the greatest mountain panorama that I've every enjoyed. The Jungfrau, the Monch, and the north face of the Eiger boldly proclaim that they are the greatest. You won't argue.

Kleine Scheidegg, an hour's hike from Mannlichen, has a lodge (with cheap dorm bunks) and an outdoor restaurant. People gather here to marvel at tiny rock climbers dangling by ropes—many of them quite dead—halfway up the icy Eiger. If money is not something you're trying to conserve, you can take the expensive ride from here to the towering Jungfraujoch ($30 R/T from Kleine Scheidegg). It's impressive, but I couldn't have asked for a more spectacular view than what Kleine Scheidegg gavé me.

From Kleine Scheidegg, you begin your hike into the next valley, the less-touristed Lauterbrunnen Valley. The hike is not difficult. My gear consisted only of short pants (watch the mountain sun!), tennis shoes, and a tourist brochure. If you have packed light, and all your luggage is on your back, then you have the good feeling that it doesn't really matter where you spend the night.

It's lunch time as you hike into your own peaceful mountain world. Find a grassy perch, and your picnic will have atmosphere that no restaurant could match. Flowers, the sun and the view all make your picnic taste *magnifique*.

Continuing downhill, you may well be all alone and singing to the rhythm of your happy footsteps. As the scenery changes and new mountains replace the ones you've already seen, after two hours you enter the traffic-free town of Wengen. Avoid the steep and relatively dull hike from Wengen to Lauterbrunnen by taking the $3 train down to the valley floor where you can continue by bus/gondola or funiclear/train to the village of Gimmelwald. (Note: this was the scenic roundabout way to Gimmelwald. For a much more direct route, skip the hike and take the train direct from Interlaken to Lauterbrunnen.)

Gimmelwald—Where Heidi Lives

The traffic-free village of Gimmelwald hangs nonchalantly on the edge of a cliff high above the floor of the Lauterbrunnen Valley. It's a small sleepy village with more cows ringing bells than people. The sounds of small avalanches on the almost touchable mountain wall across the valley, birds, waterfalls, and the crunchy march of happy hikers constantly remind you why they say, "If Heaven isn't what it's cracked up to be, send me back to Gimmelwald."

When told you're visiting Gimmelwald, Swiss people assume you mean the famous resort in the next valley, Grindelwald. When assured that Gimmelwald is your target they lean forward, widen their eyes, and ask, "How do you know about Gimmelwald?"

This ignored station on the spectacular Schilthorn gondola (of James Bond fame) should be built up to the hilt. But it's classified "avalanche zone"—too dangerous for serious building projects. So while developers gnash their teeth, sturdy peasants continue milking cows and making hay, surviving in a modern world only by the grace of a government that subsidizes such poor traditional industries. The few travelers who figure there won't be an avalanche for a few nights enjoy the Alps in their laps in a Swiss world that looks and lives the way every traveler dreams it might.

Since it allows no cars, there are only two ways to get to Gimmel-

Downtown Gimmelwald, a traffic-free Paradise

wald. Either take the $3 gondola up from Stechelberg at the far end of the Lauterbrunnen Valley, or take the Lauterbrunnen-Grutschalp funicular (a small train) up the steep wall and catch the "panorama train" to Murren. From there, Gimmelwald is a pleasant 45-minute walk downhill.

Sleep in Gimmelwald's very rugged youth hostel ($4/bed) or at the storybook chalet called Hotel Mittaghorn ($30/double with breakfast).

Gimmelwald's shacky hostel is the craziest, loosest and friendliest hostel I've ever fallen in love with. Every day its big Alp-happy family adopts newcomers and fills them with spaghetti and mountain stories. High in the Alps, this relaxed hostel is struggling to survive. Please treat it with loving care, respect its rules (and elderly Lena, who runs the place) and leave it cleaner than when you found it (tel. 036/551704).

Up the hill is the treasure of Gimmelwald. Walter Mittler, the perfect Swiss gentleman, runs a creaky chalet called Hotel Mittaghorn. It's a classic Alpine-style place with a million dollar view of the Jungfrau Alps. Walter is careful not to let his place get too hectic or big and enjoys sensitive back door travelers. He's a magnificent, but only occasional, cook, and runs his hotel alone, keeping it simple, but with class. Call Walter in advance at 036/551658. (More rooms are listed in Appendix V.)

Evening fun in Gimmelwald is found in the hostel (lots of young Alpoholic hikers and a good chance to share information on the surrounding mountains) and up at Walter's. If you're staying at Walter's don't miss his dinner. Then sit on his porch and watch the sun lick the mountain tops to bed as the moon rises over the Jungfrau.

From Gimmelwald you can ride the gondola up to the Schilthorn ($25 round trip). A revolving restaurant caps this 10,000 foot peak, and I make a point to enjoy bacon, eggs, and Alps at least once a year. The early gondola is discounted enough to pay for your breakfast. (Walter has special tickets.)

Frolic on the ridge. If you want to hike down, the first 300 yards are the most difficult. The easiest descent is just to the right of the cable car as you face down. The three-hour hike drops 5000 feet. If this is too thrilling, ride the gondola back down to Birg (the midway station) and enjoy an easier (but still steep) hike back to Gimmelwald from there. When you're ready to leave this Alpine wonderland, take the lift back down to Stechelberg, and catch a bus to Interlaken.

If you're interested in the heart of Switzerland, it's best seen from Kleine Scheidegg. If you're looking for Heidi and an orchestra of cow bells in a Switzerland that most people think exists only in dreams and storybooks—spend some time in Gimmelwald.

14: From France to Italy—Over Mt. Blanc

Europe's ultimate mountain lift towers high above the French resort town of Chamonix. The Aiguille du Midi *telepherique* (gondola) carries you to the tip of a rock needle 12,600 feet above sea level. Remind yourself that this thing has been going back and forth now for twenty-five years, surely it'll make it one more time, and get in. Chamonix shrinks as trees fly by, soon replaced by whizzing rocks, ice and snow until you reach the top. Up there no matter how sunny it is, it's cold. The air is thin and people are giddy. Fun things can happen if you're not too winded to join locals in the Halfway-to-Heaven tango.

Before you spread the Alps. In the distance is the bent little Matterhorn, and looming just over there is Mont Blanc, at 15,781 feet, Europe's highest point. Next, for your own private glacial dreamworld, and Europe's most exciting border crossing, get into the red gondola and head south. Dangle silently for 40 minutes as you glide over the glacier to Italy. Hang your head out the window, exploring every corner of your view. You're sailing a new sea.

Show your passport at Hellbrunner point (11,000 feet) and descend into Aosta, a remote valley in the north of Italy, a whole different world.

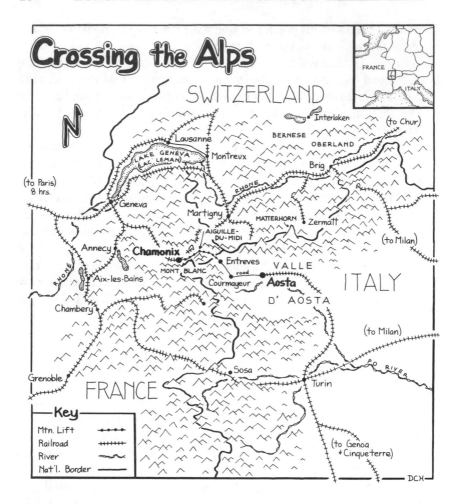

Your starting point for this adventure is Chamonix, a very convenient overnight train ride from Paris (10:30 p.m.—8:30 a.m.). Chamonix is a resort town—expensive and crowded. Most of its visitors have one thing on their minds—mountains. The town has many expensive hotels as well as several chalets offering dormitory accommodations at very reasonable prices. The youth hostel, the former barracks of the diggers of the Mont Blanc Tunnel is a good place to stay for $6 a night (tel. 531452).

From Chamonix there are enough hikes and cable car rides to keep you busy for a long time. If you came only to take the ultimate ride, get on that *telepherique* to the Aiguille du Midi. This expensive lift (about $25 round trip), which doesn't run at all in some off-season months, is

Just keep telling yourself, "It'll make it one more time."

Europe's highest and most spectacular. If the weather is good, it's worth whatever they charge. The youth hostel gives 25% discount coupons. Afternoons tend to cloud up so try to take the ride in the morning. (Call the tourist office, tel. 5053-0024, for weather and hiking conditions.)

A good plan to save a little money and enjoy a hike at the same time is to buy a ticket all the way up, but only halfway back down. This gives you a chance to look down at the Alps and over at the summit of Mont Blanc from your lofty 12,600-foot lookout. Then you descend to the halfway point where you're free to frolic in the glaciers and hike back to Chamonix at your leisure.

From the top you can return to Chamonix or continue over the mountain to Italy. If you decide to leave France from the Aiguille du Midi, remember, the last departure starts at about 2:00 p.m. The descent from Hellbrunner Point (about $10) takes you into the Valle d'Aosta. This is Italy with a French accent. A dash of France and a splash of Switzerland blend with the already rich Italian flavor to create a truly special character.

To avoid the often long wait for a bus, try to catch a ride with a fellow cable car passenger who has a car parked in Entreves, where you'll land. Ride with him to the next town, Courmayeur, or better yet, straight to the main city of the valley—Aosta.

Historic Aosta is the best place to spend the night and maybe the next

Alps from atop the Aiguille du Midi, 12,600 feet up

day. "The Rome of the Alps", as Aosta is called, has many Roman ruins. Sleep at Locanda di Rosini Renato (via d'Avisa 4, 11100 Aosta, tel. 33324 or 44286, friendly, clean, view, $25 doubles). The popular Ulisse Restaurant at Via Ed. Aubert 58 has great pizza and better prices. You'll notice that on the south side of the Alps your travel dollars become like the Italian cheese—they stretch farther. From Aosta, the train will take you to Milan and the rest of Italy.

Chamonix, Aiguille du Midi, and the Valle d'Aosta—surely a high point in anyone's European vacation.

15: Off-Beat Alps

Even those who know a Rocky Mountain high find something special, and wonderfully civilized, about Europe's Alps. When you look at them, you'd think man and mountain shared the same crib. You can hike from France to Yugoslavia finding a mountain hut or remote village for each overnight and never come out of the hills. Many times you'll walk to the haunting accompaniment of long and legato alphorns. And it seems that just when you need it most, there will be a mechanical lift to whisk you silently and effortlessly—if not cheaply—to the top of that staggering peak, where your partner can take your photo, looking very, very rugged. You'll pass happy yodelers, sturdy grannies, and pony-tailed, dirndle-skirted and singing families that should be named Trapp. And the consistently cheery greetings make passing hikers a fun part of any trek.

While the most famous corners are now solidly in the domain of tour groups and mass tourism, much of the best Alpine charm is folded away in no-name valleys, often just over the ridge from the Holiday Inns and the canned culture on stage.

Here are a few places and activities that will make your Alpine adventures much more than a lovely hike.

Extremely remote but accessible by car (barely) is the village of Taveyanne in the French-speaking part of Switzerland, two miles off the road from Col de la Croix to Villars. It's just a jumble of log cabins and snoozing cows stranded all alone at 5000 feet. The only place in town is the Refuge de Taveyanne where the Siebenthal family serves hearty meals—great fondue and a delicious *croute au fromage avec oeuf* for $7—in a prize-winning rustic setting—no electricity, low ceilings, huge charred fireplace with a cannibal-sized cauldron, prehistoric cash register and well hung ornamental cowbells. This is French Switzerland but these people speak a little English. For a special experience consider sleeping in their primitive loft—it's never full, six mattresses, access by a ladder outside, $5, tel. 025/681947.

In Western Austria, south of Reutte, lies a special treat for those who suspect they may have been Kit Carson in a previous life. Fallerscheim is a very isolated log cabin village, smothered in Alpine goodness. Drop into its flower-speckled world of serene slopes, cowbells, and musical breezes. Thunderstorms roll down this valley like it's God's bowling alley, but the blissfully simple pint-sized church on the high ground seems to promise that this huddle of houses will remain standing. The people sitting on benches are mostly Austrian vacationers who've rented cabins. For a rugged chunk of local Alpine peace, spend a night in the local Matratzen lager (simple dorm loft) "Almwirtscheft Fallerscheim" (open June-September, $5 per night, 27 beds and one outhouse, good meals, tel. 05678-5142). Fallerscheim is 4000 feet high at the end of a miserable two-mile fit-for-jeep-or-rental-car-only gravel road near Namlose on the Berwang road south of Reutte in Austria's Tyrol.

The Sommerrodelbahn is one of the great Alpine experiences. Several Alpine ski slopes are outfitted with concrete bobsled courses. Local speed demons spend summer days riding chair lifts up to "luge" down on wheeled carts with brakes. There's a Sommerrodelbahn at Chamonix in France and two in Tyrol just off the Fernpass road—one halfway between Reutte and Lermoos, the other just past Biberwier near the Shell station in the shadow of the grey and powerful Zugspitz. They are normally open daily in the summer from 8:30 a.m. to 5:00 p.m. unless it's wet. The Biberwier luge is the longest in Austria—4000 feet. The concrete course banks on the corners and even a first-timer can go very, very fast. You'll rumble, windblown and smile-creased, into the finish line with one thought on your mind—"Let's do it again!"

There's more than one way to get down an Alp

For a slower but just as invigorating activity, try joining the people of Bern for a mid-day float through their city on the Aare River. The lunchtime float is a popular tradition in the Swiss capital. Local merchants, legislators, publishers and students, proud of their clean river and their basic ruddiness, grab every hot summer opportunity to enjoy this wet and refreshing *paseo*. Visitors feel very welcome joining the locals in the ritual 20 minute hike upstream from the Swiss National Parliament building, then floating playfully or sleepily back down to the excellent and free riverside baths and pool (Aarebad). If the river is a bit much, spectating is fun and you're welcome to enjoy just the pool.

Along with staggering mountains, Switzerland is loved for its delicious chocolates. No tour of this country is complete without watching a river of molten chocolate work its way into small foil packages at a Swiss chocolate factory. The Caillers Chocolate factory in Broc, just north of Lausanne in French Switzerland, gives tours from March to October (except July) on Tuesdays, Wednesdays and Thursdays at 9:30 and at 1:30 (tel. 029/61212). The very modern and impressive Toblerone factory just outside of Bern tantalizes and treats its guests with tours on Tuesday, Wednesday and Thursday at 9:00 and 1:30, Mondays at 1:30 only, closed in July and October (tel. 031/343511). Both chocotours are free and finish with an all-you-can-savor sample time. Call to confirm tour schedules.

How does a fine Baroque church in a Bavarian setting at a monastery that serves hearty food and the best beer in Germany in a carnival setting full of partying locals sound? That's the soon-to-be-discovered Andechs monastery hiding happily between two lakes at the foot of the Alps, just south of Munich. Come with an appetite, the food is great: chunks of tender pork chain-sawed especially for you, huge and soft pretzels (best I've had), spiralled white radishes, savory sauerkraut and Andechser beer that lives up to its reputation. Everything is served in medieval proportions.

16: England's Mysterious Moors

You can get lost in England's moors. Directions are difficult to keep. It's cold. Long-haired goats and sheep seem to gnaw on grass in their sleep. The moor resists change. A castle loses itself in lush overgrowth. A church grows shorter as tall weeds eat at the stone crosses and bent tablets that mark graves.

When you tire of those disillusioning private enterprises and tourist traps like Land's End and The Devil's Toenail that charge you to park after psyching you up with many roadside announcements, boost your traveling spirit with a refreshing plunge into the stark and turnstile-free world of England's moors.

There are many. Dartmoor is the wildest—a wonderland of green and powerfully quiet rolling hills just north of Plymouth. Crossed by only two or three main roads, most of the land is either unused or shared for grazing as a "common land" by its 30,000 villagers just as they have used it since feudal days. Dartmoor is best toured by car, but it can be explored by bike, thumb or on foot. Bus service is meager. Several places rent horses ($16/day). Several National Park centers provide maps and information. The key here is to make a bed and breakfast headquarters in one of the many small towns, or check into a youth hostel in Gidleigh, Steps Bridge, or Bellever. This is one of England's most remote corners—and it feels that way. It is hard to believe that so many tourists so near are unaware of this inland treat.

Dartmoor is perfect for those who dream of enjoying their own private Stonehenge *sans* barbed wire, policemen, parking lots and hordes of tourists. Dartmoor has more Bronze Age stone circles and huts than any other chunk of England. The local Ordnance Survey maps show the moor peppered with these bits of England's mysterious past. Hator Down and Gidleigh are especially interesting.

Gidleigh is an appropriately gnarled homebase. Choosing the hostel over the local B&B, I met the warden—a monumental woman. I figured she was Mrs. Gidleigh herself, standing at the gate of her hostel which is also the post office. She told me to move my car far away. Mrs. Gidleigh instills fear and respect in those who come to her place; I felt lucky to get a bunk in the human half of the barn out back. (Castle Farm, Gidleigh, Chagford, tel. 06473/2421). Borrow her map for the hike to the nearby stone circle. (But check it carefully. She once gave the wrong map to a hostler from Hong Kong. He never returned—and she kept his Walkman.)

Word of the wonders that lurked just a bit deeper into the moors tempted me away from my hostel. I ventured in, sinking into the powerful mistical moorland. Climbing over a hill, surrounded by giant towers of ragged granite, I was swallowed up. Hills followed hills followed hills— green, growing gray in the murk. Where was that circle of stone 4000 years old?

Searching for the stones, I wandered in a world of greenery, eerie wind, white rocks and birds singing but unseen. Then the stones appeared standing in a circle. They had waited for endless centuries, not moving, waiting for me to come. In their stillness, they entertained. This is the way to see the puzzles left by civilizations past. Stonehenge doesn't quite make it.

Out on the moor, I sit on a fallen stone and let my imagination off its leash, wondering about the people who roamed England so long before written history was around to tell their story. Grabbing the moment to write, I take out my journal, thinking about the moor, the town, this circle of stones, and I dip my pen into the cry of the birds, the chill of the air, a timeless wind—and write.

17: Dingle Peninsula—A Gaelic Bike Ride

Be careful—Ireland is seductive. In many areas the old culture seems to be winning its battle with the twentieth century and stress is a foreign word. I fell in love with the friendliest land this side of Sicily. It all happened in a "Gaeltacht".

A Gaeltacht is a national cultural preserve, where the government is actively fostering the continued survival of the old Irish culture. Shaded green on many maps, these regions are most common on the West coast of the Emerald Isle. "Gaeltacht" means Gaelic-speaking. You will find the Gaelic culture alive, not only in the language but working the fields, singing in the pubs and in the weathered faces of the traditionally dark-clad Irish who live there. A Gaeltacht gives you Ireland in the extreme.

Dingle—green, rugged, and untouched—is my favorite Gaeltacht. It's Ireland's western-most point, quietly living the way it wants to. While nearby Killarney and the famous "Ring of Kerry" bustle with noisy tourists, Dingle Peninsula ages peacefully, offering an escape into the real Ireland.

Drive, take the bus or hitchhike to Dingle town. It's a good place to spend your first Irish night if you land at nearby Shannon airport. From the town of Tralee, you'll pass over a ruggedly scenic mountain pass. Depending on the weather, you'll be dazzled by the lush views, or you'll creep slowly through milky fog, seeing nothing past the road's dark edge.

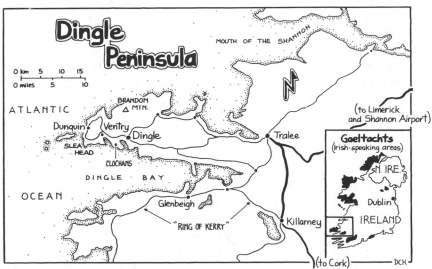

Dingle town has character. In a very Gaelic manner, it's quiet, salty and enjoyable. A weather-beaten friendliness will warm you, even on the coldest of wet mornings.

Find a good bed and breakfast. I enjoyed the hospitality of Mrs. Kathleen Farrell's Corner House at Dykegate St. Dingle, County Kerry, tel. 066/51516. Any resident of Dingle should be happy and able to direct you to a good "B & B", like Mrs. Farrell's. A cozy bed, a huge breakfast and lots of tea shouldn't cost you more than $15. The cheapest beds in town ($7) are found at the Westgate/Westlodge Hostel, Dingle's friendly, private hostel (tel. 51476). The town's tourist office (tel. 51188) is helpful.

After breakfast, find a bike to rent. Your landlady can direct you to a bike rental place. For two dollars a wheel, you're mobile for the day. Pack a picnic, your camera and a raincoat. The weather on this distant tip of Ireland is often misty, foggy and rainy. It's as wet as it is green—and I've never seen a greener land.

Bicycle around the peninsula. Follow the coastal road to the little town of Ventry. Chat with the "chatty" Irish you'll meet along the roadside. Those accents are music.

Continue along to Slea Head, the closest point in Europe to America. The rugged coastline stretches in both directions, offering magnificent views of the treacherous black-rock cliffs. Crashing surf, distant boats and the countryside (lush and barren all at once) complete this memorable picture. Sheep graze, bored by the quiet clouds constantly covering and uncovering the hills. An elfish black-clad Gaelic man might brogue about his arthritis, point out a landmark or sing you a song.

Be sure to explore some of the many *clochans,* or beehive huts. These mysterious stone huts were built without mortar by seventh-century monks in search of solitude. The huts are especially exciting when it's just you and a hut in a desolate world of dark, heavy mist.

Pedal on to Dunquin. Stop by Kruger Kavanaugh's Gaelic Pub and order a pint of something very Irish. If the weather's nice, find a quiet stream off the road a wee bit, and enjoy your picnic sitting on a rock.

Now pedal up the hill and coast back down into Dingle town. You have finished your circle around the magical Dingle Peninsula.

For your evening fun, find a "singing Gaelic pub". Try O'Flaherty's which has traditional music nearly every night, or the more ad-libbed folk music sessions at Mrs. Nelligan's Pub. (Women traveling alone need not worry—you'll become part of the pub family in no time). Here you will enjoy traditional music that has not yet been bastardized for the tourist. A tin whistle, a fiddle, a flute, goatskin drums and bad voices that sound

Ireland's top tourist attraction—the friendliest people in Europe

better as the night goes on will awaken the leprechaun in you. The atmosphere is as thick as the head on your pint of Guinness. Drink it all in. If an Irishman buys you a drink, you might offer him a Gaelic toast. Lift your glass and say "SLOYNtuh!" (spelled phonetically). Before you leave, be sure to thank him by saying, "go ra MA hagut."

Live Gaelic music, plenty to drink and a robust crowd can be a great way to end your day in Dingle. Ireland will seduce you. Let it. Enjoy it. You may never be the same.

Section 3:
Misunderstood Regions and Countries

18: Rothenburg and the Romantic Road, Germany's Medieval Heartland

The best way to connect the castles of the Rhine and the *lederhosen* charm of Bavaria is by traveling the unforgettable "Romantische Strasse". On the Romantic Road (and especially just off it) where no unfamiliar car drives through unnoticed and flower boxes decorate the unseen side of barns, visitors find the Germany most come to see. Church steeple masts sail seas of rich rolling farmland, and fragrant villages invite you to slow down. At each village, ignore the signposts and ask an old woman for directions to the next town—just to hear her voice and enjoy the energy in her eyes. Thousands of tourists have passed through, yet so few stop to chat.

This is one "back door" that is well discovered. But, even with its crowds, this part of Germany, peppered with pretty towns today because it was such an important and prosperous trade route 600 years ago, is a must.

A car gives you complete freedom to explore this heartland of medieval Germany—just follow the green "Romantische Strasse" signs. The most scenic sections are Bad Mergentheim to Rothenburg, and Landsburg to Fussen. For those without wheels the convenient Europabus tour (free with a Eurailpass) opens this door to small-town Germany.

Buses leave daily in both directions connecting Frankfurt/Wiesbaden with Munich (late March through early November) and Wurzburg with Fussen (June through September). Any Frankfurt—Munich train ticket is good on this bus. Otherwise, the bus from Munich to Frankfurt costs about $60 (the same as a second class train ticket). The trip takes 11 hours,

274

and three of those are yours to explore the fairytale towns of Rothenburg ob der Tauber and Dinkelsbuhl. You can break your journey anywhere along the road and catch the same bus the next day. Ticket reservations are necessary only for peak-season weekends (tel. 069/7903240 three days in advance).

Whenever you're traveling, it's wise to lay the groundwork for your smooth departure in advance. For instance, upon arrival in Munich (or Fussen near the famous Neuschwanstein castle) ask at the train or tourist information office exactly where and when the bus leaves the next morning and if a reservation is advisable. Then, you'll wake up on departure morning and calmly step onto the bus to begin one of the best days of your trip.

Rothenburg, Germany

The Romantic Road bus drivers are often characters. Twice I've had an eccentric guy named "Charlie Brown". Wearing a black top hat and blowing his whistle, he seems to know everyone he passes on the road. He waves and happily greets people all day long. At one point, his faithful canine friend, Snoopy, hops on the bus for a short ride. At Donauworth, as the bus crosses the baby Donau (Danube), he slips in his cassette of "The Blue Danube Waltz". The group on board loosens up, and you have time to talk to and enjoy the other travelers and build some friendships. This isn't just any bus ride.

Rothenburg

While the bus passes through many loveable little towns, Rothenburg is the most loveable. This is probably the most touristy town in Germany—and for good reason. I've yet to find a better-preserved medieval town. Rothenburg is a joy even on the most crowded day. In the Middle Ages, when Frankfurt and Munich were just wide spots in the road, Rothenburg was Germany's second largest city with a whopping population of 6000. Today it's her best-preserved medieval walled town, enjoying tremendous tourist popularity without losing its charm.

For those on the bus tour (or for a general orientation), here's Rothenburg in 90 minutes: From the bus stop, climb onto the medieval wall and hike clockwise to Rodertor (the second large gateway). From here follow the cobbles into the town center and continue through the Market Square straight down Herrengasse to the end of the castle garden for a glorious view of the "Tauber Riviera". By this time any normal person will have decided to leave the bus and spend the night. (Rooms listed in Appendix V.) But if you've got more willpower than common sense, shop and eat your way back through the town center to your bus in time to carry on down the Romantic Road.

Those trapped within the wondrous walls might actually hear the sounds of the Thirty Years War still echoing through the turrets and clock towers. Europe's most exciting medieval town is easily worth two nights and a day, if you've got them. And those spending the night enjoy the city without its daily hordes of big city day trippers.

Too often Rothenburg brings out the shopper in visitors before they've had a chance to appreciate the historic city. True, this is a great place to do your German shopping (visit Anneliese Friese' shop, 2 doors left of the tourist office—friendly, discount with this book and the best money exchange rates in town), but first see the town. The tourist infor-

mation office on the market square has guided tours in English. A local
historian, who's usually an intriguing character as well, will bring the
ramparts alive. A thousand years of history are packed between the
cobbles.

After your walking tour orientation you'll have plenty of sightseeing
ideas. First on my list is a walk around Rothenburg's medieval wall. This
mile and a half walk offers great views and is ideal before breakfast or at
sunset. For the best view of the town and surrounding countryside, make
the rigorous but rewarding climb to the top of the Town Hall Tower.

Don't miss Rothenburg's fascinating Medieval Crime and Punish-
ment Museum. It's full of old legal bits and pieces, instruments of punish-
ment and torture and even a special cage—complete with a metal gag for
nags—all well explained in English.

St. Jacob's Church contains a glorious 500-year-old Riemenschneider
altarpiece. Riemenschneider was the Michelangelo of German wood-
carvers, and this is the one "must see" art treasure in town.

For a peaceful break from the crowds take a countryside walk through the Tauber Valley. The trail leads from Rothenburg's pleasant castle gardens to the cute, skinny 600-year-old castle/summer home of Mayor Toppler. It's furnished intimately and is well worth a look. Notice the photo of bombed out 1945 Rothenburg on the top floor. Across from the castle a radiantly happy lady will show you her 800-year-old water-powered flour mill called the Fuchsmuhle. From here you can walk on past the covered bridge and huge trout to the peaceful village of Detwang, which is actually older than Rothenburg, and has a church with another impressive Riemenschneider altarpiece.

Rothenburg's little sister is Dinkelsbuhl, another wonderfully preserved medieval town an hour to the south. Old walls, towers, gateways and the peaceful green waters of the moat protect the many medieval jewels of architecture that lie within. The bus tour stops here giving you plenty of time for lunch at a typical restaurant (serving Frankonian specialties and Dinkelsbuhl beer) and for exploring, camera in hand, the old cobbled streets. Dinkelsbuhl celebrates the colorful medieval Kinderfest (Childrens' Festival) in mid-July (from the weekend before the 3rd Monday through the weekend after).

The Romantic Road has much more. If you order now you'll get Wurzburg with its fine Baroque Prince Bishop's Residenz—the Versailles of Franconia, and its glorious chapel. You can see another lovely carved altarpiece by Riemenschneider near Creglingen. To the south is Germany's best example of Baroque church architecture at the Wies Church, near Oberammergau (scaffolded until 1990), and Mad King Ludwig's Disneyesque Neuschwanstein castle near Fussen.

The Romantic Road is a quick, comfortable, inexpensive and easy way to see two of Germany's most beautiful towns and it's the best way to connect the Rhine and Bavaria.

19: Dungeons and Dragons—Europe's Nine Most Medieval Castle Experiences

Castles excite Americans. Since we have none in the USA, medieval castles are a popular European vacation target. From Ireland to Israel and from Sweden to Spain, European castle thrills lurk in countless dark nooks and dank crannies.

In Germany, the Rhine River is lined with castle-crowned hills.

There's even a castle built in the middle of the river. These can be enjoyed conveniently by train, car or boat (the best fifty mile stretch is between Koblenz and Mainz). To the south, Bavaria has many intriguing castles.

Castles line the Loire and guard every curve of the Mediterranean. From Spain, France, Italy and Yugoslavia to the impressive Crusader castles of Rhodes and Acre in the East, you'll find countless feudal fortresses in every direction.

Europe's forgotten castles, unblemished by turnstiles, postcard racks and coffee shops, are ignored by guidebooks. The aggressive traveler will find them by tapping local information sources, like the town tourist office and the friendly guy who runs your hotel or pension.

Here are nine medieval castle experiences, where the winds of the past really howl.

Carcassonne, France

Before me lives Carcassonne, the perfect medieval city. Like a fish that everyone thought was extinct, somehow Europe's greatest Romanesque fortress-city has survived the centuries.

Carcassonne's Medieval Ramparts.

I was supposed to be gone yesterday but here I sit—imprisoned by choice—curled in a cranny on top of the wall. The wind blows away the sounds of today and my imagination "medievals" me. The moat is one foot over and one-hundred feet down. Small plants and moss upholster my throne.

Twelve-hundred years ago Charlemagne stood below that wall with his troops—besieging the town for several years. A cunning townsperson saved "La Cite" just as food was running out. She fed the town's last bits of grain to the last pig and tossed him over the wall. Charlemagne's forces, amazed that the town still had enough food to throw fat pigs over the wall, decided they'd never succeed in starving the people out. They ended the siege and the city was saved. Today the walls that kept Charlemagne out open wide for visitors.

Carcassonne, medieval wonderland of towers, turrets, and cobbled alleys, is located in southwest France near the boring little country of Andorra. It's a castle and a walled city rolled into one—and a refreshing break after the touristic merry-go-round of the French Riviera and the intensity of Paris.

Carcassonne has a fine little youth hostel offering $8 beds (tel. 6825-2316), and its Hotel Aragon (15 Montee Comberleran, 11000 Carcassonne, tel. 68/471631) has good doubles for about $40. Your dinner expenses are up to you. I spent $25 for a lavish feast in the Romanesque dining hall of the Hotel de la Cite one night and $3 for ravioli, melon, bread and tea at the hostel the next. And, of course, there are the peasants who munch bread, cheese and wine among the ramparts while tossing crumbs to moat-birds and thinking of Charlemagne.

Warwick Castle, England

From Land's End to John O'Groats, I searched for the best castle in Britain. I found it. Warwick castle has much more than a fairytale exterior. It offers the visitor so much, the $6 admission fee is actually a bargain.

Like nearby Stratford, Warwick is "upon the Avon". Once you get by its moat, now a lush green park, Warwick (pronounced: "war-ick") will entertain you from lookout to dungeon. There's something for every taste—a fine and educational armory, a terrible torture chamber, a knight in shining armor posing on a horse, a Madame Tussaud re-creation of a royal weekend party, an 1898 game of statue-maker, and a grand garden park patrolled by peacocks who welcome picnickers.

Eltz Castle, Germany

Germany's best medieval castle experience is the Eltz Castle, above the Mosel River between Cochem and Koblenz. One of the very few Rhine/Mosel area castles never destroyed by the French, Berg Eltz is incredibly well-preserved and elegantly furnished. You'll learn here how even the lives of the Middle Age's rich and famous were "nasty, brutish and short" (as were many of the rich themselves). The approach to Berg Eltz is part of the thrill. You'll hike from the car park through a mysterious forest long enough to really get in a medieval mood, and then all of a sudden it appears, all alone—nothing but the past engulfed in nature— Berg Eltz. (It's a steep hour's hike from the nearest train station, Moselkern.)

Rheinfels Castle, Germany

Once the mightiest of all the Rhine castles, today Rheinfels is an intriguing ruin overlooking the pleasant medieval town of St. Goar. (Rooms listed in Appendix V.) Study and follow the helpful English information sheet and map before diving in. A flashlight is handy if you want to explore some of Rheinfels' several miles of spooky tunnels. The castle museum has a reconstruction of the castle showing how it looked before the French flattened it. Louis XIV destroyed all but one of the castles that line Germany's Rhine. (That castle is Marksburg which is great but lies on the inconvenient side of the river and allows visitors only as part of German language tours.)

Chateau Chillon, Switzerland

This wonderfully preserved 13th century castle set romantically at the edge of Lake Geneva near Montreux is worth a side trip from anywhere in southwest Switzerland. Follow the English brochure from tingly sit-on-the-medieval-window-sill views through fascinatingly furnished rooms. The dank dungeon, serious weapons and 700-year-old toilets will excite even the dullest travel partner. One of Switzerland's best youth hostels is a ten minute stroll down the lakeside promenade towards Montreux (tel. 021/9634934).

Reifenstein Castle, Italy

For an incredibly medieval kick in the pants, get off the *autobahn* one hour south of Innsbruck at the Italian town of Vipiteno/Sterzing.

Reifenstein guards the valley with her time-pocked sister, and offers castle connoisseurs the best-preserved (i.e., not prettied-up) original medieval castle interior I've ever seen. The lady who lives in Reifenstein castle takes groups through in Italian, German and only *un poco* English (tel. 0472/65879, tours at 9, 10, 11, 2 and 3 p.m.). You'll be lost in the mossy past as she explains how the cistern collected water, how drunken lords managed to get their key into the keyholes, how prisoners were left to rot in the dungeon (you'll look down the typical only-way-out hole in the ceiling) and you'll see the only original knights' sleeping quarters (rough hewn plank boxes lined with hay) in existence. The lady of Reifenstein gave me my most unique and intimately medieval castle experience ever.

Moorish Ruins of Sintra, Portugal

Just outside Lisbon, overlooking the sea and the town of Sintra, are the ruins of an 800-year-old Moorish (Moslem) castle. Ignored by the tourists who flock to the glitzy Pena Palace, a castle capping a neighboring hilltop, the ruins of Sintra offer a unique combination of scramble-up-and-down-the-ramparts fun, atmospheric picnic perches and desolation

"Mad" King Ludwig's Neuschwanstein Castle

with a view surrounded by an enchanted forest. With a little imagination it's hundreds of years ago, and you're under attack.

Castle Day—Neuschwanstein (Bavaria) and the Ehrenburg Ruins (Reutte in Tyrol)

Four of my favorite castles—two famous, two unknown—can be seen in one busy day. "Castle Day" takes you to Germany's "modern" Disney-like Neuschwanstein castle and the much older Ehrenburg ruins across the Austrian border in Reutte.

Home-base is the small Tyrolian town of Reutte, which is situated very close to the German border is three scenic hours by train west of Innsbruck. Reutte is less crowded than Fussen and has a helpful tourist information office with a room-finding service (open until 6 p.m., tel. 05672/2336) that can set you up in a private home "any day of the year" for $12. Reutte's cheapest beds are in its fine little youth hostel (open June 15 to August 25, tel. 05672/3039, friendly, clean, non-members accepted), and the best splurge hotel is the elegant old world Goldener Hirsch ($45 doubles, right downtown, tel. 05672/2508, ask for Helmut or Monica).

From Reutte, catch the early bus across the border to Fussen, the German town nearest to Neuschwanstein. Then take a local bus to Neuschwanstein, the greatest of King Ludwig II of Bavaria's fairy tale castles. His extravagance and romanticism earned him the title "Mad King Ludwig" (and an early death). His castle is one of Europe's most popular attractions. Get there early. The castle opens at 8:30, a good hour before the tour groups attack.

Take the fascinating (and required) English tour. This castle, only 100 years old, is a textbook example of 19th century Romanticism. To insult the middle ages, people who were glad they were finally out of them named that culture "Gothic" or barbarian. Then, all of a sudden, in the 1800s it became hip to be square, and Neo-Gothic became the rage. Throughout Europe old castles were restored and new ones built—with chivalry on the wallpaper. King Ludwig II put his medieval fantasy on the hilltop not for defensive reasons—but because he liked the view.

The lavishly wall-papered interior with damsels in distress, dragons, and knights in gleaming armor, is enchanting. (A little knowledge of Wagner's operas goes a long way in bringing these stories to life.) Ludwig had great taste—for a "mad" king. Read up on this political misfit—a poet, hippie king in the age of Bismarck and "realpolitik". He was found dead in a lake, never to enjoy his dream come true. After the tour, climb

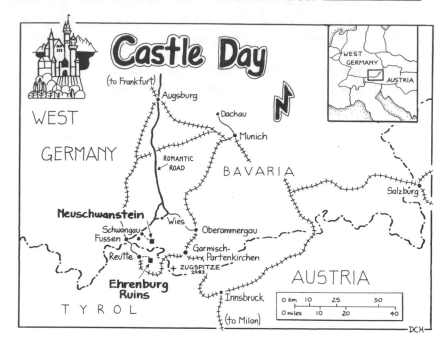

further up the hill to Mary's Bridge for the best view. There is nothing quite like the crazy, yet elegant castle of Bavaria's mad king.

Ludwig's boyhood home, the Hohenschwangau Castle at the foot of the hill, is worth a visit and offers a better look at Ludwig's life and far fewer crowds. Like its more famous neighbor, it costs about $3 and takes about an hour to tour.

This is a busy day. Thinking ahead, you noted the time your bus returns to Reutte so catching it is no problem. By lunch time you've crossed back into Austria and are ready for a completely different castle experience.

Pack a picnic and your camera and, with the help of some local directions, walk thirty minutes out of town to the brooding Ehrenburg ruins. You'll see two hills, one small and one larger, each crowned by a ruined, but real, medieval castle.

The Kleine Schloss, or small castle, is on the smaller hill. It's pretty ruined but wonderfully free of anything from the twentieth century—except for a great view of Reutte sleeping peacefully in the valley below.

The Grosse Schloss, or large castle, is perched atop the biggest hill (you can't see it from a distance) eerily overgrown and even more ruined. This is quite a hike above the small castle but worthwhile if you have time to get romantic. It's best with a cloud shroud in a spooky mist. This is especially thrilling if you've ever dreamed of medieval knights in distress and damsels in shining armor. You have your own castle—complete with sword ferns. Lower your hair; unfetter that imagination.

Back down in Reutte, you'll find your castle reconstructed on restaurant wallpaper. Ask Helmut at the Goldener Hirsch where you can find a folk evening full of slap dancing and yodel-foolery. A hearty dinner and an evening of local Tyrolian entertainment is a fitting way to end your memorable "Castle Day".

20: Alsace

The French province of Alsace stands like a flower-child referee between Germany and France. Bounded by the Rhine river on the east and the softly rolling Vosges Mountains on the west, this is a lush land of villages, vineyards, ruined castles and an almost naive cheeriness. Wine is the primary industry, topic of conversation, dominant mouthwash, perfect excuse for countless festivals and a tradition that provides the foundation for the rest of the Alsatian folk culture.

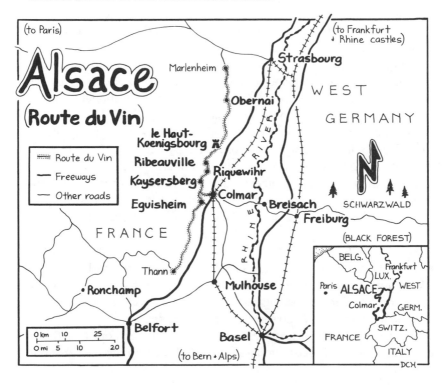

Because of its location, natural wealth, its naked vulnerability and the fact that Germany thinks the mountains are the natural border and France thinks the Rhine river is, nearly every Alsatian generation has weathered an invasion. A thousand years as a political pawn between Germany and France has given the Alsace a hybrid culture. This Gallic-Teutonic mix is seen in many ways. Restaurants serve sauerkraut with fine sauces behind half-timbered Bavarian gables. If you listen carefully you'll notice that Alsatian French is peppered with German words. On doorways of homes you'll see mixed names like "Jacques Schmidt", or "Dietrich Le Beau". Most locals who swear do so bilingually and many of the towns have German names.

Alsace's wine road, the "Route du Vin", is an asphalt ribbon tying ninety miles of vineyards, villages and feudal fortresses into an understandably popular tourist package. The dry and sunny climate makes for good wine and happy tourists. It's been a wine center since Roman days. As you drive through 30,000 acres of vineyards blanketing the hills from Marleheim to Thann you'll see how vinocentric this area is. This is the source of some of France's finest wine.

During the October harvest season all Alsace erupts into a carnival of colorful folk costumes, traditional good-time music and Dionysian smiles. I felt as welcome as a local grape picker, and my tight sightseeing plans became as hard to follow as a straight line.

Wine-tasting is popular throughout the year. Roadside "degustation" signs invite you into the wine "caves" where a local producer will serve you all seven Alsatian wines from dry to sweet with educational commentary if requested. Be sure to try the Alsatian champagne called *Cremant*. "Cave-hopping" is a great way to spend an afternoon on the "Route du Vin". The more expensive wines cost nearly $5 a bottle. Who ever thought French wine-tasting could be a poorman's sport?

The small caves are fun but be sure to tour a larger wine co-op. Beer-drinking Germans completely flattened many Alsatian towns in 1944. The small family-run vineyards of these villages returned as large, modern and efficient co-operatives. Little Bennwihr is a co-op of 211 people. They are proud to show you their facilities which can crush 600 tons of grapes a day and turn out 14,000 bottles an hour. No tour finishes without taking full advantage of the tasting room. Bennwihr has a wine tradition going back to Roman times. Its name is from the Latin "Benonis Villare" or Beno's estate—and Beno served up a great Reisling.

If you can pick grapes you can get a job in October. For a hard day in the vineyards you'll get room and board, $30 and an intimate Alsatian social experience lubricated liberally, logically, by the leading local libation. (Sorry, I won't do that again.)

There's more to Alsace than meets the palate. Those centuries of successful wine production built prosperous and colorful villages. Countless castles capped hilltops to defend the much invaded plain, and wine wasn't the only art form loved and patronized by local connoisseurs.

Alsatian towns are unique, historic mosaics of gables, fountains, medieval belltowers and gateways, cheery old inns, churches and ancient ramparts. Geared for the tourist trade they offer plenty of budget one and two star hotels (around $20 per double) and ample opportunity to savor the Alsatian cuisine. Colmar is the best homebase town. Riquewihr, Kaysersberg (home of Dr. Albert Schweizer), Eguisheim and Ribeauville are just a few of the storybook towns you'll be sure to enjoy. Several Alsatian castles are also worth touring. Climb the tallest tower and survey Alsace, looking as it has for centuries—the endless vineyards of the "Route du Vin".

Colmar

My favorite city in Alsace, Colmar, sees very few American tourists. Popular with German and French travelers, this well-preserved old town of 70,000 is the perfect base for exploring the villages, castles and "Route du Vin".

Historic beauty was usually a poor excuse to be spared the ravages of World War II. But it worked for Colmar. The American and British military were careful not to bomb the half-timbered old burghers' houses, characteristic red and green tiled roofs and cobbled lanes of Alsace's most beautiful city.

Today Colmar not only survives, it thrives—with historic buildings, impressive art treasures, and the popular Alsatian cuisine that attracts eager palates from all over Europe. And Colmar has that special French talent of being great but cozy at the same time. School girls park their rickety horse carriage in front of the city hall ready to give visitors a three-dollar clip-clop tour of the old town. Antique shops welcome browsers, and hotel managers run down the sleepy streets to pick up fresh croissants in time for breakfast.

Colmar offers heavyweight sights in a warm small-town package. By the end of the Middle Ages the walled town was a thriving trade center filled with rich old houses. The wonderfully restored tanners' quarters is a quiver of tall narrow and half-timbered buildings. The confused roof tops struggle erratically to get enough sun to dry their animal skins. Nearby is "La Petite Venice", complete with canals and a pizzeria.

For maximum local fun remember Colmar goes crazy during its August winefest and for two weekends in September called the "Sauerkraut Days". Feasting, dancing, music and wine—Alsatian style.

Colmar combines its abundance of art with a knack for showing it off. The artistic geniuses Grunewald, Schongauer and Bartholdi all called Colmar home.

Before Frederic Bartholdi created our Statue of Liberty a century ago, he adorned his hometown with many fine, if smaller, statues. Don't miss the little Bartholdi museum offering a good look at the artist's life and some fun Statue of Liberty trivia.

Four hundred years earlier Martin Schongauer was the leading local artist. His "Virgin of the Rose Garden" has given even hockey players and state troopers goose bumps. Looking fresh, crisp and new, it's set magnificently in a gothic Dominican church. I sat with a dozen people silently as if at a symphony. Schongauer's Madonna performed solo on center stage, lit by 14th century stained glass, with a richness and tenderness that could only come from another age—a late-gothic masterpiece. Even if your sightseeing has worked you to the point where you "never want to see another Madonna and Child", give this one a chance.

The Unterlinden museum is one of my favorite small museums in Europe. Housed in a 750-year-old convent next to the Tourist Office, it's the best collection anywhere of Alsatian art and folk treasures. Exhibits range from Neolithic and Gallo-Roman archeological collections to the modern art of Monet, Renoir, Braque and Picasso. It's a medieval and Renaissance "homeshow". You can lose yourself in a 17th century Alsatian wine cellar complete with presses, barrels and tools.

The highlight of the museum (and for me, the city) is Grunewald's gripping Isenheim Altarpiece. This is actually a series of paintings on hinges that pivot like shutters. Designed to help people in a hospital—long before the age of pain-killers—suffer through their horrible skin diseases, it's one of the most powerful paintings ever. Stand petrified in front of it and let the agony and suffering of the crucifixion drag its gnarled fingers down your face. Just as you're about to break down and sob with those in the painting, turn to the happy ending—a psychedelic explosion of resurrection happiness. It's like jumping from the dentist's chair directly into a jacuzzi. We know very little about Grunewald except that, through his paintings, he's played tether ball with human emotions for five hundred years. For a reminder that the Middle Ages didn't have a monopoly on grief, stop at the museum's full-sized cloth copy of Picasso's famous "Guernica".

Colmar has a helpful tourist information center providing city maps, guides and accommodations help. They can also suggest side trips around Alsace's "wine road", into Germany's Black Forest and nearby Freiburg or even a tour of the Maginot Line.

Finding a room should be easy. My favorite is Hotel-Restaurant Le Rapp, downtown at 16 rue Berthe Molly (tel. 416210). Bernard is the owner and perfect French gentleman. He offers $30 doubles and classy Alsatian cuisine in an elegant dining hall. Named after a hometown boy who became one of Napoleon's top generals, Le Rapp—like Colmar—is hard to beat.

21: French Cuisine

Cultures express themselves differently around the world. Switzerland is savored in the mountains. Music is Austria's forte and Italy immerses you in great art. Japan tunes you in to the beauties of sensuality and simplicity, and France is the world's great taste treat.

A visitor to the Alps needs a book of hikes. Those going to Italy will find an art history book handy. And, if you're going to France, you should have a list of regional culinary specialties. This chapter tastes better than it reads. It's basically a check list of each region's most exciting dishes, cheese and wines. Use it, consider each item a local art form—a Botticelli for your belly—that should be experienced next time you're eating your way through France.

Provence (The Rhone Valley) and the Cote d' Azur (French Riviera) are famous for *Bouillabaisse,* a fish and shellfish stew in white wine, garlic, saffron and olive oil. Other popular dishes include the onion and anchovy tart with black olives called *Pissaladiere;* an eggplant, tomato, pepper, onion, and garlic stew served hot or cold called *Ratatouille;* and *Brandade de Morue,* a blend of pureed fish with olive oil and spices. Banon cheese is made locally from goat or cow milk. (Try it, ewe like it.) A popular sweet is Nougat, made from sugar and almonds. The most important regional wines to sample are *Cotes de Provence* (rose), *Tavel* (rose), *Cotes du Rhone* (red, rose or white), and *Chateauneuf du Pape* (red or white).

The Basque country, straddling the French-Spanish border on the Atlantic coast eats, speaks, and lives its own way. The *Poulet Basquaise*

chicken in a hot pepper sauce and the *Jambon de Bayonne,* a raw, slightly salty ham are local specialties, as are duck and goose pates. The Basques are proud of their *Fromage de Pyrenees,* made from cow's milk, and their popular local wine, *Jurancon.*

In Bordeaux you have, of course fine local wines and truffles. Also, try *Entrecote Bordelaise,* a rib-eye steak in a mushroom, red wine, shallots and local marrow sauce. North of Bordeaux is Cognac. Bet you know what to drink there.

In Bourgogne, southeast of Paris, you'll picnic in class with *escargots* (snails), *foie gras* (goose liver pate with truffles), Burgundy wines, and of course, spicy Dijon mustard.

After a long day of chasing chateaux on the Loire, find a cozy restaurant and treat yourself to *Andouilles,* a spicy tripe sausage (don't look tripe up in the dictionary, just eat it), *Anguilles* (eels), a *Tarte fromagere* (cheese tart) and macaroons for dessert. The Loire is famous for its wines. Try *Vouvray, Muscadet* and *Sancerre*.

In the French Alps and Savoie, Fondue and *Raclette* are two melted cheese specialties. *Arbois-Jaune* is the wine to try.

In Normandy, the adventurous glutton will want to try Tripes *a La Mode de Caen* (tripe cooked in the oven with calf's feet, vegetables and apple brandy)—a meal in itself. The more timid tasters are sure to enjoy crepes (for both dinner and dessert) here. The locals wash these tasty thin pancakes down with cider (usually alcoholic). Before turning in, have a glass of *Calvados,* a very powerful apple brandy.

In Brittany sample the seafood, shellfood and *Far,* a sweet cake made with prunes and brandy. *Crepes* are also popular here. Purists go for *crepe beurre et sucre* (just butter and sugar).

In the north of France, the people eat a slimy sausage called *Ouillette* and *Frites/Moules* (French fries and mussels). Wash everything down with local beer.

Alsace, on the German border, has an exciting cuisine of its own. Many dishes have a German twist, like *Choucroute garnie* (sauerkraut with ham, bacon and sausage). Try the onion tart and the rhubarb tart as well as the powerful muenster cheese. Alsatian wine is world famous. Explore the region's "Wine Road" and taste them all. I like the *Gewurztraminer* and the *Riesling*.

In nearby Lorraine, real men eat quiche. The people of Lorraine turn small yellow plums into a dandy brandy (*Mirabelle*) and a tart (*Tarte aux Mirabelles*).

To the west is Champagne (and plenty of it) and even further west is Paris, famous for its onion soup and Brie cheese.

This "list" is far from complete, but it's a good start. Remember, the French eat lunch from 12 to 2 and so should you. In evening time, eight to nine is the time to dine. Tips are included in the price unless otherwise indicated (*service non-compris*), and you call a waiter with a polite *"garcon s'il vous plait,"* or *"mademoiselle"*. To ask for the bill, just scribble on your palm with an imaginary pencil and ask *"l'addition?"* (pron: lah dee zee oh). Budget time to linger over a meal like the French. The Michelin Red Guide is the ultimate guide to French restaurants, and the most serious Francofoodophiles don't leave home without it. Any restaurant displaying a *Relais Routiers* recommendation is a truck driver's choice— *magnifique! Bon appetite!*

22: In the Shadow of Venice— Grado, Palmanova, Chioggia

Tourists generally zip from Munich, Vienna, or Salzburg straight to Venice and then, "logically", down to Florence or Rome. On my last visit to Italy I enjoyed the perverse thrill of by-passing Venice and focusing on a few of its neglected in-the-shadow-of-the-superstar neighbors.

Just south of Austria near the Italian city of Udine, and a stone's throw from the scenic new Salzburg-Venice autobahn, you'll find some fascinating towns.

Gemona was near the epicenter of a tragic 1976 earthquake. Broken clocks around town memorialize the awesome minute that took 300 of the townspeople and most of its buildings. Today it's a sort of Steven Spielberg Italy—rebuilt, clean, new, and sleek, but according to its old Renaissance designs. Scaffolding and dusty work crews give it a back-stage feeling as the town charges forward with an impressive confidence. Wind up its main street to the parking lot just below the newly crumbled castle. Surrounded by medieval carvings and modern rubble, the church leans, but stubbornly refuses to fall. Inside is a fascinating photo essay of the earthquake and its aftermath.

A little farther south is Palmanova—1593's planned city of the future. From the sky, this Venetian Renaissance fortress city looks like a big stone snowflake. Its moated, symmetrical outer walls contain an orderly interior. Each slice of the town has its own small square and feeds into the huge hexagonal central square. The church is a textbook example of pure Renaissance planning. Apparently, our modern world can't improve on this bold product of 400 years ago—you won't find a 20th century building anywhere.

On the coast just north of Venice's lagoon is a town that calls itself the "Mother of Venice"—Grado. Born like Venice, on an island, but much earlier (in Roman times), Grado is now connected to the mainland by a causeway. Hordes of Europeans flock to Grado's lovely beaches each summer, but off season its 10,000 residents relax quietly.

Five miles inland from Grado are the very quiet and underrated Roman ruins of the town of Aquileia. In the time of Christ, Aquileia was a busy port and a Roman provincial capital. After an illustrious 600 years, Attila the Hun descended upon Aquileia and raped, pillaged and ruined it. Today it slumbers, politely entertaining its few guests with huge chunks of a former harbor, ruins of its forum, amphitheater and baths. Its basilica is carpeted with mosaics dating from 313 (just after Emperor Constantine legalized Christianity). In this ancient church and the fascinating underground world excavated around it, you'll wander among 700 square yards of Roman mosaic symbols and Bible stories.

Finally, for a taste of Venice without its crowds, explore Chioggia. This pleasant town, an hour's drive south of Venice (or a two hour vaporetto cruise) is Italy's top fishing port. You'll find canals, peaceful alleys, breezy laundry, crumbly buildings and old churches. Except for a few cars, Chioggia is Venice's shadow, but without the tourist crowds and much cheaper. Ponder the canal from the summit of an ornate marble bridge. Picnic on the crusty deck of an old fishing boat, and savor your cappuccino in a bar where the tourist is still an oddity.

23: Peloponnesian Highlights— Overlooked Greece

Stretching south from Athens is the Peloponnesian Peninsula. This land of ancient Olympia, Corinth and Sparta has more than its share of historic rubble, but it also offers plenty of fun in the eternal Greek sun with pleasant fishing villages, sandy beaches and bathtub-warm water.

Epidavros, state of the art acoustics

Just two hours south of Athens by car or bus is the Peloponnesian port town of Nafplion. Small, cozy and easy to know, it's a welcome relief after the black-hanky smoggy intensity of Athens. Not only is Nafplion itself fun, but it's a handy home base for exploring some of Greece's greatest ancient sights.

Nafplion's harbor is guarded by two castles, one on a small island and the other capping the hill above the town. Both are wonderfully flood-lit at night. The hill castle, an old Venetian outpost from the days she ruled Europe economically, is the best-preserved castle of its kind in Greece—well worth the 999-step climb. From the highest ramparts you can see several Aegean islands (great one-day side trips by boat from Nafplion) and deep into the mountainous interior of the Peloponnesian Peninsula. Below you lies an enticing beach with clear, bathtub-warm water.

Nafplion has plenty of hotels, and its harbor is lined with restaurants specializing in fresh seafood. An octopus dinner cost me $4—succulent! The next night my dinner featured snapper. He smiled through the entire meal.

The infamous resin-flavored retsina wine is a drink you'll want to experience—once. Maybe with octopus. The first glass is awful. The third glass is dangerous—it starts to taste good. If you drink any more you'll feel it all the next day—it permeates your body like DMSO.

For a change, on my third night I left Nafplion's popular waterfront district and had a memorable meal in a hole-in-the-wall joint. There was no menu, just an entertaining local crowd and a nearsighted man who, in a relaxed frenzy, ran the whole show. He scurried about, greeting eaters, slicing, dicing, laughing, singing to himself, cooking, serving and billing. Potato stew, meatballs, a plate of at least thirty tiny fried fish with lime and unlimited wine cost $7 for 2—and could have fed 4.

Nafplion is just a short drive from two important classical sights: Epidavros and Mycenae.

Epidavros, just 18 miles northeast, is the best-preserved ancient Greek theater. Built 2500 years ago to seat 14,000, it's still used each summer to house a popular drama festival reviving the greatest plays of antiquity. Try to see Epidavros either early or late in the day—the marvelous acoustics are best enjoyed in near solitude. From the most distant seat you can hear the beep beep of your partner's digital watch down on the theater floor.

Thirty minutes in the other direction from Nafplion are the ruins of Mycenae. This was the capital of the Myceneans of Trojan war fame who dominated Greece a thousand years before the age of Socrates.

You're a guest of honor at a Greek wedding festival

As you tour this fascinating fortified citadel, remember that these people were as awesome to the ancient Greeks of Socrates' day as the generation of Socrates is to us. The classical Greeks marveled at the huge stones and workmanship of the Mycenean ruins and figured, "Man no one could build with such colossal rocks, this must be the work of the giant Cyclopes." Mycenean building style was called "Cyclopian" architecture during Greece's Golden Age.

Visitors today can climb deep into a cool ancient cistern, explore the giant tholos tombs and inspect reconstructed pots near the North Gate next to a pile of shards that looks like a spilled jigsaw puzzle. The tombs, built 1500 years before Christ, stand like huge stone igloos with smooth subterranean domes forty feet wide and forty feet tall. The most important Mycenean artifacts, like the golden "Mask of Agamemnon", are in the National Museum back in Athens.

Finikoundas

The prize-winning Peloponnesian hide-away is the remote village of Finikoundas. Located on the southwest tip of the peninsula between the twin Venetian fortress towns of Koroni and Methoni, Finikoundas is big enough to have a good selection of restaurants, bed and breakfast places (*domatio* in Greek), a few shops and a business life of its own, but not big enough to draw the typical resort buildup with its traffic, crowds and

THE **PELOPONNESIAN PENINSULA**

← TO CORFU
  & BRINDISI, ITALY
DELPHI
EVIA
RIO
PATRAS
ISTHMUS OF CORINTH
DAFNI
CORINTH
PIREAUS
ATHENS
OLYMPIA
MYCENAE
ARGOS
EPIDAVROS
ZAKINTHOS
DIMITSANA
NAFPLION
POROS
CAPE SOUNION
GREAT BEACH
HYDRA
IONIAN
MISTRA
SPETSES
TO AEGEAN ISLANDS
SEA
SPARTA
METHONI
KORONI
MONEM-VASSIA
FINIKOUNDAS
PIRGOS DIROU CAVES
0 KM 50 80
0 MI   50
KITHIRA
YUG. BUL. TUR.
ALB.
GREECE
CORFU
TUR
ATHENS
CRETE
0 KM 200
DCH

noise. It's just right for your Greek holiday retreat.

Finikoundas has plenty of private rooms for rent. Plan to spend $8 for a cozy room a few steps from the beach. This was the best beach I found on the Penninsula, and the swimming was fine—even in October.

After a little Apollo-worshipping, I wandered through town in search of Dionysus, at just the right waterfront restaurant. The place I found couldn't have been more "waterfront". Since the fishing village had no dock, its Lilliputian fishing boats were actually anchored to the restaurant. I settled my chair comfortably into the sand and let the salty atmosphere take over. I dined amid rusty four-hooker anchors, honorably retired old ropes and peely dinghies as weak wavelets licked my table's legs.

A naked 20-watt bulb dangled from the straw roof which rotted unnoticed by Greeks and a few perpetually off-season Germans who seemed to be regulars. I couldn't help but think that if all mankind lived as simply as these Greeks we'd have more leisure and less tension.

Cuisine in a village like this is predictable—fresh seafood, Greek salad and local wine. After a few days in Greece you become a connoisseur of the salad, appreciating the wonderful tomatoes, rich feta cheese and even the olive oil drenching—er, dressing.

Almost within splashing distance of my table, Greek boys in swim suits not much bigger than a rat's hammock gathered around a bucketful of just-caught octopi. They were tenderizing the poor things to death by whipping them like wet rags over and over on a big flat rock. They'll be featured momentarily on someone's dinner plate—someone else's.

Evening in any Mediterranean town is a pleasant time of strolling and socializing. The streets buzz with easygoing activity. Dice chatter on dozens of backgammon boards, entrepreneurial dogs and goal-oriented children busy themselves as a tethered goat chews on something inedible in its low-profile corner. From the other end of town comes the happy music of a christening party. Dancing women fill the building while their children mimic them in the street. Farther down, two black-clad elderly women sit like tired dogs on the curb.

Succumbing to the lure of the pastry shop, I sat down for my daily honey-soaked baklava. I told the cook I was American. "Oh," he said, shaking his head with sadness and pity, "you work too hard." I assured him, "Right, but not today."

24: Diverse Yugoslavia

Imagine a country the size of Oregon with seven distinct peoples in six republics who speak five languages, with three religions (Orthodox, Catholic, and Muslim), two alphabets (Latin and Cyrillic) and one government. That's Yugoslavia, a fascinating cultural cocktail offering the visitor as much diversity, contrast and thrills per mile, minute and dollar as any European country.

When the "Iron Curtain" was dropped, Americans filed Yugoslavia away in their minds somewhere between Bulgaria and bleak. But the 22 million Yugoslavians are pioneering an independent economic course mixing capitalism and socialism. Their success has replaced most of the dreariness that tints their eastern neighbors with signs of "prosperity" (fancy hotels, sprawling resorts, traffic jams, modern shopping centers) and a spirit of pride and determination to maintain their relative freedom and prosperity.

From a traveler's point of view, Yugoslavia is Western—not Eastern—and, with a little planning and creativity, travel here can be more

exciting than travel elsewhere in Western Europe—and only a little more difficult.

Study. To appreciate this country you should think of it as many little countries—Slovenia, Croatia, Kosovo, Serbia, Bosnia-Hercegovina— each with its own features, heritage, Nathan Hales and Barbra Streisands. Cross each mini-border with fanfare. History is very close to these people. Their union was formed in 1918. One-fifth of the people were killed fighting for it in WWII. Today, parts of the land are chattering into the computer age while others are stuck in the mud of the past.

Getting around can be tedious. The trains and buses get you where you'll need to go—slowly. While they'll win no awards, they are cheap and offer plenty of boredom or intrigue—depending on what you're looking for. I'd rather drive a car. Bringing a car in from the north or renting within requires only an American driver's license.

Driving in from Greece is trickier. Before my trip, I was told that cars with Greek plates weren't allowed in. As usual, some on-the-spot research overcame this limitation. For $50 and my bank card's security, a large Athenian car rental agency (Inter-rent) did the necessary paperwork, got the permit and rented me a car to take into Yugoslavia—provided I returned it to Greece.

When Yugoslavia rations gas, tourists are exempt. We can buy gas coupons at banks, borders and better hotels everywhere. Roads are small and windy but decent and sparsely traveled. On my last visit I drove a thousand trouble-free miles and took full advantage of my rental car to boldly go where no tour bus had gone before to explore the most remote corners of Europe's last frontier. (Definition of touristic frontier: where village children mob a visitor's car out of friendly curiosity.)

While most foreign food is exotic if you spend enough, even simple Yugoslavian cuisine will leave a good taste in your memory for years to come. Choosing from strudel and baklava on the same menu, you're constantly reminded that this is a land where East meets West. On Lake Ohrid, you'll find a tasty kind of trout found nowhere else. The south is the land of paprikas. Markets are full of colorful peppers, so you're likely to find a couple of the red, green or yellow specialties even on your breakfast plate. In the north you'll find entire lambs routinely roasting on festive skewers. In Muslim sections of the country, restaurants offer tasty Turkish cuisine, and on the touristic Adriatic coast you'll find everything from fresh seafood to pizza parlors to fast-food havens for the timid tourist. Meals range from two to ten dollars and a good bottle of local wine is very cheap. The water is drinkable throughout the country. Yugoslavia's socialism shows through in its telltale lack of citrus fruits and its lousy ersatz chocolates.

Hotels are government regulated and generally cheap. Big city hotels charge up to $80 for rooms while good doubles cost about $20 in smaller towns. The local term for bed and breakfast is *sobe* and, for $10 per person, these private rooms are a great deal. Shop around since the government controls the price but not the quality. If you pay in dollars you usually score big points with your host. Dollars buy things their money can't—like gas and travel.

Outside of tourist areas and big cities, few locals speak English. A little German goes a long way since many Yugoslavians worked in Germany or had to study that language during the War. Take half an hour to learn the Cyrillic alphabet if you'll be traveling in the South. If you do your homework, you'll know "PECTOPAH" spells "Restoran", and in Yugoslavia that spells relief to a hungry traveler.

Dubrovnik

Dubrovnik is Europe's most romantic city. Set on Yugoslavia's sparkling Dalmatian coast, laced together by a massive wall with amazing Old World architectural unity, it is indeed the "Pearl of the Adriatic".

Dubrovnik is the most cosmopolitan place in Yugoslavia—and the most touristed. But it's a living fairy tale that shouldn't be missed.

Dubrovnik's present day charm is the sleepy result of its no-nonsense past when she was the second city of the grand Venetian Empire. Her Titian paintings and traffic-free marble avenues are the legacy of a shrewd and independent city, a trading power that bought off the Ottoman invaders and freed its slaves in the 15th century.

Originally, Dubrovnik was two towns, one on the mainland, the other on a tiny island. When the narrow strait separating the two was filled in and made into the main street and the towns were joined by a huge 18-foot thick wall, a united Dubrovnik rose to prominence. Today more visitors than merchants cross over the wooden drawbridge and under the Gothic arch into the traffic-free glory of old Dubrovnik.

Dubrovnik's individual sights are pleasant, but nothing to jump ship for—several convents, a few works by famous painters, some very mediocre museums and Europe's oldest pharmacy (1317). The attraction here is the city itself. Orient yourself with a walk around the wall. This one-mile walk culminates with the best overall view at the Minceta Tower.

The *Placa,* or "Main Street", bisects the circle formed by the wall. The *Placa* is the heartbeat of the city, an Old World shopping mall by day and a sprawling cocktail party after dark where everybody seems to be doing the traditional *korzo,* or evening stroll. Flirting, ice cream licking, flaunting and gawking—it's like "cruising" without cars.

The Lindo Folk Dance Company puts on Dubrovnik's "really big shoe" twice a week. A little folk dancing often can go a long way, but this group whirled, stomped, screamed and smiled for two frenzied hours—and I still wanted more. I've never seen such a rainbow wardrobe of folk costumes and so much bubbly dancing energy packaged so atmospherically under 500-year-old stone arches. This fast-paced show at the Revelin Fort is the best four dollars you can spend in Dubrovnik.

It seems that nearly all of Dubrovnik's 60,000 people are involved in the tourist trade, either feeding, bedding or selling. In peak season I'd swear there are two visitors for each local person. Nevertheless, this queen of Yugoslavian tourism handles her crowds well. There always seems to be good food, enough beds and plenty of quiet corners for those who want them.

Dubrovnik's hotels are crowded and expensive. I always go the *sobe* (pron: so-beh) route. In the case of Dubrovnik, the room-finding service at the tourist office is a hindrance. You'll do best by wandering the back streets or the bus station and letting it be known you're in need of *sobe,*

Choose between ancient, very colorful but gloomy private rooms in the old town or remarkable comfort in more modern local-style houses just outside the wall. I found a desireable neighborhood and asked the first woman I saw, "*Sobe?*" She pointed to the next door. The lady there told me her rooms were all taken but she took me down the street where, for $10, I was finally set up—in someone's house with their 1940s wedding picture staring right down on me in that big double bed.

Dubrovnik can wine and dine with the best of Mediterranean resort towns. I explain my needs to my landlady (small, untouristy place where locals go for a special time) and choose her recommendation over any guidebook favorites. It was a winner—Rozarij Restaurant (Zlatarska 4, tel. 23791) has the best fish in the old town. Their mixed grill (for two people) comes with four different fish lined up on a big plate. Add a paprika salad, Trappist cheese (a must), creme caramel dessert and plenty of red house wine, and you'll enjoy a tasty ten-dollar finale to a thrilling day.

Kosovo—The Yugoslavian Albania.

Albania, crouching between Greece and Yugoslavia, is the recluse of countries. Recently it broke relations with its only ally—China. Americans aren't allowed in, and it looks like its totalitarian rulers are doing a great job of keeping out the "evil" Western influence.

Though we can't visit Albania we can see its people, since a third of all Albanians live in the remote Yugoslavian district of Kosovo which borders Albania on the north. Kosovo is served by several small, winding but decent roads. A hairy bus ride connecting two of Europe's dullest cities, Skopje and Titograd, cuts through the heart of this fascinating, most remote corner of Europe. The ride is long and exhausting, but the mountain views and intimate glimpses of village life make the time fly. As your bus climbs higher into the mountains, the twentieth century fades. You'll see people doing their laundry on rocks grooved by their ancestors' dirty socks. Those people seem to live their entire lives up there—stranded in the past.

Stop at the entertaining town of Pritzren. The hotel on the main square charges $12 per person, with breakfast. Sorry, you can't spend more.

The Kosovan-Albanian culture is so different from ours that even everyday things take on a fresh playfulness. I often envy wide-eyed toddlers excitedly exploring things we adults see as mundane. In this respect, Pritzren can make you a child again. You're culturally blindfolded, and they've rearranged the furniture. Everything is different, a challenge and a surprise.

Since donkey carts have no headlights, the setting sun dictates rush hour. Oxcarts loaded with colorfully dressed peasant women return from the fields, and the town streets fill with people.

Turkish and Muslim influence is very strong; the Yankee impact is minimal. This is the only part of Europe that doesn't sing American pop music. Skull-caps and minarets, shish kebabs and rice pudding, goofy men and hidden women are all reminiscent of Turkey.

Without a list of museums and palaces to see, you have to be more creative in your "sight"-seeing. For lack of anything better to do on one particular corner, I enjoyed a shoeshine. This was an event, and a crowd gathered. One proud businessman made sure everyone knew he could speak English. An English-speaking Kosovan is rare. Take advantage of this willing source of local information.

Later on I let a barber give me an old-fashioned shave—like one you'd see on "Gunsmoke". He was a real artist, dressed in a tie and a white lab coat with two eager apprentices. He trimmed my beard lovingly and refused to accept any payment. As I left, he pointed to a painting on the wall of a similarly trim-bearded sultan and made some joke about a harem. Normally in the Muslim world my red beard earns me the nick-name "Ali Baba".

Always nearby looms the border of the real Albania with its fierce dogs, bald mountains, no-nonsense guards and desolate "no man's land". The Kosovans and all Yugoslavians have their share of economic and political problems, but with the devastation of World War II still fresh in their minds, they treasure their peace. Nestled as they are between the muzzled peoples of Bulgaria and Albania, they enjoy relative freedom and economic success. A visit to Kosovo is a thought-provoking experience.

Plitvice—Yugoslavia's Grand Canyon

The Plitvice National Park, south of Zagreb, is one of Europe's great-est natural wonders—a kind of Grand Canyon and Niagara Falls rolled into one. There's nothing like this grand canyon of sixteen terraced lakes laced together by waterfalls. Countless cascades and strangely clear and colorful water make this park a misty natural wonderland.

You can enjoy a whole day picnicking, rowing, exploring behind "bridal veil" falls and climbing stone stairways that are losing their battle with the busy Plitvice waters. Children love Plitvice and even Mom and

Plitvice National Park, Yugoslavis

Dad scamper and feel kind of frisky. Public buses serve Plitvice from many cities including Zagreb. (Plitvice is closed in the winter.)

These three highlights of Yugoslavia—Plitvice, Dubrovnik and the bus ride through Kosovo—can be part of your trip from Central Europe to

Greece or vice versa. Most people take the boring marathon train ride through Yugoslavia via its dull capital, Belgrade. While this is the fastest way to Athens (short of flying) it will seem like a million years.

A more interesting six-day plan would be: take the train from Central Europe to Zagreb, spend the night there and travel to Dubrovnik by bus, spending some time in Plitvice, Split (with Diocletian's Palace), and Korcula (a mini-Dubrovnik and the birthplace of Marco Polo); after two nights in Dubrovnik, take the bus to Titograd where, the following day, you venture by bus into Kosovo; from Skopje you can catch the night train to Athens. This trip can also be done in the opposite direction. This isn't Eurail country and transportation across Yugoslavia will cost $40 or $50. There are also plenty of reasonable boats from ports like Split and Dubrovnik to Italy. Whichever way you do it, you can be sure you've seen the best of Yugoslavia.

25: Eastern Europe, Melting the Iron

Europe has an eastern half—a whole different world filled with 120 million people and a rich and fascinating culture. Most tourists get within two or three hours of the East—but few venture in. Those who do, find a uniquely modern side to Europe and, in some places, more old Europe than they ever dreamed possible.

The East is as rich culturally as Europe's West. It's much less flashy and, frankly, less appealing to the average American tourist. The new society is almost by definition dreary, gray and stoney-faced. At least, that's the impression one gets coming into this advertising-free society from our Pepsi ad and Marlboro billboard world. But things are changing. A few years ago, only people on society's lowest rung could be openly warm and close to a Western visitor. I was told, "They choose to live that way so nothing can be taken from them." Today, there's a new openness. A taste for Western styles is hip. And even well-placed proponents of the socialist status quo can be seen waving their flags in new Levis.

Travel in Eastern Europe is a package deal with rewards and pitfalls. The wonders of so many families struggling to make do in a Soviet-dominated system that ignores what we call "free market forces" can't help but impress and forever broaden the visitor. You'll find an admirable strength, enviable warmth and a resilient nationalism in the local people as soon as you break through the bureaucratic and official crust.

Eastern Europe is a challenge to the Western tourist traveling without a tour. Independent travel—as we all know—is very bourgeois. To the socialist, individuality is a vice while the masses matter most. A socialist holiday is when all workers go to the prescribed best beach or mountain resort (and each country has one). They become refreshed and recharged and return to their job. Large groups get service first. The single adventurer gets left-overs at best. If I were a Bulgarian hotel clerk you would be little more than a temptation, a language problem and a hassle to me. Your business would mean nothing. I wouldn't work to accommodate you. But I would wonder how you got so much money. (The bold price list behind hotel reception desks puts me into the "capitalist" category—paying more than "socialist" guests and getting less respect.)

German is the handiest second language, spoken by many who were in school during the Nazi years. English is the language of the young educated and more Western-oriented people. All students must study Russian, but few speak it. In fact, many Westerners who speak Russian find their Eastern European travels go better if they don't use it.

An enjoyable visit to Eastern Europe requires an open mind, patience and flexibility. The Soviet and socialist worlds are generally misunderstood by Americans. A healthy approach to travel in this world is to consider the Soviet subjugation of Eastern Europe as a buffer zone that Russia perceives as necessary in a century that so far has brought her two devastating capitalist invasions. Regardless of what's "right" or what

works, their Marxism or Leninism is not fundamentally wicked, but an attempt at equality. For example, while some American cities are almost sinking in rarely used backyard swimming pools, a socialist city would have one grand people's sports pavillion. A socialist will remind the American capitalist that if he divided the miles he drives in his car by the hours he invests in it (buying, using, maintaining, etc.,) he travels about four miles per hour. While America defines oil rigs in Saudi Arabia as "vital to our national interest", the socialist accepts the fact that cars aren't for everyone and enjoys an effective and very cheap government subsidized public transit system—and a world free of traffic congestion.

While travel in the USSR is more carefully controlled, you can travel freely through most of these countries staying where you like and doing pretty much exactly as you please. Most of these countries require a visa and some have a minimum daily expenditure requirement. These policies change with the political tide, so check with your travel agent before departing. Visas can be purchased in the USA, in any European capital or sometimes at the border. Most East European aembassies process tourist visas within two or three days. Visas for Yugoslavia are issued free and easy at the border.

Local tourist information is basically propaganda—designed to steer you into areas each government would like you to see. Be sure to take in a guide book from the West. I find Frommer's *East Europe* guidebook very helpful, but Fodor's not. *Let's Go Europe* is the only one I've found with the guts to tell you how to function and not be manipulated.

After so many Men From Uncle and Impossible Missions in our blood, Eastern European travel does offer a special James Bond thrill. Foreign mail is screened and, to a varying degree, an eye is kept on visiting tourists. But I've always felt completely safe in Eastern Europe. The risk and consequences of any questionable cultural exchange is willingly borne by the subjects of these governments. A lunch with you is the average Eastern European's next best thing to a plane ticket to London or California. To dissident-types, it's a quick recharge for their spirit struggling to remain free.

Demographically, Eastern Europe is a hodgepodge. Political, racial and linguistic boundaries only vaguely resemble each other, but the related problems have taken a back seat to even more immediate concerns since the Soviet army "liberated" these people from the Nazis in 1945. The date the USSR freed each country from fascism marks the begining of the modern age and is now each country's national holiday. While many would argue that the Soviets "liberated" Eastern Europe from the frying pan directly into the fire, many are grateful to the Soviets for ending their Hitler nightmare. Every city in every Warsaw Pact country has a central mounument glorifying the Russian rulers of Eastern Europe. Locals who wish their "liberators" would go home have learned that these reminders and frustrations are most effectively fought not with Molotov cocktails but with jokes, patience and pragmatism.

As you travel through Eastern Europe try to find the most remote villages and regions. The same places that most successfully resist the modern world are also least affected by whichever government happens to be in power. According to East European "hillbillies", the governmental tune is always the same—only the musicians change.

Be approachable. English-speaking broad-minded locals will come out of the woodwork. Universities are great places to meet multi-lingual people who want to talk. Traveling alone, I've listened to the Voice of America in attics, been interviewed for a local college newspaper and explained the lyrical messages of Beatle tunes to eager teenagers. Approach very young and very old people and those on society's bottom rung—folks who aren't worried about social and official acceptance. Break the ice. We are fairytale people living in a skyscraper world speeding to a Hollywood beat and unknowing victims of our passionate materialism. Locals will look at you and wonder about movie star presidents, drive-in restaurants, Dr. Ruth and how we can go anywhere if our whole world is "private property".

26: Ignored Bulgaria

Have you ever been to Bulgaria? Known a Bulgarian? Received a letter from Bulgaria? Have you ever even had a nice thought about Bulgaria? Public relations with the USA isn't a Bulgarian priority. But there are five million Bulgarian people and most of them would love to meet you.

I stumbled into Bulgaria and returned each summer for the next five years. It grabs you in a strange melodramatic happy/sad way. The most subservient people of Eastern Europe, mind-clutched by Mother Russia, welcome the Western visitor with curious glances and a bureaucracy that makes my post office line seem speedy.

Every visitor to Bulgaria needs a visa. They can be obtained in any European capital city, but it can take several days. It's better to get one before you leave the States. (The Bulgarian consulate in Washington

D.C. can help you with this, call them at 202/387-7969.)

As a tourist you'll experience the same frustrations that Bulgarians do as citizens. You'll see first-hand a society that looks East and dreams West. Sofia is the Paris of Eastern Europe. A quiet capital of monuments, huge churches and wide yellow-cobbled boulevards, the streets just separate the side walks. There aren't many cars.

Sofia is the "big time" in Bulgaria. Notice the fashions, the style of this society's elite, browse through the department stores, sip coffee in the most elegant cafe you can find. Wander through the university. Listen to the men talking sports in the park and notice gypsies and country people gawking just like you. Under the big red star lies George Dimitrov, the local Lenin, pudgy and waxed under glass and receiving visitors most days.

Plovdiv, Bulgaria's most historic town, is just a two hour train ride away from Sofia. The stark "Stalin gothic" of Sofia takes a back seat to Plovdiv's mellow wooden balconies drooping over coarse cobbled streets. Plovdiv is cozy. Its computerized fountain pulsates to the beat of watered-down pop music as the young gather around doing their gangly best to be decadent. The center of town is a walking mall. People browse silently, talk in hushed tones and vicariously enjoy impossible luxury goods in window displays. It's a sad society of healthy birds—with clipped wings.

Take the bus into the hills. Find the farms and villages where people are closer to the earth and the government fades. Restaurants fill with rough-hewn lumberjack types, smoke and folk music. This bawdy brew is a Breugel painting come to life. In the countryside you walk with dancing bears, clap to gypsy bands and find people more relaxed, open and easy going.

For vacation, Bulgarians are dumped into a funnel and land on the Black Sea coast. Each socialist country has its premier resort area and none can hold a candle to the resorts of the West. As a visitor, you are interested in the country and not its escape. Skip the beach.

Gubrovo is Bulgaria's "Knott's Berry Farm" offering the best peek into what's left of the rich local folk culture. Here the folk crafts are honored as endangered species and the visitor is free to wander, observe, learn and, of course, buy.

Every culture has its comic scape-goats. Americans poke fun at Poles, and Norwegians at Swedes (and vice versa). Bulgarians joke about stupid, cheap-skate Gubrovians who, to save money on sweeps, let a cat down the chimney. ("Where is your wedding ring?" "My wife is wearing it this week.")

Bulgaria is complex and difficult to understand without a local friend. And a local friend is one consumer item that is plentiful in Bulgaria. You are a precious window to the West, and if you're approachable you'll never be lonely. People will stalk you for hours to establish a friendship. They collect western comic books and rock albums, listen regularly to the Voice of America and play the game of freedom in their minds. Many Bulgarians have been to London so many times in their dreams that they talk about it like they once lived there. But they know that for now a trip to the West can only be a fantasy.

While Americans would make lousy pawns, it's a valuable experience to spend a few days in a land where there is no alternative. Bulgaria is a battleground of old and new, east and west, full of warm people handling life's dilemmas realistically in a land of denial.

27: Nazi Sights in Europe

Fondue, sangria, Monet, Big Ben . . . a trip to once-upon-a-time Europe can be a fairy tale. It can also give you a glimpse at a nightmare from our recent past—fascism and its remains. While few travelers go to Europe in order to dwell on the horrors of Nazism, most understand the value of visiting the memorials of fascism's reign of terror and of honoring the wish of its survivors—"never forget".

Considering the devastating impact WWII had on Europe, it's surprising how little is left in the way of memorials. But anyone interested can learn more about the Nazi era and what fascism did to Europe by visiting some of these sights.

Of the countless concentration camps, Dachau, just outside of Munich is most visited. While many visitors complain that it's too "prettied-up", it does give a powerful look at how these places worked. This first Nazi concentration camp (1933) is the most accessible to travelers and is a very effective voice from our recent but grisly past, warning and pleading "Never Again"—the memorial's theme. Upon arrival, pick up the mini-guide and notice when the next documentary film in English will be shown. The museum, the movie, the chilling camp-inspired art, the reconstructed barracks, the ovens built (but never used) for crema-

Memorial at the Dachau Concentration Camp

tions and the memorial shrines will chisel into you the meaning of fascism. Dachau is free, open 9:00 a.m. to 5:00 p.m. and closed Mondays.

Auschwitz, or Oswiecim, near Krakow in Poland, and Mathausen, near Linz on the Danube in Austria, are more powerful and less touristed. Mathausen town sits cute and prim on the romantic Danube at the start of the very scenic trip downstream to Vienna. But nearby at a now still quarry linger the memories of a horrible slave-labor camp. Less tourist-oriented than Dachau, Mathausen is a solemn place of meditation and continuous mourning. Fresh flowers adorn yellowed photos of lost loved ones. The home country of each victim has erected a gripping monument and a visitor finds himself in a gallery of artistic grief resting on a foundation of never forget. Mathausen, open daily from 8:00 a.m. to 5:00 p.m., offers an English booklet, a movie and a fine museum.

Two powerful memorials that fit easily into most itineraries are the Memorial de la Deportation in Paris and Anne Frank's House in Amsterdam. To remember the 200,000 French victims of Hitler's camps, Paris has built a moving memorial on the tip of the Ile de la Cite just behind Notre Dame. A visit to this memorial is like entering a work of art and its modern power and brute symbolism are etched on the mind of every visitor. Anne Frank's home, made famous by her diary, gives the mind-boggling statistics of fascism the all-important intimacy of a young girl who lived through it and died from it. Even those bah humbug-types who are dragged in because it's raining and their partner read the diary find themselves caught up. Before you leave that behind-the-hidden-staircase world you'll get a look at fascism today in Europe and in the USA. The people of the Anne Frank house make it clear that the only way fascism could ever happen again is if we don't think it could ever happen again.

While Hitler controlled Europe each country had a courageous if small resistance movement. All over Europe you'll find streets and squares named after the martyrs of the resistance. Oslo and Copenhagen have Nazi resistance museums. If you're fascinated by modern European history as I am you'll find these to be two of Europe's most interesting museums.

Fascist bits and Nazi pieces of Hitler's Germany survive—but only barely. In Berlin you'll find the Reichstag building which burned down mysteriously, giving Hitler the excuse every fascist needs to blame the commies and supercede the law; the Great Synagogue (which was burned on Krystalnacht in 1938); the site of Hitler's bunker (where he committed suicide in the last days of the war); and four small "mountains" made of saturation-bombed rubble. While you can sample some fascist architecture at the Haus der Kunst, Munich's modern art museum, the best look at a fascist building is in Rome where you can wander through Mussolini's futuristic suburb called E.U.R. and the bold pink houses of fascist Italy's Olympic Village.

In Nuremberg the ghosts of Hitler's showy propaganda rallies still rustle in the Rally Grounds (now Dutzendteich Park), down the Great Road, and through the New Congress Hall. The local tourist office has a handy booklet called "Nuremberg 1933 to 1945."

Berchtesgaden is any German's choice for a great mountain hideaway—including Hitler's. The scanty remains of his Obersalzburg headquarters with its extensive tunnel system thrill many a WWII buff.

Knowing you can't take on the world without a great freeway system, Hitler started Germany's *autobahn* system. While you're zipping through Bavaria you may pass the first autobahn reststop right on Herrenchiemsee between Munich and Salzburg. Now a hotel for U.S. military personnel, it's still frescoed with *"Deutschland uber alles"* themes. Take the Feldon exit and politely wander around—the dining room has the best art.

Possibly the most powerful sight of all is the Martyr Ville, Oradour-sur-Glane in central France. This town, fifteen miles out of Limoges, was machine-gunned and burned on June 10th, 1944. Nazi SS troops, seeking revenge for the killing of one of their officers, left all 642 townspeople dead in a blackened crust of a town under a silent blanket of ashes. Oradour-sur-Glane has been left as an eternal reminder of the reality of war. Like so many other victims of fascism in our century, they beg for the present to learn from our past. When you visit, the only English word you'll run across is on the sign that greets every pilgrim who enters, *"Souviens-toi . . .* remember."

28: Northern Ireland

Make your visit to Ireland complete by including Northern Ireland. Ulster, as the six counties of Northern Ireland are commonly called, is only a two-hour train ride from Dublin and offers the tourist a very different and very Irish world.

Most of the tourist industry ignores "war-torn" Northern Ireland. The media blows the trouble out of proportion, leading people to believe that nowhere in Ulster is there peace. That's exciting but false. These British-controlled counties of Ireland are a secret enjoyed and toured mainly by its own inhabitants.

Of course, people are being killed in Northern Ireland—about as many as are being killed in New York City. Car accidents kill more Northern Irishmen than do bombs or guns. If you want trouble, you can find it. But, with common sense, travel in Ulster is safe. You'll see many signs of the violence. Armored cars, political graffiti and bomb-damage clearance sales tell the story of the on-going troubles. Friends you meet may show you the remains of a bombed-out customs house or the flowers that mark a spot where someone was assassinated. But no tourist has ever been injured by "the troubles". People I've sent to Ulster give it rave reviews.

Here's a three-day plan that will introduce you to a capital city of 400,000 (including the British Army's occupation forces), the best open-air folk museum in Ireland, a once prosperous and now rather sleepy beach resort and some powerful,if subtle, mountain beauty complete with villages, ancient stone walls and shepherds. At the same time you'll get a firsthand look at "the Irish problem"—a tragedy in an otherwise happy land. Ulster lacks the dazzle of the Riviera but it charms more intimately. You'll meet some of the friendliest people on earth and learn first-hand about their struggle.

Pick up a map of Northern Ireland and Belfast at the Dublin tourist office. Since trains leave from both cities several times a day you could even make Belfast a day-trip from Dublin. (Northern Ireland is not cov-

Belfast—barbed wire and national fire

ered by the Eurailpass. That segment of the journey costs about ten dollars each way.) Belfast is also connected daily by bus and ferry to Glasgow in Scotland.

A strange peace dominates Belfast. Surrounded by police check points, the pedestrians-only "safe zone" in the city center bustles along oblivious to the problem. Many streets reek of the Industrial Revolution. Buildings that are a potential IRA target are protected by heavy metal screens. Religion is preached on billboards and through bullhorns. Promises of a better life through Jesus and pacing soldiers add to this strange urban stew. Only the visitor gawks at troops in bullet-proof vests. Before leaving the city center pick up some information at the tourist office on High Street.

Enjoy the walk to Queen's University past the Town Hall with its massive exterior and impressive interior. Near the university visit the Botanical Gardens and the Ulster Museum. The museum has some interesting traditional Irish and contemporary art and a good exhibition on the history of Ulster—from the North's perspective, of course.

Belfast is really just a busy industrial city (witness the world's largest cranes towering over the harbor). Plan to see Belfast quickly and get out by mid-afternoon, taking the twenty-minute bus ride to Cultra and the Ulster Folk Museum. Buses leave twice an hour from the Oxford Street station near the train station. Avoid Belfast, especially the waterfront, at night. Unruly teenagers roam wild in the streets, even less ruly than the IRA.

The Ulster Folk and Transport Museum at Cultra is the best museum of its kind in Ireland, offering the closest look possible at old and traditional Irish lifestyles. Assembled in one huge park (like the open-air museums so popular in Scandinavia) are cottages and buildings from all over Ireland. Only here can you actually walk into an old schoolhouse, weaver's cottage, farmhouse—in fact, an entire old Irish village—with each structure traditionally furnished and warmed by a turf fire. Buy the guidebook, wander for three hours and you'll learn a lot about the culture of old Ireland. Any questions your guidebook doesn't answer can be answered by the man who attends each building. He'll talk about leprechauns or simply chat about the weather or sports. The neighboring Transport Museum specializes in turf sleds, horse-drawn carriages and old cars. When you've finished the museum catch the same bus you came in on and continue on into the town of Bangor.

Formerly a stylish resort town, Bangor is a pleasant place to spend the evening. Take one of the bed and breakfast places ($15) right on the waterfront on Queen's Parade. My host made certain I knew just where to find the pubs, the dancing and the outdoor gospel singing. I ended up discussing—and solving—the problems of the world with my new friends until 2:00 that morning. For an especially good look at the Irish, a touch of politics and a service you can understand, go to church on Sunday morning.

After Bangor, travel south down the Ards peninsula alongside the Strangford Lough, a haven for migratory birds. At Portaferry take the little ferry across the bay and continue south to Castlewellen or Newcastle. You'll pass through Downpatrick where St. Patrick lies under a large but unimpressive stone.

Now you have reached the mysterious and beautiful Mourne mountains. Explore the villages and the soft, green rolling "mountains" of 3000 feet. It's a land rich in folk history and tradition and equally rich in hospitality. Ask questions—the more you know about the Mournes the more beautiful they become.

Newry and the border area between Ulster and the Republic of Ireland are two trouble spots, so pass quickly, heading southward to Dundalk where a train will zip you back to Dublin.

Now you can send your family and friends a postcard announcing that you have toured Northern Ireland, had a blast—and survived.

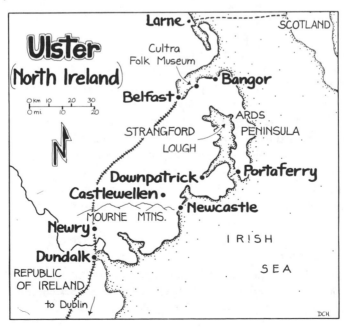

Section 4:
Front Door Cities—
Back Door Angles

29: London—A Warm Look at a Cold City

I have spent more time in London than in any other European city. It lacks the grandeur of Rome, the warmth of Munich and the elegance of Paris, but it keeps drawing me back. Its history, traditions, markets, people, museums and entertainment combine to make it the complete city. The thrill just doesn't wear off.

Of course, London is no secret. Everybody knows to see the Halls of Parliament and the Tower of London. But for many travelers, London is their first stop and it can be brutally overwhelming. The ideas in this chapter soften and warm this hard and cold city. (See Appendix V for budget hotel listings).

The list of sights in London is endless. The famous tourist attractions need no discussion here. I will mention a few parts of London that I think are particularly characteristic—yet are often overlooked by those who visit—with some ideas on how to enjoy them.

It's very important to orient yourself in this great city. On the day you arrive, I advise taking the two-hour "Round London Sightseeing Tour". This is the best possible fast and cheap introduction to London. Buses leave hourly from Picadilly Circus, Marble Arch and Victoria Station. Choose the "escorted" tour, which included a very entertaining commentary. From this double-decker bus tour you can see most of the major landmarks while getting a feel for the city.

On your first evening in London take yourself on a brief "London-by-night" walking tour. Romantic London is seen at night when the busy 20th century gives way to quieter streets and floodlit monuments. It would be a pity to see London and not treat yourself to the golden Big Ben against

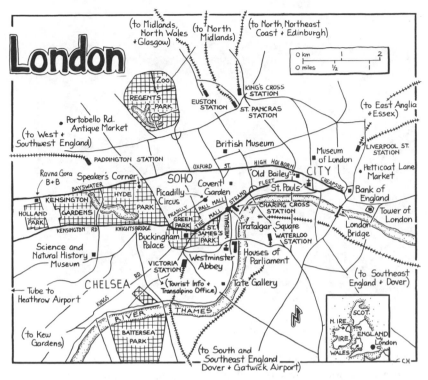

a black night sky. Walk from Picadilly Circus to Trafalgar Square and down Whitehall to Westminster. Cross the bridge and turn left to view the floodlit Halls of Parliament and "Ben" from the riverside promenade. With a little imagination, London will glow with this same evening charm in the days that follow. The bus tour and this London-by-night walk provide the foundation for a very successful stay in one of the world's most exciting cities. (The walk is also a great way to spend your jet-laggy first evening if you've just flown in.)

London is too big to grasp comfortably. See it as the old town without the modern, congested and seemingly endless sprawl. After all, most of the visitors' London lies between the Tower of London and Hyde Park—about a three mile walk.

Another great way to cut it down to size is to nibble at it one bite at a time by taking a series of very focused, two-hour walking tours of the city. For about $3, local historians meet small groups for a good look at one page of the London story (as announced in fliers at the tourist office or in "What's On" and London's other periodical entertainment guides).

A picnic at London's Kew Gardens.

Companies like "Streets of London", and "London Walks" will guide you through the world of London's plague, Dickens' London, Roman Londinium or Jack the Ripper's London. "Pub Crawl" walks are also very popular.

London is, in many ways, a collection of villages. Even today, many of these corners of the city maintain their individuality. Chelsea is still very colorful. Often compared to Paris' Left Bank, this is London's once-Bohemian, now-Yuppie quarter. Soho, which lies north of Piccadilly Circus, is a juicy and intoxicating combination of bustle, sleaze, markets, theater and people. It is London's Greenwich Village.

The most central square mile of London—and all of Britain—is the "City" of London. This is London's "Wall Street". You might want to take advantage of the interesting (and free) tours given at the Stock Exchange. Nearby, if you are interested in the traditional British system of justice, you can visit the Central Criminal Courts, nicknamed "Old Bailey". Powdered wigs, black capes and age-old courtesies, my Lord, make the public trials well worth a visit.

Try a pub lunch with the Fleet Street business crowd at Ye Olde Cock Tavern where Dickens imbibed and where he gave his last reading just a few weeks before his death.

The Tate Gallery is a must. It has a wonderful collection of British painters (particularly Blake and Turner) and a modern collection including Picasso, Moore, Rodin, Van Gogh and nearly all the major Impressionist and 20th century painters. Give yourself an art history lesson by taking one of the free tours available throughout the day. History buffs shouldn't miss the Museum of London. It offers a very well organized chronological walk through London—from Roman Londinium to World War II.

The British love their gardens, and their favorite is the peaceful and relaxing Kew Gardens. Cruise down the Thames or take the subway to Kew for a respite from the city and a good look at the British people. Don't miss the famous Palm House built of glass and filled with exotic tropical plant life. A walk through this hothouse is a veritable walk through a tropical jungle—in London.

Nearly every morning there's a market thriving somewhere in London. There are different markets for fish, fruit, antiques, clothing and plenty of other things. Petticoat Lane (miscellany on Sunday mornings), Portobello Road (antiques on Saturday mornings), and Camden Lock (hip crafts and miscellaneous. Saturday and Sunday 9:00 a.m. to 6:00 p.m.) are just a few of the many colorful markets that offer you just one more of London's many faces (but not much in the way of bargains). After visiting

An atmospheric English public house—or "pub"

Petticoat Lane's market on Sunday morning, I really enjoy an hour of craziness at Speaker's Corner in Hyde Park. By late morning there are usually several soapbox speakers, screamers, singers, communists or comics performing to the crowd of onlookers. The Round London bus tour leaves from Speaker's Corner. If you catch it at 9:00 Sunday morning it will drop you off at 11:00—for the late morning, early afternoon prime time action. Sundays are otherwise frustrating sightseeing days in London, as nearly all museums are only open from about 2:00 p.m. to 5:00 p.m.

When you are in London (or elsewhere in England) you will have a great opportunity to make your own brass rubbing. The tourist information people (tel. 730-3488) can direct you to a "brass rubbing centre" where you can be taught how to make your own rubbing. You can choose from a selection of replica memorial brasses depicting knights and ladies from the distant past. You get all the necessary instruction and materials for only three or four dollars. Just cover the brass with your paper, grab your wax and rub away. In twenty minutes you'll have a meaningful souvenir that is suitable for framing.

I think one reason I never grow tired of London is its great theater. The London visitor always has a stunning array of first-class plays to choose from. I have seen many memorable performances, including *Harvey* with Jimmy Stewart, *The King and I* with Yul Brenner, *My Fair Lady*, *A Chorus Line, Cats, Starlight Express* and *Les Miserables*. You get the quality of Broadway at a fraction of the cost.

Try to buy your tickets several days in advance. Avoid the $2 booking charge by buying your ticket at the theater rather than from a ticket office. This is easy since most of the theaters are located within a few blocks of each other in the area between Piccadilly Circus and Trafalgar Square. You are more likely to get the best ticket selection by buying from the theater. I generally order one of the cheaper tickets. Most theaters aren't big enough to have bad seats. Many times I've found that the people just a row of two in front of me paid nearly twice what I did. If you don't like your seat, there are ways to improve your lot. I've been in London theaters that sound like a sifter as soon as the lights go down—the people with the cheaper seats move up, filling the unsold, more expensive seats.

If a performance is sold out (and many will be) you can nearly always get a ticket if you try. Ask the ticket salesperson how to get a "no-show" ticket. It will generally involve a wait, but a few tickets are usually left unclaimed just before curtain time. You may also want to ask about the availability of "standing room only" tickets.

A London play will probably cost anywhere from $10 to $50. I've chosen plays carefully, with the help of local recommendations, and have always felt that I got more entertainment than I paid for. On Leicester Square there's a half-price day-of-show ticket booth that is popular with budget tourists. I've never seen tickets to anything exciting on sale there and would happily avoid it and its savings to enjoy the play of my choice. No visit to London would be complete without spending some time in one of London's colorful and atmospheric pubs. They are an integral part of the English culture. You'll find all kinds of pubs, each one with its own personality. My favorite is the Clarence, located on Whitehall, just a block from Trafalgar Square. Try the different beers (if you don't know what to order, ask the bartender for a half pint of his favorite), order some "pub grub" and talk to the people—enjoy a "Public House". Enjoy London.

30: Bath, England—Elegant and Frivolous

Bath is the most underrated city in England, if not all of Europe. Two hundred years ago this city of 80,000 was the Hollywood of Britain. Today the former trend-setter of Georgian England invites you to take the 90-minute train ride from London and immerse yourself in its elegant (and frivolous) past. Enjoy a string trio over tea and scones, discover the antique of your dreams and trade your jungle of stress for a stroll through the garden.

If ever a city enjoyed looking in the mirror, Bath's the one. It has more government-protected buildings per capita than any town in England. The entire city is built of a warmtone limestone it calls "Bath stone". The use of normal bricks is forbidden, and Bath beams in its cover-girl complexion.

Bath is an architectural chorus line. It's a triumph of the Georgian style, with its buildings as wrapped up in competitive elegance as the society they housed. If you look carefully you'll see false windows built in the name of balance and classical columns that supported only Georgian egos. The rich could afford to put feathered hats atop the three-foot hairdos of their women. The very rich stretched their doors and ground floors to accommodate these women. Today many families are nearly impoverished simply by the cost of peeling the soot of the last century from these tall walls.

Good-looking towns are not rare, but few combine beauty and hospitality as well as Bath. It is a town that makes everything easy. The town square is a quick walk from the bus and train station. This square is a pincushion of tourist landmarks including the Abbey, the Roman and medieval baths, the royal "Pump Room" and a very helpful tourist information office.

A fine way to experience the elegance of Bath is to stay in one of its best B&Bs. My favorite is Brock's Guest House. If you can afford the $20 per person splurge, it'll be the rubber ducky of your Bath time. Marion Dodd just redid this 1765 home. It's quiet, friendly and couldn't be better located at 32 Brock St. just between the Royal Crescent and the "Circus", tel. 0225/338374.

A good day in Bath starts with a tour of the historic baths. For two thousand years this hot mineral water has attracted society's elite. Then enjoy a high tea with live classical music in the nearby Pump Room before catching the 10:30 city walking tour.

Free walking tours leave from the square nearly every morning at 10:30. There are several guides. Some are real characters, so make a quick survey and follow the most animated tour leader. These volunteers are as much a part of Bath as its architecture. A walking tour gives your visit a little more intimacy, and you'll feel like you actually know a "Bather".

For lunch try the Crystal Palace Pub just down the street from the Abbey (11 Abbey Green). A hearty ploughman's lunch served under rustic timbers or in the sunny courtyard will cost four dollars. This "Pub grub" is so British it'll give you an accent. Blimey!

The afternoon should include a walk through three centuries of fashion in the Costume Museum. There's an entire room for each decade enabling you to follow the evolution of clothing styles right up to Twiggy, Charles, Princess Di and Boy George. The guided tour is excellent—full of fun facts and fascinating trivia. For instance, haven't you always wondered what the line, "Stuck a feather in his cap and called it macaroni" from "Yankee Doodle" means?

You'll find the answer (and a lot more) in Bath—the town whose narcissism is justified.

31: York—Vikings to Dickens

Historians run around York like kids in a candy shop. But the city's sights are so well organized that even those who aren't historians find themselves exploring the past with the same fascination they'd give a hall of fun house mirrors.

Like most British tourist offices, York's takes good care of you. They find rooms, change traveler's checks and give out road maps and pamphlets on sights, side trips, events and organized guided walks. (Rooms listed in Appendix V.)

The guided walks, leaving morning, afternoon and evening, offer a wonderful—and free—introduction to the city. To save museum and shopping hours and enjoy a quieter tour, try to take the evening walk. The excellent guides are usually chatty (in a fun way) and very opinionated. By the end of the walk you'll know the latest York city gossip, which "monstrosity" the "insensitive" city planners are letting be built next and several ghost stories.

With the introductory tour under your belt and your pockets full of exciting sightseeing brochures, you're getting the hang of York and its history. Just as a Boy Scout counts the rings in a tree, you can count the ages of York by the different bricks in the city wall—Roman on the bottom, then Danish, Norman, and the brand-spanking "new" addition . . . from the 14th century. On Butcher's Street you'll recognize the rusty old hooks hiding under the eaves. Eight hundred years ago, bloody hunks of meat hung here dripping into the gutter which still marks the middle of the lane.

If you've read the sightseeing brochures, you know that Henry VIII, in his self-serving religious fervor, destroyed nearly everything that was Catholic—except the great York Minster. It was spared only because Henry needed a grand capital church for North England. And you know why in York a street is called a gate, a gate is a bar and a bar is a pub. ("Gate" is a Viking word. In Norway today streets are called *gade*. "Pub" is short for public house. And, well, I remembered two out of three.)

York's three major sights are its huge and historic church, or Minster, the York Castle Museum and the new Jorvik Viking Museum.

The Castle Museum is a walk with Charles Dickens. The England of the 18th and 19th centuries is cleverly saved and displayed in a huge collection of craft shops, old stores, living rooms and other intimate glimpses of those bygone days. The shops are actually stocked with the merchandise of the day. An extra bonus is to tail English grannies as they remember those good old days—now on display in this museum.

Walls bridge centuries, and each room gives you an intimate peek into a period. Three centuries of Yorkshire interiors in the "Period Rooms" paint a cozy picture of life centered around the hearth with a peat fire warming huge brass kettles and the aroma of fresh baked bread soaking into the heavy open-beamed ceilings.

Old World main street, York's Castle Museum

After walking through the evolution of romantic valentines, you can trace the development of farming, milling and brewing equipment. Early home lighting methods are fascinating, progressing from simple rush lights and candles through crude whale-oil lamps to more modern lamps and into the age of electricity. Imagine—electricity! An early electric heater has a small plaque explaining, "How to light an electric fire— switch it on!"

Musicians enjoy the museum's many historical keyboard, brass and mechanical instruments. And everyone enjoys the glass harmonica, a group of glass bowls you massage with wet fingers to make an eerie series of notes.

Kirkgate is the museum's most popular exhibit. As towns were being modernized in the 1930's, the museum's founder, Dr. Kirk, collected whole shops intact, all fully stocked, and reassembled them here. You can wander through a Lincolnshire butcher's shop, a Bath bakery, a coppersmith's shop, a toy shop and a barbershop. I never realized that the barber pole came from the days when a barber was a kind of surgeon. The pole's colors were symbolic of cutting not hair but skin: red for arterial blood, blue for veinous blood and white for the bandage.

The original merchandise captured my attention more than the old buildings. A general store well-stocked with groceries, candy, haberdashery and a sports shop with everything you'd need to fit in on a 19th century archery, cricket, skittles or tennis court. In the confectionary, you'll browse through mouth-watering "spice pigs", "togo bullets", "hum bugs" and "conversation lozenges".

York's violent past is evident as you walk through rooms and rooms of swords, centuries of firearms and many styles of armour and military uniforms. The costume collection walks you through the closets of the last three centuries showing each period's clothing styles incorporated into contemporary furniture and room scenes.

Children of all ages are endlessly entertained by the toy collection. Dolls of the past come with porcelain heads, real hair and fine miniature clothing. You can hear the earliest baby squeak "Mama". Early games are on display including a ping pong set called "whiff-waff". Primitive steam and gas driven cars are permanently parked near ancient gravity-fed petrol pumps and an early garage.

The York Castle Museum is the closest thing in Europe to a time tunnel experience, except, perhaps, for the Jorvik Viking Exhibit just down the street.

A thousand years ago York was a thriving Viking settlement called Jorvik. While only traces are left of most thousand-year-old Viking settlements, Jorvik is an archeologists' bonanza, the best preserved Viking city ever excavated.

The exhibit combines the Pirates of the Caribbean cleverness of a Disney ride with the abundant harvest of this dig. First you travel back a thousand years in time. Rolling backwards in a little train car for two, you descend past the ghosts and cobwebs of fifty generations. Cromwell . . . Shakespeare . . . Anne Bolyn . . . the mob passes and your car flips around. It's the year 988. You're in Jorvik.

Slowly you glide through the reconstructed village. Everything—sights, sounds, even smells—have been carefully recreated. You experience as closely as possible a Viking village.

Then you pass into the actual excavation site, and your time-traveling train car rolls you past the actual remains of what you just saw reconstructed. The stubs of buildings, the piles of charred wood, the broken pottery are a rotten and time-crushed echo of a thriving town.

Finally the ride is over and you come to the museum. Glass cases display and clearly explain artifacts from every aspect of Viking life—clothing, cooking, weapons, clever locks, jewelry, even children's games.

The gift shop—the traditional final stage of English museums—capitalized nicely on my newly-developed fascination with Vikings in England.

32: Lisbon

Lisbon is a wonderful mix of now and then. Old wooden trollies shiver up and down its hills, bird-stained statues mark grand squares and people sip coffee in art nouveau cafes.

Present-day Lisbon is explained by its past. Her glory days were the 15th and 16th centuries when explorers like Vasco da Gama opened up new trade routes making Lisbon Europe's richest city. Later, the riches of Brazil boosted Lisbon even higher. Then, in 1755, an earthquake leveled the city, killing over 20% of its people.

Lisbon was rebuilt on a strict grid plan, symmetrical, with broad boulevards and square squares. The grandeur of pre-earthquake Lisbon survives only in Belem, the Alfama and in the Bairro Alto districts.

While the earthquake flattened a lot of buildings and its colonial empire is long gone, Lisbon's heritage is alive and well. Barely elegant outdoor cafes, exciting art, entertaining museums, the saltiest sailors' quarter in Europe and much more, all at bargain basement prices, make Lisbon an Iberian highlight. (Recommended Places to Stay listed in Appendix V.)

Come, follow me through a day in Lisbon.

After breakfast, taxi to the Alfama, Europe's most colorful sailors'

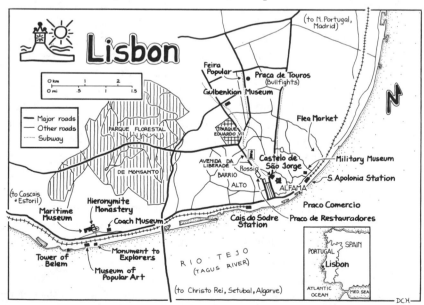

Fish market in Lisbon's Alfama

quarter. This is my favorite European cranny. It was the Visigothic birth-place of Lisbon, a rich district during the Arabic period and now the salty home of Lisbon's fisherfolk. One of the few areas to survive the 1755 earthquake, the Alfama is a cobbled cornucopia of Old World color. Visit during the busy midmorning market time or in the late afternoon/early evening when the streets teem with the local people.

Wander deep. This urban jungle's roads are squeezed into tangled stairways and confused alleys; bent houses comfort each other in their romantic shabbiness and the air drips with laundry and the smell of clams and raw fish. You'll probably get lost but that doesn't matter—unless you're trying to stay found. Poke aimlessly, sample ample grapes, avoid rabid-looking dogs, peek through windows. Make a friend, pet a chicken, read the graffiti, study the humanity ground between the cobbles. Taste the *blanco seco*—the local dry wine.

Gradually, work your way up the castle-crowned hill until you reach a little green square called Maradouro de Santa Luzia. Rest here and enjoy the lovely view of the Alfama below you. By now it's noon, and you should be quite hungry (unless you took more than pictures in the Alfama market). Across the street from Maradouro de Santa Luzia is Restaurante Farol de Santa Luzia, a busy little working-class restaurant full of babble and hungry Portuguese. Treat yourself to a huge plate of boiled clams and cockles (the house specialty) and anything else that looks good.

If you climb a few more blocks to the top of the hill you'll find the ruins of Castelo Sao Jorge. From this fortress, which has dominated the city for almost fifteen hundred years, you enjoy a commanding view of Portugal's capital city. For the second half of your day grab a taxi and ask to be taken to Torre de Belem (the Belem Tower). The Belem District, 4 miles from downtown (take trams #15, 16 or 17), is a pincushion of important sights from Portugal's Golden Age, when Vasco da Gama and company made her Europe's richest power.

The Belem Tower, Portugal's only purely Manueline-style building (the ornate Portuguese Renaissance style, built 1515), once protected Lisbon's harbor and today symbolizes the voyages that made her powerful. This was the last sight sailors saw as they left and the first one they'd see when they returned loaded down with gold, diamonds and venereal diseases. Nearby, the giant Monument to the Discoveries honors Henry the Navigator and Portugal's leading explorers. Across the street the Monastery of Jeronimos is possibly Portugal's most exciting building. This giant church and cloisters are a great example of how the Manueline style combines Gothic and Renaissance features with motifs from the sea—the source of the wealth which made this art possible. The elegant cloisters are by far my favorite in Europe.

The Portuguese bullfight is a brutal affair that many enjoy because "they don't kill the bull". The fight starts with an equestrian duel—fast bull against graceful horse and rider. Then the fun starts. A colorfully clad eight-man team enters the ring stringing out in a line as if to play leapfrog. The leader yells at El Toro and, with adrenalin sloshing everywhere, they charge each other. The speeding bull plows into the leader head on (the horns are wrapped so he doesn't get gored—just mashed) and his thud, thud, thud picks up the entire charging crew, like a hydroplane bouncing over waves.

The crew wrestles the bull—who by this time must be wondering where these lemming idiots came from—to a standstill and one man grabs the tail. Victory is theirs when they leap off the bull and the human, still hanging onto the tail, kind of water skis behind the bull. This thrilling display of insanity is repeated with six bulls. After each round, the bruised and battered head man limps a victory lap around the ring.

Portugal's top bull ring is in Lisbon, and there are fights a couple of days a week throughout the summer. These are the usual sights; cultural can-cans you can find in any guidebook. But with some imagination, your sightseeing can also include Portugal in action—live, if not on stage.

Go into a bar as if your poetry teacher sent you there on assignment. Observe, write, talk, try to understand and appreciate; send your senses on a scavenger hunt. The eating, drinking and socializing rituals are fascinating.

My favorite Lisbon evening was at the "Feira Popular". This Popular Fair rages nightly until 1:00 a.m. from May through September. Located on Ave. da Republica at the Entrecampos metro stop, it bustles with Portuguese families at play. I ate dinner surrounded by chattering Portuguese families ignoring the ever present TVs while great plates of fish, meat, fries, salad and lots of wine paraded frantically in every direction. A seven-year-old boy stood on a chair and sang hauntingly emotional folk songs. With his own dogged clapping, he dragged an applause out of the less-than-interested crowd and then passed his own shabby hat. All the while, fried ducks drip, barbecues spit and dogs squirt the legs of chairs while somehow local lovers ignore everything but each other's eyes.

33: Oslo

On May 17th, Norway's national holiday, Oslo is bursting with flags, bands, parades and blond toddlers dressed up in colorful traditional ribbons, pewter and wool. But Oslo has plenty to offer the visitor even without its annual patriotic bash. Oslo is fresh, not too big, surrounded by forests, near mountains and on a fjord. And Oslo's charm doesn't stop there. Norway's largest city, capital and cultural hub is a smorgasbord of history, sights, art and Nordic fun.

An exciting cluster of sights is just a ten-minute ferry ride from the City Hall. The Bygdoy area reflects the Norwegian mastery of the sea. Some of Scandinavia's best preserved Viking ships are on display here. Rape, pillage and—ya sure ya betcha—plunder was the rage a thousand

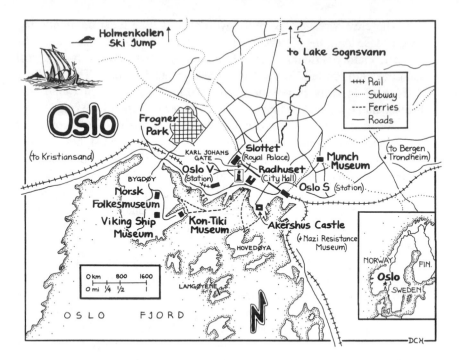

years ago in Norway. There was a time when much of a frightened Western Europe closed every prayer with "and deliver us from the Vikings, amen." Gazing up at the prow of one of those sleek time-stained vessels, you can almost hear the shrieks and smell the armpits of those redheads on the rampage.

Nearby, Thor Heyerdahl's balsa raft, the Kon-Tiki, and the polar ship Fram exhibit Viking energy channeled in more productive directions. The Fram, serving both Nansen and Amundsen, ventured further north and south than any other ship.

Just a harpoon-toss away is Olso's open-air *Folkemuseum*. The Scandinavians were leaders in the development of these cultural parks that are so popular around Europe now. One hundred and fifty historic log cabins and buildings from every corner of the country are gathered together in this huge folk museum. Inside each house a person in local dress is happy to answer questions about traditional life in that part of Norway. Don't miss the 1100 year old wooden stave church.

Oslo's avant-garde city hall, built 35 years ago, was a collective effort of Norway's greatest artists and designers. Tour the interior. Over 2000 square yards of bold colorful murals are a journey through the collective mind of modern Norway.

Norway has given the world two great modern artists, Edvard Munch and Gustav Vigeland. After visiting Oslo, many tourists become Vigeland fans—or even "Munchies". Frogner Park, behind the royal palace, features 150 bronze and granite sculpture groups representing 30 years of Vigeland creativity. The centerpiece of this Nordic sculpture garden is the impressive 60-foot tall totem pole of bodies known as the "Monolith of Life". This, along with the neighboring Vigeland Museum, is a must on any list of Oslo sights.

Oslo's Munch museum is a joy. It's small, displaying an impressive collection of one man's work rather than stoning your powers of absorption with art by countless artists from countless periods. You leave the Munch museum with a smile, feeling like you've really learned something about one artist, his culture and his particular artistic "ism"—Expressionism. Don't miss "The Scream", which captures the fright many feel as our human "race" does just that.

You can explore 700 years of local history in Oslo's Akershus Castle. The castle houses a fascinating Nazi resistance museum. The "Freedom Museum" shows how one country's spirit cannot be crushed regardless of how thoroughly it's occupied by a foreign power.

Oslo has been called Europe's most expensive city. I'll buy that. Life on a budget is possible only if you have plenty of information and take advantage of money-saving options that are available. Remember, budget

Vigeland's Monolith of Life, Frogner Park

tricks like picnicking and sleeping in dormitory-type accommodations offer the most exciting savings in the most expensive cities—like Oslo. Oslo is very expensive but you're not getting less for your dollar. In Oslo you have no choice but to buy rooms that are efficient, clean and pleasant. It's a kind of forced luxury. Know your budget alternatives, bring a little extra money and enjoy it.

Language problems are few. The Norwegians speak more and better English than any people on the continent. My cousin attends the University of Oslo. In her language studies she had to stipulate: English or American. She learned American—and knows more slang than I do.

One Day For The Fjords?

If you go to Oslo and don't get out to the fjords, you should have your passport revoked. Take the "Norway in a Nutshell" day trip from Oslo. Every morning northern Europe's most spectacular train ride leaves Oslo for Bergen. Cameras smoke as this super-scenic transport roars over Norway's mountainous spine. At Myrdal a little 12-mile spur line drops you 2800 thrilling feet to the little town of Flam for Norway's ultimate natural thrill, Sognefjord. The best of the fjord is yours as the post boat takes you up one narrow arm and down the next to the town of Guavangen where buses shuttle you back to the main train line at Voss.

From there, return to Oslo or carry on into Bergen for the evening (doubling back to Oslo, if necessary, on the night train). The whole trip is a snap; just follow the tourist office's brochure.

34: Stalking Stockholm

If I had to call one European city "home" it would be Stockholm. Green, clean, efficient and surrounded by as much water as land, Sweden's capital is underrated by most tourists, landing just above Bordeaux, Brussels and Bucharest on their checklists. Stockholm grabs the future but clings to its past.

While progressive and frighteningly futuristic, Stockholm respects its heritage. Daily mounted bands parade through the heart of town to the royal palace announcing the changing of the guard and turning even the most dignified tourist into a scampering kid. The Gamla Stan (Old Town) celebrates the Midsummer festivities (June 21, 22) with the down-home vigor of a rural village, forgetting that it's the core of a gleaming twentieth-century metropolis.

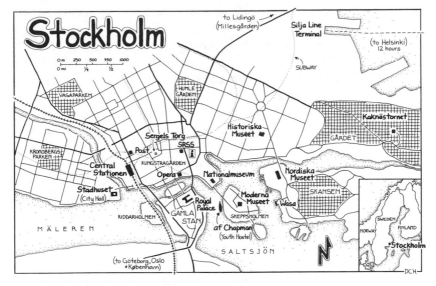

Stockholm is a place to "do" as well as see.

The culture and vitality of Sweden is best felt at Skansen. An island park of traditional and historic houses, schools and churches transplanted from every corner of the country, Skansen entertains with live folk music, dancing, pop concerts, a zoo, restaurants, peasant-craft workshops and endless amusements. It's a smorgasbord of culture enjoyed by tourists and locals alike.

Nearby is the Wasa, the royal flagship that sunk ten minutes into her maiden voyage 350 years ago. While not a good example of Viking sea-worthiness, the Wasa is incredibly intact in her super-humidified display house and is a highlight on any sailor's itinerary.

The "Carl Milles Garten" is a striking display of Sweden's favorite sculptor's work. Strong, pure, expressive and Nordic, Milles' individual style takes even the most uninterested by surprise. Hanging on a cliff over-looking the city, this sculpture park is perfect for a picnic.

A sauna is Sweden's answer to support hose and a face lift. It's as important as a smorgasbord in your Swedish experience. "Simmer down" with the local students, retired folks and busy executives. Try to cook as calmly as the Swedes. Just before bursting, go into the shower room. There's no "luke cold" and the "trickle-down theory" doesn't apply—only one button bringing a Niagara of liquid ice. Suddenly your shower stall becomes the Cape Canaveral launch pad, and your body scatters to every corner of the universe. A moment later you're back together. Rejoining the Swedes in the cooker, this time with their relaxed confidence, you now know that exhilaration is just around the corner. Only very rarely will you feel so good.

Consider a few side trips from Stockholm. Just a subway-ride away is Farsta, a trip into the future—if many urban planners get their way. You surface in the hub of this ultra-ordered suburb. Apartment complexes circle you in careful formation. Department stores, parks, transportation facilities and schools are placed conviently, and all the people know just where to go—like worms after the rain. It makes you wonder whether such scientific packaging is the only answer as our continually more advanced society deals with ever-larger crowds.

While most visitors make sidetrips to the enjoyable (but overrated) towns of Uppsala and Sigtuna, a quick visit to Helsinki is more exciting. Finland's capital, just an overnight boat-ride away, is Scandinavian only by geography. Its language is completely unrelated and culturally there's nothing "yah sure ya betcha" about Finland. Getting to Helsinki is a joy. The daily or nightly ships ($35 or free with a Eurailpass) feature lavish smorgasbords, dancing and the most enchanting island scenery in Europe.

Stockholm is notoriously expensive. But with a few tips you can manage fine on a budget. When traveling by train, try to arrive in the morning when setting up is easiest and least expensive. That means taking the overnight run from Oslo or Copenhagen. Scandinavia, always thinking ahead, located its capitals a very convenient ten-hour train rides apart.

Survey your guidebook's listing of budget accommodations. Upon arrival telephone the hotel of your choice (or use the room finding service in the station). In Stockholm I phone the Af Chapman youth hostel, a classic "cutter ship" permanently moored five minutes from downtown. The Af Chapman, with eight-dollar bunks, is one of Europe's most popular hostels. It holds 30 beds a day for drop-ins and is usually full by midmorning.

Don't leave the Stockhlom station without feasting at the ritzy Centralens Restaurant which serves an eternal smorgasbord every morning for the price of an open-face sandwich and a cup of coffee anywhere else in town.

After this culinary smorgasm, waddle over to Europe's most energetic tourist information office, The Sweden House (Sverigehuset). Besides all the normal tourist help, this organization will do everything short of whipping you with birch twigs in the sauna. They have a "Meet the Swedes at Home" program, an English library and reading room, free pamphlets in English on any aspect of the Swedish culture you could want to study, daily walking tours through the old town and more. Pick up the usual lists of sights and maps as well as the handy "This Week in Stockholm", a periodical entertainment guide in English. The Sweden House, in Kings Garden a few blocks from the station, is open daily in the summer from 9:00 a.m. to 9:00 p.m.

Finally, take advantage of tourist transportation passes. Stockholm's 3-day pass gives you free run of its excellent bus and subway system as well as unlimited entrance to Skansen.

Stockholm's floating youth hostel

Section 5: Beyond Europe - Maximum Thrills Per Mile, Minute and Dollar

35: Morocco—Plunge Deep

Walking through the various *souks* of the labyrinthian medina, I found sights you could only dream of in America. Dodging blind men and clubfeet, I was blasted with a collage of smells, sounds, sights and feelings. People came in all colors, sizes, temperaments and varieties of deformities. Milky eyes, beggars, stumps of limbs, sticks of children, tattooed women, weather-aged old men with a twinkle behind their bristly cheeks, grabbing salesmen, inviting craftsmen, enticing scents, half-bald dogs and little boys on rooftops were reaching out from all directions.

Ooo! Morocco! Slices of Morocco make the Star Wars bar scene look bland. And it's just a quick cruise from Spain. You can't, however, experi-

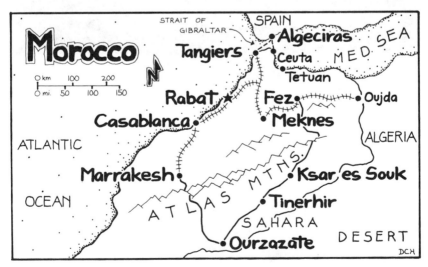

ence Morocco in a day-trip from the Costa del Sol. Plunge deep and your journal will read like a Dali painting.

While Morocco is not easy traveling, it gets rave reviews from those who plug this Islamic detour into their European vacation. Here are some tips and a suggested itinerary.

Skip Tangiers and the Moroccan "Tijuanas" of the north coast. Tangiers is not really Morocco; it's a city full of con-men who thrive on green tourists. Take the boat from Algeciras or the much more pleasant town of Tarifa in Spain to Tangiers (buy a round trip ticket), where you'll find the quickest connections south to Rabat. Power your way off the boat, then shove through the shysters to the nearby train station. They'll tell you anything to get you to stay in Tangiers ("No train until tomorrow," "Rabat is closed on Thursdays," etc.) Believe nothing. Be rude if you have to. Tangiers can give you only grief, while the real Morocco lies to the south. Try to make friends with a Moroccan traveler on the boat who won't be a con-man and who'll usually be happy to help you slip through the stressful port of entry.

Rabat is a good first stop in Morocco. This most comfortable European city in Morocco lacks the high-pressure tourism of the towns on the north coast. Stay at the Hotel Splendid near the medina, 2 Rue du XVIII Juin, tel. 232-83. It's a favorite of Peace Corps workers.

Taxis are cheap and a real bargain when you consider the comfort, speed and convenience they provide in these hot, dusty and confusing cities. Eat and drink carefully in Morocco. Bottled water and bottled soft drinks are safe. I had "well-cooked" written in Arabic on a scrap of paper and ordered meat cooked that way for safety. I found the *couscous* disappointing but the *tajine* and omelets uniformly good. The Arabs use different number symbols. Learn them. Morocco was a French colony, so French is more widely understood than English. A French phrasebook is very handy. Travel very light in Morocco. You can leave most of your luggage at your last Spanish hotel for free if you plan to spend a night there upon your return from Africa.

After Rabat, pass through Casablanca (the movie is great, the city is not) and catch the "Marrakesh Express" south. You'll hang your head out the window of that romantic old train and sing to the passing desert.

Marrakesh is the epitome of exotic. Take a horse-drawn carriage from the station downtown where you can find a hotel near the Djemaa el Fna, the central square of Marrakesh, where the action is. Desert musicians, magicians, storytellers, acrobats, snake charmers, gamblers and tricksters all perform, gathering crowds of tribespeople who have come

to Marrakesh to do their market chores. As a tourist, you'll fit in like a
clown at a funeral. Be very careful, don't gamble and hang onto your wallet. This is a trip into another world—complete with pitfalls.

You can spend an entire day in the colorful medina, or marketplace.
Wander aimlessly from souk to souk (there's a "souk" for each area of
trade, such as the dyers' souk, the leather souk, and the carpet souk).

In the medina you'll be followed—or "guided"—by small boys who
claim to be "a friend who wants to practice his English". They are after
money, nothing else. Make two things crystal clear: you have no money
for them and you want no guide. Then completely ignore them. Remember, while you're with them, these boys get commissions for anything you buy. Throughout Morocco you'll be pestered by these obnoxi-
ous hustler-guides.

I often hire a young and easy-to-control boy who speaks enough English to serve as my interpreter mainly because it seems that if a tourist is "taken" the other guides leave you alone—and that in itself is worth the small price of a guide.

The market is a shopper's delight. Bargain hard, shop around and you'll come home with some great souvenirs. Government emporiums usually have the same items you find in the market, priced fairly. If you get sick of souks, shop there and you'll get the same price—haggle-free.

From Marrakesh, consider an exciting seven day loop to the south and ultimately to Fez. While buses are reliable and efficient throughout Morocco, this tour is best by car and it's easy to rent a car in Marrakesh to be dropped in Fez. Do some comparative shopping.

Drive or catch the bus south, over the rugged Atlas Mountains, to a region that no longer faces the Mediterranean. This is Saharan Morocco. Explore the isolated oasis towns of Ouarzazate, Tinerhir and Er-Rachidia. If time permits, the trip from Ouarzazate to Zagora is an exotic mud brick pie.

These towns each have a weekly "market day" when the tribespeople gather to do their shopping. Unless you enjoy goats' heads and honeydew melons there isn't much more than pictures that a tourist would want to take. Stay in Tinerhir's Hotel du Todra and climb to the roof for a great view of the busy marketplace below.

Venture out of town into the lush fields where you'll tumble into an almost Biblical world. Sit on a rock. Dissect the silence. A bearded old man in a white robe and turban might clip-clop slowly past you. He seems to be growing side-saddle out of his weary donkey and his eyes are as wide as yours. Suddenly, six Botticelli maidens flit like watercolor confetti across your trail and giggle out of sight. Stay tuned. The show goes on.

Bus rides in this part of Morocco are intriguing. I could write for pages about experiences I've had on Moroccan buses—good and bad—but I don't want to spoil the surprise. Just ride them with a spirit of adventure—and your fingers crossed.

Saharan Adventure

From Er-Rachidia, a very long day's drive south of Fez, a series of mud-brick villages bunny hop down a lush river valley and into the Sahara. Finally, the road melts into the sand and the next stop is, literally, Timbuktu.

The strangeness of this Alice in a sandy wonderland world, uncontrolled, can be overwhelming—even frightening. The finest hotel in Erfoud, the region's major town, will provide a much needed refuge keeping the sand, heat waves and street kids out and providing safe-to-eat and tasty local food, reliable information on the region and a good bed ($20 doubles).

But the hotel is only your canteen and springboard. Explore! An overabundance of persistent local "wanna-be guides" may cause you to lock your car doors. Choose one you can understand and tolerate, set a price for his services ($5 or $6) and, before dawn, head for the dunes.

You'll drive to the last town, Rissani (market days: Tues, Thurs, Sun), and then farther south over 15 miles of natural asphalt to the oasis village of Merzouga. There's plenty of tourist traffic at sunrise and in the early evening so hitching is fairly easy. A couple of places in Merzouga rent spots on their terrace for those who spend the night. Since a civil war is smoldering in the desert you may have to show your passport.

Before you, glows a chain of sand dune mountains. Climb one. It's not easy. I seemed to slide further backward with each step. Hike along a cool and crusty ridge, observe bugs and their tracks and watch mini sand avalanches you started all by yourself. From the great virgin summit, savor the Sahara view orchestrated by a powerful silence. Your life sticks out like a lone star in a black sky. Tumble, roll and slosh your way down your dune. Look back and see the temporary damage one person can inflict on that formerly perfect slope. Then get back in your car before the summer sun turns the sand into a steaming griddle, though off season, the mid-day desert sun is surprisingly mild.

Merzouga is full of people, very poor people. The village children hang out at the ruins of some old palace. A rag tag percussion group gave us an impromptu concert. The children gathered around us tighter and tighter as the musicians picked up the tempo. The smiles, the warmth and the sadness mixed very intimately. A little Moroccan Judy Garland saw out of one eye—the other was as cloudy as rice pudding. One gleaming six-year-old had a tiny sleeping brother slung on her back. His crusty little face was covered with flies—he didn't even flinch. We had a bag of candy to share and tried to get 40 kids into an orderly line to march by one by one. Impossible. The line degenerated into a free-for-all and our bag became a *pinata*.

Only through the mercy of your guide can you find your way back to Rissani. Camels loiter nonchalantly—looking very lost and not caring. Cool lakes flirt from the distance—a mirage—and the black hardpan road stretches endlessly in all directions. Then with a sigh we were back in Rissani, where the road starts up again.

For us, it was breakfast time, and Rissani offered little other than some very thought-provoking irony. My friends and I could find no "acceptable" place to eat. Awkwardly, we drank germ-free Cokes with pursed lips, balanced bread on up-turned bottle caps and swatted legions of flies. Funny, we were by far the wealthiest people in the valley—and the only ones unable to enjoy an abundant variety of good but strange food.

From our seats we saw a busy girl rhythmically smashing date seeds, three stoic, robed elders with horseshoe beards and a prophet wandering through with a message for all that he was telling to nobody.

Back at the hotel, we shared the Walkman and went for a swim, resting and recharging before our next Saharan plunge.

Sahara Nightlife

Desert-dwellers and smart tourists know the value of a siesta during the hottest part of the day. But a Saharan evening is the perfect time for a traveler to get out and experience the vibrancy of African village life. We drove ten miles north of Erfoud to a fortified mud brick oasis village. There was no paint, no electricity, no cars—only people, mud brick and palm trees. Absolutely nothing other than the nearby two-lane highway hinted of the 20th century.

We entered like Lewis and Clark without Sacajawea, knowing instantly we were in for a rich experience. A wedding feast was erupting. The whole town buzzed with excitement. Everyone was decked out in colorful robes and shiny smiles. We felt very welcome.

The teeming street emptied through the medieval gate and onto the field where a band was playing squawky oboe-like instruments and drums. A large circle of ornately dressed women made high siren noises with tongues flapping like party favors. Rising dust diffused the lantern light giving everything the feel of an old photo, and the darkness focused our attention on a relay of seductively beautiful snake-thin dancers. A flirtatious atmosphere raged, cloaked safely in the impossibility of anything transpiring beyond coy smiles and teasing twists.

Then the village's leading family summoned us for dinner. Pillows, blankets, a lantern and a large round filigreed table turned a stone cave into a warm lounge. The men of this family had traveled to Europe and spoke English. For over two hours, the women prepared dinner and the men entertained. First the ritualistic tea ceremony. Like a mad chemist, the tea specialist mixed it just right. With a gleam in his eye and a large spike in his hand, he hacked off a chunk of sugar from their coffee can-sized master lump and watched it melt into Morocco's basic beverage. He tested it reverently, added more sugar and let me test it. When no more sugar could be absorbed, we drank it with cookies and dates. The sweeter the better. Then the hashish pipe came out and was passed around with all the fanfare of a pack of Juicy Fruit. Our shocked look was curious to them. Next, a tape deck brought a tinny clutter of music, from Arab and tribal Berber music to James Brown, Reggae and twangy Moroccan pop. The men danced—splendidly.

Finally the meal came. Fourteen people sat on the floor circling the round tables. Nearby a child silently waved a palm branch fly fan. A portable wash basin and towel were passed around to start and finish the meal. With our fingers and gravy-soaked slabs of bread, we grabbed spicy meat and vegetables. Everyone dipped eagerly into the delicious central bowl of *couscous*.

So far the Moroccan men dominated. Young girls took turns peeking around the corner and dashing off—much like teeny-boppers anywhere. Two older women in striking black-jewelled outfits were squatting attentively in the corner, keeping their distance and a very low profile. Then

Morocco in a rented bus. Why not?

one pointed to me and motioned in charades, indicating long hair and a backpack. She held up two fingers and hand-signalled a small person. I had been in this same village in the '70s. I had longer hair, a backpack and was traveling with a very short partner. Could she remember us? I scribbled "1978" on a scrap of paper. She scratched it out and wrote "1979." Wow! She remembered my 20-minute visit six years before! I can only conclude that people in remote lands enjoy a visiting tourist and find the occasion at least as memorable as we do. So many more doors open to the traveler who takes along that assumption.

After a proud tour of their schoolhouse, we were escorted across the field back to our car which had been guarded by a silent white-robed man. We drove away reeling with the feeling that the memories of this evening would be our most precious souvenir.

And Back to Europe

From Er-Rachidia, the gateway to this wondrous desert valley, return to our world by catching the bus over the Atlas Mountains to Fez or Meknes. Fez, along with Marrakesh, is a must. Both of these towns give you royal and big-city Morocco at its best.

From Fez you can catch the air-conditioned train back to Tangiers. If you bought a round-trip boat ticket from Spain you can just walk onto the boat. Without a ticket, you'll have to buy one at the Tangiers ticket office—no easy matter. If they will only sell you a ticket for a later boat (to prolong your stay in lovely Tangiers) you'll have to buy it. Try using that ticket for the next boat out. It will probably get you on.

After your trip you'll always remember that swing through Morocco as the adventure that bumped the rest of your world a couple of rungs up the ladder of normalcy.

36: The Best Way from Athens to Turkey

Turkey is the last frontier of European tourism. It's a rich land. I need a slice of Turkey in each trip—but not too much of it. Like Thanksgiving leftovers, a week or ten days of Turkey is just about right.

The best thing about Athens is the boat to Turkey. While so many people get as far east as Athens, very few realize how accessible and exciting Turkey is. My feeling is that every trip to the Greek Islands should include a visit to the west coast of Turkey. If you're looking for cultural thrills, remember, Turkey is farther from Greece culturally than Greece is to the USA.

The best way to get to Turkey from Athens is to sail. Athens is one of Europe's most notorious tourist traps—it's very crowded. See what's important (Acropolis, Agora, Plaka, and National Museum)—and leave!

A convenient way to get to Turkey is from the island of Rhodes, which in itself is well worth a visit. This Crusader city takes you back into medieval Europe as well as any place in Europe. From Rhodes you can take a small Turkish boat to the enjoyable resort town of Marmaris on the southwest tip of Turkey. From here (or Kusadasi), modern buses can take you anywhere in Turkey (including Istanbul, where trains leave daily for Germany and Western Europe).

Or catch a boat to the island of Samos. The 13-hour boat ride arrives in the morning. You can buy a sleeping berth or sleep free under the stars

or inside. Be quick to stake out a couch to sleep on. A third-class ticket will cost about $15. It's a good idea to pack a picnic for the ride (Piraeus, Athens' port town, has a good market near the harbor). Food purchased on board is expensive.

Samos (180 square miles, 60,000 people) is my favorite Greek island: green, mountainous, diverse and friendly. It's crowded with tourists, but not as bad as many other Greek islands. Bus transportation on the island is fine. Vathi, a charming town of narrow, winding lanes creeping out of the sea and up the hillside, is a fine homebase. Many streets are too narrow for cars, which preserves the quiet Greek atmosphere. Learn to play backgammon with the locals—they'll love you for it.

Rent a motorbike to explore the island of Aesop. You can see the desolate Temple of Hera, one of the Seven Wonders of the Ancient World; Pythagorian, the hometown of Pythagoras; untouched mountain towns like Pandhrosen, and forgotten old monasteries. Wild fig trees beg to be tasted, and old Greeks lead grape-laden donkeys down empty country roads. Samos has plenty of good beaches and local restaurants to enjoy as well. A motorbike is a worthwhile ten-dollar splurge.

Now you've reached the end of Greece; the brown mountains of Turkey dare you to cross the narrow channel, to trade the grapes of Samos for the more exotic fruits of Turkey.

Turkey is enjoyable because it's different enough to be exciting and interesting, but not so different that it's uncomfortable or stressful. The people, while most wear a Western facade in clothes, are definitely Oriental in mind. I don't know if they're bored or happy or apathetic or what, but the entire country—at least the male population, which is what the traveler sees—is "into" certain things like worry beads, disdain for American capitalism, imperialism and fascism; drinking tea and spending a great part of their lives playing cards, dominos or backgammon; smoking; stepping on the heels of their shoes (wearing them bent down); being about two days unshaven; keeping pictures of Ataturk on their walls and hanging around together.

Not only is the Turkish culture more exotic than any European culture, it's very cheap—much cheaper than Greece. Turkey has a bad ("Midnight Express") image but travelers and locals alike find that the new rifles-on-nearly-every-corner police state has made the country more stable, safe and relaxed. Turkey offers some of the finest classical ruins anywhere and it's not overrun by tourists like the more famous corners of Greece. (Although it's rapidly becoming a German vacation zone.)

Greeks and Turks mix like Christians and Muslims. Border crossings are more difficult and expensive than they have to be. The Greek government levies a heavy tax on each Greek island to mainland Turkey ticket sold, to discourage this easy exit from their country. They'd rather the tourist backtrack through Athens, contributing still more money to the industry that is Greece's number one source of foreign revenue—tourism.

There's a daily boat from Samos to Kusadasi in Turkey. The two-hour ride costs around twenty dollars which, while unfair, is still worth it. You'll land very close to what, in my opinion, is Turkey's greatest archaeological sight—Ephesus (Efes). It would be a crime to be in Samos and miss the home of the Ephesians, even if you aren't particularly interested

in Roman ruins. If you're going to the Greek islands, go to Rhodes or Samos, and for some real spice, include a side trip into Turkey.

37: Eastern Turkey

The town—I never saw a name—had one wide dusty road, and on each side for about 200 or 300 yards, mud brick houses. Cow dung, dried into innocent-looking, large, rough loaves, was piled into neat mounds in every yard. Ducks, dogs, chickens and children roamed around like they owned the place, while women loaded pails of water onto their balancing sticks at the well. Oxen pulled huge wagons of hay, and every few minutes a proud horseman would gallop bareback down the street. This town had no electricity, no paint or advertisements on the walls, no cars or trucks and only one small general store.

We were definitely big news. Boldly, like victorious but humane generals, we sauntered through the town, greeting people from house to house, shooting pictures, shaking hands and acting quite sure of ourselves. Throngs of villagers gathered around us. We were moved to entertain. We sang and danced, becoming the village stars. A cute little girl caught my eye and she became my very embarrassed friend.

Carl found a wonderfully spunky old lady, colorfully dressed and the epitome of good health. She invited us into her spotless house, and soon half the village had crowded in after us. The window filled with faces struggling to get a look at the visitors. Our friend brought us homemade honey, still in the waxy comb; bread; stringy, powerful and delicious cheese and tea. I was visibly tickled, I'm sure. By popular demand, I danced, dragging in the laughing old lady to the delight of a house full of Turks.

Most tourist maps of Turkey show plenty of places in the western half but an empty void in the east. From the looks of the map, there's nothing there. But the only thing that Eastern Turkey has virtually nothing of is organized tourism. It's a wild and fascinating land that very few people even consider visiting. Here even the simplest activities become games or adventures. A walk down the street or a visit to the market becomes an exotic journey. Each meal is a first, every person an enigma, every day an odyssey.

Eastern Turkey presents the visitor with challenge after challenge. Communication is difficult. English is rarely spoken. Since many Turks have worked in Germany, German is the most valuable European language. Distances are great and transportation, while cheap, is quite rugged. Most western women are comfortable here only with a male partner. Modern accommodations are virtually nonexistent; there just isn't enough demand to support tourist hotels. You'll be an oddity—the constant center of attention. People will stare and follow. Privacy will be found only in your hotel room—if you have drapes.

Nevertheless, exploration of Eastern Turkey is a special travel thrill and those who visit scheme to return. The people are curious, basically friendly and helpful. Communicaton requires creativity. A Turkish vocabulary of twenty or thirty words is essential. Hotels and restaurants, in modest Turkish style, abound and it's impossible to spend much money. Bus companies with modern Mercedes-Benz buses offer frequent and very cheap transportation to all corners of Turkey from all corners of Turkey. Smaller buses called *dolmuses* will take you anywhere the larger buses won't. Erzurum, Eastern Turkey's major city, is only a $12 bus ride from Istanbul. This 24-hour marathon ride drops you in a land that all of a sudden makes Istanbul seem mild.

If you're looking for excitement and a very different culture, Eastern Turkey's rewards far exceed the costs associated with traveling there. There are few tourist sights as such (museums, tours, famous buildings, etc.), but everything about Eastern Turkey combines to sweep you into a whole new world. You're given a close look at the traditional Moslem culture in towns with more horse traffic than cars. The streets are the man's domain while unliberated women appear in public only as walking gunny sacks.

A photographer will go through a lot of film.

Some Hints to Make Your Visit Easier

Good information is rare in Eastern Turkey. By all means, locate some literature on the area here in the USA. Study and know what interests you. Take a good map with you.

Eat carefully. Find a clean-looking restaurant and venture into the kitchen. Choose your food personally by tasting and pointing to what you like. Establish the price before you eat. Joke around with the cooks—they'll love you for it. Purify your water with iodine, Halazone or by boiling it. Bottled soft drinks and boiled *chai* (tea) and coffee are cheap and safe everywhere. Watermelons are a great source of safe liquid. If you order a glass of tea, your waiter will be happy to "process" your melon, giving it to you peeled and in little chunks on a big plate.

Learn to play backgammon before you visit Turkey. Backgammon, the local pastime, is played by all the men in this part of the world. Join in. It's a great way to make a lot of friends in a teahouse, the local hangout.

Really get away from it all. Take a minibus (*dolmus*) and ride into the middle of nowhere. Get off at a small village. If the men on the bus think you must be mistaken or lost to be getting off there, you've found the right place. Explore the town, befriend the children, trade national dance lessons, be a confident extrovert. Act like an old friend returning after a ten-year absence—you'll be treated like one.

Making friends in Eastern Turkey

I make a habit of loitering near the property of a large family. Very often, the patriarch, who is proud to have a foreign visitor, will invite me to join him cross-legged on his large, bright carpet in the shade. The women of the household bring tea, then peer at us from around a distant corner. Shake hands, jabber away in English, play show-and-tell, take pictures of the family, and get their addresses so you can mail them a copy. They'll never forget your visit—neither will you.

People will be staring at you all day long. To keep from going insane, be crazy. Keep a sense of humor. Joke with the Turks. Talk to them, even if there's no hope of communication. One afternoon, in the town of Ercis, I was waiting for a bus and writing in my journal. A dozen people gathered around me, staring with intense curiosity. I felt that they needed entertainment. I sang an old Hoagy Carmichael song, "Huggin' and a-Chalkin'." When the bus came, my friend and I danced our way on board, waving goodbye to the cheering fans. From then on I entertained (with a terrible voice) most of Eastern Turkey.

This is an exciting land—and a tremendous way to spice up your trip. Never again, in your mind, will you associate Turkey with cranberries.

38: The Treasures of Luxor, Egypt

On my rented one-speed, I pedaled through Luxor happily blowing in the breeze, catching the cool shade and leaving the stifling heat with the pesty *bakshish* beggar kids in the dusty distance.

Loading onto the old ferry, the man in the engine room hits the groaning motor into gear with a rock and in a few minutes the noisy city life is gone and the Nile has taken me back into a lush brown and green world of reeds, sugar cane, date palms, mud huts and a village world amazingly untouched by the touristic bustle of Luxor.

I like the far side of the Nile. An irrigation ditch leads me into a village where I am truly big news on two wheels. People scurry, grabbing their families to see the American who chose them over Tut. It was a royal welcome. They would have given me the Key to the Village—but there

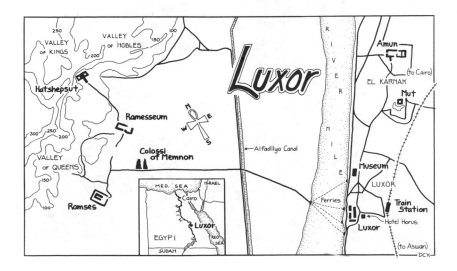

were no locks. Smiles lit by glittering eyes kept the sunset lingering as a memorable evening began.

From Athens, Cairo is just a ninety-minute flight or a day at sea, and you're in a whole new world. Economy or student boat and plane tickets from Athens to Egypt are reasonable at about $100 each way. For the best possible price, buy your ticket in Athens. These tickets are not advertised outside of Greece.

I spent more time in and around Luxor than in any European small town, and I could have stayed longer. On top of the village thrills, there's

tremendous ancient ruins. The East Bank offers the tourist two famous temple sites: the Temples of Amun, Mut and Khonsu at Karnak, one mile north of Luxor and the Temple of Luxor which dominates the town of Luxor.

And the West Bank, because of an ancient Egyptian belief, has all the funerary art, tombs and pyramids. It was only logical to bury the dead on the west bank, where the sun sets. Across the Nile from Luxor is an area rich in tombs, temples and ruins. Be selective, buying tickets for the most important sights at the ticket office near the ferry landing. The Temple of Queen Hatshepsut, Deir el-Medina, the Ramesseum, the Colossi of Memnon and the Valleys of the Kings, Queens and Nobles are just some of the many monuments from Egypt's ancient past that await you. You will become jaded sooner or later, so don't waste your powers of absorption on anything less than important.

Luxor town itself has plenty to offer. Explore the market. You can get a very inexpensive custom-made kaftan with your name sewed on in arty Arabic, if you like. A trip out to the camel market is always fun (and you can pick up a camel for half the USA price). I found the merchants who pester the tourists at the tombs across the Nile had the best prices on handicrafts and instant antiques.

Take an evening cruise on the Nile in a *felucca,* the traditional sailboat of this area, for just a few dollars an hour. Relaxing like Cleopatra in your private felucca in the cool beauty of a Nile sunset is a very romantic way to end the day and start the night. For me, five days in a small town is just asking for boredom. But Luxor fills five days like no town its size.

Here's a good plan:

Five Days in Luxor

Day 1. Your train from Cairo arrives at 5:00 a.m. Even though it's too early to check in, leave your bags at a hotel, telling them you'll return by midmorning to inspect their rooms. Take a horse carriage to the temples at Karnak while it's still cool. The cool of these precious early hours should never be wasted. Check into a hotel by midmorning. Explore Luxor town. Enjoy a felucca ride on the Nile at sunset.

Day 2. Cross the Nile and rent a taxi for the day. It's easy to find other tourists to split the transportation costs. If you're selective and get an early start, you should be able to see everything you want at a relaxed tempo by noon. That's a lot of work, and you'll enjoy a quiet afternoon back in Luxor.

One of the most interesting ways to see Egypt.

Day 3. Arrange through your hotel an all-day mini-bus trip to visit Aswan, the Aswan Dam and the important temples (especially Edfu) south of Luxor. With six or eight tourists filling the mini-bus, this day should not cost over twelve dollars.

Day 4. Rent bikes and explore the time-passed villages on the west side of the Nile. Bring water, your camera and a bold spirit of adventure. This was my best Egyptian day.

Day 5. Enjoy Luxor town. Tour the excellent Luxor museum. Take advantage of the great shopping opportunities here. Catch the overnight train back to Cairo.

Egypt seems distant and, to many, frightening. It's actually quite accessible and, with a few tips, there's a reasonable chance you'll survive and even enjoy your visit.

The overnight train ride from Cairo to Luxor is posh and scenic—a fun experience itself. A second-class air-conditioned sleeping car provides comfortable two-bed compartments, fresh linen, a wash basin and wake-up service. Make a reservation for this ride at least three days in advance, both ways. In the crazy Cairo ticket office, be patient and persistent and tip (bribe) if necessary.

In the cool months (peak season) hotel reservations are a good idea. Off season, in the sweltering summer months, there are plenty of empty rooms. Air conditioning is found only in the luxury hotels, and these rooms are relatively expensive at about $50 per double. Modest hotels with a private shower, fan and balcony offer doubles for around than $15. A cot in the youth hostel, for a couple of dollars, is rock bottom in price—and comfort. The Hotel Horus' central location (Maabed El Karnak Street, tel. 2165), showers, fans, good clean restaurant, friendly and helpful management and priceless (i.e., safe to drink) cold water machine make it a real bargain (double rooms for about $20). Hotel Horus is just across the street from the impressive Temple of Luxor and a three minute camel ride from the Nile.

Egypt is not a place where you should save money at the expense of comfort and health. A little extra expense will bring a lot of comfort.

Eat well and carefully. With the terrible heat, your body will require plenty of liquids. Water from drinkable sources is safe (e.g., water which is served in good restaurants). Pepsi and the local cola, *Sico,* are safe and very cheap. Watermelons are cheap, safe and quite quenching. Cool your melon in your hotel's refrigerator. Choose a clean restaurant. Hotels generally have restaurants comparable to their class and price range.

Transportation in and around Luxor is a treat. The local taxis are horse-drawn carriages. These are very romantic, but, as usual in Egypt, you must drive a hard bargain and settle on a price before the driver "moves 'em out". Some Egyptians will overcharge anyone who will overpay. You can cross the Nile from dawn until late at night on the very old Nile ferry. This "Tourist Fary", as the sign reads, costs only pennies. Sit on the roof and enjoy the view with the local crowd.

Transportation on the West Bank of the Nile (across from Luxor) consists of donkeys, bicycles and automobile taxis. You can rent donkeys for the romantic approach to the tombs and temples of West Thebes. The desert heat will melt the romance, and you may feel like a first-class ass sitting on your dusty donkey. Bikes, for the cheap and hardy, are a possibility for touring the ruins and tombs. An automobile taxi is the quickest and most comfortable way to see the sights of West Thebes. When split between four tourists, a taxi for the day is a very reasonable way to go. To save money and make friends, assemble a little tour at your hotel. You will enjoy the quick meet-you-at-the-ferry-landing service of the taxi, and in one day, adequately cover Luxor's Westbank sights.

Survival on the Nile during the heat of summer is easier if you follow a few hints. The "day" generally lasts from 5:00 a.m. until 12:00 noon. The summer heat, which they say can melt car tires to the asphalt, is unbearable and dangerous after noon. Those early hours are prime time: the temperature is comfortable, the light is crisp and fresh and the Egyptian tourist hustlers are still sleeping. The afternoon should be spent indoors or in the shade. Wear a white hat (you can buy them there) and carry water. An Egyptian guidebook is a shield proving to unwanted human guides that you need no "help".

You must constantly be on the budgetary defense. No tip will ever be enough. Tip what you believe is fair by local standards and ignore the inevitable plea for more. If you ever leave them satisfied—you were ripped off. Carry candies or little gifts for the myriad of children constantly screaming *"Bakshish!"* ("Give me a gift!") Hoard small change in a special pocket so you'll have tip money readily available. Getting change back from your large bill is like pulling teeth—on a duck.

About the Author

Rick Steves graduated with honors degrees (magna justa barely) in European History and Business Administration from the Univesity of Washington—but that's not where he received his education.

His true education was gained during seventeen years of European travel. From Ireland's Dingle Peninsula to the oasis towns of Saharan Morocco; from Swedish Lapland lit by the midnight sun, to the ornate subways of Moscow; from the scalps of the Alps to the beaches of Greece, Steves has crisscrossed Europe. With budgets ranging from $3 to $35 a day, he has had no choice but to learn the tricks of budget travel. He travels with finesse. Armed with the philosophy that the less you spend, the closer you get to the real Europe, budget travel has been a joy as well as an education.

Author of ten travel guidebooks, Steves spends three or four months a year in Europe where he leads tours, researches new travel guides and still enjoys just traveling. The rest of the year is spent in Seattle, where he writes a weekly newspaper column, keeps a busy lecture and consulting schedule, and dreams about his next trip.

Send Me a Postcard—Drop Me a Line

Thousands of trips are shaped by this book. I take that as a very heavy responsibility and do my best to keep every page conscientious and up to date. Things do change, however, and travelers are always making new discoveries. I would really appreciate any corrections, additional ideas and discoveries, comments, criticisms and feedback of any kind. All reader correspondence will receive a reply and the latest edition of our Back Door Travel Newsletter.

If you would like to share your discoveries with other "Back Door" readers or help me improve the next edition of ETBD, please send a card to **Europe Through the Back Door,** 120 4th North, Edmonds, WA 98020. Thanks and happy travels!

A New Enlightenment Through Travel

Thomas Jefferson said, "Travel makes you wiser but less happy." I think he was right. And "less happy" is a good thing. It's the growing pains of a broadening perspective. After exposure to new ways of thinking and finding truths that didn't match those I always assumed were "self-evident" and "God-given", coming home gave me culture shock in reverse. I've shared with you a whole book of my love of travel. Now let me take a page to share with you some thoughts on how travel has given me a new way of thinking.

The "land of the free" has a new religion—materialism. Its sophisticated priesthood (business, advertising, military and political leaders) make its goal unsustainable growth. The specter used to keep the flock in line is the Communist threat. And like all religious zealotry, the result is ignorance and unquestioning obedience. And while the Golden Rule of Christianity and nearly every other major religion is "Love thy neighbor as thyself", the new Golden Rule is "Have it all!"

Sure, greater wealth would be wonderful, but the only way for 5% of the planet's people (the USA) to get more than the 40% we already take of the global economic pie (or even maintain what we already have, for that matter) is to get more and more aggressive.

As individuals and as a society, I see us making bad investments. We're making serious and far-reaching personal and environmental sacrifices for more and more material wealth. While it's hard to tie it all in, especially in one page, I have a strong sense that materialism, war, poverty and politics are interrelated.

Whoa! What happened to me? Did the young Republican with the history degree who voted for Reagan in 1980 go off the liberal deep end? Or, as Jefferson said, did I "travel and become wiser but less happy"?

I traveled. And travel gave me new perspectives. Like the early astronauts, I saw a planet with no boundaries. It's a tender green, blue and white organism that will either live together or it will die together. I saw that I'm just one of five billion equally precious people. And by traveling I've seen humankind as a body, which somehow must tell its fat cells to cool it because nearly half the body is starving and the whole thing is threatened.

I've found that "full utilization" of travel experience requires information that our system doesn't promote. Expose yourself to some radical thinking. You'll find a very free world where anchormen aren't cute and ignorance is not bliss. My ideas are from lots of travel and books like *Small Is Beautiful* (Schumacher), *The Fate Of The Earth* (Schell), *Food First* (Lappe), *The Future In Our Hands* (Dammann, $6 ppd from my office), *Bread For The World* (Simon), and the newsletters of small peace groups.

A new enlightenment is needed. Just as the French Enlightenment led us into the modern age of science and democracy, the new Enlightenment will teach us the necessity of realistic and sustainable affluence, global understanding, peaceful co-existence and controlling nature by obeying her.

I hope that your travels will give you a fun and relaxing vacation or adventure, and also that they'll make you an active patriot of the planet. The future is in our hands.

Rick Steves

Appendix I— A Checklist of Sights

This list is very arbitrary and by no means complete. The places mentioned are just some of my favorites that I would recommend to you. In past editions, many readers have commented that they found this very helpful as a checklist for their trip plans.

Museums and special places that have impressed me . . .

AUSTRIA

Wien (Vienna)
Tourist Info near Opera
Hofburg
Schloss Schonbrunn
Kunsthistorisches Museum
Grinzing
Rathauskeller, City Hall
  restaurant
Danube Cruise – Melk to Krems,
  free with Eurail
Mauthausen Concentration Camp
  near Linz

Salzburg
Castle
Hellbrunn Castle, trick fountains
Baroque cathedral
Mozart's birthplace
Music festival, late July
  through August

Innsbruck
Alstadt – Old Town
Tiroler Folk Museum

Graz
Laudeszeughaus, medieval
  armory

Reutte
Ruins of Ehrenburg castle

BELGIUM

Brussells
La Grand Place
African museum
Kriek, Faro – local beer
Musee d'Art Ancien, Flemish
  masters
Place du Jeu de Balle, flea market
Eat mussels

Brugge
Markt, Belfry view
Groeninge and Gruuthuse
  museums, Flemish art
Begijnhof, peaceful old "nunnery"
Lacemaking school

Antwerp
Cathedral
Rubens' house
Namur – nice town, great hostel

DENMARK

Copenhagen
Tivoli May 1–Sept. 17 amusement
  park

Christiania, commune
National Museum
Nazi Resistence Museum
Carlsberg Brewery Tour
Stroget – blonde-watching
    shopping street
Nyhavn – jazz
Walking tour by Helge Jacobsen –
    "Copenhagen on Foot"

Hesingor
Louisiana, modern art, north
Frederiksburg Castle

Roskilde
Viking Ships
Cathedral

Odense
Hans Christian Andersen land
Billund – Legoland
Aero Island

ENGLAND

London
Houses of Parliament, tour
Westminster Abbey
Westminster Hall, oak ceiling
#10 Downing Street
Trafalgar Square, museums
Piccadilly
Soho
British Museum
Imperial War Museum
Victoria and Albert Museum
Hyde Park, Speaker's Corner
St. Paul's Cathedral
"The City"
Stock Exchange
"Old Bailey" Courthouse
Tower of London, tour, jewels
Museum of London
Tate Gallery, modern art
The Theaters, near
    Shaftsbury Ave.
Kew Gardens
Covent Garden
Greenwich Maritime Museum
    and ships
Antique Markets
City walking tours,
    listed in "What's On"
Brass Rubbing

Canterbury
Cathedral

Cinque Ports
Rye

Dover
Castle

Battle
Battle (of Hastings) Abbey
Bodiam Castle

Brighton
Royal Pavilion
Palace Pier and promenade

South Downs
Beachy Head

Arundel
Castle
Mr. Potter's Curiosity Museum

Salisbury
Cathedral, Magna Carta
Stonehenge
Avebury stone circles

Bath
Roman and Medieval Baths
Pump Room, tea and scones
Royal Crescent, Circus
Assembly Rooms, Costume
    Museum
Bath Abbey
Scrumpy – local cider
Walking Tours, free
American Museum

Wells
Cathedral

Glastonbury
Abbey

Tintagel
Castle, hostel, King Arthur

Oxford
University, walking tours
Blenheim Palace

Cotswald Villages
Stanton, Stanway – cutest
Stow-on-the-Wold, headquarters
Cirencester, Roman city, museum
Ironbridge Gorge, Industrial
    Revolution

Cambridge
University, walking tours
King's College Chapel
Choose over Oxford

Durham
Norman (Romanesque) cathedral

York
Walled city, walking tours
Minster
York Castle Museum, out-
standing
Jorvik Viking Exhibit

Hadrian's Wall, near Haltwhistle
Once Brewed, hostel,
museum, fort

FINLAND

Helsinki
Temppelliaukio Church
Finnish Design Center
Floating Market
Lutheran Cathedral

Scenic Stockholm-Helsinki cruise
Savonlinna Lake District
Retretti Museum

FRANCE

Paris views:
Tour Eiffel
Tour Montparnasse
Arc de Triomphe, museum and
view on top
Notre Dame
Sacre Coeur
Pompidou Center
Samartaine dept. store

Ile de la Cite
Notre Dame
Ste.-Chapelle, stained glass
Conciergerie
Deportation monument

Left Bank
Sorbonne University
Latin Quarter
Les Invalides, military museum,
Napoleon's tomb
Rodin Museum
Les Egouts (sewers tour)

Right Bank
Galeries Lafayette, shopping
American Express Co., mail
service
Jeu de Paume, Impressionism
Palais du Louvre, greatest art
museum
Musee d'Orsay
Sacre Coeur, Place due Tetre
Musee de Cluny
Marmottan Museum (Monet)
Chagall ceiling in opera
house

Side Trips
Versailles, greatest palace, Le Hameau
Fontainebleau, Napoleon's Palace
Chantilly, great chateau
Giverny – Monet's garden
Chartres, Malcolm Miller tours,
greatest Gothic church
Vaux-le-Vicomte

Rouen
walking tour
well-preserved town

Bayeaux
Tapestry, Battle of Hastings
Cathedral
Arromanches, D-Day landing
museum
Omaha Beach

Mont. St. Michel

Carcassonne
Europe's greatest medieval
fortress city

Avignon
Palais des Papes

Arles, Nimes
great Roman ruins

Nice
Chagall Museum

Loire Valley
Chateaux country
Tours – home base
Chambord, Chenenceau,
Azay-le-Rideau, Chinon
Amboise – Close Luce (Leonardo
exhibit)

Alsace
Route du Vin, Alsacian wine road,
  "degustation" – tasting
Riquewihr, Equisheim,
  Kayserberg
Colmar – Unterlinden Museum

Reims
Champagne caves
Cathedral, gothic, Chagall
  stained glass

GERMANY

Munich
Marianplatz
Residenz
Alte Pinakothek
Deutsches Museum
Stadtmusuem
Nymphenburg Palace
Mathaser's Beerhall
Dachau
Olympic Park / BMW Museum

Oberammergau
Die Weis Church, Bavarian
  Baroque
Theater tour
Woodcarver shops

Fussen
Neuschwanstein, Mad King
  Ludwig's castle
Hohenschwangau

Berchtesgaden
Salt Mine tour
Konigsee cruise
Kehlstein – Hitler's hideaway
  and view

Rothenberg
Rathaus tower view
Folterkammer, torture museum
Walk the wall
Riemenschneider altarpiece
Walk to Detwang village

Bodensee
Meersburg, town and castle
Tropical island of Mainau
Lindau, Venice of the North
Boats free with Eurail

Aachen
Charlemagne's Cathedral

Koln / Cologne
Cathedral – next to station
Romisch-Germanisches Museum

Moselle Valley
Cochen Castle and town
Berg Eltz
Trier, Roman town
Overnight in Zell

Rhine Cruise
Bingen to Koblenz
St. Goar – best hour ride
St. Goar, walk to Rheinfels Castle
Bacharach, castle hostel,
  nice town

Bonn
Beethoven's Haus

Wurzburg
Frankish culture museum
Residenz – Baroque palace

Berlin
Museum of the wall
  (escape attempts), at Checkpoint Charlie. East Berlin over
  Checkpoint Charlie

East Berlin
Pergamon Museum (East)
Brandenburg Gate
Museum for Deutsche Geschicte
  (socialist view of history) (East)

GREECE

Athens
Acropolis, temples, museum
Agora, Temple of Hephaistos
Plake, old town, shopping,
  nightlife
National Archeological Museum
Lykavittos Hill – take funicular,
  sunset, view

Near Athens
Temple of Poseidon, Cape
  Sounion
Dafni wine festival,
  late summer, monastery,
  Byzantine mosaics
Delphi ruins

Peloponnese
Old Corinth, Acro Corinth

Mycenae
Nafplion
Epidauros
Olympia
Mystra Byzantine ruins
Pirgos-Darou Caves, Mani
Finikous – best beach town,
   SW coast
Back Door villages: Dimitsana,
   Dafni

Islands
Mykonos, Delos
Crete, Palace and Museum of
   Knossos, Gorge of Samaria
Rhodos, crusader city, boat
   to Turkey
Samos
Patmos – special at Easter
Santorini
Best Athens day trip: Hydrofoil
   to Hydra
Corfu

Northern Greece
Meteora Monasteries
Metsovo – Romanian town

IRELAND

Dublin
National Museum
Trinity College
General Post Office
Hurling Match, Dog Racing
Guinness tour
Kilmainham Jail

Rock of Cashel

Gaeltachts
Gaelic Pubs
Dingle, Aran Islands

Belfast
Ulster Museum and Art Gallery
Cultra Folk Museum
Northeast coast

ITALY

Rome
Pantheon
Piazza Navona, night life
Castel Sant Angelo
Campidoglio Hill, Museo
   Capitollino, city history

Forum
Colosseum
Mamertine Prison, St. Peter's
   Prison
Santa Maria della Concezione,
   Cappuchin crypt, bones
St. Peter's Cathedral
Vatican Museum, Sistine Chapel
National Museum, near station,
   ancient art
Museo Etrusco
Baths of Caracalla, open-air opera
Tivoli, Villa D'Este
Tivoli, Hadrian's Villa
Ostia Antica, ancient port town

Milan
Duomo, cathedral, roof top
Santa Maria delle Grazie,
   Leonardo's Last Supper
Galleria – Victorian shopping mall
side trip: Mantova town

Venice
Grand Canal
Basilica of San Marco
Doge's Palace
Traghetti gondola
Campanile, bell tower
Basilica del Frari, Donatello's
   St. John the Baptist
Peggy Guggenheim Collection,
   modern art
Burano, lace town

Florence
Duomo, baptisery
Bargello
Palazzo Vecchio
Uffizi Gallery
Santa Croce
Accademia
Pitti Palace
Medici Chapel
gelati

San Gimignano

Ravenna
best Byzantine mosaics

Siena

Assissi
Basilica di San Francesco

Orvieto
Duomo
Etruscan Museum
Etruscan tombs
bus to Bagnaregio, walk to
Civita di Bagnaregio

Naples
Pompeii
Herculaneum
National Archeological Museum

Paestum
Greek Temple Site, in Italy

Palermo
Monreale Cathedral mosaics
Cappuchin catacombs – bones

Agrigento
Greek ruins

Syracuse
Greek ruins

NETHERLANDS

Amsterdam
Rijksmuseum, Rembrandt
Van Gogh museum
Ann Frank's House, Nazi
Resistance
Beginhof
Red Light District
Canal tour
Leisdeplein, nightlife

Alkmaar, Edam
cheese

Arnhem
Hoge-Veluwe Nat'l Park
Kroller-Muller museum,
modern art

Zaandijk
windmills

Den Haag
Peace Palace
Madurodam, mini-Holland
Torture Museum
Scheveningen beach resort town
Bali restaurant – Rijstafel

NORWAY

Oslo
Radhuset, city hall tour

Nazi Resistance Museum,
Akershus
Bygdoy – Viking ships, Fram
Kon Tiki, Ra, Open Air Folk
Museum
Munch Museum
Frogner Park, Vigeland
Sculptures, Vigeland Museum
Holmenkollen – skijump, museum

Oslo-Bergen scenic train
Flam side trip, cruise
to Gudvangen – best of fjords

Bergen
Bryggen
Hanseatic League Museum
Mt. Floien
Fantoft Stave Church
Troldhaugen, Edvard Grieg
Gamla Bergen

Trondheim
Nidaros Cathedral
Music Museum

PORTUGAL

Lisbon
Alfama, sailor's district
Castelo Sao Jorge
Belem Tower
Hieronymite Monastery
Monument to Explorers
Coach and Maritime Museum

Sintra
Moorish castle ruins
Pena Palace

Obidos
walled town

Salema
best town on Algarve, near Sagres

SCOTLAND

Edinburgh
Castle
Royal Mile, Robert Burns,
Walter Scott, Robert Louis
Stevenson
National Modern Art Gallery
Folk music in pubs
Festival – late summer

SPAIN

Madrid
Prado Museum, Bosch, Goya
Puerto del Sol
Palacio Real, royal palace
Plaza Mayor, night life
El Rastro, Sunday flea market

Segovia
Aqueduct, Roman
Alcazar, castle
Cathedral

Salamanca
Plaza Mayor, Spain's best square

Toledo
El Greco's House and museum
Museo de Santa Cruz,
    Santo Tome
Cathedral, sacristy (take tour)

Seville
Alcazar
Cathedral, Giralda
Piazza d'Espana
Weeping Vigin alterpiece

Ronda
Pileta Caves

Estepa
Convent's hilltop chapel, excellent

Cordoba
Moorish architecture

Granada
Alhambra, Generalife

Barcelona
Picasso House, museum
Gaudi architecture
Ramblas
Montserrat Monastery

SWEDEN

Stockholm
Sverigehuset (Sweden House,
    tourist info)
Gamla Stan, old town
Djurgarden, Wasa
Skansen, Grona Lund,
    open air folk museum
Historiska Museet
Kulturhuset
Sauna
Millesgarden, Carl Milles
    sculpture
Planned suburbs – Farsta
Af Chapman hostel

SWITZERLAND

Bern
Modern Art Museum
Old Town
Toblerone chocolate factory tour
    (tel. 031/343511)

Zurich
Kunsthaus, modern art
Swiss National Museum

Luzern
Medieval covered bridges
Rigi – mountain view

Berner Oberland
Best Alps, south of Interlaken

Murten
Walled Town
Broc Caillers chocolate factory
tour (tel. 029/61212)

Gruyeres
Walled town, cheese

Lake Geneva
Chateau de Chillon
Free Eurail cruise

WALES

Cardiff
St. Fagan's Open Air Folk
    Museum
Caerphilly, Europe's 2nd
    largest castle
St. David's Cathedral,
    Welsh speaking
Aberystwyth

Caernarfon
Castle

Snowdon
National Park
Miniature railways
    Slate mine tours
Ruthin Castle medieval
    banquet

Appendix II—
European Festivals

Each country has a "4th of July" celebration. A visit to a country during its national holiday can only make your stay more enjoyable.

Austria	Oct. 26	Morocco	March 3
Belgium	July 21	Netherlands	April 30
Bulgaria	Sept. 9	Norway	May 17
Czechoslovakia	May 9	Poland	July 22
Denmark	April 16	Portugal	April 25
Egypt	July 23	Romania	Aug. 23
Finland	Dec. 6	San Marino	Sept. 3
France	July 14	Spain	Oct. 12
East Germany	Oct. 7	Sweden	April 30
Greece	March 25	Switzerland	Aug. 1
Hungary	April 4	Turkey	Oct. 29
Ireland	March 17	USSR	Nov. 7
Italy	June 2	West Germany	June 17
Luxembourg	June 23	Yugoslavia	Nov. 29
Malta	Dec. 13		

EUROPEAN FESTIVALS

Austria
Salzburg Festival, July 26-Aug 30. Greatest musical festival, focus on Mozart

Belgium
Bruges, Ascension Day. Procession of Holy Blood. 3 p.m. (40 days after Easter). 1,500 locals in medieval costume.
"Adriaan Brouwerfeesten," last Sat & Sun in June. Beer festival in Oudenaarde, nice town 35 mi W of Brussels.
"Ommegang," 1st Thurs in July. Brussels' Grand Place. Colorful medieval pageant.

Denmark
Tivoli, May 1-Sept. 15. Always a festival. Copenhagen.
Midsummer Eve, June 23 & 24. Big festivities all over Scandinavia, bonfires, dancing, burning of tourists at the stake.

Roskilde Rock Festival, last weekend in June or 1st in July. Annual European Woodstock, fairground atmosphere, big acts. Roskilde, 20 mi W of Copenhagen.

Hans Christian Andersen Festival, mid July-mid Aug in Odense. Great family entertainment. Danish children perform fairy tales.

England

Jousting Tournament of Knights, last Sun & Mon in May at Chilham Castle near Canterbury. Medieval pageantry, colorful.

Allington Castle Medieval Market, 2nd or 3rd Sat in June in Maidstone (30 mi SE London). Medieval crafts and entertainment.

Druid Summer Solstice Ceremonies, June 20 or 21. Stonehenge, Hoods and white robes, rituals from midnight to sunrise at about 4:45 a.m.

Alnwick Medieval Fair, last Sun in June to next Sat. Medieval costumes, competition, entertainment. Alnwick, 30 mi N of Newscastle.

Haslemere Early Music Festival, 2 Fridays before 4th Sat in July. 16th-18th c. music on original instruments. 40 mi S of London.

Sidmouth Int'l Folklore Festival, 1st to 2nd Fridays of August, 300 events, 15 mi E of Exeter.

Reading Rock Festival, last weekend in August. England's best. 40 mi W of London.

Nottingham Goose Fair, 1st Thurs-Sat in Oct, one of England's oldest and largest fairs. Nottingham.

Guy Fawkes Day, Nov. 5. Nationwide holiday.

France

Fetes de la St. Jean, around June 24, 3 days of folklore and bull running in streets. St. Jean de Luz (on coast, S of Bordeaux).

Tour de France, first 3 weeks of July, 2,000 mile bike race around France ending in Paris.

Maubeuge Int'l Beer Festival, Thursday before July 14 for two weeks. Great entertainment and beer in largest beer tent. In Maubeuge near Belgian border.

Bastille Day, July 13 & 14. Great National Holiday all over France. Paris has biggest festivities.

Great Festival of Corouaille, 4th Sun in July. Huge Celtic folk festival at Quimper in Brittany.

Alsace Wine Fair, 2nd & 3rd weekends in Aug in Colmar.

Festival of Minstrels, 1st Sun in Sept. Wine, music, folklore, etc. in Ribeauville 35 mi S of Strasbourg.

Fete d'Humanite, 2nd or 3rd Sat and Sun of September. Huge communist fair color festivities — not all red. Paris.

Germany

Der Meistertrunk, Sat before Whit Monday. Music, dancing, beer, sausage in Rothenburg o.d.T.

Pied Piper's Procession, Sundays, 1:00 p.m. all summer, Hamlin (where else?).

Ayinger Volksfest, 2nd thru 3rd weekend in June. White bear, concerts and Maypole dancing at Aying, 15 mi SE of Munich.

Freiburger Weinfest, last Fri thru following Tuesday in June. Wine festival in Black Forest town of Freiburg.

Kinderzeche, weekend before 3rd Mon in July to weekend after. Festival honoring children who saved town in 1640's. Dinkelsbuhl.

Trier Weinfest, Sat to 1st Mon in Aug. Trier.

Gaubondenfest, 2nd Fri in Aug for 10 days. 2nd only to Oktoberfest. Straubing 25 mi SE of Regensburg.

Der Rhein in Flammen, 2nd Sat in Aug. Dancing, wine and beer festivals, bonfires. Koblenz to Braubach.

Moselfest, last weekend in Aug or 1st in Sept. Mosel wine festival in Winningen.

Backfischfest, last Sat in Aug for 15 days. Largest wine and folk festival on the Rhine in Worms.

Wurstmarkt, 2nd Sat, Sept, through following Tuesday. And 3rd Fri through following Monday. World's largest wine festival in Bad Durkheim, 25 mi W of Heidelberg.

Oktoberfest, starting 3rd to last Sat in Sept through 1st Sun in Oct. World's most famous beer festival, Munich.

Greece

Epidaurus Festival, approx 1st of July to 1st of Sept. Greek drama and comedy. 2,500 yr old amphitheatre. Epidaurus, 100 mi SW of Athens.

Rhodes Wine Festival, 1st Sat in July through 1st Sun in Sept. Great variety of Greek wines. Arts, handicrafts, music, dancing. Rhodes.

Dafni Wine Festival, 2nd Sat in July through 1st Sun in Sept. Many varieties of wine, music, dancing, restaurant. Nominal cost. Special bus from Koumoundourou Square. 5 mi from center of Athens.

Ireland

Pan Celtic Week, 2nd through 3rd weekends in May. Singing competitions, bagpipes, harps, stepdancing, wrestling, hurling. Killarney.

Fleadh Cheoil na h-Eireann, last weekend in Aug. Ireland's traditional folk musicians. National festival, locale changes yearly.

Italy

Sagra del Pesce, 2nd Sunday in May. One of Italy's great popular events, huge feast of freshly caught fish, fried in world's largest pans. Camogli, 10 mi S of Genoa.

Festa dei Ceri, May 15. One of the world's most famous folklore events, colorful pageant, giant feast afterwards. Gubbio, in hill country, 25 mi NE of Perugia.

"Palio of the Archers," last Sun of May. Re-enactment of medieval crossbow contest with arms and costumes. Gubbio, 130 mi NE of Rome.

"Palio," July 2 and Aug 16. Horse race which is Italy's most spectacular folklore event. Medieval procession beforehand. 35,000 spectators. Siena, 40 mi SW of Florence.

Joust of the Saracen, 1st Sun of Sept. Costumed equestrian tournament dating from 13th c. Crusades against the Muslim Saracens. Arezzo, 40 mi SE of Florence.

Historical Regatta, 1st Sun of Sept. Gala procession of decorated boats followed by double-oared gondola race. Venice.

Human Chess Game, 1st or 2nd weekend in Sept on even-numbered years. Medieval pageantry and splendor accompany re-enactment of human chess game in 1454. Basso Castle in Marostica, 40 mi NW of Venice.

Carneval, Lent season before Easter, especially Venice.

Netherlands

Kaasmarkt, Fridays only from late April to late Sept. Colorful cheese market with members of 350 yr old Cheese Carriers' Guild. Alkmaar, 15 mi N of Amsterdam.

North Sea Jazz Festival, weekend of 3rd Sun in July. World's greatest jazz weekend. 100 concerts with 500+ musicians. Den Haag.

Norway

Constitution Day, May 17. Independence parades and celebration. Oslo.

Midsummer, June 23-24. "Jonsok Eve" celebrated with bonfires, beer, open-air dancing, boating. Nationwide.

Horten Festivalen, 1st Sun in July. Small festival features all kinds of music, esp rock. Located 50 mi S of Oslo in Horten and reached by train & bus from the Oslo West station.

Portugal

Popular Saints Fair, June 12, 13; 23, 24; 28, 29. Celebration of 3 favorite saints. Parades, singing, dancing in streets, bonfires, bullfights. Lisbon.

Feirade Santiago, July 25-Aug 8. Celebration for patrons saint featuring feast day, cultural events, folklore, bullfights. Setubal, 20 mi SE of Lisbon.

Romaria de Senhor da Nazare, 2nd weekend in Sept. 3 colorful processions in picturesque fishing village. Daily bullfights, market, nightly folk music, dancing. 70 mi N of Lisbon. Nazare.

Scotland

Beltane Festival, approx 3rd week of June. Ancient festival dates from Celtic sun worship festival and is combined with annual Common Riding. Peebles, 25 mi S of Edinburgh.

Inverness Highland Gathering, 2nd Sat in July. Athletes in kilts, bagpipers, traditional dancing. Inverness, 160 mi NW of Edinburgh.

Edinburgh Festival, 3rd to last Sun in Aug through 2nd Sat in Sept. World's most comprehensive performing arts festival. Edinburgh.

Argyllshire Highland Gathering, 4th or last Thurs in Aug. Athletics, dancing, piping competition. Oban, 95 mi NW of Glasgow.

Cowal Highland Gathering, last Fri and Sat in Aug. One of the largest Highland Gatherings. Complete highland festivities. Dunoon, on coast west of Greenock and 25 mi (via ferry connection) NW of Glasgow.

Braemar Royal Highland Gathering, 1st Sat in Sept. Largest and most famous highland gathering with Royal Family in attendance. Braemar, 60 mi W of Aberdeen.

Spain

Int'l Music and Dance Festival, approx early July. Classical music and ballet in courtyard of the Alhambra. Leading performing arts festival in Spain. Grenada.

Running of the Bulls, July 6-14. World-famous "encierros," (running of the bulls), accompanied by religious observances, processions, jubilant festivities. Pamplona.

St. James Fair, approx July 15-31. Festivities, fireworks, fairs, cultural events. Santiago de Compostela, 390 mi NW of Madrid.

El Encierros de Cuellar, last Sun in Aug through following Wed. Spain's oldest running of the bulls event. Dances, bullfights. Cuellar, 35 mi N of Segovia.

Sweden

Midsummer, Fri and Sat nearest June 24. Dancing, games, music during height of summertime when days are longest. Nationwide, and throughout Scandinavia.

Asele Market, 2nd or 3rd weekend in July. Laplanders' most important folk festival for 200 years. Asele, 400 mi N of Stockholm.

Ancient Gotland Athletic Games, Sat and 2nd Sun in July. Ancient sports contests between Norsemen. Stanga (Gotland) 25 mi SE of Visby.

Switzerland

Landsgemeinde, 1st Sun in May. Largest open-air parliamentary session. Glarus, 40 mi SE of Zurich.

Montreux International Jazz Festival, 1st through 3rd weekends in July. Comprehensive annual musical events featuring top artists. Montreux.

William Tell Plays, 2nd Thurs in July through 1st Sun in Sept. Dramatic presenta-

tions retelling the story of William Tell. Open-air theatre. Interlaken.
Swiss National Day, Aug. 1. Festive national holiday! Parades, concerts, bell
ringing, fireworks, yodeling, boat rides. Nationwide.

Yugoslavia

Hay Making Day, 1st Sun. in July. Competition in hay making, horseracing,
stone throwing. Folk costumes. Kupres, by bus from Banja Luka (55 mi),
Split (65 mi), or Sarajevo (75 mi).
Zagreb International Folklore Festival, next to last Sun through last Sun in July.
One of Europe's largest folklore revues. Zagreb, 230 mi NW of Belgrade.

These are just a few of Europe's countless folk and music festivals. Each country's
National Tourist Office in the USA will send you a free calendar of events. The best
book I've seen for a listing of the great festivals of Europe is Playboy's *Guide to Good
Times: Europe*, $2.95. ISBN 0-872-16819-0.

Appendix III— Sample Train Trips

Sample European Train Trips

How long they take and how much they cost in 1988

From .... To		2nd Class (One Way)	Journey Time (Hours)	Trains daily (approx)
Amsterdam	Brussels	$ 22	3½	19
	Frankfurt	54	6	7
	Copenhagen	94	12	4
	Munich	101	12	7
	Paris	47	5½	8
	Vienna	132	15	2
	Zurich	104	11	5
Athens	Munich	99	39	2
	Beograd	41	20	3
Barcelona	Marseilles	41	8	3
	Madrid	40	8	4
	Rome	107	20	2
	Paris	86	12	3
Berlin	Hamburg	34	3½	3
	Brussels	89	10	3
	Warsaw	34	9	2
	Paris	111	14	4
Brindisi	Rome	43	7	4
	Patras	83	17	2
Kopenhavn	Koln	94	11	7
	Oslo	66	10	4
	Rome	228	31	4
	Paris	135	14	5
	Stockholm	52	8	7
Madrid	Lisbon	32	9	2
	Seville	32	6	3

Oslo	Paris	99	16	5
	Trondheim	65	8	5
	Stavanger	69	9	3
	Bergen	57	7	4
Paris	Marseilles	68	5	7
	Rome	115	17	4
	Venice	91	13	5
	Vienna	132	15	4
	Zurich	56	7½	6
Rome	Venice	41	6	10

1st Class tickets cost about 50% more than 2nd Class.

There are faster and slower trains—these times are average.

Any journey of 6 hours or longer can be taken overnight.

From this list you should be able to estimate the time and money required for any European train journey. Remember times and costs of journeys per inch on the map are roughly similar at equal latitudes. So to estimate time and cost of a southern journey, compare it to a southern entry on this list. Northern trains are faster and more expensive. Don't worry about more exact information until you get to Europe. Plan with this chart, cocky confidence and a spirit of adventure.

Every year the Rhine steamer schedule changes slightly but this one (taken from the Cook Continental Timetable) should be close. The best cruise is from St. Goar to Bacharach. The best longer segment is from Koblenz to Mainz. Notice for example how you could depart from Koblenz at 9:00, de-boat at 11:55 in St. Goar for lunch and to climb through its castle, and sail on at 4:30 p.m., arriving in Mainz at 9:00 p.m. in time to catch your night train to Copenhagen, Vienna or Rome. Also notice the extra schedule information keyed in below. This Rhine cruise is just one of many extras included free with your Eurailpass.

Rhine Cruise

Table 700   KÖLN-DÜSSELDORFER DEUTSCHE RHEINSCHIFFAHRT AG
KD GERMAN RHINE LINE

Rhine Line steamer timetable (Table 700), downstream and upstream schedules between Koblenz, St. Goar, Bacharach, Bingen, Rüdesheim, Mainz and Frankfurt/Main, with service-day codes.

A— Daily, Apr. 20–30.
B— Suns., May 1–June 2.
C— Daily, May 1–Sept. 18.
D— Daily, April 20–Oct. 30.
E— April 21, 3? and daily April 25–Sept. 18.
G— Daily, Sept. 19–Oct. 30.
H— Daily, Sept. 19–Oct. 2.
J— Daily, Oct. 3–30.
K— Daily, April 20–Oct. 2.
L— Daily, May 1–Oct. 2.
M— Daily, June 12–Sept. 18 (not Koblenz-Boppard on Sats.).
N— Daily except Weds. May 1–Sept. 18.
O— Express service, daily except Mons., May 1–Oct. 2 by hydrofoil Rheinpfeil. Also runs Apr. 21, 22, 28, 29, Oct. 8, 9, 15, 16, 22, 23, 29, 30. Special fares apply.
P— Mons., Tues. and Thurs., July 11–Aug. 18 also June 13, 20, 27, July 4, Aug. 22, 29, Sept. 5, 12.

Q— Daily Sept. 19–Oct. 2, also Sats. and Suns. July 10–Aug
R— Daily, Oct. 3–9.
S— Daily, June 12–Sept. 18, except Aug. 27, Sept. 3, 10, 1;
T— Daily, Sept. 19–Oct. 9.
W— Daily, May 8–Oct. 16.
Y— Daily, May 8–Sept. 11.
Z— Daily, Espt. 12–Oct. 15.
AA—Daily, Sept. 12–Oct. 16.
BB—Daily, Oct. 3–30.
b— Daily except Mons., July 10–Aug. 21.
d— Rhine/Moselle excursion to/from Kobern (Moselle).
‡— Fast ship, supplement payable (not applicable between and Koln Sept. 2).
§— Fast ship, supplement payable only from to Mainz.

Appendix IV— Eurail User's Guide

What Your Agent May Not Tell You: If you buy a train pass read this very carefully.

Coverage and Duration

Your Eurailpass gives you unlimited travel on all the national train lines in Europe except Great Britain and Yugoslavia. That's over 100,000 miles of track!

Your pass also gives you many extras that some Eurailers never know about. Read the Eurail map and handbook (free with your pass) very carefully. These extras include international boat crossings (Denmark-Sweden, Sweden-Finland, Ireland-France, Italy-Greece), scenic river trips (Rhine, Mosel, Danube), lake rides in Switzerland, the Romantic Road bus tour in Germany, Expressway buses in Ireland, buses run by the train companies (German, Austria, Switzerland), and more.

Your pass is valid non-stop for its duration. 15 days would mean, for instance, from June 1st until midnight June 15th. A one month pass goes by the date number (e.g., August 8 – midnight September 7). If you start a one month pass in a 31 day month, you get 31 days. Starting in February leaves you short.

Starting Your Pass

Eurail passes are open-dated. You can start it on the day of your choice but only within six months of its date of issue, as shown stamped on the pass (e.g., a pass issued on March 1 must be validated before September 1).

The man at any train station ticket window can validate your pass (or direct you to a special Eurail window that will). Give him your pass (which you should sign in front of him), your passport, and a slip of scratch paper with the dates you figure should be entered. He will stamp the pass, enter your passport number, and fill in the dates on both the pass itself and on the connected "stub." Since he may be sloppy and an error by him on your pass would cause untold problems, that slip with your dates on it is a wise precaution. (Remember the European system of dating: day/month/year – day/month/year, e.g., 3/6/88–2/7/88 is June 3 to July 2nd.

Your Validation Slip, Proof Stub, and Lost Passes

The detachable stub of your pass is very important. Leave it intact until your pass is validated. At that time the man who validates your pass should tear it off and give it to you. Keep this stub separate from your pass (like you keep the proof coupons separate from your traveler's checks). I think it's wise for traveling partners to store their stubs in the other person's plastic Eurail sheath.

This validation slip has two purposes: 1) A conductor may ask to see it to substantiate any info on your pass. If anything looks fishy your stub can clear matters up. Many people doctor the validation dates.

Success in this game is nearly impossible with the new validation stubs. Also, if someone is using a stolen pass, the conductor knows they probably won't have the stub. 2) If you lose your pass it is replaceable if you present your stub and a sad story to a Eurail aid office (listed on your Eurail map). Even with the stub, replacing a lost pass is a first class hassle. Hang onto your pass as if it were non-replaceable.

Refunds

Once your pass has been validated it cannot be refunded. Unvalidated passes can be 85% refunded if returned to the agent you bought it from within one year of its date of issue. If you get to Europe and decide you don't want to use your pass, that's fine—but it'll cost you 15% of the pass price.

1st Class vs. 2nd Class

If you're 26 or older, you have a 1st class pass—forced luxury. Those under 26 can opt for the 2nd class Youthpass. With the Youthpass you get exactly the same coverage with all the extras—except you travel in the 2nd class compartments. "1st class people" can travel 2nd class freely. 2nd class pass holders must pay the difference to ride 1st class. 1st class costs 50% more than 2nd (i.e., to upgrade a $50 second class ride, you'd have to give the conductor $25). 1st class enjoys the special bonus of no supplemental payments on Europe's super trains (TGV, IC, Euro-city, Rapidos, etc.) 2nd class travelers will almost inevitably be hit up for a few surprise "supplementos" during their trip.

In general, trains have 1st and 2nd class cars—all traveling at exactly the same speed. 1st class cars, marked with a yellow line above the windows, are less crowded, more roomy, with plusher upholstery and filled with other Eurail travelers (mostly Yankees) and Europeans who paid 50% extra so they wouldn't have to mingle with common folk. The soldiers and nuns are partying in 2nd class. 1st class is most advantageous on overnight rides (better chance to stretch out) and during peak season (July and August) and holiday periods when crowds can create problems.

Reservations

Generally, train reservations make as much sense as calling ahead for a Big Mac. Don't. If you want reservations anyway, get them in the city you'll be leaving from at the time of your arrival there. It's easy, but you'll have to wait in line and spend a dollar or two. Reservations are not required except in Spain and Norway and on certain fancy trains (IC, Euro-city, TGV and any train marked on the schedule with an R.) Remember, reservations must be made at least several hours in advance. In 15 years of Eurail travel, I think I've made 20 or 30 reservations. On many of those rides I walked through several empty cars to find that special seat with my number on it. Reservations from the USA are crazy.

Couchettes

Most overnight trains have "sleeping cars" full of beds. They range from ridiculously expensive luxury compartments to simple couchettes. A couchette (pron. "coo-SHETT") is one bed in a triple bunk (6 beds per compartment or room). For about $12 you get sheets, a pillow and blankets, and up to five roommates of either sex. While couchettes can be booked well in advance, from just about anywhere, 24 hours is generally ample lead time to get a reservation. I like to book my rolling bed on the day I arrive in a town. 1st class or 2nd class Eurailpass holders get the same simple couchette for that $12 price.

If you decide en route that you wish you had a bed, the conductor on board will set you up and take your money—if a bed is available. France has special "Cabine 8" cars which offer semi-couchette seats—almost like beds—for just the cost of a seat reservation. For maximum head room, baggage space and privacy, I request top bunks whenever possible.

Station Info Office and Timetables

Every station has an information desk (or at least a ticket window that will serve as one). Confirm your major travel plans here. More times than I care to admit, I've misread those easy-looking schedules. To overcome any language problem, give the man a written-out plan of your trip as you understand the schedules (e.g., Paris - Lyon 14:20 - 17:36, track 7?). He will affirm your plans or correct them.

There are plenty of schedules in Europe. The conductor has one, the stations are wallpapered with them and most countries have handy national schedule booklets available for a small price. In the stations you'll see arrival and departure schedules. You're looking for departures. Usually, departure schedules are yellow, arrivals are white.

The complete schedule is the Thomas Cook Continental Timetable. You can buy it new (expensive), or get an old one, which works just fine. It's handy (and makes you very popular on the train) but it's too bulky for me. A very handy easy-to-carry condensed Eurail timetable comes free with each pass. That is sufficient.

Basic Train Schedule Symbols

⊠ Change trains
✗ Weekdays
⊣ Couchette car
Ⓡ Seat reservation compulsory
† Sundays and public holidays
iċ Intercity 1st/2nd class with supplement
        (except in Switzerland)

Any funny mark you don't understand means: "Be careful, there's something funny about this particular train."

The intro to the Cook's Timetable explains all schedule symbols very thoroughly. Schedule literacy is most helpful.

Britain

Of course, Great Britain is not covered on your Eurailpass. It's a great place to use a car with about the cheapest car rental rates in Europe—$120/week with unlimited mileage. Or you can get a Britrail pass from your travel agent at home—$166 for 8 days, $249 for 15 days, $369 for one month. While you can't buy Britrail passes in Britain, it's quite easy (and often a bit cheaper than USA prices) to buy them from a travel agent on the European continent. They can issue you one on the spot for local currency. In most ways, Britrail passes work like Eurails.

The Norway Line boat from Newcastle, England, to Bergen or Stavanger, Norway takes about 20 hours, goes only May 22 to October 17, three times a week and costs about $80 (or much more if you insist on buying it in the USA. It almost never fills up but if you plan to use it, get your ticket and confirm your plans as much in advance as is convenient in London or Oslo. (In England, tel. (632)-585555). There's also a boat from Harwich, England to Esbjerg, Denmark.

Off the Track—a few miscellaneous tips

—Each particular car is labeled with its destination. Cars often split from the train at various locations during the journey. If you walk from car to car, remember to check your new car's travel plans.

—Your Eurail map is very handy. Bring it and use it.

—The Eurail pass is good for subway rides in Copenhagen, Hamburg and some in Munich.

—Conductors roam the trains regularly. They are generally friendly and helpful. They can help you with connection info, arrival times, couchettes, and any train-related problems you may have. When he enters your compartment and says something in another language, he probably wants to see your ticket. Just flash your pass. Conductors growl when they see shoes on the seats.

—Many seats will be reserved. Check for reservation tags. If you sit in a reserved seat, you may be booted out at the last minute and find all previously unclaimed seats occupied. Many reservations are never used, once you're rolling, go ahead and sit there. Some reservations are for just a segment of the journey. This segment is usually noted on the reservations tag.

—Train toilets dump right onto the track. Don't use them in stations. They start out clean and well stocked with supplies and deteriorate as the ride progresses. 1st class toilets are best. Toilet paper quality ranges from wax paper to sandpaper. Normally, lights at the end of the car tell you if the can is free.

—Whenever you take an inner-city bus ride, show your pass before buying the ticket. Pleasant surprises abound.

—The book called "The Eurail Guidebook"

is not good for backdoor travelers. It's misleading in too many ways.

—Make a habit of doing everything you can upon arrival in a station to clear the way for a smooth and efficient departure.

—A few key mountain train lines are not covered by your Eurail pass. Since they are private lines (not national) they don't even appear on your Eurail map. The most important are in Switzerland from Brig-Goschenen-Disentis (completing the very scenic Chur to Martigny trip), and from Martigny southwest to Chamonix in France. Draw these in on your Swiss map inset. These and other private lines (shown on Swiss rain maps available free at any Swiss station) cost a few dollars, but are generally worthwhile.

—Irish trains are inconvenient, but many handy Irish buses are covered by your pass. Learn specifics upon arrival.

—The Italy-Greece boats charge a $10 peak season supplement (June 1-September 1) and should be reserved in advance during this period (try the AmExCo office in Athens or visit an Adriatica office three days before you sail. In Florence on Via Conservatorio near Santa Maria Novella). Be careful. Your trip is covered *only* on the Adriatica and Hellenic lines. Con men from other companies will try to lure you onto their boats and charge you when it's too late to turn back. The trip is very crowded from July 15 to Aug. 15.

—If you won't be validating your pass for awhile, tape it to the inside back cover of your passport for safekeeping. Then disconnect it when you "turn it on." Be careful not to "deface" your passport.

—Also for safety, keep your train pass in your moneybelt (available at Europe Through the Back Door). If you'll be using your pass several times in a day, store it in a *buttoned* shirt or pants pocket.

—Non-smoking cars are clearly marked. In many trains, red seats are for smokers, green seats are not.

—Technically, you're supposed to show your passport with your pass. Don't bother unless the conductor asks. He rarely will.

—Train water is not for drinking, and food is expensive on board. Bring a picnic with you. Window seats have small collapsible tables.

Eurail Usage Strategies

To "stretch" your pass life, consider these tips.

—When coming from London to Paris, pay to get to Paris ($14 from the coast) and start your train pass only when you leave Paris. The English Channel crossing is not covered on your pass anyway. Start or finish your Continental travels in Belgium and Holland. Distances in this region are short, ticket prices reasonable and travel here rarely justifies the use of a Eurail pass.

—End your pass upon completion of boat rides to either Ireland or Greece. Train travel is rather lousy (and cheap) in both countries. You'll do better on buses or boats. Europe's best hitchhiking is in Ireland.

—Consider an open-jaws flight plan into London and home from Athens. Or finish your Eurail time in Greece and get a cheap flight, bus or train back to London ($100-$160 depending on your endurance, luck and age).

—Most travel agents provide a handy pocket-sized European train schedule booklet with each pass sold. If yours doesn't get one by sending a card to: Eurailpass, Box 10383, Stamford, CT 06904-2383.

Eurailpasses are supposed to be purchased outside of Europe. If you need one in Europe a friend can get one for you easily in the USA and mail it to you in Europe or some Eurail aid offices (in major cities) issue them for an extra fee to those who can prove they reside outside of Europe.

—Choose the most scenic stopover. Many times if you're going from B to F you'll have to change from train B-E to train A-F. You may have a two-hour stopover in either town C or town D. Know your stopover options and which town offers the most entertaining layover.

—Spend the night on the "wrong"—but less crowded—car. If you're sleeping on the popular B-E train and everyone seems to be E-bound, you may want to avoid that nocturnal crush by making a much less crowded F-bound car your rolling home for the night. Remember, one train starting in B will commonly have both E- and F-bound cars. It will split in D. The conductor can tell you what time. Let's say the train leaves B at 22:00, splits at D at 6:00, and arrives in E at

8:00. You can stretch out in a less crowded F-bound car until 6:00, then move in with those E-bound sardines for the last two hours of the ride.

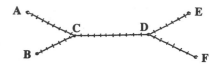

Beyond Eurail

While the Eurailpass gives you unlimited rail travel in 16 countries and is far and away the most popular pass for Americans, many people are not aware that each country has special discounts and passes; anyone traveling extensively in that country can save a bundle by using them. Many of these passes aren't advertised in the U.S. I've listed a few rough prices but things are changing so fast I've left many out. Your travel agent has up-to-date prices and conditions for all train passes listed here.

GENERAL EUROPE

Interail—One month, unlimited travel in all Eurail countries plus Great Britain, Morocco, Yugoslavia, Romania and Hungary. You must be under 26 and prove at least 6 months residency in Europe. Gives only 50 percent reduction in country where purchased, so buy in a small country. A good deal if you can prove residency—tough with a US passport. $250 (less than a Eurail Youthpass, but only gives 50 percent discount on ferries that are free with Eurail. For two months, Eurail is a better deal.)

Bige, Eurotrain, Transalpino tickets—Not actually a pass. One-way tickets with unlimited stops along the way. Up to 2 months to complete trip. Must be under 26. Savings of up to 50% on regular 2nd class fares. Available at student travel agencies and many train stations. Sample fare: London to Istanbul = $170. Pick up information in the Transalpino office in London's Victoria Station.

GREAT BRITAIN

Britrail Pass—8 days: adult $149, youth $130. 15 days: adult $249, youth $209. 22

days: adult $319, youth $269. One month: adult $369, youth $309. (First class costs 30 percent more.) You can't buy this in Britain. Buy in the USA or on the Continent (cheaper in Europe than in the USA—any travel agency can issue it on the spot). Kids 5-15 pay ½ price, under 5 are free, and senior citizens (60 and over) pay about 2nd class price for 1st class pass. Remember, you can rent a car for a week for the same price as a one week Britrail pass.

Other British Rail Specials (usually cheaper than the Britrail):

½-Fare Cards—30 to 50% off any ticket. Valid one year. Must be under 24, student (ISIC card required), senior citizen, or disabled available at Britrail centers in England for $20. *Cheap Day Returns*—For one-day excursions. Some restrictions apply (e.g. you must depart after 10 a.m.). *Triple Ticket*—3-day returns to S. England from London for approx. $20. *Other Specials*—Ask at station or tourist office. (e.g., Rt to Edinburgh from London = $45.)

British Bus Pass—Much cheaper than Britrail, but less comfortable. Available in London. Not good on some smaller lines. Consider purchase of individual bus tickets instead.

Freedom of Scotland Pass—Only good in Scotland. Unlimited travel on rail only (1 week $70 or 2 weeks, $100). *Highlands and Islands Travelpass*—unlimited travel on most rail, buses, ships. (7 days $75, 14 days $110). *Irish Rambler*—Valid on buses and trains in Republic of Ireland only. (8 days $100, 15 days $140).

FRANCE

France Railpass—Must buy outside France. Unlimited travel in France. Includes subway and bus pass for Paris. Second class tickets cost: 4 non-consecutive days out of 15—$69, 9 days out of 30—$130, 16 out of 30—$170. (First class prices: $89, $190, $250 respectively).

BELGIUM, NETHERLANDS, LUXEMBOURG – BENELUX

Benelux Tourrail—Unlimited rail travel in all 3 countries on any 5 days in a 17-day period. (1st class, adult = $90, youth (under 26) = $60. Distances are short in these countries, but regular fares are quite expensive, so this pass is a good deal (esp. the youth pass). *Belgian 5/17 Card* —Must buy in Belgium. Unlimited travel for 5 days out of 17 – $45. *Netherlands Ranger Passes*—Must buy in Netherlands. (2nd class, 3 day = $40 = $55.

WEST GERMANY

DB Tourist Karte—Must buy in W. Germany. Unlimited travel for 4, 9 or 16 days on trains & buses, Rhine & Mosel cruises. Includes discount on RT ticket to Berlin and free bike rentals. *Tramper Monats Ticket*— Must buy in W. Germany. Unlimited 2nd class travel for one month on all trains & buses. Must be under 22 or under 26 with student ID. Cost of one N-S trip almost pays for it. *Senioren Pass*—Women over 60 & men over 65 get 50% discount. Buy cheaply at any German station. *National Netzkarte*— Must buy in W. Germany. Unlimited travel for one month. *Rosarot Billet*—Special discount round trip ticket good for any journey inside West Germany.

SWITZERLAND

Swiss Holiday Card—Must buy outside Switzerland. Unlimited travel on trains, postal buses and lake steamers in Switzerland. Discount (50%) on many scenic (& expensive) privately owned mountain railways and cable cars not covered by Eurail. (2nd class, 4 days = $94, 8 days = 109, 15 days = $131, 1 month = $183; 2nd class. Kids 6-15 pay ½ fare). Money saved on mountain lifts alone can make this pass worthwhile. *Regional Holiday Tickets*— Must buy in Switzerland. Valid for 15 days, allowing free travel for 5 days and ½ price travel for the remaining 10 days (you choose which days you pay and which you ride free). Available for several different regions in Switzerland, including Bernese Oberland! ($22-79). *Half-Fare Travel Card*— Good for 1st and 2nd class on all national and some private lines. (15 days $35, 1 month $45) students, youths and seniors get the half fare card for much less. *Day Cards*—Unlimited travel on all national railroads. (4 days $80; 10 days $160).

AUSTRIA

Austria Ticket—Must buy in Austria or major stations in Switzerland or W. Germany. Unlimited travel on trains & postal buses and some boats & mountain railways. (Adult version called Bundes-Netzkarte second class: 9 days = $122, 16 days = $147, 1 month = $234; 2nd class, youth 16-26, 9 days = $70; 16 days = $100). *Senior Citizen Half Fare*—For women 60 & over and men 65 & over. Half price for train and bus tickets with $14 card you can buy at any station or post office in Austria.

SCANDINAVIA

Nordturist Pass—Must buy in Scandinavia. Unlimited train travel for 21 days and 50% discount on ship crossings (boats from Denmark to Germany and Denmark to Sweden are free) 1st = $280, 2nd = $200. Great if your trip is limited to Scandinavia —much cheaper than Eurail. Each of the Scandinavian countries has special prices for seniors (65 and over), groups, families and extensive travel within that country. Finland also offers a Finnrail pass for 8, 15 or 22 days of unlimited 1st or 2nd class travel.

ITALY

Italian Tourist Pass—Must buy outside of Italy. Unlimited rail travel for 8, 15, 21 or 30 days first and second class. *Kilometric ticket*—Must buy in Italy. Good for 20 trips totalling 3000 kilometers (2000 miles) in a 2-month period. Can be used by more than one person. (1st class $180, 2nd class $105) *Family Ticket*—Must buy in Italy. Four or more family members traveling together receive 30 percent off. Italian train prices are low even without these specials. (Rome to Venice, $33, 2nd class)

SPAIN, PORTUGAL and GREECE

These countries have "kilometer tickets", senior discounts, and unlimited travel passes. Buy them locally. Normal ticket prices are already very low. Train service is pretty bad. Consider buses, car rental or just pay as you go.

Appendix V—
Back Door
Accommodations

This book is not written as a directory-type guidebook. John Muir Publications' 22 Day Series lists nitty-gritty information on what to see, how to get there, where to eat, stay, etc. The *Let's Go* series of guidebooks is also very good for back door-style hotel listings. Nonetheless, here are a few recommendations.

South Spain

Accommodations in these towns are meager. You can sleep very cheaply in any town in a private home. Just ask around for *camas* or *casa particular*. Hotels are clearly rated throughout Spain. You'll see blue and white plaques on the door explaining that place's classification. The categories are, in roughly descending order of luxury and price, H (*hotel*), HS (*hostal*), HsR (*hostal-residencia*), P (*pension*), CH (*casa de huespuedes*), and F (*fonda*). Hotels and *hostales* are further distinguished by ratings of one to five stars (five being best). While prices correspond to the blue plaque, standards of cleanliness and comfort may vary. While Estepa has no hotels, you may want to spend the night in one of these places:

Grazalema: Hostal Grazalema, $30 doubles, tel. 111342; **Zahara:** Hostal Marques de Zahara, $30 doubles, classy, tel. 956/137261; **Arcos:** El Convento is the only reasonable place in the old town center, friendly, fine rooms, meals and view, tel. 956/702333; The Hotel Los Olivos is a poor man's ($40) parador on the edge of town, San Miguel #2, with $40 doubles, tel. 956/700811.

The Cotswold Villages

Stow on the Wold is the ideal home-base town; Croyde Bed and Breakfast (Norman and Barbara Axon, Evesham Road, tel. 0451/31711, very friendly); The Pound (Sheep St. tel. 30229); and the great youth hostel right on the central square (tel. 0451/30497). In a very remote location nearby: The Guest House in village of Guiting Power, tel. 04515/470.

Europe's Best-Preserved Little Towns

Toledo: Hotel Maravilla, 7 Barrio Rey, tel. 223300, $30 dbls, great place; Fonda Segovia (Calle de Recoletos 2, tel 211124, $12 dbls), fine youth hostel, tel 224554, $3 per person); Hostal de Cardenal, a 17th century palace, Paseo de Recaredo 24, tel. 224900, $40 dbls, good splurge; **Obidos:** plenty of *quartos* for $18 per dbl. Casa do Poco tel. 62/95358, $30 dbl.; **Brugge:** Hotel St. Christophe Nieuwe Gentweg 76, tel. 050/331176, $40 dbl; Hotel Singe d'OrZand 18, tel. 333109; Hans Memling Hotel: Kuiperstr 18, tel 332096

Cinqueterre, Italy's Riviera

Vernazza Pension Sorriso, the only place in town, is my homebase. ($28 per person for bed, breakfast and dinner, 19018 Vernazza, 5 Terre, La Spezia, tel. 0187/812224, English spoken). If that's full or too expensive, Sr. Sorriso—the godfather of local beds, who has all the business he can handle—will usually help you find a private room ($15 per person). Asking around town and at the local bars is often cheaper. Vagabonds camp at the picnic tables on the Monterosso trail (check bags at the station for 50 cents, showers on the beach).

In **Riomaggiore,** Hotel Argentina is above the town on Via di Gasperi #27 tel. 0187/920213, $25 doubles. The restaurant in the center of Riomaggiore can usually find you a bed in a private home for $10. There is a new unofficial hostel in Riomaggiore run by Rosa Ricci, speaks no English, $8 per person, lockers and cooking facilities, tel. 0187/92050, just a block inland from the station, Via Signorini 41.

In **Manarola,** Marina Piccola is located right on the water (tel. 0187/920103, $35 doubles).

When all else fails, try Monterosso with its many hotels or stay in nearby towns like Lerici, Pisa or big and bustling La Spezia and commute into the villages by train. Lerici has several reasonable harbor-side hotels and a daily boat connection to Vernazza. Boat in, train home. Pisa, with its famous tipsy tower has plenty of hotels and is a short and direct train ride away.

Salema, Portugal's Sunny South Coast

Reservations normally not necessary, plenty of private rooms (*quartos*). The brown tiled building up the "*quartos* street" has 8 doubles for $15 each (see "Romen" on the buzzer, tel 65128, no English). A British couple run a rather stuffy but nice place, Restaurant Pension Mare, $20 doubles, minimum three nights, tel. 082/65165. You can camp with a low profile on the beach, showers available in town center.

The Berner Oberland, Heart of the Swiss Alps

Gimmelwald: Walter Mittler's Hotel Mittaghorn tel. 036/551658, a wonderful experience, youth hostel, tel. 551704, and Pension Gimmelwald tel. 551730). **Lauterbrunnen:** Masenlageer Stocki, tel. 551754, a cheap dorm; Schutzenbach Campground with dorm huts,tel. 551268; Naturfreundehaus Alpenhof, tel. 551202, a dorm in **Stechelberg; Wengen:** Chalet Schweizerheim Garni, tel. 551581. **Interlaken:** Balmer's Herberge, student-type dorm and cheap hotel, tel. 036/221961. Dorms at **Kleine Scheidegg** can be booked through local tourist offices.

Rothenburg and the Romantic Road

Rothenburg: Hotel Goldene Rose, Spitalgasse 28, tel 09861/4638, $30 dbl. Herr Moser's zimmer:, Spitalgasse 12, tel. 5971, $25 dbl. Gastehaus Raidel: Wenggasse 3, tel. 3115, $30 dbl; Pension Poschel: Wenggasse 22, tel 3430, $25 dbl.; Herr Ohr's zimmer: Untere Schmiedgasse 6, tel. 4966, $25 dbl.; youth hostels: tel. 4510.

Dungeons and Dragons, Nine Great Castles

Rheinfels Castle: In **St Goar;** Hotel Landsknecht, tel. 06741/1693. Hotel Montag: tel. 1629; Frau Wolter's zimmer: Schlosberg 24, tel. 1695; Frau Schwarz's zimmer: Heerstr 86, tel. 7585;youth hostel: tel. 388; **Bacharach:** Hotel Kranenturm, Langstr 30, tel. 06743/1308; Gerturd Aman's zimmer: Oberstr. 18, tel. 1271;youth hostelin Stahleck castle, tel. 1266

London—A Warm Look at a Cold City

All places listed are in my favorite neighborhood on the north edge of Holland Park, just west of Hyde Park. Hotel Ravna Gora, 29 Holland Park Avenue, WII, tel. 727-7725, well-worn, friendly, a bit eccentric, cheapest decent rooms in town, $40 dbl.; Holland Park Hotel, 6 Ladbrook Terrace, WII 3PG, tel. 727-8166, cozy, great value, hotellesque, $48 dbl.; Abbey House Hotel, 11 Vicarage Gate, tel. 727-2594, $50 dbl. classy-cozy; Vicarage Private Hotel, 10 Vicarage Gate, tel. 229-4030, $48 dbl, classy-cozy too; Alba Guest House, 53 Pembridge Villas, tel. 727-8910, funky, family-run, $45; Holland House youth hostel, in Holland Park, tel. 937-0748.

York, From Vikings to Dickens

Each of these small guest houses or Bed and Breakfast places are a short walk from the train station, tourist office and town center and charge from $15 to $20 per person with a huge breakfast.

York Lodge Guest House, Hilary and Keith Meadley, 64 Bootham Crescent, Bootham, York, tel. 0904/54289; The Blossoms, 28 Clifton Road, tel. 52391; Briar Lea Guest House, 8 Longfield Terrace, tel. 35061; Longfield House, 2 Longfield Terrace, tel. 27321; St. Mary's Hotel, 17 Longfield Terrace, tel. 76972; Langford House, 11 St. Mary's, tel. 53573.

Day in Lisbon

Europe's cheapest capital. Decent $20 doubles abound. My favorite hotels are: Downtown, in the Baixa and Rossio area.

Public transportation is very inexpensive and taxi rides are cheaper than bus rides in the rest of Europe. Lisbon is ten hours from Madrid by train (go overnight) and 24 from Paris. This is a fine place to end your trip. Consider an open jaws flight plan—for instance, into London and home from Lisbon.

Residencia Campos, Rua Jardim do Regedor 24, tel. 320560, $12 dbls; Pensao Norte, Rua Das Douradores 159, tel. 878941, $12 dbls; Hotel Suisso Atlantico, Rua da Gloria 3-19, tel. 361713, $25 dbls. And in the old town districts of Chiado and Bairro (more colorful but borderline seedy) Residencial Camoes, Trav. Poco da Cidade 38, tel. 367510, $15, great place; Pensao Duque, Calcada do Duque 53, tel. 363444, funky, rugged, dingy, verrry old, $10 dbls; Residencial Nova Silva, Rua Victor Cordon 11, tel. 324371, $20 dbls, great place.

Oslo

City Hotel, Skippergatan 19, tel. 413610, $60 dbl with breakfast; Sjomannshjem, a "retired seaman's hotel" and a great value, Tollbugt 4, tel. 412005, $35 dbl; The MS Hakon Jarl Hotel, a refurbished steamer luxury hotel with one cheap room with no plumbing, the "writer's room" costs only $45 for two with breakfast, Radhusbrygge 3, tel. 424345; The Haraldsheim youth hostel, 4 Heraldsheimveien, tel. 155043, $15 per bed; St Katarinahjemmet, a convent open to tourists in summer, Majorstuveien 21B, tel. 601370, $35 for modern dbls.

Appendix VI— European Weather

Here is a list of average temperatures and days of no rain. This can be helpful in planning your itinerary, but I have never found European weather to be particularly predictable.

1st line: ave. daily low; 2nd: ave. daily high; 3rd: days of no rain

		J	F	M	A	M	J	J	A	S	O	N	D
AUSTRIA		26°	28°	34°	41°	50°	56°	59°	58°	52°	44°	36°	30°
Vienna		34°	38°	47°	57°	66°	71°	75°	73°	66°	55°	44°	37°
		23	21	24	21	22	21	22	21	23	23	22	22
BELGIUM		31°	31°	35°	39°	46°	50°	54°	54°	50°	44°	36°	33°
Brussels		42°	43°	49°	56°	65°	70°	73°	72°	67°	58°	47°	42°
		19	18	20	18	21	19	20	20	19	19	18	18
DENMARK		29°	28°	31°	37°	44°	51°	55°	54°	49°	42°	35°	32°
Copenhagen		36°	36°	41°	50°	61°	67°	72°	69°	63°	53°	43°	38°
		22	21	23	21	23	22	22	19	22	22	20	20
EGYPT		42°	44°	50°	59°	69°	70°	73°	73°	71°	65°	54°	45°
Luxor		74°	79°	86°	95°	104°	106°	107°	106°	103°	98°	87°ᵇ	78°
		31	28	31	30	31	30	31	31	30	31	30	31
FINLAND		17°	15°	22°	31°	41°	49°	58°	55°	46°	37°	30°	22°
Helsinki		27°	26°	32°	43°	55°	63°	71°	66°	57°	45°	37°	31°
		20	20	23	22	23	21	23	19	19	19	19	20
FRANCE		32°	34°	36°	41°	47°	52°	55°	55°	50°	44°	38°	33°
Paris		42°	45°	52°	60°	67°	73°	76°	75°	69°	59°	49°	43°
		16	15	16	16	18	19	19	19	19	17	15	14
		40°	41°	45°	49°	56°	62°	66°	66°	62°	55°	48°	43°
Nice		56°	56°	59°	64°	69°	76°	81°	81°	77°	70°	62°	58°
		23	20	23	23	23	25	29	26	24	22	23	23
GERMANY		29°	31°	35°	41°	48°	53°	56°	55°	51°	43°	36°	31°
Frankfurt		37°	42°	49°	58°	67°	72°	75°	74°	67°	56°	45°	39°
		22	19	22	21	22	21	21	21	21	22	21	20
GREAT BRITAIN		35°	35°	37°	40°	45°	51°	55°	54°	51°	44°	39°	36°
London		44°	45°	51°	56°	63°	69°	73°	72°	67°	58°	49°	45°
		14	15	20	16	18	19	18	18	17	17	14	15
GREECE		42°	43°	46°	52°	60°	67°	72°	72°	66°	60°	52°	46°
Athens		54°	55°	60°	67°	77°	85°	90°	90°	83°	74°	64°	57°
		24	22	26	27	28	28	30	30	28	27	24	24
IRELAND		35°	35°	36°	38°	42°	48°	51°	51°	47°	43°	38°	36°
Dublin		47°	47°	51°	54°	59°	65°	67°	67°	63°	57°	51°	47°
		18	17	21	19	20	19	18	18	18	19	18	18
ITALY		39°	39°	42°	46°	55°	60°	64°	64°	61°	53°	46°	41°
Rome		54°	56°	62°ᵈ	68°	74°	82°	88°	88°	83°	73°	63°	56°
		23	17	26	24	25	28	29	28	24	22	22	22
PORTUGAL		47°	57°	50°	52°	56°	60°	64°	65°	62°	58°	52°	48°
(Lagos/Algarve)		61°	61°	63°	67°	73°	77°	83°	84°	80°	73°	66°	62°
		22	19	20	24	27	29	31	31	28	26	22	22
		46°	47°	49°	52°	56°	60°	63°	64°	62°	57°	52°	47°
Lisbon		56°	58°	61°	64°	69°	75°	79°	80°	76°	69°	62°	57°
		22	20	21	23	25	28	30	30	26	24	20	21

1st line: ave. daily low; 2nd: ave. daily high; 3rd: days of no rain

	J	F	M	A	M	J	J	A	S	O	N	D
MOROCCO Marrakesh	40°	43°	48°	52°	57°	62°	67°	68°	63°	57°	49°	52°
	65°	68°	74°	79°	84°	92°	101°	100°	92°	83°	3°	66°
	24	23	25	24	29	29	30	30	27	27	27	24
Tangiers	47°	48°	50°	51°	56°	60°	64°	65°	63°	59°	52°	48°
	60°	61°	63°	65°	71°	76°	80°	82°	78°	72°	65°	61°
	21	18	21	22	26	27	31	31	27	23	20	21
NETHERLANDS Amsterdam	34°	34°	37°	43°	50°	55°	59°	59°	56°	48°	41°	35°
	40°	41°	46°	52°	60°	65°	69°	68°	64°	56°	47°	41°
	12	13	18	16	19	18	17	17	15	13	11	12
NORWAY Oslo	20°	20°	25°	34°	43°	51°	56°	53°	45°	37°	29°	24°
	30°	32°	40°	50°	62°	69°	73°	69°	60°	49°	37°	31°
	23	21	24	23	24	22	21	20	22	21	21	21
SPAIN Madrid	33°	35°	40°	44°	50°	57°	62°	62°	56°	48°	40°	35°
	47°	51°	57°	64°	71°	80°	87°	86°	77°	66°	54°	48°
	22	19	20	21	22	24	28	29	24	23	20	22
Barcelona	42°	44°	47°	51°	57°	63°	69°	69°	65°	58°	50°	44°
	56°	57°	61°	64°	71°	77°	81°	82°	67°	61°	62°	57°
	26	21	24	22	23	25	27	26	23	23	23	25
Malaga	47°	48°	51°	55°	60°	66°	70°	72°	68°	61°	53°	48°
	61°	62°	64°	69°	74°	80°	84°	85°	81°	74°	67°	62°
	25	22	23	25	28	29	31	30	28	27	22	25
SWEDEN Stockholm	23°	22°	26°	32°	41°	49°	55°	53°	46°	39°	31°	26°
	31°	31°	37°	45°	57°	65°	70°	66°	58°	48°	38°	33°
	23	21	24	24	23	23	22	21	22	22	21	22
SWITZERLAND Geneva	29°	30°	35°	41°	48°	55°	58°	57°	52°	44°	37°	31°
	39°	43°	51°	58°	66°	73°	77°	76°	69°	58°	47°	40°
	20	19	21	19	19	19	22	21	20	20	19	21
TURKEY Antakya area	39°	41°	45°	51°	59°	66°	71°	72°	66°	58°	51°	43°
	57°	59°	66°	74°	83°	89°	93°	94°	91°	84°	73°	61°
	23	21	25	25	27	28	30	30	29	28	25	24
YUGOSLAVIA Belgrade	27°	27°	35°	45°	53°	58°	61°	60°	55°	47°	39°	30°
	37°	41°	53°	64°	74°	79°	84°	83°	76°	65°	52°	40°
	23	22	24	21	22	21	25	24	24	23	23	22
Dubrovnik	42°	43°	47°	51°	58°	64°	69°	69°	65°	58°	51°	46°
	52°	53°	57°	63°	71°	78°	83°	83°	76°	69°	60°	55°
	23	21	23	23	26	26	28	28	25	23	21	21

Metric Conversion Table
Approximate

1 inch	= 25 millimeters	1 ounce	= 28 grams
1 foot	= 0.3 meter	1 pound	= 0.45 kilogram
1 yard	= 0.9 meter	Temp. (F.)	= 9/5 C + 32
1 mile	= 1.6 kilometers	1 kilogram	= 2.2 lbs.
1 sq. yd.	= 0.8 square meter	1 kilometer	= .62 mile
1 acre	= 0.4 hectare	1 centimeter	= 0.4 inch
1 quart	= 0.95 liter	1 meter	= 39.4 inches

BACK DOOR CATALOG

ALL ITEMS FIELD TESTED, HIGHLY RECOMMENDED,
COMPLETELY GUARANTEED AND DISCOUNTED BELOW RETAIL.

The Back Door Suitcase/Rucksack $60.00

At 9"x21"x13" this specially designed, sturdy functional bag is maximum carry-on-the-plane size (fits under the seat). Made of rugged waterproof Cordura nylon, with hide-away shoulder straps, waist belt (for use as a rucksack), top and side handles, and a detachable shoulder strap (for toting as a suitcase). Lockable perimeter zippers allow easy access to the roomy (2200 cu. in.) central compartment. Two outside pockets are perfect for books and other frequently used items. Over 8,000 Back Door travelers have used these bags around the world. Rick lives out of one for 3 months at a time. Comparable bags cost much more. Available in navy blue, black, grey, or burgundy.

Moneybelt $6.00

Required! Ultra-light, sturdy, under-the-pants, nylon pouch just big enough to carry the essentials comfortably. I'll never travel without one and I hope you won't either. Beige, nylon zipper, one size fits all, with instructions.

Catalog . . . . Free

For a complete listing of all the books, products and services Rick Steves and Europe Through the Back Door offer you, ask us for a copy of our 32-page catalog. It's free.

Eurailpasses

With each Eurailpass order we offer a free taped trip consultation. Send a check for the cost of the pass you want along with your legal name, a proposed itinerary and a list of questions and within two weeks we'll send you your pass, a taped evaluation of your plans, and all the train schedules and planning maps you'll need. Because of this unique service, we sell more train passes than anyone on the West Coast.

Back Door Tours

We encourage independent travel, but for those who want a tour in the Back Door style, we do offer a 22-day "Best of Europe" tour. For complete details, write to us at the address below.

All orders will be processed within one week and include a one year's subscription to our Back Door Travel newsletter. Add $1.00 postage and handling to each order. Washington state residents add 7.8% sales tax. Sorry, no credit cards. Send checks to:

Europe Through the Back Door
120 Fourth Ave. N. • Edmonds, WA 98020 • (206) 771-8303

PUBLICATIONS

People's Guide to RV Camping in Mexico, Carl Franz $12.95   (91-5)   356 pp.

The sequel to *The People's Guide to Mexico*, this revised guide focuses on the special pleasures and challenges of RV travel in Mexico. An unprecedented number of Americans and Canadians have discovered the advantages of RV travel in reaching remote villages and camping comfortably on beaches. Sept '88

The On and Off the Road Cookbook, Carl Franz $8.50   (27-3)   272 pp.

Carl Franz, (*The People's Guide to Mexico)* and Lorena Havens offer a multitude of delicious alternatives to the usual campsite meals or roadside cheeseburgers. Over 120 proven recipes.

The Shopper's Guide to Mexico, Steve Rogers & Tina Rosa $9.95   (90-7)   200 pp.

The only comprehensive handbook for shopping in Mexico, this guide ferrets out little-known towns where the finest handicrafts are made and offers shopping techniques for judging quality, bargaining, and complete information on packaging, mailing and U.S. customs requirements. Sept '88

The Heart of Jerusalem, Arlynn Nellhaus $12.95   (79-6)   312 pp.

Denver Post journalist Arlynn Nellhaus draws on her vast experience in and knowledge of Jerusalem to give travelers a rare inside view and practical guide to the Golden City—from holy sites and religious observances to how to shop for toothpaste and use the telephone.

Guide to Buddhist Meditation Retreats, Don Morreale $12.95   (94-X)   312 pp.

The only comprehensive directory of Buddhist centers, this guide includes first-person narratives of individuals' retreat experiences. Invaluable for both newcomers and experienced practitioners who wish to expand their contacts within the American Buddhist Community. Sept. '88

Complete Guide to Bed & Breakfasts, Inns & Guesthouses, Pamela Lanier
$13.95   (82-6)   520 pp.

Newly revised and the most complete directory, with over 4800 listings in all 50 states, 10 Canadian provinces, Puerto Rico and the U.S. Virgin Islands. This classic provides details on reservation services and indexes identifying inns noted for antiques, decor, conference facilities and gourmet food.

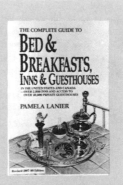

THE COMPLETE GUIDE TO
**BED &
BREAKFASTS,
INNS & GUESTHOUSES**
IN THE UNITED STATES AND CANADA
—OVER 2,800 INNS AND ACCESS TO
OVER 10,000 PRIVATE GUESTHOUSES
PAMELA LANIER

All-Suite Hotel Guide, Pamela Lanier
$11.95   (70-2)   312 pp.

Pamela Lanier, author of *The Complete Guide to Bed & Breakfasts, Inns & Guesthouses,* now provides the discerning traveler with a listing of over 600 all-suite hotels. Indispensable for families traveling with children or business people requiring an extra meeting room.

Elegant Small Hotels, Pamela Lanier $13.95   (77-X)   202 pp.

This lodging guide for discriminating travelers describes 168 American hotels characterized by exquisite rooms and suites and personal service par excellence. Includes small hotels in 35 states and the Caribbean with many photos in full color.

Gypsying After 40, Bob Harris $12.95 (71-0) 312 pp.

Retirees Bob and Megan Harris offer a witty and informative guide to the "gypsying" lifestyle that has enriched their lives and can enrich yours. For 10 of the last 18 years they have traveled throughout the world living out of camper vans and boats. Their message is: "Anyone can do it'!!

Mona Winks, A Guide to Enjoying the Museum of Europe, Rick Steves $12.95 (85-0) 356 pp.

Here's a guide that will save you time, shoe leather and tired muscles. It's designed for people who want to get the most out of visiting the great museums of Europe. It covers 25 museums in London, Paris, Rome, Venice, Florence, Amsterdam, Munich, Madrid and Vienna.

Europe Through The Back Door, Rick Steves
$12.95 (84-2) 404 pp.

Doubleday and Literary Guild Bookclub Selection.

For people who want to enjoy Europe more and spend less money doing it. In this revised edition, Rick shares more of his well-respected insights. He also describes his favorite "back doors" — less visited destinations throughout Europe that are a wonderful addition to any European vacation.

Europe 101, Rick Steves & Gene Openshaw $11.95 (78-8) 372 pp.

The first and only jaunty history and art book for travelers makes castles, palaces and museums come alive. Both Steves and Openshaw hold degrees in European history, but their real education has come from escorting first-time visitors throughout Europe.

Asia Through The Back Door, Rick Steves & John Gottberg $11.95 (58-3) 336 pp.

In this detailed guide book are information and advice you won't find elsewhere — including how to overcome culture shock, bargain in marketplaces, observe Buddhist temple etiquette and, possibly most important of all, how to eat noodles with chopsticks!

Traveler's Guide to Asian Culture, John Gottberg $12.95 (81-8) 356 pp.

John Gottberg, *Insight Guide* editor and co-author with Rick Steves of *Asia Through the Back Door,* has written for the traveler an accurate and enjoyable guide to the history and culture of this diverse continent. Sept. '88

Guide to Bus Touring in the U.S., Stuart Warren & Douglas Block $11.95 (95-8) 256 pp.

For many people, bus touring is the ideal, relaxed and comfortable way to see America. The author has had years of experience as a bus tour conductor and writes in-depth about every aspect of bus touring to help passengers get the most pleasure for their money. Sept. '88

Road & Track's Used Car Classics edited by Peter Bohr $12.95 (69-9) 272 pp.

Road & Track contributing editor Peter Bohr has compiled this collection of the magazine's "Used Car Classic" articles, updating them to include current market information. Over 70 makes and models of American, British, Italian, West German, Swedish and Japanese enthusiast cars built between 1953 and 1979 are featured.

Automotive Repair Manuals

Each JMP automotive manual gives clear step-by-step instructions, together with illustrations that show exactly how each system in the vehicle comes apart and goes back together. They tell everything a novice or experienced mechanic needs to know to perform periodic maintenance, tune-ups, troubleshooting and repair of the brake, fuel and emission control, electrical, cooling, clutch, transmission, driveline, steering and suspension systems, and even rebuild the engine.

How To Keep Your VW Alive $17.95 (50-8) 384 pp.
How To Keep Your VW Rabbit Alive $17.95 (47-8) 440 pp.
How To Keep Your Honda Car Alive $17.95 (55-9) 272 pp.
How To Keep Your Subaru Alive $17.95 (49-4) 464 pp.
How To Keep Your Toyota Pick-Up Alive $17.95 (89-3) 400 pp. April '88
How To Keep Your Datsun/Nissan Alive $22.95 (65-6) 544 pp.
How To Keep Your Honda ATC Alive $14.95 (45-1) 236 pp.

ITEM NO.			TITLE	EACH	QUAN.	TOTAL
		·				
		·				
		·				
		·				
		·				
		·				

Subtotals _____

Postage & handling (see ordering information)* _____

New Mexicans please add 5.625% tax _____

Total Amount Due _____

METHOD OF PAYMENT (circle one)   MC   VISA   AMEX   CHECK   MONEY ORDER

Credit Card Number   Expiration Date

☐☐☐☐☐☐☐☐☐☐☐☐☐☐☐☐   ☐☐ - ☐☐

Signature X _____

Required for Credit Card Purchases

Telephone: Office ( )_____ Home ( )_____

Name _____

Address _____

City _____ State _____ Zip _____

See reverse side for Ordering Information

ORDERING INFORMATION

Fill in the order blank. Be sure to add up all of the subtotals at the bottom of the order form, and give us the address whither your order will be whisked.

Postage & Handling

Your books will be sent to you via UPS (for U.S. destinations), and you will receive them in approximately 10 days from the time that we receive your order.

Include $2.75 for the first item ordered and add $.50 for each additional item to cover shipping and handling costs. UPS shipments to post office boxes take longer to arrive; if possible, please give us a street address.

For airmail within the U.S., enclose $4.00 per book for shipping and handling.

ALL FOREIGN ORDERS will be shipped surface rate. Please enclose $3.00 for the first item and $1.00 for each additional item. Please inquire for airmail rates.

Method of Payment

Your order may be paid by check, money order or credit card. We cannot be responsible for cash sent through the mail.

All payments must be in U.S. dollars drawn on a U.S. bank. Canadian postal money orders in U.S. dollars also accepted.

For VISA, Mastercard or American Express orders, use the order form or call (505) 982-4078. Books ordered on American Express cards can be shipped only to the billing address of the cardholder.

Sorry, no C.O.D.'s.

Residents of sunny New Mexico add 5.625% to the total.

Backorders

We will backorder all forthcoming and out-of-stock titles unless otherwise requested.

Address all orders and inquiries to:

JOHN MUIR PUBLICATIONS
P.O. Box 613
Santa Fe, NM 87504
(505) 982-4078

All prices subject to change without notice.